Twentieth-Centu

MW01274066

Twentieth-Century Marxism outlines and assesses the Marxist tradition as it developed in the twentieth century, and considers its place and standing as we move into the twenty-first century.

The book is divided into three parts examining Marxism historically, geographically and thematically.

- *Part I* analyses early Marxism in Russia and Europe as it developed after the death of Marx. Lenin, Trotsky, Luxemburg, Kautsky, Bernstein and the schools of thought associated with them are all examined.
- *Part II* deals with thinkers, debates and movements that followed the early Marxism focused on in Part I. It includes chapters on Marxism in Europe, the Soviet Union, Africa, Asia and Latin America.
- *Part III* is concerned with more contemporary debates in relation to Marxism and its standing and role today. The chapters in this section consider various themes including the relationship between theory and practice in Marxism, democratic procedure and liberties, Marxism as an economic critique of capitalism and Marxist methodology.

This book provides a thoughtful and stimulating contribution to debates about the role of Marxism today and its future direction.

Daryl Glaser is Associate Professor in the Department of Political Studies, University of Witwatersrand, South Africa.

David M. Walker teaches political theory at the University of Newcastle, UK.

Contributors: Howard Chodos; Joseph Femia; Nick Knight; Daniel Little; Ronaldo Munck; Fikret Adaman; Yahya M. Madra; Mark Sandle; Alan Shandro; Rick Simon; Ian Thatcher; Jules Townsend.

Twentieth-Century Marxism

A Global Introduction

Edited by Daryl Glaser and David M. Walker

Routledge
Taylor & Francis Group

LONDON AND NEW YORK

First published 2007 by Routledge
2 Park Square, Milton Park, Abingdon, Oxon OX14 4RN

Simultaneously published in the USA and Canada
by Routledge
711 Third Avenue, New York, NY 10017, USA

Routledge is an imprint of the Taylor & Francis Group, an informa business

© 2007 Editorial selection and matter: Daryl Glaser and David M. Walker;
individual chapters: the contributors

Typeset in Times New Roman by Prepress Projects Ltd, Perth, UK

British Library Cataloguing in Publication Data
A catalogue record for this book is available from the British Library

Library of Congress Cataloging in Publication Data
A catalog record for this book has been requested

ISBN 10: 0–415–77283–4 (hbk)
ISBN 10: 0–415–77284–2 (pbk)
ISBN 10: 0–203–94062–8 (ebk)

ISBN 13: 978–0–415–77283–9 (hbk)
ISBN 13: 978–0–415–77284–6 (pbk)
ISBN 13: 978–0–203–94062–4 (ebk)

Contents

11   Marxist theory, Marxist practice   196

DARYL GLASER

12   Marxisms and capitalisms: From logic of accumulation to articulation of class structures   212

YAHYA M. MADRA AND FIKRET ADAMAN

13   Marxism and method   230

DANIEL LITTLE

Acknowledgements

More than most books an edited collection is a collaborative venture, and thanks are due first and foremost to all our authors both for the quality of their contributions and for their patience in what has been a lengthy process to get their work into print. Special thanks are owed to Howie Chodos, who has been involved from the outset and has had a big hand in the development of the project. His knowledge, astuteness, hard work and friendship have all been vital ingredients in the making of this book.

Thanks also to Lucy Robinson for a helping hand when we needed one, and to Craig Fowlie, Natalja Mortensen, Andrew R. Davidson and everyone at Routledge and Prepress Projects for all the hard work that goes into the final process of turning a manuscript into a printed book.

Contributors

Fikret Adaman teaches economics at Bogazici University, Istanbul. His research areas include the socialist calculation debate, democratic planning, participatory decision-making, ecological economics and the political economy of the environment. His articles have appeared in, among others, *International Review of Sociology, Studies in Political Economy, New Left Review, Cambridge Journal of Economics, Review of Political Economy, Economy and Society* and *Journal of Economic Issues*.

Howard Chodos is a senior analyst with the Parliamentary Research and Information Services in Ottawa. He has written numerous pieces on Marxism and other topics, including articles in *Historical Materialism, Critical Sociology* and *Studies in Marxism*.

Joseph Femia is Professor of Political Theory at the University of Liverpool. He is the author of several books, including *Gramsci's Political Thought* (1981), *Marxism and Democracy* (1993) and *Machiavelli Revisited* (2004). He has held Visiting Fellowships at Yale and Princeton, as well as a Visiting Professorship at the European University Institute in Florence.

Daryl Glaser, formerly of the University of Strathclyde, Glasgow, now lectures at the University of Witwatersrand, Johannesburg. His interests include democratic theory, applied political philosophy and South Africa. He is the author of *Politics and Society in South Africa* (Sage 2001). He has also published in a wide range of international and area-studies journals including *African Affairs, Ethnic and Racial Studies, Ethnicities, Journal of Southern African Studies, Global Society, Political Studies* and *Review of International Studies*.

Nick Knight works in the Department of International Business and Asian Studies at Griffith University in Brisbane, Australia, where he teaches Asian studies, Chinese politics and research methods. He has written widely on Marxism in China, and particularly on the origins, development and logic of the Marxism of Mao Zedong. His books on this subject include *Mao Zedong on Dialectical Materialism: Writings on Philosophy, 1937* (1990), *Li Da and Marxist Philosophy in China* (1996), *Critical Perspectives on Mao Zedong's Thought* with

Arif Dirlik and Paul Healy (1997), and *Marxist Philosophy in China: From Qu Qiubai to Mao Zedong, 1923–1945* (2005). He is also the author of *Understanding Australia's Neighbours: An Introduction to East and Southeast Asia* (2004). He is currently researching the Chinese Communist Party's ideological response to globalization.

Daniel Little is Chancellor of the University of Michigan-Dearborn. He serves as professor of philosophy at UM-Dearborn, faculty associate at the Inter-University Consortium for Political and Social Research within the Institute for Social Research at the UM-Ann Arbor, and center associate at the Center for Chinese Studies, UM-Ann Arbor. He has written extensively on a range of topics including Marxism, philosophy of science, Chinese studies and economic development. The most recent of his several books is *The Paradox of Wealth and Poverty: Mapping the Ethical Dilemmas of Global Development* (Westview Press 2003), a discussion of some of the normative issues raised by processes of economic development in the developing world.

Yahya M. Madra teaches history of economics and political economy at Gettysburg College. He has published in *Journal of Economic Issues, Rethinking Marxism, Birikim, Toplum ve Bilim, Psychoanalysis, Culture and Society* and in a number of edited volumes published by Kluwer Press and Black Rose Books. His research fields are economic methodology, Marxian economic theory and Lacanian psychoanalysis. He is currently completing his doctoral dissertation, *Late neoclassical economics: The persistence of theoretical humanism in contemporary economic theory*, at the University of Massachusetts, Amherst. He is also part of the editorial collective of *Rethinking Marxism*.

Ronaldo Munck is Professor of Sociology and Theme Leader for internationalization, interculturalism and social development at Dublin City University, where he also heads the university's citizenship and community engagement strategy. He has written widely on Marxism (including *Marx @ 2000: Late Marxist Perspectives*, Zed Books 2002) and on Latin America (most recently *Contemporary Latin America*, Palgrave 2003). His recent work has focused on the impact of globalization: *Globalisation and Labour: The New 'Great Transformation'* (Zed Books 2002); *Globalization and Social Exclusion: Towards a Tranformationalist Perspective* (Kumarian Press 2004); and *Globalization and Contestation: The New Great Counter-Movement* (Routledge 2007). He is currently working on globalization and migration in Ireland and edits the journal *Translocations: The Irish Migration, Race and Social Transformation Review* (www.imrstr.dcu.ie).

Mark Sandle works in the Faculty of Humanities at De Montford University, Leicester, UK. He teaches Russian and Soviet history, and also introductory history for first-year students. He is the author of a number of books including *A Short History of Soviet Socialism* (1999) and *Communism* (2006). His specialist interests lie in the field of intellectual and cultural history. He is about to embark on a project to write a cultural history of Novosibirsk.

Alan Shandro teaches political philosophy at Laurentian University, Sudbury, Canada and is a member of the editorial board of *Science and Society*. He has published a number of articles on Marxist political thought and is currently completing a book on Lenin and the logic of hegemony.

Rick Simon is Senior Lecturer in European Politics at Nottingham Trent University. His interests are in processes of democratization and the nature of the Russian state. He is the author of *Labour and Political Transformation in Russia and Ukraine* (2000).

Ian D. Thatcher is Reader in Modern European History at Brunel University. His latest books include *Trotsky* (2003), *Late Imperial Russia: Problems and Prospects* (2005) and *Reinterpreting Revolutionary Russia* (2006).

Jules Townshend is Professor of Political Theory at Manchester Metropolitan University. His latest book, with Simon Tormey, is *Key Thinkers, from Critical Theory to Post-Marxism* (Sage 2006).

David Walker teaches political theory at Newcastle University and is the author of *Marx, Methodology and Science* (2001) and, with Daniel Gray, *An Historical Dictionary of Marxism* (2006).

Introduction

David Walker

The century of Marxism

The twentieth century was the century of Marxism. Regimes claiming the name covered much of the globe: Afghanistan, Albania, Angola, Benin, Bulgaria, China, Congo, Cuba, Czechoslovakia, East Germany, Ethiopia, Guinea-Bissau and Cape Verde, Hungary, Kampuchea, Laos, Mongolia, Mozambique, North Korea, Poland, Romania, Somalia, the Soviet Union, Vietnam, Yemen and Yugoslavia all boasted Marxist governments for periods in the twentieth century. Hundreds of political organizations and parties proclaimed themselves to be Marxist or Marxist inspired, including, to name but a few, the British Communist Party, the Communist Party of the United States of America, the South African Communist Party, International Workers of the World, the Fourth International, the Khmer Rouge and Sendero Luminoso.

The twentieth century also saw Marx's original ideas inspire the creation of a lexicon of terms denoting Marxist ideological variants such as Bolshevism, Menshevism, Leninism, Stalinism, Trotskyism, Maoism, Castroism, Austro-Marxism, analytical Marxism, structuralist Marxism and Marxist humanism, to note just some of the more prominent ones. In addition, the use of Marxist ideas extended well beyond the field of politics to not just the more predictable areas of sociology, economics, history and philosophy – areas in which Marx himself wrote significant works – but also such diverse fields as psychology, anthropology, ecology and geography. Corresponding to this spread and development of Marxist ideas and influence there was a spectacular growth in the literature on Marxism, Marxists, Marxist organizations, movements and regimes, and Marxist perspectives on almost everything within the fields of social science, natural science and the arts. It is difficult to overestimate the impact of Marxism on the world in the twentieth century. Arguably, it contributed more than any other political ideology to the shape of the political and intellectual landscape of the last century, with the possible exception of liberalism.

Marxism in the nineteenth century

The origins of Marxism are found, though, in the century before last. In the nineteenth century Karl Marx and Friedrich Engels produced the body of works that were to provide the basis for the Marxist movement and ideology. In his writings Marx outlined what became known as his theory of historical materialism, an approach to the study of history and society that focuses on the productive or economic sphere of society as the key to understanding the nature, development and trajectory of the society as a whole. According to orthodox interpretations of Marx's theory, the manner of production in a society shapes the character of the political and legal institutions, the morality and the prevailing ideas. Production, in this reading of Marx's model, is basic to society, and changes in the way a society produces alter the nature of that society. For example, the change from manual labour and simple tools as the means of production to the use of machinery and steam power saw society transform from feudalism to capitalism. This in turn saw a change in the political and legal institutions, and the religious, moral and social attitudes of society. Hence, religion no longer insisted on the divine right of kings, and all the ideas of classical liberalism concerning liberty of the individual, freedom of conscience, freedom of contract, the free market and competition came to dominate society as feudalism gave way to capitalism.

Marx also gave a trenchant analysis of the society of his time, capitalism, which he characterized in terms of commodity production, private ownership of the means of production, and the free market. Marx identified contradictory tendencies within capitalism that would inevitably lead to its collapse. The pursuit of profit that drove capitalism forwards would also ultimately destroy it by making the rate of profit steadily decline over time, with economic crises recurring, each time more acute, until a catastrophic collapse brought the entire capitalist structure crashing down. At the same time as these underlying economic forces were at work a struggle between rulers and ruled was taking place. Capitalists, the ruling class, and workers, the oppressed masses, were in constant conflict, their interests irreconcilable. Ultimately, Marx expected the victory of the workers over the capitalists and of socialism over capitalism in a process of revolutionary change.

In the course of and alongside the development of his theory of historical materialism and his analysis of capitalism, Marx, in a profound but unsystematic way, developed distinctive conceptions and theories of the state, class, revolution, human nature, alienation and ideology. He mounted penetrating critiques of capitalism, classical economics, liberalism, anarchism, non-Marxian socialism, religion and the thought of contemporary European philosophers, notably the Hegelian idealists.

This very brief, and, hence, necessarily simplified, account of the main thrust and themes of Marx's thought indicates something of the nineteenth-century foundations of the twentieth-century Marxist ideological developments described and discussed in this book. Underdeveloped or outdated aspects of Marx's thought in particular attracted the attention of twentieth-century thinkers and activists inspired by Marx, with topics such as imperialism, the Third World, women's emancipation, and culture prompting great outpourings of theorizing and writing. But even the most central of Marx's ideas, such as historical materialism and class, have not been immune to the efforts of twentieth-century Marxists to update them, revise them and improve them.

In the nineteenth century, both as an ideology and a political movement, Marxism was far from dominant or pre-eminent on the European stage, let alone globally. For example, the League of Communists for which Marx and Engels produced the *Communist Manifesto* was a small group of German émigrés living in London, which fell apart after 1850. The *Manifesto* itself made virtually no impact at all when it was published in 1848. As for the other political organization with which Marx is most closely associated, the First International (The International Working Men's Association, to give it its full name) only lasted from 1864 to 1876 and, despite Marx's increasing influence within it, was never a Marxist organization as such. It contained a broad range of groups including followers of Bakunin, Mazzini, Proudhon and Blanqui, and political perspectives ranging from Mazzinian nationalism to Anglo-French positivism, with varieties of anarchism, socialism and even freemasonry also stirred into the pot. The Paris Commune of 1871 drew the attention of a wider audience to Marx as a result of his strong defence of the Commune in writings and speeches. He was identified by newspapers and commentators as a leading and dangerous radical, closely associated with the Paris Commune despite having had nothing to do with its instigation and organization. However, even after this publicity, Marx's death in 1883 passed all but unnoticed, except for a brief paragraph in *The Times*. Only with the German Social Democratic Party adopting a Marxist outlook in 1891 and the steady growth of the largely Marxist Second International in the last decade of the nineteenth century did Marxism as an ideology and as a movement begin to gain significance.

In the nineteenth century, then, Marxism was a marginal ideology struggling for ascendancy within the radical organizations and currents of the time. A fledgling movement in the latter half of the nineteenth century, it took the German Social Democratic Party and, above all, the Bolsheviks in Russia to instigate the transformation of Marxism from a sect to a mass, and ultimately a global, movement in the twentieth century.

The death of Marxism?

Born in the nineteenth century, Marxism came of age in the twentieth, and, according to some, the last century also saw its death. In 1989 the Berlin Wall was breached, marking the end of the Marxist regime in East Germany. In the same year Zbigniew Brzezinski's book *The Grand Failure: The Birth and Death of Communism in the Twentieth Century* (1989) was published, in which he argued that communism had failed and its demise was inevitable. Seemingly fulfilling Brzezinski's prediction, in 1991 the Marxist regime in the Soviet Union collapsed, its communist empire in Europe already fallen. By the 1990s the Afro-Marxist regimes had largely fallen or capitulated to outside pressure to abandon their ideological commitment. In 1992 Francis Fukuyama published a book, *The*

End of History and the Last Man (1992), in which he argued that Marxism was defeated and that capitalism had triumphed over its ideological adversary. Fukuyama described Marxist doctrine as 'discredited' and 'totally exhausted'. In 1999 Andrew Gamble began a book on Marxism with a chapter titled 'Why Bother with Marxism?' in which he wrote, 'Marxism is widely perceived to be in crisis, and many believe the crisis is terminal. Marxism it is said had had a long run and now its energies are spent and its usefulness is long past. It is time to return Marx to the nineteenth century where he belongs' (Gamble *et al.*, 1999: 1).

The 'death of Marxism thesis' suggests that the story of Marxism has come to an end and that any lingering doubts about the futility and falsity of Marxism have now been dispelled. Marxist theory and practice have been discredited. Furthermore, Marx died well over 100 years ago, and he wrote the *Communist Manifesto* more than 150 years ago. The world of Marx was very different from the world of today, politically, economically and socially, so there can be little of interest or relevance in Marxism now. The *Communist Manifesto* must be seen for what it is, simply a historical document, and any truth there may have been in Marx's ideas no longer applies in the twenty-first century.

Proponents of this death of Marxism argument overlook several points. First, self-proclaimed Marxist governments continue to exist, most notably, at the time of writing, in China and Cuba. Also, Marxist parties and Marxist-inspired organizations have continued to be active into the twenty-first century, the Zapatistas in Mexico to name but one significant example of a group with Marxist influences. In addition, in a number of former communist countries there is anecdotal, electoral and opinion poll evidence of a growing nostalgia for the 'good old days' of communism and of significant support for communist parties and policies.[1] Second, Marxism is a living tradition that has changed and spread in different directions, so that although nineteenth- and even twentieth-century Marxism may be dated, just as nineteenth- and twentieth-century liberalism is, twenty-first-century Marxism is not so easily dismissed as irrelevant. Third, the influence of Marxist ideas in a vast range of fields should not be underestimated, and the impact of Marxism even in areas seemingly some distance from politics, areas such as geography and the arts, has already been noted. Finally, there is the issue of the discrediting of Marxism by reference to the practice of communist regimes. That is to say, those pronouncing the death of Marxism argue that the failings and ultimate fall of the Soviet Union show the falsity of Marxism. At the very least, proponents of this view need to show that Marxist theory entails the practice seen in the Soviet Union, and also that the failings and collapse of the Soviet Union were due to its Marxism and not to other factors.

However, it is fair to say that contemporary Marxists in one sense at least face a greater challenge than that faced by their predecessors. For now they are confronted with either defending or explaining the deeds done in the name of Marxism: the 'Great Terror' of Stalin's purges, the brutalities of Mao's 'Cultural Revolution', and the 'Killing Fields' of Pol Pot. Now, also, the absence of a successful and sustained Marxist revolution and the persistence of capitalism must be accounted for.

Marxism: a twenty-first-century perspective

The beginning of the twenty-first century is an appropriate time to make an audit of Marxism, and, in particular, to review the ideas and theories that have built on Marx's thought in the course of the twentieth century. In looking at a variety of schools of Marxism it is implicitly accepted that Marxism is no monolith; there is an irreducible plurality of Marxisms. This book is not an attempt to identify an authentic Marxist tradition, but, rather, it is a bid to explain and assess the range of important strands of Marxist thought that emerged in the twentieth century.

Although representing a range of viewpoints and being far from uncritical of Marxism, the contributors to this book share a sense that Marxism as a body of thought and as a political movement is profound and important. In general there is a sense that, far from having died, Marxism is alive and at least tolerably well. At the very least it contains ideas and insights worthy of consideration. The failures of communism and the flaws in Marxist theorizing should not mask the fact that Marxist thought still has something to offer to contemporary politics and scholarship, and is likely to remain an important political and intellectual reference point well into this century also. Marxism remains a developing tradition, and what the various authors show, in writing about the different Marxisms that have emerged, is that Marxism is tremendously adaptable. For an ideology that has been criticized for being dogmatic, it is remarkable how flexible and varied it has proved to be. As early as 1899 it was 'revised' by Eduard Bernstein. It was then 'Russified' in Russia, 'Sinified' in China, and adapted to local conditions wherever it spread, by Che Guevara and José Carlos Mariátegui in Latin America, by Mao Zedong and Ho Chi Minh in Asia, and by Amilcar Cabral and Frantz Fanon in Africa to highlight but a few examples. This range and variability of Marxisms is reflected in the book, and it is an important feature of this work that a truly global picture of Marxist thought is presented, avoiding the tendency in much literature on Marxism published in the English-speaking world to be too Eurocentric or 'Americocentric'.

The structure of the book falls into three parts mixing chronological, geographical and thematic approaches. Part I deals with early Marxism and looks specifically at Lenin and Leninism, the 'right-wing' Marxism of the Mensheviks, Karl Kautsky and Eduard Bernstein, and the 'left-wing' Marxism of Leon Trotsky and Rosa Luxemburg.

Chapter 1 provides a robust defence of Lenin and Leninism by Alan Shandro, who argues that criticisms of Lenin have been based on misreadings and misunderstandings of him, failing to take into account the contexts in which he wrote his various works. The collapse of Soviet communism has meant a facile dismissal of Leninism and the reduction of Lenin to little more than a caricature, with a serious consideration of his ideas being avoided. Focusing particularly on three of Lenin's major works, his *What is to be Done?*, *Imperialism: the Highest Stage of Capitalism* and *State and Revolution*, Shandro seeks to give Lenin's ideas the serious consideration they deserve. He defends Lenin's ideas on spontaneity and the vanguard party, on imperialism, and on constitutional order and democratic rights. He rejects the criticism that *What is to be Done?* lays the theoretical foundation for the subordination of workers to an intellectual elite, arguing instead that Lenin was committed to a dialectical interplay between the masses and the leadership, and that his views on the need for a vanguard party have to be considered in the context of the absence of proletarian hegemony. Shandro also asserts the continued relevance of Lenin's views on imperialism, and suggests that the logic of Lenin's argument requires a political stance open to criticism. Throughout, Shandro emphasizes Lenin's insistence that 'concrete situations be analyzed concretely'. Far from suffering from the 'sin of intellectual pride', as his critics suggest, Lenin did not lay claim to absolute knowledge or a philosophy of certainty; he was not dogmatic, but saw the fluidity of reality as necessitating constant re-examination of circumstances and the assumptions governing his analyses.

Ian Thatcher provides a historical comparison of Trotsky and Luxemburg. Left communism as a whole he characterizes as revolutionary, libertarian, councilist, anti-Stalinist and anti-parliamentarian. Luxemburg he finds more libertarian than Trotsky and ultimately more patient and principled, believing principles without power to be better than power without principles. In particular, Luxemburg will not sacrifice her commitment to democracy in order to achieve socialism, and consistently opposes the substitution of a vanguard party for the full involvement of the masses in revolution. Trotsky, on the other hand, while having a more lasting influence within Marxism and despite his writings being of great importance in the project of constructing a non-Stalinist Marxism, suffers from his closeness to Lenin. Thatcher suggests that Trotsky 'could never be truthful about how Stalin and Stalinism emerged from Lenin and Leninism.'

Jules Townshend offers a qualified defence of right-wing Marxism, a school which he notes has been widely criticized and condemned from within the Marxist tradition. Cautious, unheroic and history's losers, right-wing Marxists such as the Mensheviks, Kautsky and Bernstein nevertheless made significant contributions to Marxism. For Townshend, right-wing Marxism, unlike other strands of Marxism, never lost sight of the crucial link between democracy and socialism through which workers' self-emancipation was to be achieved. They also brought a realism to the Marxist project, attempting to adapt Marxism to new conditions and to respond to the impact of modernity. Bernstein, in particular, upheld the critical spirit of Marxism and opened up space for moral advocacy in his bold revisions of Marxism. 'The twenty-first century may prove a little kinder to right-wing Marxist reputations than the twentieth,' suggests Townshend.

The thinkers and debates considered in Part II are in the main chronologically after those discussed in Part I, but Part II follows a more geographical structure. It contains chapters on Soviet and Eastern bloc Marxism, Eurocommunism, Western Marxism, African Marxisms, Asian Marxisms and Latin American Marxisms.

In his chapter on Soviet and Eastern bloc Marxism, Mark Sandle focuses on 'the development, consolidation, crisis and eventual collapse of "official" Marxism in the Soviet bloc.' He notes that as an official belief system Soviet Marxism–Leninism held a monopoly position with all divergent views censored. Cut off from all criticism and meaningful debate, intellectual ossification was inevitable. Soviet Marxism, because of the dominant political position of the Soviet Union, was enormously influential, but because it became 'a dogmatic, stylized set of empty formulae bearing no relation to reality,' and was 'little more than a thinly veiled rationalization of the monopoly of power of the [Communist Party of the Soviet Union]' it failed to endure past the collapse of the Soviet system in 1991. But this is not the whole story, according to Sandle. There were innovations in such areas as ethics, logic and philosophy of history, and there were developments of Marxist theory of the transition from capitalism to communism and the nature of the transitional (socialist) and end (communist) societies. In addition, the contributions in the post-Stalin era, particularly in Czechoslovakia and Yugoslavia (most notably the Praxis school), should not be overlooked.

The path of Eurocommunism is traced by Rick Simon, who notes its attempt to find a 'third way' between Soviet-style communism and Western European social democracy. Simon characterizes Eurocommunism in terms of its critical stance towards Soviet Marxism, an emphasis on different national roads to socialism, an acceptance of the need for democracy and human and civil rights, and a commitment to using liberal democratic institutions to achieve socialism. He criticizes the failure of Eurocommunists to generate an enduring theoretical framework, suggesting this was a product of their over-emphasis on strategy, alliances and national peculiarities. The very term 'Eurocommunism' implies a coherence and identity that was apparent rather than real, and Eurocommunism is essentially a phenomenon representing a phase in the crisis of world communism. Simon concludes, 'Ultimately socialism can only be constructed on a global scale. By emphasizing national distinctiveness to the detriment of the global dimension, Eurocommunism could only follow a reformist path.'

In a wide-ranging chapter covering such heavyweight thinkers as Georg Lukacs, Karl Korsch, Antonio Gramsci, Max Horkheimer, Theodor Adorno, Herbert Marcuse, Jean-Paul Sartre and Louis Althusser, Joseph Femia adopts a largely critical approach to Western Marxism. Femia acknowledges the achievements of Western Marxism as a varied body of theory, particularly in its critique of scientistic philosophy and positivist social science. However, Femia questions the coherence of Western Marxist thought, arguing that the attempts of its exponents to introduce non-Marxist elements into Marxism amounted to an implicit critique of the Marxist project, and, hence, we should not be surprised to see the trajectory of Western Marxists, such as Habermas, from Marxism to post-Marxism. In a damning conclusion he writes, 'If the point of revolutionary theory is to change the world, then Western Marxism must be judged a failure.'

Daryl Glaser in his account and analysis of African Marxism begins by looking at African socialism and its links and overlaps with African Marxism. He moves on to provide an informative exposition of Marxist theory on Africa, and of the development of Marxism in African countries (ironically one key means of transmission being imperialism). The diversity of forms of Marxism is highlighted, reflecting the very different conditions operating in different African countries, most notably the developed capitalist and feudal class systems found in South Africa and Ethiopia respectively. Glaser argues that, while a standard formula based on Leninist and Soviet teaching was applied by African Marxist governments, there were also some distinctive contributions made by Africa's Marxist movements and regimes, for example General Mohammed Siad Barre's synthesis of Marxism and Islam, Ben Bella's 'arabo-Islamic' socialism, the Eritrean People's Liberation Front and Tigray People's Liberation Front's views on secession, Sékou Touré's experiments with mass-party forms, and the Madagascan Marxists' partial electoral pluralism.

In discussing the decline and fall of Afro-Marxism Glaser notes the relatively brief lifespan of most of the Marxist regimes in Africa (from the 1970s to the 1990s), which has led the overwhelming majority of both participants and observers to judge the Marxist project in Africa a failure. Glaser notes the difficulty in diagnosing this failure given that it is not easy 'to separate out the effects of Marxism's inadequacies and of Africa's malaise.' Nevertheless, Glaser identifies such problems as resource scarcity, hostile countries surrounding the Marxist regimes, over-ambition, impatience and political ineptness on the part of their leaders, and, above all, the limitations of their Leninist-style democratic theory and practice as key factors in the failure of Afro-Marxism. For Glaser the shortcomings of Afro-Marxism do not mean that Africa must embrace neo-liberal capitalism or that Marxism has no place in the future of the continent. In the socialist project of generating sustainable economic growth, deepening democracy and limiting social inequality, it may yet be necessary 'to consult Marxism, if not to devise a new political order, then at least to provide a clear-sighted analysis of the new pattern of class inequality that has formed on the ruins of discarded socialisms.'

Nick Knight writes, 'it is one of the great ironies in the history of the Marxist tradition that Marxism has had a greater political impact in Asia than any other region of the globe.' He lists Russia, China, North Korea, Vietnam, Cambodia, Laos, India, Indonesia, Malaysia, Japan and the Philippines as countries that have had Marxist governments or important Marxist movements. Although Marx was a 'quintessentially European intellectual' his thought contains universal elements, most importantly a method based on a material perspective focusing on production, and a critique of capitalism, a system that has spread to every pocket of the world. These universal elements appealed to Asian Marxists. Marx's specific writings on Asia have largely been ignored by Asian Marxists, who have preferred to draw inspiration from Lenin's works that suggested that national, anti-colonial revolutions were a key part of the struggle for world revolution. Knight focuses on the thought of Mao Zedong and Ho Chi Minh as the most significant Asian Marxists. He notes how they both sought to adapt Marxism to local conditions, and combined nationalism or patriotism with Marxism. Ultimately, Mao and Ho were successful revolutionaries, but rather less successful in building socialism, and this points to Knight's overall assessment of the impact of Marxism on Asia: Marxism worked as a theory of revolution, but not as one of socialist construction. It is noteworthy that since the deaths of Mao and Ho both China and Vietnam have pursued policies more accommodating to capitalism.

There are some parallels in Marx's views on Latin America and his views on Asia. In both instances he displays an extremely Eurocentric viewpoint and this is brought out strongly by Ronaldo Munck in his chapter. To give one quotation from Marx highlighted by Munck: 'We have witnessed the conquest of Mexico and have rejoiced at it . . . It is to the interests of its own development that Mexico will in future be placed under the tutelage of the United States.' Munck provides an account of the contributions of thinkers probably less well known in Europe, including Juan Justo and José Carlos Mariátegui, both of whom attempted to 'Latin Americanize' Marxism, with the latter becoming known as the continent's Gramsci. He also discusses Cuba, the Sandinistas in Nicaragua, the Renovadores in Chile and the Zapatistas in Mexico. Suggesting that Latin American Marxism is 'consumed' in the developed countries as a series of icons – think of Che Guevara as little more than a poster image – Munck argues that its intellectual contribution is overlooked. In particular, theories of radical democracy, the 'national-popular', and dependency theory have all been developed within the Latin American Marxist tradition. Looking to the future, Munck notes the possibilities for the creative development of Marxism freed up by the collapse of Soviet communism, but remains sceptical about the value of Marxism as a guide to action in Latin America.

The contributors in Part III endeavour to engage with recent issues and debates in Marxist thought. Howard Chodos discusses the relationship between Marxism as theory and Marxist-inspired practice, and picking up on related themes Daryl Glaser reflects on the theory and practice of Marxism, and in particular issues of epistemology and democratic procedure. Yahya Madra and Fikret Adaman stress economics more in their consideration of Marxist analyses of capitalism, and Daniel Little looks at the key area of Marxism and method, and the extent to which Marxism has something methodologically distinctive and useful to offer.

In looking at the experience of attempts to put the Marxist vision of socialism into practice, Chodos notes the failure of historical communism to survive the twentieth century intact. Either it collapsed, as in the case of the Soviet Union, or it was drastically changed, almost out of recognition, as in the case of China. He also notes the economic failings and widespread human rights violations of communist regimes. Whilst acknowledging that there is no straightforward relationship between theory and practice, Chodos suggests that the historical record 'can legitimately be said to call into question the validity of the Marxist project itself.' Focusing on the Soviet Union, Chodos examines the record of historical communism and draws up an historical balance sheet. The massive loss of life, both intended and unintended, the economic waste and inefficiency, and the environmental devastation all lead Chodos to conclude that 'the Soviet experiment constitutes a massive failure.'

Probing further into the nature of historical communism and its link with Marxist theory, Chodos develops his own characterization of historical communist regimes and identifies the role of the party and the fusion of the economic and social spheres as key in creating the structure of social accumulation of communist regimes. The link between the practice of historical communism and Marxist theory, and Chodos does claim a link, lies in the combination of specific elements of Marxist theory. For Chodos it is a Marxist teleology, a belief in the scientific character of Marxism, and a Manichean view of both the world and historical struggle, all allied to the concentration of enormous political and economic power in the hands of a ruling elite that led to the disastrous record of historical communism.

However, according to Chodos, the fate of historical communism is not inevitable and its defects can be avoided by taking certain steps. First, Marxist regimes must not allow what he terms 'refeudalization', that is the fusion of economy and polity, to take place. Second, there must be genuine democracy with real political competition (multiple parties and free expression). Third, the socialist project must in principle be reversible through democratic means; the legitimacy of socialism depends on it being freely chosen and the people must be allowed the option of rejecting it. Fourth, human rights and freedoms must be inviolable. Fifth, whereas the core dynamics of capitalism must be changed, not everything capitalist has to be altered. Finally, and perhaps from a Marxist perspective most controversially of all, socialism must no longer be defined in terms of the rule of the working class. As Chodos concludes, 'if there is to be a future for Marxist-inspired socialism, a way must be found to initiate the transition to classlessness without the intermediate phase of working-class power.'

Glaser in his chapter focuses 'on the metatheoretical background of Marxist theory and action rather than on the content of a viable Marxist theory, methodology, analysis or programme.' He notes the poor economic performance, the democratic deficit and the appalling human rights record of Marxist states, an overall history that should concern adherents to an ideology that stresses the link between theory and practice. After rejecting the view that it is Marxism's self-proclaimed scientific approach and epistemology that is the root of the totalitarianism displayed by Marxist states, Glaser puts forward two rules for Marxists translating Marxist theory into practice: first, knowledge must be viewed as provisional; second, binding decisions must be consent-based. In order to avoid the failings of twentieth-century Marxist practice and to ensure that Marxism does no harm, but rather is of benefit in the future, Marxists must be committed to the tenet that all knowledge is provisional and democratic procedures must be followed. In acknowledging that knowledge is provisional Marxists must accept that there is no warrant to 'force people to be free' – what is being forced upon people may turn out to be mistaken. In committing to procedural democracy Marxists achieve legitimacy and give expression to the provisionality of knowledge rule. Glaser goes on to discuss the three roles of Marxism, as interpreter, 'politico' and Legislator, roles that again show the need for Marxists to be procedural democrats. For Glaser, Marxism must follow democracy-friendly rules of conduct and can 'contribute to democracy construction and other socially desirable projects.' A socialist radicalism coupled with principled proceduralism points to a twenty-first-century Marxism.

In looking at Marxist economics and analyses of capitalism, Madra and Adaman stress that there is no one, homogenous critique of political economy, but instead there is a multiplicity of Marxist theories. They focus on two of the principal Marxist approaches or projects, each with very different implications: capital accumulation theories and class exploitation theories. 'Whereas the former project is committed to the analysis of capitalism as a crises-ridden process of wealth accumulation, the latter can be described as the institutionally specific analyses of different class structures (capitalist, feudal, slave, independent, or communal) and their articulation,' write Madra and Adaman. In addition to discussing these two approaches they provide an introduction to basic concepts of Marxian economics and a discussion of colonialism and imperialism from the viewpoint of Marxian economics. Madra and Adaman emphasize the political implications of different Marxist theories of capitalism, arguing that 'the way in which we theorize the economy affects the ways in which we devise political strategies of social transformation.' Accumulationist theories point to the state and capitalist corporations as key locations for struggle, whereas class exploitation theories direct attention to 'the multiplicity of forms of exploitation and domination within contemporary social formations,' and also suggest possibilities of 'imagining and enacting communal (and maybe even independent) class structures and democratic forms of governance today – as opposed to waiting for the terminal collapse of capitalism.' A key insight suggested is that the economy, whether of the world as a whole or of a specific country or region, even in the age of capitalism is not wholly capitalist. Non-capitalism exists in parts of the Third World, but also in the informal sector, households and some local communities where local public goods are provided by communal labour. For Madra and Adaman the richness, relevance and possibilities for further development are the most salient features of Marxian economic theories. The class exploitation approach in particular has opened up new avenues for constructive political action, which, when combined with the insights of the more orthodox Marxist accumulationist approach, gives a Marxian economics for the twenty-first century.

In the final chapter of the book Little looks at the contributions to social scientific methodology of both Marx and later Marxists, including Althusser, Poulantzas, Gramsci, the critical theorists and materialist historians, and finishing with the school of analytical Marxism. Summarizing Marx's influence on twentieth-century social science, Little usefully provides lists of themes and substantive methodological maxims for social research that constitute Marx's contribution. These include emphasizing and focusing on class, production, technology, property, alienation and exploitation. Overall, Little sees Marx as offering not a tight prescriptive body of methodological tenets, but, rather, a loose set of prescriptions, a heuristic that directs us to be flexible in applying materialism, to look at material institutions, class, power, exploitation and domination, to be aware of 'contradictions' in social formations and to seek underlying causes and structures. In short, Marx provides 'a loose research programme, inspired by a congeries of hypotheses, insights, and salient powerful interpretations.' For Little this 'style' (rather than method) of inquiry is eclectic and plural, and still has much to offer.

In the course of the book contributors describe the record of Marxist thinkers and schools of thought in the twentieth century and put forward criticisms and defences of various aspects of Marxist thought. For some, such as Femia and Munck, there is much to criticize and reject, whereas others, Shandro and Townshend for example, offer more sympathetic accounts of Marxism, or at least of aspects of it. This critical survey leads into a discussion of aspects of recent Marxist theory, where the contemporary relevance of Marxism is most directly broached. Chodos, Glaser, Madra and Adaman, and Little all point to a role for Marxism in the twenty-first century. Mindful of its history, failings and lacunae, they all suggest directions for development and ways in which Marxist theory might still prove fruitful. The century of Marxism has not quite given way to the century of post-Marxism.

Note

1 To give just a few examples of electoral support for communism: the Party of Demo-cratic Socialism, the successor to the East German Communist Party, secured close to 9 per cent of the vote in the 2005 general election, including over 25 per cent of East German votes cast; in the Czech Republic the Communist Party of Bohemia and Moravia polled 18.5 per cent of the vote in the 2002 parliamentary elections; in Russia the Communist Party of the Russian Federation polled 12.6 per cent of the vote in Duma elections in 2003; in Moldova the Communists' Party of the Republic of Moldova holds power, having polled 46 per cent of the vote in 2005. In a poll of over 2000 Russians in 2004 by the reputable Yuri Levada Analytical Center, 67 per cent 'regretted the fall of the Soviet Union'. In another survey 71 per cent of Russians 'strongly' or 'somewhat' approved of the former communist regime with 41 per cent responding either 'somewhat agree' or 'strongly agree' to the statement 'We should return to communist rule' (Rose, 2005).

References

Brzezinski, Z. (1989) *The Grand Failure: The Birth and Death of Communism in the Twen-tieth Century*. London: Macdonald.
Fukuyama, F. (1992) *The End of History and the Last Man*. London: Penguin.
Gamble, A., D. Marsh and T. Tant (eds) (1999) *Marxism and Social Science*. London: Macmillan.
Rose, Richard (ed.) (2005) *New Russia Barometer XIV: Evidence of Dissatisfaction*. Stud-ies in Public Policy No. 402. Glasgow: University of Strathclyde.

Part I

1 Lenin and Marxism

Class struggle, the theory of politics and the politics of theory

Alan Shandro

Berlin 1989: the wall dividing East and West is broken down and the props of 'actually existing socialism' will crumble in surprisingly rapid succession. As the icons of Marx and Lenin come tumbling down across Eastern Europe and the former Soviet Union, Western cartoonists vie with each other in producing variants of one image: gangs of workers and peasants, armed with hammers and sickles, angrily chasing after the two startled and bewildered communist thinkers.

What was their transgression that it should call forth such retribution? There are those for whom the Bolshevik revolution and the social order to which it gave rise are to be understood as the poisoned fruit of a criminal will to power. The story suggested by the cartoons, however, is probably more influential and certainly more interesting. The communists are caught unawares, victims of misguided confidence in the truth of their theory, despite all evidence to the contrary. So overweening was this confidence that, not only were they willing to reconstruct entire societies upon the promise of a theory, they would impose their blueprint with massive violence, violating the aspirations and the experience of the very people in whose name the promise had been proffered. The anger of the workers and peasants was directed, then, at the betrayal of a promise but also, through this, at the theoretical arrogance that stood behind the promise. The offence of Marx, and especially of Lenin, was the original sin of intellectual pride.

Something like this story also runs through the academic literature on Marx and Lenin, evident in the current practice of attributing to Lenin a claim to 'absolute knowledge', a 'philosophy of certainty' (see, for example, Harding, 1996: 219–42). It is a story with some rhetorical force; it can appeal to the virtues, grounded in plebeian experience, of modesty and tolerance. Its intellectual power, however, is dubious; in it Marxist and Leninist ideas are criticized only by implication, or rather by insinuation. What matters about those ideas is that they were imposed with arrogant disregard for popular aspiration and experience; from the anger of the workers and peasants we can infer the falsity of the ideas. No need, then, to investigate the ideas themselves; we already know, from the experience of their victims, the truth about them. And should the contradictions of our own quotidian experience tempt us to test its limits, we already know what might lie beyond and can prudently resist the temptation. Never mind that empathy for the experience of the victims and fear of what lies beyond the familiar confines of our own experience have been mobilized more than once since the wall came down on behalf of wars of imperial conquest.

The terms in which Marxists and their adversaries have understood the movement of the class struggle and debated the appropriate strategies and institutions continue nonetheless to shape debates and divisions in working-class and popular movements and thereby enter into the present context of political action. They can enter consciously or unconsciously; where, as in the case of Lenin, they are permitted entry only in forms so highly abstracted and even caricatural as effectively to repress the logic of political debate, careful and critical re-examination is particularly called for. Furthermore, just because political actors in the tradition of classical Marxism have had to engage with the difficulties and uncertainties of situating themselves politically and theoretically in determinate moments of the class struggle, one can hope to derive from their example analytical tools that can be brought to bear upon present moments; I would argue that Lenin's almost dogged insistence that concrete situations be analysed concretely makes him exemplary in this regard. There could be no more propitious moment for a critical re-examination of the substance of the thought beneath the symbol.

The politics of class consciousness

The *locus classicus* of the original Leninist sin of intellectual pride is the thesis, formulated in *What Is To Be Done?*, that socialist consciousness must be imported into the spontaneous working-class movement from without. Conventional wisdom, preoccupied with the question of who is the bearer of consciousness and perhaps for that very reason unduly confident that it already knows what is meant by spontaneity and consciousness, can read this claim as the theoretical foundation for the subordination of the workers to an intellectual elite. Yet, if Lenin's claim is read, as he insisted, in the context of his argument as a whole, then it will be seen to bear very different implications.

The context invoked in Lenin's argument is defined by the intersection of three principal trends: the spontaneous upsurge of the nascent Russian working-class movement; the appearance of a liberal-bourgeois opposition with the evident ambition of contending for hegemony in the impending democratic revolution; and the emergence in social-democratic ranks of a tendency, dubbed 'Economist', to place a narrow construction upon the political tasks and the political consciousness of socialists in the democratic revolution and thereby, Lenin argued, subordinate the working-class movement to the hegemonic strategy of the bourgeoisie. The intersection of these trends yields a working-class movement subject to two spontaneous tendencies. The first is grounded in the social relations of capitalist production, toward socialist consciousness, whereas the second is driven by the pervasive diffusion of bourgeois ideology and the adaptability of bourgeois strategy, toward 'trade-union consciousness'. Lenin's claim is that the latter tendency 'spontaneously' predominates over the former.

To appreciate the force of this claim, we need to look at the logic of the interplay between these tendencies. The claim is *not* that the workers are some-how compelled to restrict themselves to narrow economic demands and forms of struggle. In the course of their spontaneous struggles, the workers may very well innovate in ways that challenge the parameters of bourgeois hegemony and even, on occasion, breach them. Spontaneous innovation is met, however, by the reformulation of the parameters of bourgeois hegemony. This allows a reorganiza-tion of bourgeois strategy and the spontaneous imposition of bourgeois ideology onto the struggle of the workers. It is here that Economism played a pivotal role. Bourgeois hegemony need not depend upon denial of the class struggle and the Economists did not necessarily or even usually advocate the reduction of political to economic struggle; indeed, their stance could be and often was articulated in very revolutionary terms. Perhaps better termed 'spontaneism', this trend con-sisted of the accommodation of socialist politics to the spontaneous movement of the class struggle, that is to lines, forms and trajectories of conflict prescribed by, or at least recoverable by, bourgeois hegemony.

Accommodation to bourgeois hegemony thus proceeds spontaneously, not through a failure of proletarian commitment to the struggle for socialism, which Lenin never questioned, but through failure to mount a political project of pro-letarian hegemony. Such a project presumes socialist consciousness, understood in Lenin's argument as consciousness of 'the irreconcilable antagonism of [the workers'] interests to the whole of the modern political and social system' (1961 [1902]: 375). Socialist consciousness would have to draw upon Marxist theory and could not be brought to bear upon the class struggle in the absence of an organized leadership informed by that theory and able to apply it ambitiously and with confidence. It could not arise simply from the workers' spontaneous experi-ence because that experience is structured both by the reality of class antagonism and by the bourgeois ideological construction of such antagonism as somehow reconcilable. Since both terms of this contradictory couple can take on novel forms beyond the current experience of the participants, the irreconcilability of the antagonism can only be grasped theoretically.

Why could the workers themselves not grasp Marxist theory spontaneously? Lenin's explicit answer was that they could do it, better in fact than the intel-lectuals. They would do so, however, not in the mass, but as individuals, and having become conscious, they would find themselves in a position analogous to that occupied by the initial, intellectual, carriers of Marxist theory, confronting the challenge of bringing consciousness to bear upon the contradictory logic of the spontaneous movement. At stake in Lenin's thesis of 'consciousness from without' was not an issue in the sociology of knowledge concerning the bearer of socialist consciousness, but the strategic, or better, meta-strategic, issue of the terms in which Marxist political actors – intellectuals or workers – can come to grips with their own situation within the class struggle and position themselves to act effectively upon it.

His distinction between spontaneity and consciousness is not a transposition into political terms of an ontological distinction between matter and mind or of a social-scientific distinction between base and superstructure or even of a sociological distinction between workers and intellectuals. It invokes, rather, the contradictory combination of a complex set of forces and tendencies in a concrete conjuncture of political struggle in which the class struggle, and, with it, working-class consciousness, cannot but develop unevenly. The thesis of consciousness from without is an attempt to think through the implications of this unevenness for political action and political leadership of the working-class movement. It provides the conceptual underpinnings for the distinctive Leninist injunction to concrete analysis of the concrete situation and it mandates, accordingly, the reflexive adjustment of consciousness to the shifting lines and logic of the struggle for hegemony. Thus, paradoxically, it generates the possibility of opening Marxist theory to unexpected innovation and diversity in the spontaneous movement of the class struggle (see Shandro, 1995).

The struggle for hegemony

Lenin would deploy the analytical framework first set to work in *What Is To Be Done?* across successive conjunctures of the political struggle and this would enable him to work out an increasingly concrete conception of the political project of proletarian hegemony. This work is not to be understood as a mere evolution of ideas but required a sustained engagement with the activity of the spontaneous movements of the masses, workers and peasants, as the experience of the 1905 revolution may serve to illustrate. In response to the unexpected breadth and the radicalism of peasant land seizures, Lenin would distinguish two possible trajectories of revolutionary development according to the alliance of class forces necessary to propel each. A proletarian–peasant path would lead to a thoroughgoing destruction of the political and social institutions underpinning the Tsarist order, whereas a landlord–bourgeois path would result in a compromise preserving as much of these institutions as was consistent with the evolution of Russian capitalism. If the interests of workers and peasants were, on this analysis, aligned, how the proletariat might establish its hegemony in and through such an alliance remained unclear. The Marxist party of the proletariat, though gaining influence rapidly among the workers, had little presence in the vast Russian countryside.

It is in the context of this problem that Lenin would approach the spontaneous movement of the proletariat. Organizing themselves into soviets, the workers spontaneously reorganized the space of political life: opening the process of political decision-making to the scrutiny of the popular masses, they encouraged the masses to enter politics; merging the social, economic and cultural demands and grievances of the people in the assault upon the autocratic regime, they palpably expanded the range of political struggle; dispensing with formalities that barred the path to participation in the struggle, they facilitated the confluence of popular forces in all their contradictory diversity. In all these ways, they restructured the terrain of political struggle along lines that enabled the Marxist vanguard party more effectively to pursue the political project of proletarian hegemony.

For Lenin's Menshevik rivals, by contrast, the phenomenon of the soviets was conceived as a forum for the self-education of the workers in practical politics, for working-class self-activity, that might culminate in the formation of a real mass party of labour. What was most fundamentally at stake in the institution of the soviet, thus understood, was the relation between the working class and its political party rather than the more inclusive agenda of the democratic revolution and the struggle to overthrow the power of the autocratic state. The distinctiveness of Lenin's position is thrown into relief by his critique of this Menshevik view: to take the political self-education of the workers, conceived in abstraction from the strategic logic of the class struggle for hegemony and thus from the prospect of counter-revolutionary violence, as the guiding aim is to assume an educational forum sheltered somehow from the intervention of state power. But to base a political education upon such an assumption, since it abstracts from a fundamental reality of politics, can only be self-defeating. Further, inasmuch as it is self-defeating, it opens avenues for the deployment of bourgeois influence in the working-class movement. The order of analysis is reversed in Lenin's approach and the meaning of political education correspondingly transformed; the workers can gain a real education in politics only by tackling whatever tasks are imposed by the logic of the real political struggle. The material available for the demanding work of socialist political education is supplied by the historical movement and the present reality of the class struggle; in this struggle the ruling class is no mere static backdrop against which workers and revolutionary intellectuals work out their project of socialist self-education: just as workers spontaneously innovate in the course of their struggles, rulers innovate, through their ideological and political representatives, in response. The process of working out a socialist political education is one in which the adversary is inevitably and actively present. To reckon without this presence, as the Mensheviks did, is to assume, in the very terms of one's struggle for hegemony, the position of the subaltern (see Shandro, 2001).

Vanguard and masses play different, possibly harmonious, but sometimes necessarily contradictory, parts in the logic of the class struggle. The very weight of organized numbers in motion, of the masses, can lead to the emergence of unforeseen political forces, positions and possibilities. But a position staked out today can always be transformed in accordance with the strategic calculation of an adversary. So the struggle for hegemony presumes the ability to adapt to the changing conjuncture of political struggle, to combine awareness of the underlying forces that shape the logic of struggle with openness to the possibility that other actors, adversaries or allies, will innovate in the course of the struggle. Leadership in the class struggle thus demands a conscious vanguard, sensitive to the struggles of the masses yet willing and able where necessary to oppose its political analyses to their spontaneous movement. The objection can be raised that this claim simply provides a sophisticated rationale for minority dictatorship. This objection would be persuasive, however, only if the concepts and distinctions that underpin this Leninist claim did not afford a superior analysis of the logic of the class struggle. The question of the truth of the analysis is, in this sense, unavoidable but here, as elsewhere, this question does not arise from a claim to know some absolute truth but 'relative truths, pertaining to perfectly definite facts, with which alone [Lenin] operate[s]' (Lenin, 1961 [1904]: 477).

The logic of imperialism

The role of Marxist theory, as understood by Lenin, was not simply to indicate the aim of the struggle but to situate that aim in the context of action, in the class struggle, and reflexively to revise it in accordance with the logic and the concrete circumstances of that struggle. Marxism was not simply an injunction to action – go, workers, go! – but a guide to action. Lenin's analysis of imperialism aimed to provide revolutionary Social Democrats with the means to reorient themselves theoretically in a new and critical conjuncture in which erstwhile comrades had aligned themselves with the war effort of one or another of the contending imperialist powers.

To that end, it was designed to explain the connection between the logic of capitalist development, the war and the crisis of international socialism. That imperialism is characterized in Lenin's principal work on the subject as 'the highest stage of capitalism', 'the eve of the socialist revolution' (1964 [1916a]: 187), is no mere afterthought or rhetorical flourish; it not only coheres with the political aim of his analysis – if imperialism is the eve of the socialist revolution, political identification with the social-democratic allies of empire is unthinkable – but is built into its conceptual logic. Imperialism possesses this characteristic, however, not in virtue of an alleged inability to stimulate technological progress or enhance economic growth – Lenin distanced himself in no uncertain terms from any such claim (see 1964 [1916a]: 300) – but because it restructures the arena of class struggles, extends the contradictions of capitalist production to the farthest corners of the world, and thus irreversibly reorganizes the pattern of contradictions that would shape the transition to socialism. His analysis turns not upon some empirical dogma concerning the level of production attained at a certain point in time but upon an account of how monopoly grows out of capitalism and how the movement of imperialist contradictions in turn grows out of the social form of monopoly capitalism in which production is organized and moves. Class struggle thus remains central in his account of the transition to socialism.

Inextricably bound up with the socialization of production, monopoly capitalism embodies the possibility of socially planned production and hence raises the spectre of socialism but, in the context of private appropriation, socialization only renders competition more conscious, more strategic, more intense, thus more political – and consequently more dangerous. The inherently expansive character of capitalism assumes, with the advent of monopoly, the predominant form of the export of capital and thus the worldwide extension of the social relations of capitalist production. The export of capital and the corresponding implantation of the machinery of imperial domination call forth movements of resistance in which class struggles mesh with opposition to national and colonial oppression and draw the peoples of the colonies into a global arena of struggle. Since the development of capitalism becomes increasingly uneven, shifts become inevitable in the relative strength of contending imperialist powers and, once the world is divided between the powers, struggles to shift the division in accordance with a new relation of forces can be settled, ultimately, only by force. Imperialism is thus the highest stage of capitalism in the further sense that it extends the contradictions of capital to the farthest reaches of the globe and pushes them, in the form of imperialist war, to their highest intensity. What is more, imperialism breeds a parasitic tendency for the decay of the social body. Although parasitism and decay are not synonymous, in Lenin's usage, with economic stagnation, they do suggest a social organism whose dominant elements depend essentially upon, but cannot exist without sapping, the productive activity of others. Imperialist parasitism signifies a set of permutations in the field of class forces, first, the growth of a class of 'rentiers' living on their holdings, without taking part in productive enterprise, guarded by a militarist machine and enveloped in an ideology of chauvinism.

Second, monopoly super-profits accrued through the super-exploitation of cheap labour in the colonies provide a material basis for the formation of a stratum of relatively well-to-do workers, a labour aristocracy, distinct from the mass of wage-labourers. The labour aristocracy assumes various shapes in the course of Lenin's analyses but what emerges across these variations is a process of division, of the hierarchical fragmentation of the working-class movement. Imperialist super-profits provide capital – and the state – with the wherewithal to concede, in forms that reflect and reproduce division and hierarchy, some of the most pressing demands of some workers. They thereby constitute a material basis for the belief that socialism is attainable through the peaceful accumulation of reforms. The resulting inability of Social Democrats to meet imperialist war with a declaration of class war disorganized the proletariat as an independent social force, allowing its fragments to be consolidated into a system of social control in which leaderless masses were confronted, as isolated individuals, with the organized power of the state. Conversely, however, the workers are constituted as a class not by the exclusion of the stratum of labour aristocrats but through the deployment of a political project that would enable the struggles of that stratum to be integrated with, and thus subordinated to, the political struggle for socialist revolution.

The forces of revolution are assembled only on the field of battle, in the course of hostilities, from whatever elements present themselves, drawn often from the ranks of opposing forces. The job of revolutionary political leadership is thus in part a *bricolage*, demanding both clear awareness of the complex ecology of battle in which one is situated and the independence of judgment to act decisively in its midst. Lenin's analysis of imperialism therefore implies a rethinking of the relation between democratic struggles and socialist revolution. Since imperialism gives rise to bourgeois movements of national liberation and a petty-bourgeois-democratic opposition, the revolutionary vanguard of the proletariat must seek to assume the political leadership of the democratic struggles of heterogeneous or even of non-proletarian strata of the people while waging a political and ideological struggle against the hegemony of petty-bourgeois democracy – more precisely, of an alliance of petty-bourgeois and labour aristocrat – in the struggle against imperialism. The socialist revolution can no longer be supposed to announce its advent through a simplification of class alignments but must instead take the form of a conjunction of the proletarian struggle for socialism with a variety of revolutionary-democratic movements. Imperialism is thus the highest stage of capitalism, finally, in the sense that there will be no socialist revolution except through political engagement in the complex, uneven and contradictory logic of the struggle for hegemony.

When it is grasped along these lines, there is no reason to suppose Lenin's theory of imperialism, at least in its broad outlines, outmoded. In fact, it can serve to point up the fact of the uneven, indeed increasingly uneven, development of capital: the division between oppressed and oppressor countries and nations has changed in shape but not in substance, and resistance to the bipolar logic of accumulation remains endemic, intense and on occasion dramatic, albeit 'variegated and discordant, motley and outwardly fragmented' (Lenin, 1964 [1916b]: 356), throughout the underdeveloped outreaches of the global order where the hegemony of capital cannot be enforced without unleashing the war engines of imperialist intervention. While almost Carthaginian conditions of social peace are imposed in the East, old and some new modes of repression and reaction are mobilized against the anticipation of new forms and fronts of opposition in the imperialist centres of the West. And those who are quite certain that the tendency to war between imperialist powers has been held in check for a long half century by something more durable than the strength of 'actually existing socialism' might do well to ponder the possibilities implicit in the increasingly bellicose unilateralism of US policy and in the growing disquiet occasioned thereby, not only in erstwhile enemies, but among nominal friends and allies as well. Lenin's theory is not, of course, a concrete analysis of the current conjuncture – that can only be a matter for the present – but its logic offers intellectual tools pertinent to such analysis.

Revolution and counter-revolution

The same logic can be found at work in Lenin's most famous work of political theory, *The State and Revolution* (1964 [1917a]). Most often discussed as though its object were to advocate an ideal type of social organization, the argument of the text is thereby assumed to turn upon a comparison between pre- and post-revolutionary institutional models, between the state and the stateless communist society of the future. Lenin's concern, however, was to think through the destruction of the state machine together with the withering away of the state as elements cohering in an integral process of revolution. He did this by distinguishing between state power – a relation of domination, constrained only by struggle and hence a dictatorship of one class over others – and the apparatus of the state – the institutional arrangements through which that relation is orchestrated – and then thinking of the movement of these terms in relation to the process of the class struggle.

Lenin understood the apparatus of the state in class societies as an institutional precipitate of the social dominance of property owners over those who must live by working for them, a transformed form of social power, alienated from the mass of society and so beyond its control. He invokes the soviets and the Paris Commune, by contrast, as forms of organization of the proletariat as the ruling class, whose proletarian character is to be sought precisely in their openness to the heterogeneous ensemble of the people. Openness – 'expansive' is Marx's term (1970 [1871]: 72), 'flexible' Lenin's (1964 [1917a]: 436) – is simply an enabling condition: the emergence of a space in which the practical concerns of the masses can be given political expression and their political aims can be debated in practical terms does not by itself accomplish the seizure of state power nor does it destroy the 'ready-made state machinery' (Marx, 1970 [1871]: 64). What it does is permit a dramatic expansion of the limits of political participation and political debate, including debate about these very issues. However, the engagement of the masses in political struggle and political debate cannot take place, he argues, without the influence of petty-bourgeois democracy, expressed both in trepidation before the revolutionary seizure of state power and in the erosion of the institutions of popular power by bureaucratic place-hunting cloaked in parliamentary bombast. The participation of the masses is thus at once an agency indispensable to the process of the socialist revolution and the object of political struggle.

Still indispensable, then, is the leadership of the Marxist vanguard of the proletariat. The promise of the soviets could be redeemed and proletarian leadership of the people consolidated, in 1917 as in 1905, only through the seizure of state power. The class struggle of the workers could be directed effectively against the power of the state, in 1917 as in 1905, only through the intermediation of a Marxist vanguard in struggle against the spontaneous influence of petty-bourgeois ideology. The full flowering of the soviets would, in 1917 as in 1905, erode the barrier between the popular masses and the state apparatus and thus also the distinction between society and the state: 'The chief thing,' Lenin tells us, is not knowledge or education or technique but 'to imbue the oppressed and the working people with confidence in their own strength,' with a conviction of their responsibility and a sense of their ability, despite inevitable setbacks, to administer the state, oversee production and ensure distribution themselves (1964 [1917b]: 114–5).

Popular self-confidence, the people's courage for politics, does not simply flourish in a romance of revolutionary self-discovery; it must be forged through the logic of the political struggle for hegemony. This requires the intervention of the vanguard of the proletariat, then, not only to educate the masses politically but also to encourage them, to lead them in the destruction of the 'ready-made state apparatus', in the struggle with counter-revolution and in the everyday work of crushing the active and passive resistance of the propertied classes, leaving them with nowhere to go and nothing to do but resign themselves to 'observing the simple, fundamental rules of the community' (Lenin, 1964 [1917a]: 479). The dictatorship of the proletariat and the withering away of the state are not, then, two separate stages but two aspects of a single process of revolutionary transformation.

Revolution is to be understood, then, not as a moment of transgression but as a process structured by the terms of the struggle with counter-revolution, a process of class struggle and the struggle for hegemony, of the proletariat 'constitut[ing] itself as the nation' (Marx and Engels, 1973 [1848]: 84), the constitution of a community in and around the working class; not as the exertion of revolutionary will but as the formation of a proletarian and popular will. Thus understood, there can be no revolution without the threat of violence and the risk of terror, of panic and irresolution, of miscalculation and of crime. These dangers simply serve to underline the indispensability of conscious intervention by an organized vanguard able to gauge the constellation of forces and act to focus the struggles of the masses.

But the real danger in the logic of revolution and counter-revolution is that violence and coercion, hunger and fear, ambition and distrust would sap the nascent roots of proletarian-popular community. For such bonds of community are a necessary condition for the vitality of the link between vanguard and masses and hence for the diagnosis and rectification of mistakes, for the punishment of crimes and the protection of the innocent. In the reality of Soviet socialism under siege, this condition was always under stress and eventually it collapsed. The confinement of the revolutionary process to the war-torn and famine-stricken outreaches of empire left the former propertied classes with many places to go. It thus nourished the ambition of counter-revolution while it pushed the besieged vanguard of the revolution into more or less vicious circles of dependence upon the assistance of bourgeois experts and upon political terror and thus it wore away at popular confidence in the emancipatory dynamic of the process. The claims of the Bolshevik leadership to knowledge came to be invested less in the fractured community of proletarians and the people than in a would-be panoptic apparatus of power, erected above the masses and increasingly resistant to criticism from without, and hence to seem incorrigible, absolute.

In the Soviet Union and in most countries that sought to follow its example (some cases, such as Cuba, perhaps as yet undecided), the logic of the struggle between revolution and counter-revolution led to the military and bureaucratic deformation of the revolutionary process and ultimately to the reversal of its democratic and socialist gains. Such an outcome imposes the question of the adequacy of Leninism to its professed revolutionary task, not simply the conquest of political power but its exercise in an emancipatory transformation of capitalist social relations of production. Critics of Lenin attribute the failure of the Soviet experiment to the very logic of his ideas whereas defenders note the ambition and the difficulty of the attempt and the particularly harrowing circumstances – isolation and intervention, famine and war, economic backwardness and illiteracy – in which the Bolsheviks took on this unprecedented work. The question has proven intractable, perhaps because there is disagreement between critics and defenders not only over clearly defined issues but also over the definition of the issues at stake. Considerations of space preclude a systematic treatment of the issues but some light may be thrown on the question by looking at how Lenin approached freedom of criticism. And once his ideas are examined with care, the shape of an adequate response will prove more nuanced than is consistent with the critics' accusation of a Leninist claim to absolute knowledge.

Class struggle and freedom of criticism

Lenin's most extensive discussion of freedom of criticism occurs in the context of the turn-of-the-century debate occasioned by Eduard Bernstein's revisionist criticisms of orthodox Marxism. Lenin's Economist adversaries, whom he regarded as 'Russian Bernsteinians', complained that the Marxist response to their criticisms was dogmatically to stifle debate. The first chapter of *What Is To Be Done?*, a frankly mocking rejoinder to this complaint, begins with an expression of perplexity that recourse to the principle of freedom of criticism should have been made by one party to a controversy between 'democrats and socialists'. Lenin's perplexity is sometimes taken as temperamental inability to appreciate the value of different perspectives and sometimes as Asiatic incomprehension of the importance of individual freedom and democracy in Western European culture. But what he finds perplexing is not the principle of freedom of criticism as such but the grounds for its use as a slogan in the given situation. He poses the following dilemma:

On one hand the slogan is advanced in response to a challenge to the very principle of freedom of criticism but, he asks rhetorically, '[h]ave voices been raised in the advanced parties against the constitutional law of the majority of European countries which guarantees freedom to science and scientific investigation?' (1961 [1902]: 352). Indeed, he goes on to argue that the unprecedented demands of struggle against Tsarist autocracy call for development of the theoretical capacity to assess the historical experiences of the class struggle critically and test them independently. Since the parameters of debate were bound to shift, theoretical struggle presumes engagement with positions occupied by theoretical adversaries and to this extent it presumes freedom of criticism. Thus, Lenin's argument presumes – although it does not theorize – a diversity of sources of criticism and the existence, if not of a constitutional law, at least of a moral consensus among 'the advanced parties' on the value of freedom of criticism.

On the other hand it is invoked in tandem with and in defence of some specific criticism, which is allegedly being suppressed, in which case the context of the criticism must be spelled out in order to see whether it warrants recourse to the principle. However, Lenin asserts, there was nothing substantially new in the criticisms advanced by the Bernsteinians, no ideas that were not already widely disseminated from political platform and university chair and readily available in learned treatise and popular pamphlet. The critics were free to advocate conciliation with the liberal–bourgeois enemy but they could not very well expect to do so as members of a group whose very reason for being was to wage a struggle against that enemy. Restrictions upon their freedom to expound their ideas as social-democratic ideas posed no threat to public discussion of those ideas. What was thus at stake in the conflict was not the pursuit of truth but a struggle for political influence within social democracy; invoking the principle of freedom of criticism while abdicating responsibility for addressing any concrete criticisms of Marxism, the Russian Bernsteinians rendered themselves effectively complicit with the logic of a liberal–bourgeois bid for hegemony. Indeed, Lenin argued, the fact that the critics campaigned not for assent to their ideas but merely for tolerance of them was tacit admission of an 'inherent falsehood' in their appeal to freedom of criticism; they traded upon the value of this freedom to the pursuit of truth while nonetheless refusing to commit themselves to the truth of their ideas and thus open themselves to refutation. In the same way that predatory wars were fought under the banner of free trade, 'freedom of criticism' served to camouflage the predatory subversion of the theoretical and political independence of social democracy. What is purported to be a truth of universal value is in fact used as an instrument for extending the domination of received ideas – and entrenched interests – by confounding the emergence of any distinct opposition to them.

Lenin's critique of the call for freedom of criticism thus relies upon two assumptions. It assumes a moral consensus, at least among 'the advanced parties', on the value of such constitutional principles as freedom of criticism and it assumes that the significance of a slogan such as 'freedom of criticism', like political watchwords and practices in general, depends upon the balance of political forces and must therefore be assessed with reference to the logic of the class struggle and the struggle for hegemony. There is, however, some tension between the two assumptions: if the antagonism of class interests really is irreconcilable, then there is nothing in the social whole that could not, in principle, be required as a weapon in the class struggle; belief in moral consensus is not exempt from such strategic assessment. To pose the same issue in more directly political terms: can one suppose a moral consensus to hold once class struggle intensifies to the point of struggle between revolution and counter-revolution? Viewed in this light, the challenge posed by Eduard Bernstein's revision of Marxist orthodoxy may be seen as an attempt to resolve the dilemma by subordinating the social-democratic conduct of the class struggle to a moral consensus around liberal-democratic or constitutional norms. Such a consensus, by conciliating the class interests of workers and liberal-bourgeois, would avoid the ravages of revolution. Thus Bernstein could establish a theoretical guarantee of liberal-democratic freedoms but only at the cost of supposing, against all evidence, that a bourgeoisie would respect the consensus even as it was dispossessed of its monopoly of the means of production.

Abstracting a liberal-democratic consensus from the dynamic of class struggle, Bernstein's approach was tantamount, in Lenin's view, to abandonment of the political independence of the working-class movement. Definitive of his political stance, by contrast, was the subordination of any such constitutional norms as freedom of criticism to the logic of the class struggle. The problem of class power is more fundamental in his political optic than the problem of the apparatus, of the institutional forms in which the struggle is embodied. This priority is expressed with brutal clarity in Lenin's definition of dictatorship – 'rule based directly upon force and unrestricted by any laws' (Lenin, 1965 [1918]: 236) – and it renders unavoidable the question whether Leninism can be consistent with constitutional order and democratic rights, the more so as the question did not remain merely theoretical. Indeed, after the Bolsheviks assumed power, even after the civil war had drawn to a close, Lenin would invoke the unfavourable conjuncture of the class struggle to restrict freedom of organization and freedom of speech. Some of the measures he authored established precedents that arguably went beyond what was necessary to the defence of the revolution, and would be used to excuse the subsequent hypertrophy of a repressive state apparatus that refused to wither away.

But the theoretical priority of the class struggle to the formation of a moral consensus does not imply that rights are simply to be treated in a purely instrumental fashion; nor does the primordial importance of the struggle for power imply either unconcern with the problem of working out constitutional forms to foster the emergence of the proletarian–popular community-in-struggle or lack of recourse in trying to address it. That the rule of the proletariat is to be unrestricted by any laws does not imply the absence of legal forms as normal conduits of proletarian rule;[1] indeed, Lenin's encouragement of the working people to take the administration of the law into their own hands was designed to discover and test out forms of rule appropriate to their newfound power, although these forms, too, would always have to be revisited in light of shifting circumstances, capacities, needs and dangers. The point is borne out by more recent events: when the people of the barrios of Caracas rose in April 2002 against the pro-imperialist coup that briefly removed the democratically elected Venezuelan president, Hugo Chavez, from office, they seized television stations that, having legitimized the coup, proceeded in its aftermath with programming as usual, and obliged them to report news of resistance to the coup. They did so, in Lenin's sense of the term, 'dictatorially', that is, they imposed their will upon the owners of the television stations by force, without seeking to gain their consent by persuasion and without regard to the authority of the law. And yet, such 'dictatorial' measures, suppressing freedom of speech, were arguably indispensable to the restoration of 'democratic' rule. One need not be insensitive to the rhetorical force of the language of democracy in order to suggest that violence is done to the texture and the logic of the political struggle of the masses by the attempt to squeeze them, analytically, into an exclusive alternative of democracy or dictatorship.

The ability of proletarian power to clothe itself in effective constitutional forms depends upon the strength and vitality of the proletarian–popular community; this, in turn, is not a given quantity but develops or degenerates in the course of the struggle of revolution and counter-revolution. The elaboration of legal and constitutional forms under the dictatorship of the proletariat is thus subject to the complex, uneven and contradictory logic of the struggle for hegemony. Success in this endeavour is not, therefore, dependent solely upon the political will of the workers and their leadership but the logic of the process bears implications for their practice, of which one is particularly apposite here. The very need to adapt one's analysis and activity to the logic of the struggle and hence to the concrete circumstances of the conjuncture indicates that the context of political action is always subject to unforeseen change. It is thus a feature of every present political conjuncture that there will be a subsequent conjuncture in which the assumptions that sustain present political action will no longer be adequate. The prospect of change imposes the necessity of re-examining both the circumstances and the assumptions governing one's analysis and, as Lenin argued, this requires criticism and therefore a political stance open to criticism. On the logic of Lenin's own argument, then, openness to criticism is a necessary rather than a contingent feature of rational political action. Its necessity, arguably, is not always adequately reflected in Lenin's post-revolutionary practice. But it is a necessity, not grounded upon some transcendent principle of deontology, but rather immanent in the logic of political action. Consequently, not only must the significance of the principle of freedom of criticism (and the institutions and practices through which it is appropriately instantiated) be assessed and reassessed in the full context of political action, the principle itself is not indefeasible.

The absence from Lenin's perspective of any guarantee more absolute than the political intelligence and maturity of the workers and their leaders may seem inadequate, particularly in light of the unfortunate history of democratic rights in the Soviet Union. But such criticism would refuse from the outset the uncertainties inherent in the practice of politics, certainly in the practice of revolutionary politics. Lenin's occasional recourse in his later years to the Napoleonic dictum, 'On s'engage et puis . . . on voit' – 'First engage in a serious battle and then see what happens' (cited in Lenin, 1965 [1923], 480) – suggests that the lesson he drew from his wartime reading of Hegel's *Science of Logic* was, on the contrary, that what can be known absolutely is simply that there are no guarantees; since no one – neither revolutionary nor Bonapartist – can hope to know everything, in particular how others will react to one's own actions, one cannot but summon the courage to act on merely relative truths, in the shadow of uncertainty.

Note

1   Although less forthright than Lenin, a bourgeois theorist like John Locke could not spell out the practical operation of the rule of law without having, in order to anchor the dictatorship of property, to invoke the expedient of prerogative, a 'power to act according to discretion, for the public good, without the prescription of the law, and sometimes even against it' (1980 [1690], paragraph 160) and the threat of enslavement for violators of private property (see 1980 [1690], paragraphs 18 and 23). In this respect, Locke remains contemporary with Lenin – and with us.

References

Harding, Neil (1996) *Leninism*. London: Macmillan.
Lenin, V.I. (1961) [1902] 'What Is To Be Done?' in *Collected Works*, volume V. Moscow: Progress Publishers.
Lenin, V.I. (1961) [1904] 'One Step Forward, Two Steps Back. Reply by N. Lenin to Rosa Luxemburg' in *Collected Works*, volume VII. Moscow: Foreign Languages Publishing House.
Lenin, V.I. (1964) [1916a] 'Imperialism, The Highest Stage of Capitalism' in *Collected Works*, volume XXII. Moscow: Progress Publishers.
Lenin, V.I. (1964) [1916b] 'The Discussion on Self-Determination Summed Up' in *Collected Works*, volume XXII. Moscow: Progress Publishers.
Lenin, V.I. (1964) [1917a] 'The State and Revolution' in *Collected Works*, volume XXV. Moscow: Progress Publishers.
Lenin, V.I. (1964) [1917b] 'Can the Bolsheviks Retain State Power?' in *Collected Works*, volume XXVI. Moscow: Progress Publishers.
Lenin, V.I. (1965) [1918] 'The Proletarian Revolution and the Renegade Kautsky' in *Collected Works*, volume XXVIII. Moscow: Progress Publishers.

Lenin, V.I. (1965) [1923] 'Our Revolution: A Propos of N. Sukhanov's Notes' in *Collected Works*, volume XXXIII. Moscow: Progress Publishers.

Locke, John (1980) [1690] *Second Treatise of Government*. Indianapolis, IN: Hackett.

Marx, Karl (1970) [1871] *The Civil War in France*. Peking: Foreign Languages Press.

Marx, Karl and Friedrich Engels (1973) [1848] 'Manifesto of the Communist Party' in Karl Marx, edited by David Fernbach, *The Revolutions of 1848*. Harmondsworth: Penguin Books.

Shandro, Alan (1995) '"Consciousness from Without": Marxism, Lenin and the Proletariat', *Science & Society*, 59 (3): 268–97.

Shandro, Alan (2001) 'Lenin and Hegemony: the Soviets, the Working Class and the Party in the Revolution of 1905' in Colin Barker, Alan Johnson and Michael Lavalette (eds), *Leadership and Social Movements*. Manchester: Manchester University Press.

2   Left-communism
Rosa Luxemburg and Leon Trotsky compared

Ian D. Thatcher

Introduction

Throughout the twentieth century one tendency within Marxism distinguished itself by its revolutionary commitment and optimism, its internationalism, and its criticism of the social democratic and orthodox Marxist–Leninist movements dominant within socialism. Left-wing Marxism (or left-communism) was resolutely revolutionary in opposition to reformist tendencies, and committedly libertarian or councilist in opposition to both Stalinist and parliamentarist strands. More ambiguously and inconsistently it distinguished its own position from that of Lenin.

Two figures stand out as emblematic of the dominant currents of left Marxism in the twentieth century: Rosa Luxemburg and Leon Trotsky. Both were revolutionaries who supported the October 1917 Bolshevik takeover. Both had a complex and changing relationship with Lenin and the Bolsheviks. Both were anti-parliamentary and in favour of a combination of vanguard leadership and workers' councils. Luxemburg, however, was the more clearly libertarian, sympathetic to spontaneous mass activity and deeply attached to the preservation of civil liberties under socialism. Trotsky was the more vanguardist and the one who, despite his anti-Stalinism, was more willing to subordinate democratic means to revolutionary ends. These two figures have had a profound influence on Marxism and Marxist thought, albeit an influence felt mainly and most strongly in fringe and minority groupings of left politics. Trotsky initiated a trend of radical and anti-Stalinist vanguardism, while Luxemburg's legacy has been more diffuse (there are few 'Luxemburgists' in the way that there are Trotskyists) but is felt and viewed positively by a range of left activists and thinkers, from the radical liberal through to the anarchist. In this chapter the complex relationship between Trotsky and Luxemburg during their lifetime is explored in order to convey a sense of what left Marxism is, and to see what light can be cast on the tensions and differences between its two main rival strands.

Reform or revolution? For a revolutionary Marxism

Although acting in different circumstances, Luxemburg and Trotsky became committed to revolutionary Marxism early in their political careers. In Luxemburg's case, her formative polemics were directed against Polish 'nationalism' and Bernstein's 'revisionism'.

In 1892 several groups united to form the Polish Socialist Party (PPS), partly in the belief that in Poland the struggle for socialism had to be combined with the winning of Polish independence. Luxemburg immediately opposed the notion that the national arena was a sufficient base for revolutionary activity. Nationalism, she pointed out, was a bourgeois ideology and, in any case, the Polish bourgeoisie was too weak to lead a national revolution. The best future for Polish socialism, she reasoned, lay in broader links with Russian socialists and the demand for Polish autonomy within a liberalized Russian Empire. These arguments were to become an integral part of the programme of Social Democracy of the Kingdom of Poland (SDKP), which Luxemburg helped to found in 1894. Although the SDKP was to remain a small organization for several years, it managed to establish itself as a recognized presence in the Second International. In 1900 it was reconstituted as the Social Democracy of the Kingdom of Poland and Lithuania (SDKPiL). It fought the internationalist corner within Polish socialism, guaranteeing a split between internationalists and nationalists. It was a battle the internationalists would ultimately win when, in 1918, the majority of the PPS was swallowed up in the formation of a Polish Communist Party.

Luxemburg's leadership of the SDKP, her articles in its newspaper *Sprawa Robotnicza*, and her forceful appearances at prominent socialist gatherings raised her profile as a revolutionary Marxist for whom any concession to bourgeois ideology was an unacceptable compromise with revisionism. In 1898 she moved to Germany, beginning an association with German socialism that would last until her death. She arrived as German comrades were grappling with Edward Bernstein's revisionist challenge to Marxist orthodoxy, which appeared in leading party journals and in book form over 1897–98. Luxemburg replied to Bernstein's arguments in the pamphlet *Reform or Revolution*, first issued in 1899 and then revised in 1908. She sought to refute his conclusions about the nature of the contemporary capitalist economy, which, Bernstein claimed, was not heading for an inevitable breakdown, and to reject his related argument for capitalism's peaceful transition to socialism through parliamentary reform, trade union activity and the cooperative movement.

From Bernstein's examples of capitalist stabilization Luxemburg discovered only further evidence for its ultimate demise. That the extension of the credit system and the formation of capitalist trusts could not save capitalism from anarchy and crisis was clear, for instance, from the fact that the economic down-turn of 1907–8 hit hardest in countries with the most developed credit systems and capitalist trusts (Luxemburg, 1937: 14). If in such instances Bernstein had revealed his profound misunderstanding of modern capitalism, his view of politics, Luxemburg believed, was completely naïve. Luxemburg found herself having to repeat what she thought of as the ABC of Marxism. Bourgeois parliaments, for example, could not serve as the means for the attainment of socialism, for they were a subordinate element in a state machine dominated by the concerns of the ruling class. The bourgeoisie would permit parliamentary social reform only if it coincided with the interests of capitalist development. Socialism via bourgeois parliaments was simply impossible (Luxemburg, 1937: 19–23). Similarly, trade unions could only defend the workers' interests within capitalism; they were not bodies for the transformation of capitalism into socialism. The impact trade unions could have was dependent upon the prevailing market situation. When the economy was in boom concessions to the workers were more likely; during recessions trade unions would be forced to defend previous gains in increasingly difficult circumstances. It was at this point that, for Luxemburg, the political struggle for domination of the state would take precedence over the economic conflict for capitalist resources (Luxemburg, 1937: 16–18, 37–8). As for cooperatives, they were banned from the most important branches of capitalist production. The cooperative movement could not change capitalism into socialism, it was no more than an 'attack made on the twigs of the capitalist tree' (Luxemburg, 1937: 36). In making this case Luxemburg was not warning workers away from parliaments, trade unions and cooperatives. She thought it was important for the proletariat to engage in reformist activity, for it was by this means that it discovered the limits of reformism and gained in political acumen (Luxemburg, 1937: 24–6, 45–7, 52). Where Bernstein perceived reformism as an end in itself, Luxemburg considered it a means to an end, as revolutionary activity by a conscious and mature working class (Luxemburg, 1937: 4, 51).[1] While Luxemburg was leading the fight against revisionism in Poland and in Germany, Trotsky played a minor role in the theoretical debates against Economism, defined by left-communists as the revisionist heresy afflicting Russian socialism. Economism was associated above all with E.D. Kuskova's *Credo* of 1899, a work which argued that workers should forget about revolutionary politics – best left to the bourgeoisie – and struggle exclusively for their own economic well-being. Trotsky worked under Lenin, as an agent for *Iskra*, the Marxist newspaper that led the fight against Economism. Its main message was to insist upon the primacy of revolutionary politics over an exclusive focus on the day-to-day concerns of the workers' economic struggles. Trotsky took up Lenin's cause with such fervour that he acquired a reputation amongst Russian Social Democrats as Lenin's cudgel (Deutscher, 1954: 76). Trotsky was, though, to fall out with Lenin over the issue of how best to advance the construction of the workers' movement in Russia. This began a period of hostility between the two that was to last until the summer of 1917.

Party organization

Of all the burning issues disputed amongst Russian Social Democrats, it was Lenin's plans for a strictly centralized vanguard body of professional revolutionaries that split the movement into Bolsheviks and Mensheviks. The division took place at the Second Party Congress of 1903, although Lenin had developed his views in writings over several years, most notably in his *What is to be Done?* of 1902. Prominent among Lenin's detractors were Luxemburg and Trotsky, the former expounding her objections in the pamphlet *Marxism versus Leninism* of 1904, the latter in his essay *Our Political Tasks* of 1904. Their case against Lenin can be reduced to three fundamental criticisms. First, professional revolutionaries may be incredibly well versed in Marxist theory, but this provides no guarantee that they will always fulfil a vanguard role. Indeed, history abounds with examples in which theorists lag behind the spontaneous development of the masses (Luxemburg, 1961: 91–2). Second, for Luxemburg and Trotsky, Lenin's scholastic view of what constitutes a party was based upon a division of labour between revolutionaries and workers in which Social Democrats were cut off from their constituency. The inevitable result was inattention to questions of political tactics faced by real workers (Trotsky, n.d.: 57–61). Marxism living in a mass movement, as a serious political force, would only emerge in Russia, Luxemburg and Trotsky argued, if the proletariat was self-active. In turn, this would occur only if the proletariat was encouraged to learn in and grow from struggle, and if the base of the party was broadened, without an artificial division of labour between professional revolutionaries and the working class (Luxemburg, 1961: 88; Trotsky, n.d.: 36, 69, 72–9, 87–8). Luxemburg and Trotsky made it clear that they perceived this as a long-term process. The proletariat would go from Tsarism into the political school of a liberal Russia before creating a socialist Russia (Luxemburg, 1961: 102; Trotsky, n.d.: 70). Along this path, the proletariat would fall under the influence of opportunism, from which no quantity of professional revolutionaries could save them (Luxemburg, 1961: 106). However, by allowing the workers to draw their own lessons in a struggle against opportunism, the movement thus generated would be healthier and stronger, for it would be based upon the independence of the working class, not slavish obedience to an intellectual elite. The third and most serious sin in Lenin's proposed party organization highlighted by Luxemburg and Trotsky was the substitution of the working class by an ever-narrower clique of professional revolutionaries. Only a proletariat raised to think independently and display its own initiative, they argued, could save socialism from the degeneration into rule by a corrupt, dictatorial elite that Lenin's conception of the party risked. Trotsky's and Luxemburg's most frequently quoted passages, normally for their 'prophetic' character, are taken from their rejection of Lenin's substitutionism:

> In the internal politics of the Party [Lenin's] methods lead ... to the Party organization 'substituting' itself for the Party, the Central Committee substituting itself for the Party organization, and finally the dictator substituting himself for the Central Committee.
>
> (Trotsky, n.d.: 77)

> Historically, the errors committed by a truly revolutionary movement are infinitely more fruitful than the infallibility of the cleverest Central Committee.
>
> (Luxemburg, 1961: 108)

The 1905 Russian Revolution

In the course of the 1905 revolution in Russia, Luxemburg and Trotsky constructed a different conception of the relationship between spontaneous mass action and political leadership, and between trade unionism and socialism. Their analyses of the revolutionary events of 1905 converge at several points, most notably in their characterization of Russia's social structure and the correlation of its class forces.[2] Both viewed liberals and peasants as anti-revolutionary; the former because they were too weak, the latter because they were too backward. The driving force of the revolution, both agreed, was the proletariat. Although only a minority of the Empire's population and having only a relatively brief history as a class, Trotsky and Luxemburg perceived the Russian proletariat to be a fully formed, conscious working class. Furthermore, dominant in its own revolution, the Russian workers' struggle to overcome autocracy had consequences for the international working class, not least because the workers of the most backward country had developed the most advanced proletarian tactics. Trotsky and Luxemburg looked at 1905 in an international perspective, stressing the implications for workers everywhere of the fate of the Russian Revolution.

There are also crucial instances in which Luxemburg and Trotsky differed over the nature of the 1905 revolution. According to Luxemburg, despite being the key revolutionary force, the immediate goal of the Russian working class remained the establishment of a bourgeois-democratic, capitalist Russia. She recognized though that the final victory of capitalism over feudalism in Russia was distinguished in important respects from the previous victorious bourgeois revolutions in the West. In Russia not only was the proletariat leading the revolution, it was also generating its own socialist slogans. It was the workers themselves, not social-democratic theoreticians, who raised the demand for an eight-hour working day alongside a democratic parliament. In this sense the Russian workers were displaying a political maturity their comrades in the West had taken several decades to acquire, or, indeed, were still in the process of acquiring. The Russian proletariat had compressed a lengthy political learning process into several months, and had put forward the most contemporary political slogans, using the most advanced forms of proletarian struggle (chiefly, the mass strike), at the very outset of Russia's bourgeois revolution.

If Luxemburg argued that the Russian proletariat could leap over their comrades in the more advanced West in their consciousness and tactics she did not think that it could leap over an historical stage. Trotsky, on the other hand, drew an opposite conclusion. For him, the Russian workers' advanced consciousness was revealed above all in the establishment of the latest form of revolutionary organization, namely the soviets or workers' councils. If it seized power, such a class would act in accordance with its thinking and introduce socialism, even in backward Russia. This belief was an integral part of Trotsky's theory of permanent revolution. In leading the Russian Revolution the proletariat would not be able to limit the field of its activity to tasks of a bourgeois-democratic nature. In Trotsky's paradigm, precisely the most backward country could be the first to realize a socialist uprising. Later he would express this paradox in the form of a law of uneven and combined development.

From their conflicting evaluations of the nature of the Russian Revolution,[3] Trotsky and Luxemburg drew different conclusions as to its international repercussions. For Trotsky, a workers' government in Russia could overcome the unfortuitous circumstances of its arrival in power only if it was aided by successful workers' revolutions in the more advanced countries of Western Europe. The interdependence of the Russian and world revolutions is another key aspect of Trotsky's theory of permanent revolution. In one scenario Trotsky envisaged Russian workers carrying the revolution westwards by force of arms. Devoid of the transfer of technology from comradely regimes, an isolated socialist government would founder on the contradiction of implementing socialism on an insufficient economic base.

Luxemburg did not deny that the Russian Revolution acted as a fillip to the German workers' movement. However, where Trotsky drew the conclusion that revolution should be placed at the top of the agenda, Luxemburg took from the Russian experience the lesson that the German proletariat should focus upon the tactic of the mass strike and its connection to the ultimate revolutionary battles that still lay in the future. It was the mass strike and the relationship between trade unions and Social Democrats that dominated Luxemburg's thinking about the significance of worker activity in Russia in 1905. At this point the role played by the soviets, so important to Trotsky's writings on 1905 (Trotsky, 1971: 103–12), seems not to have caught her attention. As we shall see, the situation was to be reversed in 1917–19. At this earlier juncture Luxemburg undertook a campaign to win over the SPD to the mass strike. She stated her case in its fullest form in the pamphlet *The Mass Strike, the Political Party and the Trade Unions* of 1906. This work rejected Lenin's somewhat simplistic distinction between economic and political struggle and between trade union consciousness and real Marxism. Luxemburg presents a much more complex interaction of various forces, economic and political, organized and unorganized workers, and party and non-party bodies in the mass strike. If at some instances, for example, economic struggle grows over into political demands, so the domination of political demands can also raise the tempo of economic strikes (Luxemburg, n.d.: 47). Although workers would be most united and sure of themselves when guided by a resolute social democracy, at the same time Luxemburg limits its influence in calling mass strikes. One should not, she writes, 'under-estimate [the] unorganized proletarian mass and their political maturity . . . in the mass strike . . . the element of spontaneity plays such a predominant role . . . because revolutions do not allow anyone to play the school master with them' (Luxemburg, n.d.: 62, 50). Luxemburg also had little patience with disputes between Social Democrats and trade union leaders over who should lead the mass strike. For her the distinction between the two was clear. Social Democrats were guided above all by the politics of revolution, trade unions by immediate economic demands. However, it was nonsense to separate the two into opposing camps because of their different functions. Each relied on the other for strength and growth, and workers looked upon them as part of one class movement. In this sense Luxemburg called for cooperation between the party and the trade union (Luxemburg, n.d.: 80). Neither Luxemburg nor Trotsky looked upon the 1905 revolution in a negative light. As revolutionary optimists, they saw it as another way in which the workers had deepened their struggle and their understanding of it. 1905 was also an important turning point in Trotsky's intellectual biography, for it was in this year that he first expounded his theory of permanent revolution. He was to be associated with this theory for the remainder of his life. Many consider it his original contribution to Marxism. 1905 was also notable for Luxemburg. In September she and other leftists persuaded the SPD to incorporate the mass strike as a political weapon in the armory of the German workers' movement. However, as she admitted in a speech of 1907 to the Fifth Congress of the RSDLP, it had proven harder to implement the resolution than to have it added to the party statute books (Luxemburg in Drabkin, 1991: 141). Indeed, Luxemburg overestimated the extent to which German comrades had been won over to the mass strike. Both German trade unions and then the SPD and its leading theoreticians rejected the mass strike as a vital ingredient of the contemporary class struggle.[4] Just how far reformism had penetrated German social democracy was made clear to Luxemburg and Trotsky by its response to the outbreak of the First World War.

The First World War

On 4 August 1914 the Social Democratic deputies in the Reichstag resolved to vote for the war credits that would fund Germany's campaigns in the First World War. Civil peace, that is the avoidance of labour–capital conflict, was declared for the duration of the hostilities. Luxemburg, Trotsky and other left-internationalists deplored this social-patriotic betrayal of Marxism. For them the real battle was to expose the war for what is was, not one of liberation, but an imperialist war. It was the clear duty of all conscientious Marxists, of whatever nationality, to explain this to the workers. Worker opposition to the war should be encouraged, preferably as a means of fomenting revolution. The Second International, which had been unable to prevent the war, lay in ruins. To answer the tasks of the moment, Marxists had not only to overcome social-patriotism in national workers' parties, they also had to work for the formation of a new, revolutionary Third International. These were not easy tasks, especially given the patriotic fervour that had captured many workers and their organizations. Compounding matters was the military censorship. Luxemburg, amongst many, spent much of the war in jail. Trotsky had relative freedom of expression in Paris. His newspaper *Nashe Slovo* was read eagerly by Social Democrats scattered across Europe. However, even he was eventually expelled from France and spent some time in a Spanish jail before making his way to New York.[5] Nevertheless the propaganda activities of the left-internationalists did give them some sense of community and, in the difficult environment of war, they developed political and psychological outlooks that informed their behaviour in the post-war period. Above all, the First World War was, for Trotsky and Luxemburg, the product of capitalism in crisis. Its upheavals, social, political and economic, were preparing the ground for social revolution. If the proletariat was to take advantage of this situation, Marxists would have to be prepared in advance. Social-patriotism in workers' circles was the main enemy. These were the broad themes on which the revolutionary-internationalists could agree. They continued to polemicize, though, over how best to advance the revolution, and what sort of revolution it would be.

According to Trotsky, the war had come about because of a revolt of the productive forces against the narrow confines of the nation-state. In other words, the European economy had become sufficiently unified to demand a Europe-wide political framework to oversee its further expansion. The war was an attempt to meet this demand, albeit in a regressive, capitalist–militaristic manner. The rapacious great powers would, for Trotsky, be unable to assert their hegemony on a stable basis. Capitalist contradictions would ensure further wars, whatever the outcome and whoever the victor. However, there was another historical alternative. If the development of the productive forces to date had made the nation-state an anachronism, it had also rendered it insufficient as a base for revolution. Should the proletariat take power in even one of the warring countries taken separately, Trotsky argued, the revolution would soon spread across Europe. The United States of Europe, in a socialist, democratic form, would be the state structure through which the proletariat would conduct its revolution.[6] This would be but a first step towards the establishment of a United States of the World. In the meantime the best slogan to win the workers from war to revolution, according to Trotsky, was peace. Before the workers could turn their weapons on the class enemies, he reasoned, they had first of all to stop pointing them at each other.

The prospects for revolution foreseen by Trotsky followed logically from his analysis of the war's causes. It was also a paradigm that strengthened his commitment to permanent revolution in Russia. In conditions of an interconnected European economy, a victorious Russian proletariat would have good reason to hope for speedy support from comrades in Germany, Britain and France. His arguments continued, however, to cause controversy amongst fellow Social Democrats. To name but a few disagreements, Lenin favoured the call for turning the imperialist war into a civil war over the slogan of peace. Lenin continued to view the Russian Revolution as a national revolution that would take a bourgeois-democratic form, even if it would be led by the proletariat and the peasantry. He continued to berate Trotsky for underestimating the revolutionary potential of Russian peasants. He rejected the notion of a United States of Europe as an immediate possibility. Despite Trotsky's subsequent claims that during 1914–17 he and Lenin had moved closer together politically, the debates of the First World War witnessed a sharpening of the conflicts separating Trotsky from Lenin and the Bolsheviks. Trotsky's views were also too revolutionary and overly optimistic for the Mensheviks. They argued that the future course of the revolution would be far more tortuous and drawn out than that suggested by Trotsky and his theory of permanent revolution.

In these debates Trotsky would often claim for himself the support of comrades in other countries. In this context he mentioned, amongst others, John MacLean in Britain, Christian Rakovsky in the Balkans, and Karl Liebknecht and Rosa Luxemburg in Germany (Trotsky, 1990: 70–9). Although he had not verified such unity in personal correspondence or contact, Trotsky was justified in viewing himself as part of a group of revolutionary internationalists. After all, Luxemburg also rejected reformism and the war, she also demanded further revolutionary upheavals and called for a new, revolutionary Third International to coordinate the revolution (Luxemburg in Looker, 1972: 187–96, 197–210, 211–26). However, in the concrete conditions of the collapse of the old regimes exhausted by total war, Trotsky and Luxemburg adopted conflicting evaluations of the revolutionary process.

The Russian and German revolutions

The fall of the Russian autocracy in February 1917 was the first real breakthrough for the revolutionary internationalists. They could, however, claim little credit for bringing it about. After all, the revolutionary leaders were in exile and there was no strong RSDLP presence in Petrograd. But after years of despair it was an event that could give them genuine hope. The establishment of a Provisional Government with a promise to organize elections on a democratic basis for a new Constituent Assembly opened up real opportunities for revolutionary agitation. The exiles, internal and external, could return to the capital, papers could be published without censorship, politics could be openly entered into.

Alongside the Provisional Government the victorious workers, peasants and soldiers began to organize their own forms of administration in soviets, workers' councils of the sort that had first sprung up in 1905. As the Provisional Government foundered from one crisis to another, the soviets became increasingly important as the foci of power. The revolutionary parties sought to guide the course of the revolution by increasing their representation in the soviets, which held elections on a continual basis.[7] The balance of power within them was in a constant state of flux. Over the course of 1917 the Bolsheviks came to win majorities in the most important of the soviets. Lenin became convinced that the time was ripe for a full transfer of power to the soviets under Bolshevik leadership. The Provisional Government that had pursued the war and dragged its feet over solving the country's pressing economic, social, and political problems should be arrested. The only way to keep the revolution moving forward was to stage a workers' revolution. Lenin was opposed by influential figures within his own party who thought such conclusions premature. He was supported, though, by a recent arrival to the Bolshevik camp, one Leon Trotsky. Although Trotsky had his doubts about the extent to which the Bolsheviks had truly internationalized themselves, in 1917 Lenin was the only party chief that came to agree with Trotsky's theory that the bourgeois-democratic revolution could grow into the socialist revolution. Concerned above all that an attempt at revolution should be made, Trotsky joined forces with Lenin. As Lenin undertook a campaign to convince his Central Committee to agree to the need for a revolution, Trotsky set about drawing up the actual plan for the transfer of power.[8] In a real sense the October Revolution was

Lenin's and Trotsky's revolution, a testimony to their powers of leadership. As Lenin had predicted, the revolution would not occur without the aid of professional revolutionaries, and, as Trotsky had long insisted, a successful revolution would seek to introduce socialism. The first years of the Russian Revolution witnessed the first attempt to construct a socialist order, with planning, a moneyless economy, discrimination against the propertied classes (no vote for them), and a glorification of all things proletarian.[9]

From afar Luxemburg greeted the February revolution not as a bourgeois revolution, but as a continuation of the revolution of 1905. The main credit for the collapse of the autocracy could therefore be given to the workers. Like Trotsky, she argued that Nicholas II's abdication marked not the end of the revolutionary process, but only its beginning. The Russian bourgeoisie wanted to continue the war to a successful conclusion. Only the further revolutionary struggle of the proletariat could advance the cause of peace (Drabkin, 1991: 296–8, 298–300).

In advocating an increase of revolutionary activity in Russia, Luxemburg also discerned a particular danger. Should the proletariat seize power and call a halt to the hostilities, it would face the wrath of the Western bourgeoisie, including the British and the French. The greatest danger though would come from Germany. The German bourgeoisie would undoubtedly seek to shore up its power and influence by crushing a workers' revolution in Russia and demanding territorial concessions. For Luxemburg, only a seizure of power by the Western European proletariat could save a fledging workers' regime in Petrograd (see Luxemburg in Looker, 1972: 227–34).

When the October Revolution actually occurred Luxemburg applauded Lenin and Trotsky's work. To them fell the honour of the first genuine attempt at a socialist revolution. They had saved the name of international socialism and exposed the reformists in the SPD as liars. After all, the SPD had premised its betrayal upon a view of the war as a battle to liberate Russia. With the Tsar gone and a socialist regime seeking a just peace, what need now to support German militarism?[10] Luxemburg's admiration for the Bolsheviks turned to disappointment when she turned her attention from the seizure of power to the way that power was used. For Luxemburg the Bolsheviks began to value the retention of power above principles.

This was evident, she argued, from several aspects of Bolshevik policy, both international and domestic. The decision to sign the rapacious peace of Brest-Litovsk that ended the war with Germany, for example, was a clear betrayal of internationalism, a sacred principle for all left-communists.[11]

It was the Bolshevik destruction of democracy, however, that most aroused Luxemburg's indignation. In his *Terrorism and Communism* of 1920, a work directed mostly at Kautsky, Trotsky defended the Bolshevik's suppression of formal democracy, most notably in the dispersal of the Constituent Assembly and the establishment of one-party rule in the soviets. 'A revolution,' Trotsky states, 'is not decided by votes . . . repression [is] the necessary means of breaking the will of the opposing side' (Trotsky, 1975: 109, 75). Trotsky came to believe that a correct revolutionary policy was the preserve of the party, not formal democracy whether practised in a parliament or in the soviets.[12] Luxemburg was horrified. It was precisely democracy, she argued, that gave meaning to the dictatorship of the proletariat. To oppose the two, as Trotsky had done, was simply wrong. The suppression of democracy would in fact doom the revolution to failure. Most importantly, the masses would be excluded from the revolution as their political rights, chiefly freedom of choice, expression and participation, were taken away. The inevitable result, for Luxemburg, would be the atrophy of all political institutions, the growth of corruption and the degeneration of the revolution. It was foolish to think, she wrote, that 'the socialist transformation is something for which a ready-made formula lies completed in the revolutionary party . . . socialism by its very nature cannot be decreed' (Luxemburg, 1961: 69–70).[13]

If democratic socialism was being undermined in Russia, Luxemburg was determined that it should guide party policy in the German revolution. Power should be captured not from above, by a small party clique, but from below, by the workers themselves. Before the German revolution could take place, Luxemburg argued that workers' councils would have to be established throughout the country, especially in the villages, where social democracy was at its weakest. Only when such a system existed and the workers understood that it was their councils that were to take over the tasks of government could a revolution be realized. Luxemburg admitted that, working from below in this way, the revolution might be delayed, but she thought it was a surer path to success (Drabkin, 1991: 375–8). Should the revolution succeed, Luxemburg tried to ensure that the Executive Committee of the soviet system of government would not be able to rule over the masses as in Russia. She recommended that the Executive Committee be elected by a Central Council that itself should be re-elected every three months. Electors had the right to recall deputies at any time. In this way 'active contact between the mass of the workers' and soldiers' councils . . . and their supreme organ of government' would be guaranteed. (Looker, 1972: 282) Apart from placing democracy at the centre of council communism, Luxemburg insisted that in taking power the soviets should try to minimize violence. If, for Trotsky, terror was inseparable from the establishment of socialism, for Luxemburg, 'ruthless revolutionary energy and tender humanity – this alone is the true essence of socialism . . . a man who hurrying on to important deeds inadvertently tramples underfoot even a poor worm, is guilty of a crime' (Looker, 1972: 261).

Conclusion

Luxemburg and Trotsky are united as left-communists and revolutionary internationalists. For all her reputation for revolutionary rhetoric, though, Luxemburg had a far more patient conception of the revolutionary process than Trotsky. They were both convinced that the future lay with socialism, and that the proletariat would emerge stronger and wiser from its temporary defeats. In this projection, for Luxemburg, the highest priority was the retention of socialist principles. Better the Russian Revolution fail with honour than prolong itself in an undemocratic form. Trotsky took longer to appreciate the truth of this outlook. He stuck it out but the more the world revolution was delayed the more he found himself fighting against corruption in and the degeneration of the Russian Revolution predicted by Luxemburg.

Unlike Luxemburg, however, Trotsky did not trace the origins of 'the revolution betrayed', which for him occurred first under Stalin, to Lenin and Leninism. Indeed, Trotsky never fully grappled with the dangers of substitutionism and Leninist vanguard theory. In re-examining the history of the Russian Revolution, for example, Trotsky did not return to the arguments set out in *Our Political Tasks*. He could never face up to the possibility that in joining forces with Lenin in 1917 he had committed an error of political judgement. Lenin remained beyond criticism.[14] All of Trotsky's post-1924 writings defend his closeness to Lenin. Such concerns only served to undermine Trotsky's analysis of Stalinism, for he could never be truthful about how Stalin and Stalinism emerged from Lenin and Leninism.

Of course Trotsky's analysis of Stalinism was about more than merely the relationship of Stalinism to Bolshevism. He wrote, for example, of the importance of such factors as Russia's history of cultural oppression and economic misery, as well as the pressure of contemporary world imperialism. Trotsky's critiques of Stalin's foreign policy, from its responsibility for the massacre of Chinese communists in the late 1920s to the inadequacies of its response to the rise of Hitler and fascism, for its consistent betrayal, in fact, of proletarian internationalism in the interests of 'socialism in one country', has made a deep and lasting impression on the historians of these issues.[15] Trotsky's calls for a further political revolution in the USSR and political and social revolutions elsewhere inspired new generations of left-communists in the post-Second World War era. Trotsky's writings were of tremendous value to socialists grappling with the problems of constructing a non-Stalinist Marxism for fighting oppression in East and West. It is of little surprise that Trotsky should have become the guru of political movements such as the Socialist Workers' Party in the UK and beyond, as well as more academic-based revolutionaries such as the Critique school at Glasgow University.[16]

One can also claim a relevance for Luxemburg and Trotsky beyond left-communism and interpretations of Stalinism. Given that both stressed the dependence of the Russian Revolution upon its expansion across the globe, one could use their writings to help explain the ultimate collapse of the USSR in 1991.[17] In other ways Luxemburg's and Trotsky's writings continue to have a contemporary resonance. One can still argue that the choice before humanity remains that between capitalism and socialism.[18] One can say that Trotsky was prescient in the view he expounded during the First World War that the successful management of the European economy needed a United States of Europe. After all, much of Europe's post-1945 political history has concerned the attempt to manage the continent's economy under the rubric of pan-European institutions. Most recently such ideas have resulted in the establishment of a European Central Bank and a single European currency. Moreover, these developments are intended to protect Europe from future wars between its leading states. During his lifetime Trotsky denied that capitalism could resolve these tasks. No doubt he himself would be surprised at the extent to which capitalists have coordinated efforts in this direction. But to date the European Union remains beset with inter-governmental conflict. Perhaps the form will survive but its future may lie in a socialist content.

If there is to be a socialist United States of Europe, Luxemburg would presumably insist that, above all, it should be arranged democratically. As a left-communist she enjoys a better reputation today than Trotsky, despite Trotsky's greater impact upon twentieth-century Marxist movements.[19] We must put this higher regard down to her everlasting commitment to democratic rights. However, Luxemburg's reputation was achieved without her ever having had to lead a revolution by participating in government. Had she ever held real power, she might well have had to compromise as the Russian Bolsheviks did, and place the leadership's belief in what was good for the revolution above the requirement for consultation with and control by the masses. Whether there ever can be a socialist upheaval that respects democracy remains an open question, and one to which the left-communists have no obviously satisfactory answer.[20] This, combined with capitalism's resilience and continued growth, has severely limited the growth of left-communism as a fighting force.

Notes

1 Here it is interesting to note James D. White's (1989) criticism of Luxemburg's anti-Bernstein tract, expressed in a review of a reissue of *Reform or Revolution?*: 'The method of argumentation employed presupposes that some ultimate truth resides in Marx's writings, and that disagreement with them is necessarily erroneous. The assumption is also present that no departure from Marxism can be a valid alternative opinion, but denotes an ideology which is alien to the working class. In this respect Rosa Luxemburg gave rise to some of the most conservative and repressive currents in socialist thought.'

2 A more detailed exposition of Trotsky's work on 1905 and the Russian Revolution more generally can be found in Thatcher (1991). The summary of Luxemburg's views has been culled from several sources including 'Revolyutsiya [1905 g.] v Rossii' in Drabkin (1991): 92–8; 'Epokhal'nye sobytiya', ibid.: 99–106; 'V zareve revolyutsii', ibid.: 106–9; 'Russkaya revolyutsiya', ibid.: 133–7; 'Rech o russkoi revolyutsii', ibid.: 137–40; 'The Revolution in Russia' in Looker (1972): 117–20.

3 Despite the fact that Luxemburg clearly disagreed with Trotsky's conception of permanent revolution, much later, in a letter of 1931 to the journal *Proletarskaya revolyutsiya*, Stalin claimed that it was precisely Luxemburg who, along with Parvus, had 'invented a utopian and semi-Menshevik scheme of permanent revolution . . . [that] was seized upon by Trotsky and turned into a weapon of struggle against Leninism' (Stalin, 1955: 93).

4 For a concise and clear account of the debates that raged around the mass strike in German social democracy see Harding, 1996: 67–70.

5 The best account of Trotsky's work and activities between 1914 and 1917 is Thatcher (2000a). The summary of Trotsky's views of this period presented here is based upon this book.

6 Trotsky did advocate the formation of one further transnational state structure, a Balkan Federative Republic for southeast Europe. This, he hoped, would solve the region's ethnic tensions.

7 For an account of the electoral history of the soviets in the first years of Bolshevik rule

see, for example, Thatcher (1995). Other parts of this chapter also cover the fate of the Constituent Assembly and elections in the Bolshevik party.

8 See, for example, White (1999).

9 The atmosphere of the times has best been summed up by Alec Nove: 'sleepless, leather-jacketed commissars working round the clock in a vain effort to replace the free market' (Nove, 1992: 68).

10 Luxemburg's positive evaluation of the October Revolution is best summarized in her *The Russian Revolution and Leninism or Marxism?* (1961: 25–40).

11 The debate that raged around the issue of a separate peace with Germany was passionate and its significance for the left-communists is often overlooked. For a study that seeks to recreate the importance of the Brest-Litovsk treaty for the left-communists in Russia see, for example, Kowalski (1991: 60–82). It is interesting to note that even a historian hostile to Marxism agrees with the left-communists that in opting for a separate peace Lenin had acted on traditional, 'realist' assumptions. This, claims Pipes (1990: 604–5), was to remain as the defining feature of Soviet foreign policy.

12 See further Trotsky's statements that one cannot be right against the Communist Party (e.g. 1963: 158; 1939: 41).

13 Of course Luxemburg was not the only left-communist to voice concerns about the fate of democracy in the Russian Revolution. For a brief account of the issues raised by left-communists from Kollantai to Shlyapnikov see, for example, White (1994).

14 For a critical reading of Trotsky's *History of the Russian Revolution* see, for example, Thatcher (1999).

15 See, for example, Tucker (1990). In chapter 10, covering Stalin's foreign policy towards Germany, Tucker begins by rejecting some of Trotsky's interpretation (223–5), but then essentially agrees with Trotsky's view that Stalin aided Hitler's rise to power (228–32).

16 The Critique school's most notable member is Hillel Ticktin. In a series of articles and books he has analysed the USSR and Western capitalism from a left-communist perspective, inspired mostly by Trotsky. For his contributions to Marxist thought Ticktin has recently been made a Professor at Glasgow. The *Critique* journal, which began publication in 1973, has run special issues on left-communists, e.g. Victor Serge, and has translated key documents from the history of the movement.

17 Here, one could follow Alec Nove's critique of left-communists for their idealistic and utopian assumptions about the feasibility of a marketless economy, based upon an assumed abundance, that could easily and efficiently be run by a democratic community of free producers. For an appreciation of Nove's critique see, for example, Thatcher (2000b).

18 Although just how difficult this is becoming is clear from Anderson (2000).

19 For very favourable evaluations of Luxemburg's life and thought see, for example, Abraham (1989); Basso (1975); Geras (1976). The most recent appreciation of Luxemburg, although in a broader context, is Fernbach (1999). For an interesting review article of biographies of Rosa Luxemburg see, for example, Edmondson (1989). Kolakowski stands out for preferring Lenin's vanguard party organization over Luxemburg's insistence on democracy. He argues that Lenin was at least consistent. After all, Luxemburg believed in scientific Marxism. If one thinks that there is only one truth then one needs a Leninist party to inform one what it is (see Kolakowski, 1978: 95–6). If, Kolakowski apart, Luxemburg is generally well thought of, Trotsky's latest biographers blame him for helping to create Stalinist tyranny. For an account of these works see Thatcher (1994).

20 This, for example, is the conclusion of a historian who was at least sympathetic enough to the left-communists to undertake a serious study of their movement: 'The ideological preconceptions of the Left Communists would have spawned a centralised, bureaucratic system, not an emancipated society in which power was diffused to the workers' (Kowalski, 1991: 188).

References

Abraham, R. (1989) *Rosa Luxemburg. A Life for the International*. Oxford: Berg.

Anderson, P. (2000) 'Renewals', *New Left Review*, 1: 5–24.

Basso, L. (1975) *Rosa Luxemburg. A Reappraisal*. London: Deutsch.

Deutscher, I. (1954) *The Prophet Armed: Trotsky 1879–1921*. Oxford: Oxford University Press.

Drabkin, Y.S. (ed.) (1991) *Roza Lyuksemburg o sotsializme i russkoi revolyutsii*. Moscow: publisher.

Edmondson, Linda (1989) 'Lives of Rosa Luxemburg', *Revolutionary Russia*, 2 (2): 35–44.

Fernbach, D. (1999), 'Rosa Luxemburg's Political Heir: An Appreciation of Paul Levi', *New Left Review*, 238: 3–25.

Geras, N. (1976) *The Legacy of Rosa Luxemburg*. London: New Left Books.

Harding, N. (1996) *Leninism*. Durham, NC: Duke University.

Kolakowski, L. (1978), *Main Currents of Marxism. II: The Golden Age*. Oxford: Oxford University Press.

Kowalski, Ronald I. (1991), *The Bolshevik Party in Conflict. The Left Communist Opposition of 1918*. Basingstoke: Macmillan.

Looker, R. (ed) (1972) *Rosa Luxemburg. Selected Political Writings*. London: Cape.

Luxemburg, Rosa (n.d.) *The Junius Pamphlet*. London: Merlin Press.

Luxemburg, Rosa (1925) *The Mass Strike, The Political Party and The Trade Unions*. Detroit: Marxian Educational Society.

Luxemburg, Rosa (1937) *Reform or Revolution*. New York: Three Arrows Press.

Luxemburg, Rosa (1961) *The Russian Revolution and Leninism or Marxism?* Ann Arbor, MI: University of Michigan Press.

Nove, Alec (1992) *An Economic History of the USSR*. Harmondsworth: Penguin.

Pipes, R. (1990) *The Russian Revolution 1899–1919*. London: HarperCollins.

Stalin, J. (1955) 'Some Questions Concerning the History of Bolshevism' in *Works*, volume 13. Moscow: Foreign Languages Publishing House.

Thatcher, Ian D. (1991) 'Uneven and Combined Development', *Revolutionary Russia*, 4 (2): 235–58.

Thatcher, Ian D. (1994) 'First Russian Biographies of Trotsky: A Review Article', *Europe–Asia Studies (Formerly Soviet Studies)*, 46 (8): 1417–23.

Thatcher, Ian D. (1995) 'Elections in Russian and Soviet History' in P. Lentini (ed.), *Elections and Political Order in Russia*. Budapest: Central European University Press.

Thatcher, Ian D. (1999) 'Trotskii's Russian Revolution Revisited', *Revolutionary Russia*, 12 (1): 157–63.

Thatcher, Ian D. (2000a) *Leon Trotsky and World War One*. Basingstoke: Macmillan.

Thatcher, Ian D. (2000b) 'Alec Nove, Soviet Planning and Market Reform, and the Need for Relevant Economics', *New Political Economy*, 5 (2): 269–80.

Trotsky, L. (n.d.) *Our Political Tasks*. London: New Park Publications.

Trotsky, L. (1939) *Their Morals and Ours*. n.p.: Pioneer.

Trotsky, L. (1963) *Trinadtsatyi s"ezd RKP(b). Stenograficheskii otchet*. Moscow: Gospolitizdat.

Trotsky, L. (1971) *1905*. Harmondsworth: Penguin.

Trotsky, L. (1975) *Terrorism and Communism*. London: New Park Publications.

Trotsky, L. (1990) *Politicheskie siluety*. Moscow: Novosti.

Tucker, Robert C. (1990) *Stalin in Power. The Revolution from Above, 1928–1941*. London: W.W. Norton.

White, James D. (1989) 'Review of Rosa Luxemburg, Reform or Revolution', *Revolutionary Russia*, 2 (2): 52–4.

White, James D. (1994) *The Russian Revolution 1917–1921. A Short History*. London: Arnold.

White, James D. (1999) 'Lenin, Trotskii, and the Arts of Insurrection: The Congress of Soviets of the Northern Region, 11–13 October 1917', *Slavonic and East European Review*, 77 (1): 117–39.

3   Right-wing Marxism

Jules Townshend

Seemingly, little of significance could be said about the 'right wing' Marxists, except for adding a few more sobriquets to an already polemical-rich Marxist lexicon: Kautsky the 'renegade', Bernstein the 'revisionist' and the Mensheviks as 'tailists'. Such epithets were not prompted by envy at their success: they were history's losers. Not only were they denied the historical success of a Lenin, they did not possess the *brio* of a young Trotsky, or Luxemburg, or Gramsci. Indeed, they did not even 'lose' heroically. There was no tragic dimension to their sacrifice, the quick deaths by rifle-butt (Luxemburg) or ice-pick (Trotsky) or a slow death via imprisonment (Gramsci). Apart from rank and file Mensheviks who refused to go into exile in the early 1920s (Broido, 1987), they were an unheroic lot, many living to a ripe old age. They were the consummate masters of caution, which immobilized rather than inspired. Yet caution can just as easily spring from hard-headedness as from cowardice, and revolutionary risk-taking can court political disaster, either as defeat or as left-wing totalitarianism. And a modicum of logic tells us that we ought to distinguish between the motives prompting argument and analysis from their actual content. The twenty-first century may prove a little kinder to right-wing Marxist reputations than the twentieth. When *glasnost* within the Marxist tradition has fully run its course their contribution may be more fully recognized.

The right-wing Marxists attempted to get to grips with the problematic legacy of the *Communist Manifesto*. Marx and Engels themselves understood that the 'general principles' of the *Manifesto* had to be adapted to particular historical conditions (Marx, 1988: 43). Thus political practice would always constitute a practical problem because circumstances were always changing. Accordingly, Kautsky constructed a socialist strategy for Germany in conditions which suggested that parliamentary democracy and the existence of a militarily strong state would provide the twin coordinates of political reckoning. The Mensheviks operated in circumstances in which parliamentary democracy had not been established and capitalism was not nearly developed enough to make a proletarian majority imminent. In developing their strategies both Kautsky and the Mensheviks drew upon what Marx and Engels in the *Manifesto* said about Germany, and a possible two-stage revolution – first, the overthrow of the absolute monarchy, feudal squirearchy and petty bourgeoisie, by the bourgeoisie with the proletariat. Then 'straightway [the proletariat should] use, as so many weapons against the bourgeoisie, the social and political conditions that the bourgeoisie must necessarily introduce along with its supremacy . . .' Thus, a bourgeois revolution would be but a 'prelude to an immediately following proletarian revolution' (Marx, 1988: 86). What Kautsky derived from this turning of bourgeois weapons against themselves was the need to strengthen democracy in Germany so that the proletariat could use it to introduce socialism. The Mensheviks on the other hand could keep more literally to this two-stage formulation, since before 1917 there was neither democracy in Russia nor a proletarian majority.

Yet at another level, and perhaps more seriously, the *Manifesto* raised unforeseen problems stemming from its revolutionary and teleological assumptions concerning the 'real' and the 'good' coalescing in the 'inevitable' overthrow of capitalism. Bernstein's response to these difficulties formed the centre of his (in)famous 'revision' of Marx. What if the working class did not inherently possess hegemonic capacities? What if capitalism could continually expand in a relatively non-conflictual way, thereby not creating the preconditions for revolution? What if the expansion of parliamentary democracy reduced social antagonism rather than increased it? Put another way, was reality itself undermining the 'general principles' of the *Manifesto*? Retrospectively we can see that the *Manifesto* was written when capitalism and parliamentary democracy were in their infancy. Marx and Engels could not anticipate the political implications arising from a developed capitalism for such democracies, nor the effects of such democracies upon workers' political aspirations. We have then the classic problem that all political ideologies have to confront in remaining historically sustainable: how to adapt to new conditions?

Before detailing their distinctive contributions to the history of twentieth-century Marxism we can acknowledge that the relationships between these 'right-wing' thinkers were complex and on many matters they were hardly univocal. Many commentators for example during and after the famous Revisionist controversy (1899–1900) within the German Social Democratic Party (SPD) saw Bernstein as abandoning Marxism altogether (the first post-Marxist?), and yet he was not expelled from the Party and later Kautsky described himself and Bernstein as 'Siamese twins' (Kellner, 1977: 179). In the factional split (1903–4) between the Bolsheviks and the Mensheviks within the Russian Social Democratic Labour Party (RSDLP), Kautsky remained neutral rather than siding with the Mensheviks (Donald, 1993: ch. 2 *passim*), although Kautsky was personally closer to the Mensheviks before and after the Russian Revolution (Donald, 1993: 251–6). We also should note that the divisions between 'right'- and 'left'-wing Marxism were complex. The relations between the Mensheviks and Bolsheviks were for the most part until 1917 merely semi-detached: both were after all members of the RSDLP, and many of those close to the Mensheviks, notably Trotsky, joined the Bolsheviks in 1917. And after the October Revolution the exiled Mensheviks were far from united in their attitudes towards it. Nevertheless, what we shall see is that the kindred 'right-wingness' of these disparate Marxists lies in their unwavering commitment to achieving socialism through democracy, especially in its parliamentary form, and a reluctance to advocate violence in the pursuit of political ends. In addition, apart from Bernstein they emphasized the 'objective' preconditions necessary for socialism and a corollary 'pessimism of the intelligence', to use Gramscian parlance, although we shall see that 'subjective' preconditions were deemed equally vital. Unsurprisingly, they were hostile to the Bolshevik 'adventure' in 1917, whatever their subsequent changes of perspective.

Karl Kautsky

Kautsky was known as the 'Pope' of Marxism until the First World War before being dubbed a 'renegade' by Lenin after his critique of the October Revolution in *The Dictatorship of the Proletariat* (1918). He was the SPD's intellectual powerhouse from the 1890s until the outbreak of the First World War in 1914, as editor of the Party's theoretical journal *Die Neue Zeit*. He was seen as successor to Marx and Engels. He was also co-author, along with Bernstein, of the Party's Erfurt Programme (1891), which influenced all the other European Social Democratic parties. He was in effect the first Marxist 'ideologist' of the first Marxist mass political party, who was expected to offer a 'world-view' in keeping with the aspirations of the late Engels, rather than pronounce on day-to-day tactics. In particular, consonant with the *Manifesto* he saw his job as enlightening the proletariat, as making it aware of its historic mission to become a ruling class (Goode, 1983: 14). His working assumption, in line with the *Manifesto*'s call to 'win the battle of democracy', was that the nexus between democracy and socialism was created by capitalism: the logic of democracy was socialism once capitalism had made the proletariat the majority of the working population (Kautsky, 1909: 7; 1913: 189–91).

Kautsky's Marxism reflected the conditions surrounding the birth of the SPD and its continued existence. German Marxists found themselves at the head of an emerging labour movement committed largely to trade union activity and piecemeal economic, social and political reforms. Retrospectively, this reformism was very much an expression of modernity: a developing, sophisticated division of labour, the growth of parliamentary democracy and large-scale political organizations (whether in the form of state or party) and the emergence of economic organizations (whether trade unions, companies or employers' organizations). In other words, there existed a potential discrepancy between revolutionary Marxist theory and working-class reformist practice. The SPD, established in 1875, seeking to represent the *whole* of the growing German proletariat, embodied this dilemma. It was an amalgam of reformists and revolutionaries. The Erfurt Programme (1891) gave simultaneous voice to potentially contradictory maximalist and minimalist aspirations, which Kautsky sought to reconcile. This task helped form the basis of his 'centrism' (Steenson, 1978: 141–54).

This attempt to maintain a middle ground was even more understandable given the situation faced by the SPD. The German state, its bureaucratic machine and its army at that time were the most formidable in the world. Socialist activity had been outlawed between 1878 and 1890, with SPD members suffering from different forms of persecution. A background fear was that calls for militant action could again drive the Party underground. Thus, winning the 'battle of democracy' had to take account of the fact that the German army could not be confronted head-on, but would have to be subverted through the democratic process itself, rendering it 'faithless to the rulers' (Kautsky, 1913: 88).

Yet the power of the German state was not the only reason for Kautsky's advocacy of a parliamentary route to socialism. It was a key process by which the working class would develop the political maturity to become a ruling class, along with activities in trade unions and local government. Not only were objective, economic preconditions necessary for socialism (socialization of production and so on), *subjective* ones were equally vital. The working class had to have the organizational cohesiveness and skills to become a ruling class, to become a fully fledged proletarian dictatorship (Kautsky, 1913: 81).

Kautsky also justified parliamentary democracy, because it was a manifestation of the growing division of labour in modern society, with its division between executive and legislative functions (Kautsky, 1913: 29; 1925: 77; Salvadori, 1979: 14). Given what he saw as the obvious benefits of an increasingly sophisticated division of labour he wanted to minimize the effects of any revolutionary rupture. The danger of violent revolution was that the productive base required for a socialist economy would be destroyed, producing a 'crippled capitalism' (Kautsky, 1925: 89). Again this was one of the virtues of a parliamentary transition, enabling socialism to be introduced in a relatively rupture-free manner.

His centrist and parliamentarist positions explain his famous political skirmishes. He opposed the Party's 'revisionist' right wing, because it threatened party unity, and Bernstein in calling for an alliance with middle-class parties blatantly challenged the *raison d'être* of the Party, as facilitating the proletariat in fulfilling its historic mission. In 1910 he campaigned against the left wing, led by Luxemburg, over the mass strike tactic aimed at broadening the Prussian franchise. He feared the response of the military–bureaucratic machine, and thought the tactic could only harm the SPD's prospects in the forthcoming elections. During the German revolution of 1918, his centrism and parliamentarism led him to refuse to opt for either parliament *or* workers' councils as the institutional embodiment of proletarian dictatorship, preferring parliament *and* workers' councils (Salvadori, 1979: 237).

The need for Party unity and his parliamentary strategy also induced Kautsky not to oppose Germany's participation in the First World War, the beginning of his Marxist apostasy in Lenin's eyes. Whilst the war lasted the social and economic issues that could bring the SPD to power through the electoral process were marginalized (Salvadori, 1979: 181–5). In calling for a 'democratic' peace Kautsky was prepared to ally himself tactically with the middle classes. His theory of 'ultra-imperialism' supported this electoral strategy, in suggesting that the First World War did not constitute the final crisis of capitalism, since capitalist powers could cooperate in exploiting the eonomically underdeveloped regions of the globe (Kautsky, 1970: 46).

Kautsky's other heretical act from Lenin's viewpoint was to oppose the Bolshevik revolution, in 1918, when its fate hung by a thread. Kautsky's case against the Bolsheviks was grounded on his parliamentary strategy and his appraisal of Russian and world conditions. He rejected Lenin's 'weak link' hypothesis that a proletarian revolution in Russia would detonate revolutions in the West (Kautsky, 1964: 64), and was hostile to the Bolshevik dictatorship, which started with the disbanding of the democratically elected Constituent Assembly in January 1918. He contended that a 'democratic' parliamentary path was the only viable one, in fostering the ruling skills of the proletariat – a vital 'subjective' precondition for socialism (Kautsky, 1964: 42). Further, in the absence of imminent world revolution only one conclusion could be drawn: economic and social conditions – a numerically small proletariat, a large peasantry and underdeveloped productive forces – rendered Russia unripe for socialism (Kautsky, 1964: 65; 1925: 63) He was also appalled by the denial of full civil and political rights to the former bourgeoisie, demonstrating the Bolsheviks' unwillingness to raise the 'whole of humanity' to 'a higher plane' (Kautsky, 1920: 180). He rejected Lenin's idea of proletarian dictatorship, which consisted of a tyrannical form of government, rather than a political 'condition' naturally arising from the proletariat constituting the majority in a democratic state (Kautsky, 1964: 45). He characterized the Soviet Union as 'state capitalist', with the state and capitalist bureaucracies 'merged into one system' (Kautsky, 1920: 202).

Bernstein

Bernstein, the father of 'Revisionism', authored the 'minimalist' demands of the Erfurt Programme. He became close to Engels as a result of his exile in England (1888–1901), during and after the period of the Anti-Socialist Laws (1878–90). He edited one of the Party's journals, *The Social Democrat*, and was strongly influenced by what he learnt and saw in England. Although influenced by neo-Kantianism and marginalist economics, whatever his disclaimers, his theoretical approach and political conclusions were uncannily reminiscent of Fabian and New Liberal thought. He implicitly saw the German labour movement economically and politically going down the road of its British counterpart. He had seen the future: it was reformist, with developed trade unions and parliamentary democracy and civil liberties. No doubt he also took his cue from the late Engels, not merely in stressing the importance of parliamentary struggle, but also by qualifying the Marxist base/superstructure model of historical explanation, thus giving much greater scope for human agency and moral argument (Steger, 1999: 187–9).

Bernstein was a 'Marxist' in the sense that, although he rejected virtually every tenet of Marxism, he saw himself as committed to its critical 'spirit'. This meant destroying the illusions that the radical intellect may harbour, especially in revolution. The 'scientific' facts convincingly demonstrated that the revolutionary elements within Marxism were doctrinaire, 'ideological', supported by a fallacious dialectical methodology. Given the Marxist belief that strategy must be condition-dependent, and modern economic, social and political conditions

were not conducive to revolution, gradualism was the only answer. His solution to
the reform/revolution dilemma, arising from the problem of Marxists heading an
emerging labour movement that was reformist rather than revolutionary, was not
Kautsky's centrism, but the removal of the dilemma altogether. Modern conditions had rendered revolution undesirable and impossible.

By ruling out revolution, he disavowed Marxism's teleological core. The
goal of socialism meant 'nothing' to him, the movement 'everything' (Bernstein,
1993: xxviii). Bernstein, a self-confessed eclectic, was prepared to ask Marxists
the hard questions and came up with knuckle-whitening answers. He based his
rejection of the orthodox historical projection upon interrelated theoretical and
empirical arguments. Facts were the crucial test of any theory, and they showed
that the dialectic and its materialist underpinning were faulty, leading either to
an ungrounded a priorism or to a tendentious view of how the future would un-
fold. For Bernstein, the dialectical method, exemplified in the 'negation of the
negation', especially when applied to understanding the future development of
such complex phenomena as society, was always in danger of involving 'arbitrary
construction' (Bernstein, 1993: 31). In truth, 'actual development is forever bringing forth new arrangements and forces, forever new facts, in the light of which
that exposition (in *Capital*, vol., 1, chapter on the historical tendency of capital
accumulation) seems inadequate and, to a corresponding extent, loses the ability
to serve as a sketch of the development to come' (Bernstein, 1993: 198). In his
view, the determinism that underpinned these predictions was becoming increasingly implausible, because humankind as a result of the development of science
was assuming greater mastery over the natural and social environment, thereby
undermining the 'iron necessity of history' (Bernstein, 1993: 18–20). The Marxist
labour theory of value which underlay its theory of exploitation was also built
upon unfounded abstraction (Bernstein, 1993: 55).

Bernstein's empirical objections to the future revolutionary scenario depicted
in the *Communist Manifesto* are well known. The growth of cartels, credit and
improved business communications prevented economic collapse. Benefiting
from improved living standards through economic growth, trade union activity
and state-organized welfare reforms meant that the proletariat was no longer
revolutionary. In any case, the working class was too internally differentiated
to become a 'dictatorship' (Bernstein, 1993: 104), and such a state became unnecessary as democracy was increasingly suppressing class government if not
classes (Bernstein, 1993: 142). Furthermore, evidence seemed to show that the
working class was not necessarily becoming the majority class in society – the
basis of Kautsky's assumption that socialism was (conditionally) inevitable. The
German peasantry was not disappearing, and neither was the middle class. At the
'meta-theoretical' level Bernstein argued that the principle of cooperation rather
than class struggle increasingly constituted the dynamic of history. If there was
a historical trajectory it was manifested in growing cooperation in society, and
socialism was a 'movement towards, or the state of, a co-operative order of society' (Bernstein, 1993: 99). He sought to blur the qualitative distinction between
capitalism and socialism by appealing to the abstract principle of cooperation.

Socialism was for him 'organized liberalism' (Bernstein, 1993: 150), whose aim was to make 'citizenship universal' (Bernstein, 1993: 146). The aim of 'socialist measures' such as the maximum working day was 'the development and protection of the free personality' (Bernstein, 1993: 147). What he wanted was the regulation of private interests so that they were not detrimental to the community. 'We [social democrats] do *not* abolish private property, we *limit* its rights' (quoted in Steger, 1997: 147).

Bernstein demolished the theoretical foundations of Marxism by looking at the empirical evidence, rejecting its dialectical method, its project of proletarian dictatorship and much else. For him, the unintended consequences of capitalism's economic and political development were not proletarian revolution, but the creation of a multi-class community which would become increasingly cooperative through the democratic process. He saw no future revolutionary implications immanent in the present. For revolutionary Marxists, the game was up.

The Mensheviks

The Mensheviks, although without an obvious figurehead, were led by Iulii Martov, Pavel Axelrod and Fedor Dan and later loosely supported by Georgii Plekhanov. They got their name as a result of the split within the RSDLP in 1903–4 over party organization, in which they were in the 'minority' (Townshend, 1996: chs 5 and 6 *passim*) The issue of party organization soon subsided, and is only significant historically because Lenin's 'Jacobinism' in this period has been viewed as a precursor to Stalin's one-party rule. Nevertheless, this debate indicates the Mensheviks' less vanguardist approach to revolution, and their firm commitment to linking democracy and socialism, stressing the importance of workers' self-activity in achieving socialism. The significance of the democracy/socialism nexus also expressed itself in the strategic differences between themselves and the Bolsheviks after 1905. Their model of socialist transition was more obviously 'European' and Kautskyan than Lenin's, as became very apparent during the course of the Russian Revolution in 1917. The Mensheviks assumed that socialism would be on the agenda in Russia only once capitalism was well developed, with workers constituting the majority of the population. With democracy in place, workers' preference for socialism could be articulated, but as long as the majority of the Russian population were peasants, the logic of democracy would not lead to socialism.

Nevertheless, whatever strategic and organizational differences existed between the Mensheviks and Bolsheviks, *until* 1917, apart from Trotsky, all Russian Marxists were convinced that the forthcoming revolution would be bourgeois, given Russia's economic structure, and were thus committed to a 'stages' strategy (first liberal democratic capitalism, then socialism). What divided them in effect was what type of bourgeois revolution was desirable and possible, which depended on their estimation of the political interests and capacities of the various social classes. Before 1917, Lenin's and the Bolshevik's radicalism stemmed from their belief that a bourgeois revolution led and organized by the bourgeoisie was unlikely: it was too disorganized and unheroic, more like the German bourgeoisie of 1848 than its French forebears of 1789. So Lenin favoured an alliance of workers and peasants within the framework of a democratic republic that would facilitate a future proletarian revolution by hastening the development of capitalism (including an agrarian dimension), thereby putting workers and peasants in a strong political position to bring about such a revolution. Unsurprisingly, they put a great premium on the role of revolutionary agency and leadership, involving an armed uprising if necessary, which would enable the working class and agricultural labourers to play an influential part in a democratic republic. In opposition to the Mensheviks, they saw the Russian peasantry, unlike its European counterpart, as a force for radicalism rather than conservatism. Although the Bolsheviks and Mensheviks both veered towards a maximalist, socialist position during the revolution of 1905, after its defeat, the Mensheviks abandoned Plekhanov's idea of the 'hegemony of the proletariat' (as did Plekhanov himself) and adopted a far more 'European' and 'objective' model of socialist transition. Thus, they envisaged the bourgeoisie making its own revolution, and like Kautsky they thought it would take time for the proletariat to mature into a hegemonic class.

The Mensheviks' 'European' and more 'objectivist' position became clearer in the course of the 1917 revolutions. For them, the February revolution that toppled the Tsar constituted the bourgeois revolution that they had expected. They hoped that the Constituent Assembly would enable the construction of a bourgeois-democratic state. But the various social grievances could not be dealt with while the war lasted, until either the Central Powers had been defeated or a negotiated 'democratic peace' had been established. A unilateral decision pulling Russia out of the war would only drive the bourgeoisie into the arms of the reaction. For them, the soviets of workers, peasants, soldiers and sailors thrown up in the course of this revolution had a limited role in ensuring that the Provisional Government did not backslide in its commitment to a democratic revolution, a view held by the Bolsheviks until Lenin's arrival at the Finland Station in Petrograd in April 1917.

Events exposed the limitations of their strategy. The war was deeply unpopular, not merely with the soldiers at the front and the relatives of the dead, but with the population at large on account of the economic havoc it was causing. The peasants, hungry for land, were in no mood for delayed gratification, and Lenin's slogan of 'Bread, Peace and Land' patently had far greater appeal. Lenin, true to Marxism, made his revolutionary strategy condition-dependent. His volte-face in 1917, rejecting any semblance of a two-stage revolution, led to his call for a worldwide socialist revolution, with Russia as the catalyst. Whereas the Mensheviks worked within the confines of a domestic analysis, Lenin started from a global perspective. The war for him was *the* crisis of capitalism. A further revolution in Russia with socialist aspirations, even if the material and social conditions were absent, could inspire a global socialist revolution. This was possible because after the February revolution the proletariat and poorer peasants were becoming increasingly radicalized. Thus, he called for the soviets, representing these two classes, to assume sovereign power He had little time for a Constituent Assembly, which might undermine this process of radicalization, disbanding it in January 1918. In sum, the Mensheviks were marginalized by events, which did not fit neatly into their abstract, revolutionary template. They had no answers to the economic, social and political crisis that gripped Russia, and became, according to Martov, 'an intelligent superfluity' after the October Revolution (Broido, 1987: 25).

Assessment

However one chooses to describe Kautsky and the Mensheviks, their thinking ought to be recognized as remaining within the framework of Marxism. Kautsky has certainly been misrepresented, as recent commentaries demonstrate (Townshend, 1989: 659–64). If he was a 'renegade' then he had been so all his political life. Over his long career he was remarkably consistent in defending a parliamentary road to socialism and the idea that revolutions could not be made at 'will'. Kautsky was as strongly committed to updating the analysis of the *Manifesto* as other Marxists, in applying its principles to specific German conditions, and to modernity generally. As a good Marxist, his concern with specificity provoked his scepticism about the possibility of socialism in Russia. The Revolution would not detonate revolutions in the West. As a consequence of this and Russia's economic backwardness, he saw a form of bureaucratic state capitalism emerging. Implicitly, he was as alive as Gramsci, who had also rejected the 'permanent revolution' scenario, to the different terrains of 'East' and 'West'. Kautsky also strongly subscribed to the democracy/socialism couplet that lies at the heart of the *Manifesto*. Here we see a consistency not just over time, but between means and ends, of how the working class was to become a ruling class, of how it was going to emancipate itself under modern political conditions.

All this is not to deny Kautsky's palpable weaknesses. This is not merely evidenced in his statist tendencies that allowed for 'political emancipation' without 'human emancipation' (Thomas, 1994: 171). He also seemed unaware of the problematic treatment of the division of labour in Marx's writings, either as a positive source for human productivity through cooperation, or as engendering individual alienation. Further, his Marxism was doctrinaire, heavily reliant on teleological thinking, with the proletariat forming a majority of the population, and automatically wanting to bring about socialism in an orderly fashion through the ballot box. He produced a fair-weather formula that was inapplicable in situations of intense social and political conflict, as occurred during and after the First World War. There may have been great consistency in his work, but his avoidance of the problem of 'dirty hands' marginalized his Marxism. His refusal to deal with the problem of violence and to acknowledge the limitations of parliamentarism has, from the point of view of socialist transition, made him ineffective. Yet, ultimately, violent strategies in the twentieth century have proved equally ineffective, and the lack of a preparedness to get hands 'dirty' nevertheless contains a virtue if those with dirty hands have forgotten what the dirty hands are actually for. The 'dirty' doer and the 'clean' critic may need each other.

Similarly, the Mensheviks could be viewed as schematic Marxists in contrast to Lenin's flexibility and concreteness. In immediate terms, the Mensheviks lost the revolutionary plot in 1917, and could be accused of seeing classes as embodying abstract categories, and of failing to put Russia within a wider, international picture. Nevertheless, the question of political appropriateness can only be tested in practice, and the pessimism of their intelligence has proved correct in the long term. Retrospectively, one can see that in terms of a global *socialist* revolution by the early 1920s there was no revolutionary plot. As Trotsky stated in 1917: 'Were Russia to stand all on her own in the world, then Martov's reasoning [that Russia was not yet ripe for revolution] was correct' (Getzler, 1967: 220). Moreover, although the Mensheviks made only a brief appearance on the historical stage, they had been successful according to their own programme. They did not think a further revolution after February was possible or desirable, and cannot be judged to have failed in a competition for which they had not entered. If they stand accused of losing the revolutionary plot, they could plausibly claim that the Bolsheviks rapidly lost the democratic plot.

The lesson here is not about who are the 'better' Marxists, the right or left? It points to the dangers of fetishizing a particular strategy. There are many examples of shifts in position made by the most 'radical' of Marxist thinkers. Lenin advocated cooperatives in Russia towards the end of his life, rather than waiting for the Western proletariat to come to the Soviet Union's aid. Trotsky regarded a stages theory as appropriate for the Chinese revolution in the mid-1920s, albeit based upon Lenin's 1905, rather than the Menshevik, formula (Lowy, 1981: 82–3), and Gramsci famously differentiated between the political terrains of Western Europe and Russia, leading him to advocate his 'war of position' (Gramsci, 1971: 238–9).

As for Bernstein, his real contribution to Marxism was as its first critical interlocutor, asking the tough questions, indicating some of its inherent weaknesses, encouraging a self-critical spirit, and showing an appreciation for the complexity of modernity. He helped puncture illusions derived from a teleological reading of history, and developed a political formula more in keeping with the Western European working classes' lack of political ambition. Although we can criticize his methodology and his illusions about the possibility of a harmonious, democratic capitalism (the product of his own teleology) he made a start in disentangling factual from normative questions, so as to distinguish properly between Marxism's 'philosophy' and 'theory' of history (Cohen, 1978: 27). Thus, we can talk more comfortably about historical directionality and possibilities, rather than exclusively in terms of 'historical missions'. Such a deconstruction of Marxism's teleological dimension can only help strengthen its democratic credentials, by abandoning a vanguardism that is buttressed by the guarantees of 'history'. And following Bernstein greater space is opened up for 'moral advocacy' (Cohen, 1988: 9). Notwithstanding Marx's great insight that moral argument can be a cloak for particular material interests, the advantage of emphasizing the importance of ethical discourse is that it more obviously reasserts the means/end link often denied in orthodox Marxism, and it helps bind identity-differentiated political agents together in a world of growing social and economic complexity, by linking the aspirations of the exploited and oppressed with the idea of a common humanity.

There are other reasons not to forget the 'right-wing' contribution to the Marxist tradition, despite its lack of success in the twentieth century. One of Marxism's insights is that ideas themselves are the product of material and social conditions – Marxism itself no less so. 'Right-wing' Marxism was a European phenomenon, and it did not travel well. Its representative in Russia – the Mensheviks – demonstrated this, experiencing only momentary glory in 1917. The Bolshevik success in 1917 marked a sea-change in the history and meaning of Marxism. Marxism as a hegemonic force was now 'Marxism–Leninism', which resonated amongst populations subject to the yoke of Western imperialism, rather than amongst the Western working class. It became a political ideology that tapped into anti-imperialist struggles and the attendant need for independent, state-organized economic development.

This brand of Marxism did not have the same appeal in Western Europe with its strong parliamentary traditions, entrenched of civil and political rights, well-developed labour movements and complex economies. One of the poignant ironies of twentieth-century Marxism is that the spectre of Kautsky lurked behind later Communist attempts to develop a parliamentary strategy in the West from the 1950s onwards, culminating in Eurocommunism in the 1970s. They thought that Lenin's model of a commune state outlined in his *State and Revolution*, in reality so alien to Soviet practice, would not win support amongst the Western working class. Indeed, there are many parallels between the final work of Poulantzas, the leading theorist of 'left' Eurocommunism, and Kautsky in 1918 in his preference for a form of state that combined parliament and citizens' committees (Poulantzas, 1978: 262). In other words, the 'centrist' wheel was subsequently reinvented, in ignorance of Kautsky's pioneering effort. Perhaps Kautsky could be regarded as the real, if unspoken, founder of a *political* 'Western Marxism' in contrast to its standardly conceived philosophical, practice-less form as defined by Perry Anderson (1976).

The inner contradictions of Marxism–Leninism were brutally exposed as events unfolded in Eastern Europe from 1989 onwards: a socialism that denied its democratic foundation could not last. Thus, perhaps these 'right-wing' losers may not be losers after all. Time may be on their side, not merely because of the need to reconnect democracy and socialism. They also attempted to fashion a socialist strategy consonant with the problems thrown up by modernity, especially its complexity deriving from an ever increasing division of labour. Perhaps the growing uniformity of political, economic and social conditions stemming from a well-developed globalized capitalism will mean that the message of 'right-wing' Marxism will fall on more sympathetic ears.

The Marxist 'right wing' then have pertinent things to say for anyone concerned with the education of the radical egalitarian impulse and intellect. What is reaffirmed, especially by Kautsky and the Mensheviks, is a genuine commitment to workers' self-emancipation through the articulation of an indissoluble tie between democracy and socialism. Second, these Marxists brought a realism, an attempt to appreciate the effect that modernity would have on the socialist project, and an acknowledgement that its construction may be beyond the lifetime of any individual socialist. If anything is to be saved of Marxism in the twenty-first century as an emancipatory ideology, a full reckoning has to be made with its own political tradition, which includes this 'right wing'. Any such work of retrieval would also be facilitated by remembering Marx's famous declaration that he was not a 'Marxist'.

References

Anderson, P. (1976) *Considerations on Western Marxism*. London: New Left Books.

Bernstein, E. (1993) (edited by H. Tudor) *The Preconditions of Socialism* [1899]. Cambridge: Cambridge University Press.

Broido, V. (1987) *Lenin and the Mensheviks*. Aldershot: Gower.

Cohen, G.A. (1978) *Karl Marx's Theory of History: A Defence*. Oxford: Clarendon Press.

Cohen, G.A. (1988) *History, Labour and Freedom*. Oxford: Clarendon.

Donald, M. (1993) *Marxism and Revolution: Karl Kautsky and the Russian Marxists, 1900–1924*. New Haven, CT: Yale University Press.

Getzler, I. (1967) *Martov: A Political Biography of a Russian Social Democrat*. Cambridge: Cambridge University Press.

Goode, P. (ed.) (1983) *Karl Kautsky: Selected Political Writings*. London and Basingstoke: Macmillan.

Gramsci, A. (1971) (edited by Q. Hoare and G. Nowell Smith) *Selections from the Prison Notebooks*. London: Lawrence and Wishart.

Kautsky, K. (1909) *The Road to Power*. Chicago: Bloch.

Kautsky, K. (1913) *The Social Revolution* [1902]. Chicago: Kerr.

Kautsky, K. (1920) *Terrorism and Communism*. London: National Labour Press.

Kautsky, K. (1925) *The Labour Revolution*. New York: Dial Press.

Kautsky, K. (1964) *Dictatorship of the Proletariat* [1918]. Ann Arbor, MI: University of Michigan Press.

Kautsky, K. (1970) 'Ultra-Imperialism' [1914], *New Left Review*, 59: 41–60.

Kellner, D. (ed.) (1977) *Karl Korsch: Revolutionary Theory*. Austin, TX: University of Texas Press.

Lowy, M. (1981) *The Politics of Combined and Uneven Development: The Theory of Permanent Revolution*. London: Verso.

Marx, K. (1988) (edited by F.L. Bender) *The Communist Manifesto*. New York: Norton.

Poulantzas, N. (1978) *State, Power and Socialism*. London: New Left Books.

Salvadori, M. (1979) *Karl Kautsky and the Socialist Revolution*. London: New Left Books.

Steenson, G.P. (1978) *Karl Kautsky, 1854–1938*. Pittsburgh, PA: University of Pittsburgh Press.

Steger, M.B. (1997) *The Quest for Evolutionary Socialism: Eduard Bernstein and Social Democracy*. Cambridge: Cambridge University Press.

Steger, M.B. (1999) 'Friedrich Engels and the Origins of German Revisionism: Another Look' in T. Carver and M.B. Steger (eds), *Engels after Marx*. Manchester: Manchester University Press.

Thomas, P. (1994) *Alien Politics*. New York: Routledge.

Townshend, J. (1989) 'Reassessing Kautsky's Marxism', *Political Studies*, 37 (4): 659–64.

Townshend, J. (1996) *The Politics of Marxism*. London: Leicester University Press.

Further reading

Ascher, A. (1972) *Pavel Axelrod and the Development of Menshevism*. Cambridge, MA: Harvard University Press.

Broido, V. (1987) *Lenin and the Mensheviks*. Aldershot: Gower.

Bronner, S.E. (1990) *Socialism Unbound*. New York: Routledge.

Donald, M. (1993) *Marxism and Revolution: Karl Kautsky and the Russian Marxists, 1900–1924*. New Haven, CT: Yale University Press.

Gay, P. (1962) *The Dilemma of Democratic Socialism: Eduard Bernstein's Challenge*. New York. Collier Books.

Geary, R. (1987) *Karl Kautsky*. Manchester: Manchester University Press.

Haimson, L. (1974) *The Mensheviks: From the Revolution of 1917 to the Second World War*. London: University of Chicago Press.

Kautsky, J.H. (1994) *Karl Kautsky: Marxism, Revolution and Democracy*. New Brunswick, NJ: Transaction Publishers.

Tudor, H. and Tudor, J.M. (1988) *Marxism and Social Democracy: The Revisionist Debate, 1896–1898*. Cambridge: Cambridge University Press.

Wilde, L. (1999) 'Engels and the Contradictions of Revolutionary Strategy', in T. Carver and M.B. Steger (eds), *Engels after Marx*. Manchester: Manchester University Press.

4 Soviet and Eastern bloc Marxism

Mark Sandle

Introduction

As the first socialist state, dedicated to the construction of a communist society, the USSR offers some unusual and fascinating perspectives on the history of Marxism, as does Eastern Europe. The Soviet state devoted a huge amount of time, resources, energy and words to the development, production, dissemination and propagation of Marxism Soviet-style. Is there an identifiable Soviet Marxist canon? What, if anything, did this massive effort contribute to the development of Marxist thought in general? In political terms, the self-identification of the Soviet state as an entity guided by, or better perhaps armed with, Marxism–Leninism, coupled with the troubled history of the USSR, has significantly shaped popular perceptions of the effects of Marxism when in power. How accurate is it to see Soviet Marxism as a sterile, dogmatic, monolithic, uncritical body of doctrine designed to rationalise the oppressive rule of the CPSU (Communist Party of the Soviet Union)? Finally, the Soviet case provides an interesting example of the shift from revolutionary doctrine to ruling ideology which Soviet Marxism underwent after 1924. How did this change impact upon Soviet Marxism?

These aspects – the nature of Marxism as ruling ideology, the development of Marxism as the 'official' ideology of the Soviet state (and of the Soviet bloc after 1945) and the impact outside the Soviet bloc of Marxism Soviet-style – makes understanding the Soviet experience crucial to any appraisal of Marxist thought in the twentieth century. This chapter will trace the development, consolidation, crisis and eventual collapse of 'official' Marxism in the Soviet bloc, and will evaluate the strengths and weaknesses of Soviet Marxism as a body of ideas. Before turning to this, it is necessary briefly to outline the paradigms for understanding Soviet Marxism.

Understanding Soviet Marxism: the paradoxes of an 'official' body of thought

An official ideology

Before turning to an appraisal of the historical development of Marxism Soviet-style, it is essential to grasp three key features. These elements are central to any analysis of Marxism in the Soviet bloc:

- the status occupied by Marxism as the 'official' belief-system of the Soviet state;
- the role and functions of Soviet Marxism within the Soviet system;
- the general content of Soviet Marxism as a body of thought.

The Soviet state had an official belief-system: Soviet Marxism–Leninism. This had a number of important implications. First, this body of ideas occupied a monopoly position; no other ideologies were allowed to be publicly disseminated or propagated. All discrepant voices or views were to be censored and silenced. In effect this meant that, for almost its entire existence, Soviet Marxism was immune to criticism from 'alien' discourses, but was also cut off from intellectual developments – both Marxist and non-Marxist – from elsewhere. The seeds for intellectual ossification were sown right at the start. Second, from 1929 onwards, there was increasing political pressure not just towards an ideological monopoly for Soviet Marxism, but also towards the emergence of one 'correct' interpretation. Criticism from within gradually died off as a result. Third, this ideology became institutionalised within the Soviet state. Intellectual life in the USSR was dominated by a vast politico-ideological complex. This was a conglomerate of departments, agencies and organisations which undertook the production, dissemination and control of ideas. In effect, there was a fusion of the worlds of knowledge and power, creating a situation of ideological monism and intensely politicising intellectual life and theoretical developments (Waller, 1988: 36–9). These factors are crucial in understanding the form and content of Soviet Marxism, and the role it played within the system.

Soviet Marxism was caught in a number of paradoxes. It claimed to be both objective and partisan: partisan because it expressed the fundamental interests and world-view of the proletariat and its vanguard (the most advanced element of the working class), the CPSU; objective because it also claimed a scientific validity for itself. Also, Soviet Marxism contained pressures both to defend and rationalise the status quo, and to promote change. On the one hand, there were clear political pressures on the development of new ideas or new interpretations: to defend the Soviet state, to rationalise the rule of the CPSU, to bolster the political authority of the General Secretary, to promote the hegemony of the USSR in the international arena. There were bureaucratic pressures at play also. A vast bureaucratic hierarchy existed to control intellectual life, and any moves to allow greater intellectual freedom or autonomy were a threat to their position. Consequently, from Stalin's time onwards, Soviet Marxism became a body of thought which existed to legitimise the distribution of power and in particular the rule of the CPSU. Any theoretical or conceptual developments had to be commensurate with this aim.

On the other hand though, the *raison d'être* of the CPSU was to lead and guide Soviet society towards communism. Its legitimacy was predicated on being able to demonstrate progress towards this goal. This required them to introduce changes or new interpretations into their ideology from time to time, in order to prevent it becoming outdated, or out of step with reality. In this sense, Soviet Marxism was a yardstick against which to measure the actions and policies of the CPSU, a guide to future developments and a constant force for change (Evans, 1993: 1–5; Scanlan, 1985: 9–16). The history and nature of Soviet Marxism can only be understood fully within this context of the intensely politicised nature of all ideological development.

From pluralism to monism: Soviet Marxism 1924–38

How did this transformation of Marxism into the official ideology of the Soviet state come about? It is tempting to see the emergence of a single official interpretation of Marxism as the outcome of Stalinist interventions in Soviet intellectual life after 1931, destroying the intellectual pluralism of the 1920s and culminating in the codification of Marxism in 1938 with the *History of the Communist Party of the Soviet Union (Bolsheviks): Short Course* (published 1939). But this temptation should be resisted. First, the intellectual 'pluralism' of Bolshevism in the 1920s should not be overstated. Although there were debates within the party across a number of issues – culture, industrialisation, the structure of peasant society, national v. international perspectives – essentially they were concerned with specifying the best means to construct socialism in the USSR. Almost all Bolsheviks operated within the same Engels-derived Marxist world-view, and shared a set of core values on the fundamentals of capitalism and the essential structures of socialism (Sandle, 1999: 199–220) Second, the pre-eminent position occupied by Lenin in terms of theoretical interpretation set a precedent for the emergence of a single correct line interpreted for the party by a single leader. Indeed, some have seen this as implicit in Lenin's conception of a vanguard party, rather than merely in Lenin's status as the dominant figure within the party hierarchy. Bolshevism's adherence to democratic centralism as an organisational and political principle had a theoretical consequence. Unity behind the party line required a single party line.

The aftermath of the death of Lenin in January 1924 and the resultant succession struggle was a crucial factor in paving the way for the emergence of a Soviet Marxist orthodoxy. Of the contenders for power, it was Stalin who first saw the importance of establishing an ideological pedigree for himself. Slowly, Lenin's ideas were transmuted into almost canonical status, particularly as a result of Stalin's series of lectures *Foundations of Leninism* in early 1924, in which he set out the fundamental principles of 'Leninism', which he termed the 'Marxism of the era of imperialism and proletarian revolution'. By defining a body of doctrine as 'Leninism', he was able to validate his own ideas, and undermine those of his opponents. In this way, an 'official' party line could be established, condemning opponents of this line to be heretics, rather than critics. Soviet Marxism became Soviet Marxism–Leninism. The driving force behind this was the succession struggle. Stalin used ideology to try to discredit the ideas of one of his opponents, Trotsky. Stalin, by defining 'Leninism', hoped to prove that there were significant ideological differences between Lenin and Trotsky, and consequently to portray himself as the heir apparent of Lenin's mantle (Evans, 1993: 29–32); although it needs to be stated at this point that the main source of Stalin's ideas was Bukharin.

The main battleground upon which this conflict was fought was the issue of 'Socialism in One Country', which was the first doctrinal innovation to be incorporated into Soviet Marxist discourse after Lenin's death. Stalin was intent on driving a wedge between Trotsky and Lenin. One of these ways was to portray Trotsky's theory of 'permanent revolution' as being at odds with Lenin's thinking. The issue debated was whether it was possible for Russia to build socialism on her own, or whether an international revolution was required so that the European proletariat could assist their Russian comrades in this task. Stalin and Bukharin, during the period December 1924 to January 1926, argued that socialism could and had to be completed in Russia, but that the final victory of socialism could not be guaranteed until the possibility of capitalist intervention was removed by the victory of the international revolution (Stalin, 1947: 156–77). The disagreement with Trotsky was really quite minor (Trotsky supported the idea of constructing socialism in Russia but argued that economic and technical backwardness would prevent this being completed) but Stalin exploited it for his own political ends. What distinguished the two theorists was faith: faith in the ability of the Russian people to construct socialism. Stalin was appealing to a pride in the achievements of the revolution, asserting that Russia was no longer dependent upon the West. Indeed Russia was now the centre of the world revolutionary movement.

The debate around 'Socialism in One Country' was resolved firmly in Stalin's favour by his defeat of Trotsky in the factional struggles of 1925–29. The ramifications for Soviet Marxism–Leninism were highly significant. 'Socialism in One Country' incorporated notions of Russian nationalism, self-sufficiency and autarky into the dominant ideological compound. Stalin had revised the definition of internationalism, prioritising the interests of the Soviet state. Under 'Socialism in One Country', the cause of world socialism was best served by constructing socialism in the USSR, by defending the revolutionary gains of 1917. There was now a complete coincidence of the interests of the international proletariat and of the Soviet state, and the former were to be subordinated to the latter. The fusion of nationalism and Marxism was complete.

Stalin's victory in the factional struggles was crucial in paving the way for the official ideological monopoly of Soviet Marxism–Leninism, and the concept of 'Socialism in One Country' was to become a core part of this orthodoxy. Two other 'innovations' were introduced into Soviet Marxism–Leninism by Stalin after Lenin's death. First, there was the idea that the class struggle became more acute the closer you got to socialism. This ran contrary to the view prevalent amongst other Marxists of the time that the class struggle begins to recede after the revolution. Stalin postulated that the 'old' classes would struggle more resolutely and desperately as their day of reckoning approached. Second, in line with an earlier view espoused by Trotsky in the debate about the use of terror after the revolution, Stalin argued that the state should become stronger the nearer the USSR got to communism. Partly this was a function of the acutening class struggle thesis, but it was also partly derived from the notion of 'Socialism in One Country'. Hostile capitalist encirclement required a strong coercive state with the ability to defend the USSR from attack (Evans, 1993: 39–40; Kolakowski, 1978: 100–1). The development of these three concepts reflects the subordination of Marxist theory to the narrow political agenda of Stalin and his programme of state-sponsored change.

There are three other noteworthy developments in the consolidation of a Stalinist orthodox interpretation of Soviet Marxism–Leninism. The first occurred in 1931. From 1929 onwards, increasing pressure was brought to bear upon intellectuals to conform to the official line, in literature, art, poetry and music. In 1931, the fields of philosophy and history were brought under the *diktat* of the official ideology. Any deviations from orthodox Leninism, or criticisms of Lenin, were castigated. Their proponents were liable to be dismissed and replaced by advocates of orthodoxy. In philosophy, this took the form of the nullification of a long-standing dispute between two groups of Soviet philosophers: *mechanists* and *Deborinists*. The party intervened and established a clear line to which all had to conform in a Central Committee resolution of 1931 (Kolakowski, 1978: 66–75; Bottomore *et al.*, 1983: 455). Similarly, in the field of history, Stalin intervened in a somewhat arcane dispute in a letter to the editors of the journal *Proletarskaya Revolyutsiya*. Defending Lenin, Stalin sought to portray any account of the history of the Bolshevik party that was in some way critical as being a 'falsification' and a Trotskyite ruse to undermine the party (Kolakowski, 1978: 92–3; Stalin, 1947: 378–89). The combined impact of these interventions was to establish the collective authority of the party, and the personal authority of Stalin in all theoretical matters. Intellectual life was now to be closely supervised and policed to ensure orthodoxy. Although the natural sciences retained a degree of autonomy well into the late 1940s, social theory, history and philosophy were squeezed into an intellectual mould.

The second development occurred in 1936. Heralding a new constitution, Stalin proclaimed that:

> Our Soviet society has already, in the main, succeeded in achieving socialism; it has created a socialist system, i.e., it has brought about what Marxists in other words call the first, or lower phase of communism.
>
> (Stalin, 1947: 548)

With the virtual completion of collectivisation and the continuation of industrialisation, Stalin asserted that the foundations of socialism had been laid: for instance socialist ownership of the means of production, abolition of exploitation and unemployment, right to work, education and leisure. This put an end to the debates about how to construct socialism, and to alternative conceptions of this 'lower phase'. This had a twofold effect. First, it established a particular method for building socialism, one that was to be imposed and imitated in many subsequent regimes. Second, it rendered the existing structures, institutions and values immune from criticism. Theoretical energies were increasingly devoted to celebrating what had been achieved, rather than critically evaluating the present.

Last, and most significantly, in 1939, in a revised version of the *History of the Communist Party of the Soviet Union (Bolsheviks): Short Course*, Stalin contributed a chapter entitled 'Dialectical and Historical Materialism'.[1] The text of the *Short Course* became the centrepiece of Soviet historical, ideological and educational life until the mid-1950s. The chapter on *diamat* and *histmat* became the officially approved world-view of the party, to which all thought had to conform and all thinkers pay fealty. This was a simplified, schematic exposition of Marxist philosophy as derived from Engels, Plekhanov, Lenin and Bukharin. Stalin set out the basic features thus.

Dialectical materialism was described as the 'world outlook of the Marxist–Leninist party'. It consisted of a dialectical method of study, and a materialistic view of the world. The former contained four components:

- nature is an interconnected and integral whole, and must be studied in this way;
- nature is in a state of continuous movement, development and change;
- the process of development is one of the transition from quantitative into qualitative changes;
- the process of development from lower to higher forms occurs as the struggle of opposites. All phenomena have inner contradictions, and the conflict between them is the key component of the developmental process (CC of CPSU, 1939: 105–9).

The major omission from this list was the idea, advanced by both Lenin and Engels, of the 'negation of the negation', of which more below. The materialist world-view embodied the following propositions:

- the world is by its very nature material;
- matter, reality, being is an objective reality, and matter is primary;
- the world is fully knowable, and this knowledge has the status of objective truth (CC of CPSU, 1939: 111–14).

Applied to human society and history, this world-view formed the basis of historical materialism. History was governed by laws, and the key to understanding these laws lay in the economic life of society. Stalin outlined that:

Hence the prime task of historical science is to study and disclose the laws of production, the laws of development of the productive forces and of the relations of production, the laws of economic development of society.

(CC of CPSU, 1939: 121)

This entailed a slavish adherence to the five-stage formation as set out by Marx in the 1859 *Preface to a Critique of Political Economy*. History was a law-governed process, which evolved inexorably through five stages: primitive communism, slavery, feudalism, capitalism and socialism. What was there, if anything, of theoretical significance in this chapter?

The dominant appraisals of the content of this piece have invariably focused upon its somewhat schematic and simplified nature. Although this is certainly an accurate perception, it is worth remembering the context and purpose for which it was written. It was part of a brief history of the CPSU, and intended as a means of popularising the essentials of the party's world-view. It was not an extended philosophical treatise. It was deliberately couched in a broadly accessible manner to make it a useful educational/propagandist tool for the party. Any criticisms of its lack of theoretical sophistication or of its being overly schematic need to be qualified by an awareness of this context. Two further criticisms have been levelled at Stalin's chapter. The first is that Stalin's definition of the dialectical method is a distortion of Engels' views as outlined in *Anti-Duhring*. Stalin removed one of Engels' propositions, 'the negation of the negation', and replaced it with two general properties of matter, whilst retaining Engels' ideas of transformation of quantity into quality, and the unity of opposites. Why?

Stalin was concerned to strip all the potential for revolutionary transformation from Marxism in order to defend and preserve what had been achieved and constructed so far. Although Stalin acknowledged the universal applicability of dialectical materialism to all societies (be they socialist, capitalist or whatever), he reinterpreted these laws in the light of the immediate political outlook of the Stalinist leadership. If the principle of the 'negation of the negation' were applied to Soviet society, then socialism, as the negation of capitalism, would in turn be negated through the development of communism. By omitting the 'negation of the negation', revolution, radical change and sharp breaks in development were all precluded.[2] Socialist society would thus develop on a harmonious, continuous, gradual basis (Evans, 1993: 52–4; Kolakowski, 1978: 93–102).

The second criticism argues that the chapter is highly reductionist, particularly in regard to historical materialism. The strict adherence to the 1859 *Preface*'s five-formation schema precluded discussion of Marx's other writings on history, most notably the discussion of the 'Asiatic mode of production'. By situating the Russian Revolution within the bounds of this schema, Stalin was able to legitimise 1917, and undermine non-Bolshevik criticisms of it as being 'premature'. To admit or acknowledge exceptions or variations in this scheme, even ones advanced by Marx, would allow room for legitimate discussion of the Soviet experience in the light of Marx's theory of history. This chapter's endorsement of the five formations through which all societies pass precluded any such discussion. Once more, the need to legitimise the regime and its leadership shaped the nature of Soviet Marxist orthodoxy.

Stalin's chapter also maintained a close affiliation with the world-view of pre-revolutionary Russian Marxism, though. The emphasis upon the scientific nature of Marxism, and of Engels in establishing an orthodox interpretation through his pamphlet *Anti-Duhring*, which was initially set out by Plekhanov and continued by Lenin, is maintained by Stalin. No mention or discussion is made of the 'early' works of Marx (the *1844 Economic and Philosophic Manuscripts*, and *Grundrisse*), which had become available to Soviet scholars only in 1932. The chapter draws heavily from both Lenin and Engels, as well as Marx.

This chapter set the parameters for discussion of theory in Soviet Marxism. As was noted above, the deification of Stalin deriving from the hideous excesses of the cult of personality reduced Soviet philosophy to paeans of praise to the all-wise Stalin. Meaningful theoretical discussion and debate all but disappeared. In all fields, the imperative was to reinforce the propositions of the *Short Course*, and to defend the party, the state and the Leader.

However, the dualistic nature of Soviet Marxism – rationalise the status quo, and provide direction for the future – ensured that new issues and developments would have to be discussed at some point. The subsequent history of Soviet Marxism – both in the USSR and Eastern Europe – testifies to the continual need to update and reinterpret Marxism in the light of new tasks and changing conditions. In particular, there were discussions of the timetable of the transition from socialism to communism, as well as the nature of different aspects of life under socialism, developments in capitalism and in foreign affairs to name but a few. The discussion set out below examines the changes introduced into the official ideology after Stalin's death. This process of theoretical renewal witnessed significant changes being introduced into the official interpretation of orthodox Soviet Marxism, as well as regional variations derived from the Eastern European experience. Interestingly, the end of the Stalinist dictatorship saw a greater degree of autonomy for the Soviet intelligentsia. This had a profoundly important impact upon Soviet Marxism, paving the way for the intellectual renewal which occurred after 1985.

The following section explores the developments in Soviet Marxism in the USSR from 1938 through to 1985, as Stalin's successors began to grapple with the theoretical legacy of the *Short Course*.

Developments in Soviet and Eastern bloc Marxism 1938–85

Mature Stalinism: consolidating Soviet Marxism 1938–53

Before looking at the changes introduced after 1953, it is worth briefly dwelling upon the developments in the late Stalinist period (1946–53). Although there were relatively few interesting theoretical innovations in the post-war period, they were underpinned by the same principles that had dominated the *Short Course*: to provide an ideological rationale for the maintenance of the status quo. In Stalin's report to the Eighteenth Party Congress in March 1939, he emphasised that he expected the lower phase of communism (socialism) to have an extended life, thus postponing the transition to the higher phase. Stalin was aware of the potentially radical changes in all areas of Soviet social, economic, political and cultural life which the transition to the higher phase would bring. In order to preclude introducing these changes, Stalin had to demonstrate that the lower phase, and its social and political structures, would remain for a long time into the future (Sandle, 1999: 260–1).

These were the themes of Stalin's two main pamphlets in this era: *Marxism and Linguistics* (1950), and *Economic Problems of Socialism* (1952). In the former, Stalin took issue with the philological theories of Nikolay Marr. Marr had postulated that language was part of the 'superstructure' and formed part of the class system. Language developed in 'qualitative leaps', not through gradual development. Stalin differed.[3] In an article in *Pravda*, he argued that language was essentially non-ideological, belonging neither to the base nor to the superstructure. He reiterated the orthodox position that the superstructure existed to serve the base (i.e. that culture was to serve the interests of the state). Additionally he rejected the idea that change came through qualitative, radical leaps. Restating his view on the dialectics from the *Short Course*, Stalin argued that qualitative changes under socialism would always take place 'gradually' (Kolakowski, 1978: 141–2).

In his latter pamphlet, Stalin introduced two significant innovations into orthodox Soviet Marxism. The first referred to the nature of contradictions under socialism. The struggle of contradictions in society was the basic motive force for change in history. Under capitalism, contradictions were antagonistic. The class contradictions of capitalist society – increasing immiserisation of the exploited majority and the increasing affluence of the exploiting minority – reflected mutually antagonistic class interests. These were resolved only through the class struggle. Under socialism, however, there were no antagonistic contradictions. Soviet society exhibited a fundamental class unity because of the abolition of exploitation. The remaining contradictions – town and country or worker and peasant – were of a non-antagonistic nature. Stalin stripped Marxian/Engelian dialectics of any notions that might legitimise radical change or 'leaps' in development (Evans, 1993: 52–4).

One final point on this latter pamphlet. Stalin argued that the objective laws of economics applied equally to both socialism and capitalism, and that the law of value still operated under socialism, which implied the continued existence of commodity–money relations under socialism (Kolakowski, 1978: 142–3). What distinguished socialism from capitalism was the end towards which economic activity was directed: the latter to profit-maximisation, the former to satisfaction of human needs.[4] Taken together, Stalin's incursions into the field of Marxist theory were highly sporadic and fitful, but with a single aim: to rationalise a programme of prolonged, gradual, balanced development which emphasised the need to consolidate the lower phase, before embarking upon the transition to communism.

From one road to many: from Khrushchev to Gorbachev 1956–85

The death of Stalin in 1953 did not usher in any immediate changes. It was not until Khrushchev revealed some of the crimes of the Stalin era in a four-hour secret speech to a closed session of the Twentieth Congress of the CPSU in 1956 that a process of intellectual renewal could begin in earnest. The main developments across the period from 1956–85 came in three areas: the timetable of the transition from socialism to communism and the nature of socialism; the development of new fields of enquiry and reassessments of key parts of Soviet Marxist orthodoxy; and finally variations on Soviet Marxism developed within Eastern Europe.

From socialism to communism

Unlike Stalin, Khrushchev showed no reticence about spelling out a specific timetable for the transition from socialism to communism. In the 1961 party programme, Khrushchev stated that during 1961–70 the USSR would outstrip the USA in production per head of population. During 1971–80, the material-technical basis of communism would be created, and by 1980 communism 'in the main' would be built (CC of CPSU, 1961: 445–590) In Khrushchev's view, socialism as a transitional society had two phases: the construction of socialism and the creation of the material-technical basis of communism. Communism itself would have two stages: basic and completed communism. How orthodox was this view of socialism and communism, and of the transition from one to the other?

In some areas orthodoxy was revised. A fundamental shift in the nature of the state was announced. According to the party programme, the construction of socialism meant the end of the era of dictatorship of the proletariat. Now, 'the state has become the state of the entire people, an organ expressing the interests and the will of the people as a whole' (CC of CPSU, 1961: 547). This was a major departure. Orthodox Soviet Marxism had always identified the state as an instrument of class rule. Now the 'all-people's state' represented all Soviet citizens. Moreover, how could the elaboration of a new state form be reconciled with the traditional belief in the 'withering away' of the state under communism? Khrushchev held to the idea of 'withering away', but interpreted it in such a way as to defend the existence of a central organ of power well into the communist phase. Khrushchev maintained that particular functions of the state would wither away (coercion and repression in particular). Other activities – economic and cultural tasks – would remain. The state would still be in existence in the era of basic communism. The advent of self-government by the people under full communism would be brought about by drawing the populace more fully into the running of the system, albeit closely guided by the party itself which would remain the central political organisation under communism (Sandle, 1999: 321–8; Evans, 1993: 92–9).

In other areas the programme affirmed orthodoxy. The central features of communism – material abundance, social homogeneity, distribution according to need – remained central to Khrushchev's vision. However, the specific meanings of these ideas were reinterpreted in such a way as to postpone the radical transformations deep into the future. Material abundance was defined not as the abolition of scarcity, but as the attainment of Western levels of consumption. Distribution according to need would not arrive until full communism. Commodity–money relations would continue to operate. Material inequality would remain, but differentials would decrease. Khrushchev's rhetoric and timetable was bold and utopian. The specifics of his vision of communism were really quite pragmatic and conservative, though. The continued existence of the state and commodity–money relations emphasises that Khrushchev, like Stalin, was keen to hedge in the transformations inherent in the task of constructing communism. Khrushchev's innovations in Soviet Marxism–Leninism exemplify the tension between the desire to preserve and rationalise the status quo, and the desire to promote change (Sandle, 1999: 321–8).

Brezhnev's leadership saw a reinterpretation of the nature of socialism and the timetable of the transition to communism. He officially endorsed a new concept – Developed Socialism – in 1971 to replace Khrushchev's idea of the 'full-scale construction of communism'. Socialism was reinterpreted. It was no longer a brief transitional period between capitalism and communism. It was a long historical phase, marked by its own laws of social development. Developed Socialism did not signal the abandonment of the end goal of reaching communism, merely another postponement. The transition to communism would be a prolonged, gradual process. No timetable was spelt out. Alongside the elaboration of a new periodisation of the post-revolutionary era, Developed Socialism also reaffirmed the central socio-political and economic values of Soviet Marxism–Leninism. In particular, the new constitution of 1977 reiterated the nature of the state under socialism (the all-people's state) and the leading role of the communist party (Evans, 1993: 105–26).

Two things link the innovations in Soviet Marxism–Leninism concerning the transition from socialism to communism under Stalin, Khrushchev and Brezhnev. The first was a continual postponement of the final stage of history: full communism. This was intimately linked to the desire of the ruling elite to avoid the potential for radical change inherent in this process. The second was the maintenance of the central institutions and organs of political power: the CPSU and the Soviet state. Theoretical developments were designed with the political needs of the ruling elite in mind. But what is interesting to note is that the Soviet leaders could not abandon the final end goal of communism from their ideology as this was the *raison d'être* of their existence. Ideas may have been subordinated to political needs, but the framework provided by Soviet Marxism had to be taken seriously by the leadership.

The growth of intellectual autonomy

The Khrushchev era witnessed some highly significant innovations in Soviet intellectual life. Khrushchev oversaw a partial separation of the worlds of knowledge and power. It became possible, albeit in selected fields and within clear limits, for intellectuals to discuss and debate new ideas and concepts. The first inklings of intellectual renewal came in 1958–59. Khrushchev set up creative collectives in order to rewrite the key historical and philosophical texts underpinning Soviet Marxism–Leninism. A new *History of the CPSU* was written, along with a new philosophical textbook, *Fundamentals of Marxist Philosophy,* and a new book on Marxist theory, *Fundamentals of Marxism–Leninism.* The first had the chapter on 'Dialectical and Historical Materialism' removed, which opened the way for a far greater degree of critical inquiry for scholars and intellectuals. The last was a much more detailed, and relatively innovative piece of work. Out of the collectives formed to produce these texts grew a number of academic institutes and research centres that quickly earned reputations as centres of innovative and creative thought. These new texts removed the rigid encasement within which Soviet Marxism–Leninism existed. This had a twofold impact upon Soviet Marxism–Leninism: it provided scope for theorists to depart from the dogmatism of the Stalinist schema, and also for explorations in new fields (Sandle, 1999: 318–21).

There are many examples of both phenomena, and space precludes a detailed treatment.[5] Perhaps the most interesting developments came amongst Soviet historians. While the official ideology stuck rigidly to the crude base/superstructure determination model and the five-formation schema, Soviet historians began to push back the boundaries. Greater attention began to be paid to the complexity of the historical process. Other socio-economic formations, outside the orthodox five, began to be analysed. The role of economic factors as determining forces in historical change also came into question, with Scanlan postulating that Soviet historians were in practice 'historical interactionists rather than historical materialists' (Scanlan, 1985: 223). Although there was something of an ideological tightening after 1969 that made discussions more difficult to undertake, it was still possible for historians and philosophers of history to debate new ideas. The late 1950s and 1960s also witnessed new concepts, ideas and fields of theory being discussed by Soviet scholars. In areas such as international relations, economics, sociology and cybernetics Soviet scholars were able to develop whole new areas of enquiry. Virtually unencumbered by a framework imposed by existing orthodoxy, these areas proved to be a fruitful area of work for Soviet scholars, demonstrating that there was some genuine creative life within Soviet Marxism–Leninism.

What these developments demonstrate is that there were a number of layers to Soviet Marxism–Leninism. At the level of the official ideology, there were changes introduced, but these were usually closely linked to the immediate political needs of the party leadership. Beneath that, it was possible for scholars to debate and publish new ideas and interpretations, although they were rarely incorporated into the official orthodoxy. From 1956 to 1985, Soviet Marxism–Leninism did demonstrate, in varying degrees, a pluralism of approaches which distinguish it from the rigid dogmatism of the Stalin years. Outside the structure of orthodoxy, there existed a small underground current of critical Marxism. However, it is always important to remember that orthodoxy always held sway, and there were clear limits on the extent to which scholars could diverge from this. Intellectual life remained subject to political control, but a slight gap had opened up which allowed for a degree of intellectual non-conformity (Scanlan, 1985: 326–35).

Soviet Marxism in the Eastern bloc: revisionism, the Prague Spring and Yugoslavian Praxis

The death of Stalin and Khrushchev's Secret Speech had a great impact in the socialist countries in Eastern Europe. The opportunity to criticise Stalinist ideology produced a variety of responses from Marxists. The difficult issue for the ideologists and political leaders of the socialist states was how much scope they had to develop a distinctive ideological and political programme, without undermining their own position at home or lapsing into 'revisionism': a form of Marxist 'heresy' in which the fundamental truths as established by Soviet Marxism–Leninism were abandoned or fundamentally altered. It was a difficult line to tread. The essential distinction lay between those who sought to criticise Stalinist dogmas by following the lead set in Moscow, and those who wished to go beyond this to criticise the fundamental structures and values of the Soviet-type regimes, albeit from a Marxist perspective. This latter group (often viewed as an underground or unofficial Marxism) were to form the nucleus of a distinctive Eastern European variant of Marxism (Bottomore *et al.*, 1983: 316–20). Unfortunately it is not possible to explore within the confines of this essay the growth of this unofficial or underground strand.[6] Betwixt these two poles lay something of an ideological grey area. Different countries and thinkers sought to explore the limits of Marxist theorising that would be tolerated either locally or in Moscow. The lines were constantly shifting. It is probably best to view Soviet Marxism in Eastern Europe in terms of a spectrum between orthodoxy and revisionism. At one end, there were Romania, Bulgaria and the GDR, who tended to stick closely to orthodoxy. At the other end were Yugoslavia and Albania who forged their own path. In between there were Poland, Hungary and Czechoslovakia. This section will trace the variations on 'official' Marxism within Eastern Europe from 1954 to 1985, particularly the fate of those countries in this ideological 'no-man's land'.

From 1955/56 onwards, there emerged a movement in Eastern Europe which sought to reform the structure, operation and ideology of the regimes but on the basis of its own professed Marxist–Leninist principles. Outside of Yugoslavia, the first expressions of this emerged in Poland and Hungary in 1956. The stimulus given to an intellectual renewal amongst Marxists by Khrushchev's Secret Speech found expression in a generalised critique of Stalinist dogma. This encompassed both party and non-party critics. The main elements of their critique were to attack the excesses and aberrations of the Stalinist form of rule. In the socio-political field, they called for greater democracy (both within the party and also in the workplace), restrictions on censorship, subordination of the secret police to the political and legal authorities, restoration of a 'normal' legal culture, and the abolition of the privileges of the bureaucracy. In the economic sphere, there were calls for greater participation by the workers in the productive process, reforms to the planning mechanism and a recognition of the need for diversity in forms of economic organisation in the countryside. In the international sphere there was a growing desire for autonomy in determining their own path of development, something which found expression in Khrushchev's recognition of national roads to socialism for the Eastern European socialist states (Kolakowski, 1978: 463–6).

Initially, this intellectual renewal rested on an attempt to rescue Leninist and Marxist principles from the distortions of Stalinism. These voices focused their criticisms upon philosophy and economics, as these two fields left unmolested the key ideological principle that underpinned the structure of power: the monopoly of political power enjoyed by the communist party. When this point appeared to be under threat – as in Hungary in 1956, Czechoslovakia in 1968 and Poland in 1980/81 – the USSR resorted to armed intervention. Philosophical criticisms attempted to eliminate determinism and to restore the subjective, human element to philosophical analysis. Economists explored ways to integrate planning with market mechanisms. As time went on, however, the broad anti-Stalinist coalition began to dissolve. Increasingly critical voices began to be heard, which attacked Leninist political and philosophical norms, and sought to restore the critical edge of Marxist social theory to an appraisal of the nature of Eastern European socialism. Interventions in intellectual life from the party authorities quickly followed the Soviet invasion of Hungary in October 1956, which drove critical Marxism 'underground' (although some Polish economists were able to discuss reforms to the economic mechanism). The 'official' ideology remained virtually unchanged. Widespread disillusionment amongst Eastern European intellectuals led many not just to abandon Leninism completely, but also to abandon any adherence to Marxism.

The experiences of Czechoslovakia were slightly different from those of Poland and Hungary. 1956 was far less of a pivotal year than in Poland and Hungary, although there were some important developments. Gradually currents of thought grew up in Czechoslovakia, drawing upon indigenous traditions and embracing philosophy, law, economics and politics. These 'revisionist' currents adopted a similar approach to those in Poland and Hungary: rejecting Stalinist dogmatism in order to rescue Marxism from these distortions. Theorists such as Mlynar, Sik, Jicinsky and Kosik began to grapple with how to revive Marxist theory, and so to rejuvenate the practice of socialism in Czechoslovakia. Echoing the views of philosophers in Poland, Hungary and Yugoslavia, Czech revisionists also denied the crude base/superstructure model and the determinism of *diamat* and *histmat*. Unlike elsewhere, the 'official' ideologists were more tolerant of this revisionist current, and considerable intellectual autonomy existed for theorists to explore new ideas, many of whom remained within the party itself. Significantly, Czech revisionist intellectuals, most notably Zdenek Mlynar, began to think and write about changes to the political system, including the possibility of elections with a choice of candidates, separation of powers, legal safeguards for the rights of individuals, and democratic accountability of office-holders. Developments came to a head with the Prague Spring of 1968, when a broad-based reformist movement, led by Alexander Dubcek, sought a series of changes, based loosely around a revisionist platform: ending of censorship, abolition of the secret police, creation of the rule of law, political pluralism. The Prague Spring was snuffed out brutally by Soviet tanks in August 1968 (McLellan, 1979: 146; Kolakowski, 1978: 466–70; Kusin, 1971: 106–23).

The crushing of the Prague Spring essentially ended the toleration of this 're-visionist' current in Marxism across the entire Eastern bloc. The scope for intellectual autonomy and creativity outside of the ideological establishment all but disappeared. Within this establishment, the 'official' interpretation of Marxism eschewed any radical changes and fell into line with the ideological framework established in the USSR: the era of Developed Socialism (although interestingly Developed Socialism actually migrated to the USSR from discussions in Eastern Europe in the late 1960s) (Meiklejohn Terry, 1984: 221–53). The 1970s really offered little more than the repetition of orthodoxy.

The most significant departure from Soviet orthodoxy amongst official ruling parties in Eastern Europe came in Yugoslavia. The Yugoslav experience is distinct from the rest of the Soviet bloc. The break with Stalin that Tito undertook in 1948 gave Yugoslav Marxists greater autonomy to develop a distinctive approach, although a similar clash between radical thinkers and the ideological establishment also occurred. The Yugoslav Communist Party (YCP) began to forge a distinctive model of socialism which differed from that of the Soviet model in promoting a more decentralised, workers' self-management approach. This in turn entailed a variant of market socialism, as the YCP sought to combat the bureaucratism of Soviet socialism. This ethos found a philosophical resonance in the emergence of the *Praxis* group in Yugoslavia in 1964. *Praxis* was the name given to a journal devoted to the exploration of alternatives to orthodox Marxism.

The basic starting point of the *Praxis* group was similar to that of revisionists elsewhere: the attempt to recover the humanist essence of Marxism by returning to the texts and issues of the early Marx: alienation, the human being as a creative agent and emancipation through creative labour. They rejected the deterministic and mechanistic approach of the Stalinist *diamat* and *histmat*, and sought to bring about human self-realisation through a sustained critique of all the institutions and practices which oppressed and exploited the individual, under both socialism and capitalism. This critical edge of the *Praxis* group brought it into conflict with the political and ideological establishment, and by 1975 the journal had been closed down and many of its contributors removed from their posts (Kolakowski, 1978: 474–8; McLellan, 1979: 147–8; Markovic and Cohen, 1975: 1–38).

The experience of Marxism in Eastern Europe from 1953 to 1985 demonstrates the complexities of a belief-system which is an intellectual apparatus that at one and the same time both criticises the prevailing structures of power and defends that power structure. For a short time (1953–56/57) the 'thaw' produced a critique of Stalinist dogma which united the ideological establishment and the Marxist intellectuals outside the establishment. The revisionist agenda – humanist, anti-bureaucracy, anti-deterministic – soon exhausted its usefulness for the ideological and political elites once their political position had been consolidated, leading to the divorce between 'official' and underground Marxism in Eastern Europe. Orthodoxy reasserted itself very rapidly, and fell into line with the post-Stalinist line propounded by the CPSU. But the continuation of critical thinking amongst Marxist intellectuals in Eastern Europe testifies to the continued vitality of Marxist doctrine.

The demise of Soviet Marxism–Leninism 1985–91

Within six years of coming to power, Gorbachev had overseen the collapse of the communist system and the disappearance of the USSR. *Perestroika* had been a process of deconstruction, rather than reconstruction. Somewhat lost amidst the chaos and flux of these events was the demise of Soviet Marxism–Leninism, both as the official ideology of the Soviet state and as a belief-system in its own right. Significantly, this demise had become apparent before the demise of the communist system itself. As the position of the ruling group underwent radical changes, so too did its ideology, leading ultimately to its collapse (Sandle, 1999: 371–422). How did this happen?

The erosion of Marxism–Leninism occurred as a direct result of the vast political, social, economic and cultural changes unleashed by *perestroika*. In particular, the processes of *glasnost* (openness) and democratisation created the preconditions for ideological and political pluralism within the Soviet system after 1988. In this situation, it was no longer possible or appropriate for the Soviet state to possess one exclusive official ideology, and to prevent the public dissemination of alternative ideologies and belief-systems. Inexorably, Soviet Marxism–Leninism lost its status as the 'official' ideology of the Soviet state.

In these conditions, the CPSU was forced to modify and adapt Marxism–Leninism in order to try and compete in the new political and intellectual climate. By importing an array of new beliefs, ideas and values, the essential philosophical principles and ideas of orthodox Soviet Marxism–Leninism – *diamat* and *histmat* – were destroyed. A couple of examples will suffice to illustrate this. The CPSU abandoned its commitment to the Stalinist interpretation of dialectical materialism, without lapsing into an idealist position. It maintained its belief that being existed independently of consciousness, and that the world was knowable. However, it eschewed the ontological aspects (that matter was primary and the mind secondary). In this sense it rejected the orthodox position. This shift had been conditioned by the humanistic and ethical interpretation of socialism developed by Gorbachev: the emphasis in 'Humane Democratic Socialism' on the need to concentrate on humanistic not class values, and to emphasise the importance of the needs and interests of individuals. Moral and existential issues were now treated as crucial issues to be addressed. No longer were the norms and beliefs of an individual's life defined purely by their material situation and their social relations. This is best exemplified by the party's public retreat from scientific atheism as a key component of its world-view. In its place, the party put respect, tolerance and dialogue with believers (Sandle, 1997).

Similarly, there was also a retreat from historical materialism in its orthodox form. Theorists began to question whether the historical process was at all times a linear, law-governed one which went through the five phases identified by Marx. The base/superstructure formula was increasingly viewed problematically, and many rejected the idea that the key and sole source of development in history was the conflict between productive forces and the relations of production. Inexorably, other key components of Soviet Marxism–Leninism came into question. The teleological element – that history was moving towards a pre-ordained end – was abandoned. Capitalism and socialism were no longer diametrically opposed social systems. Proletarian internationalism was replaced by a rather woolly commitment to 'all-human values'.

By the time the CPSU came to draw up a new Party Programme (its basic statement of faith) in July 1991, the key components of the orthodox interpretation of Marxism–Leninism had been eroded. The principles and values which constituted the core of Gorbachev's vision of 'Humane Democratic Socialism' – common human values, reassessments of capitalism, socialism and communism, greater emphasis upon the individual and upon spiritual issues – gradually undermined and displaced the central pillars of Soviet Marxism–Leninism: the teleology of historical materialism, proletarian internationalism and ontological materialism. The new synthesis represented little more than a form of social democracy. In the drift from scientific to ethical socialism, not only did orthodox Soviet Marxism–Leninism disappear, but the CPSU became a party based only partially on the teachings of Marx, Engels and Lenin. In the draft 1991 programme, it was stated that, 'while restoring and developing the initial humanist principles of the teaching of Marx, Engels and Lenin, we include in our ideological arsenal all the wealth of our own and world socialist and democratic thought' (Sandle, 1999: 416). Orthodox Soviet Marxism was dead.

Soviet and Eastern bloc Marxism: an appraisal

The short life of Soviet Marxism–Leninism was a curious one. Thousands of hours and millions of words, great effort and energies were poured into the development, production dissemination and propagation of its ideas both at home and abroad. It exerted a great influence over the communist movement, both in the USSR and Eastern Europe and elsewhere. Millions of people were brought up in an educational system infused, explicitly and implicitly, with the values and world-view of Soviet Marxism. Yet by 1991 it had few adherents, was seen as a dogmatic, stylised set of empty formulae bearing no relation to reality, and was perceived as contributing little or nothing to the world Marxist canon. It appeared to be little more than a thinly veiled rationalisation of the monopoly of power of the CPSU. The cynicism and apathy of the Soviet people by the late 1970s and early 1980s appeared to demonstrate the enormous irrelevance of Marxism to their everyday lives.

Much of the above is, of course, irrefutable. A great deal of damage to intellectual life (and to intellectuals) was perpetrated by the Soviet state, which generally tended to reward conformity and persecute critical and innovative thinking. Much of the widespread disillusionment with Marxism stems from the popular identification of Marxism and the Soviet system. This picture does need qualification, though, if we are to appraise Soviet Marxism–Leninism accurately. Although it was at times a highly dogmatic, formulaic set of doctrines, it did maintain a degree of intellectual autonomy and vitality. The Soviet state committed huge resources to the production of a sustained analysis of the post-revolutionary state, of the timetable of the transition from capitalism to communism, and of the nature of the transitional society and (to a lesser extent) the final end-point of history: communism (although much of this thought was shaped by the political needs of the CPSU). In addition, in the ideologically less sensitive areas of philosophy, there was a good deal of autonomous scholarship which developed Marxist approaches in areas such as ethics, logic and the philosophy of history (Scanlan, 1985: 326–33). The post-Stalin 'thaw' produced a period of relative intellectual creativity which produced a form of diversity and pluralism within Soviet Marxism–Leninism. The monolithic nature of Soviet Marxism–Leninism needs to be qualified.

The most compelling testament to the continued vitality of Soviet Marxism, in spite of the extensive political controls and pressures on intellectual developments, is the process of ideological reform after 1985. Many of the ideas which came (briefly) to hold sway after 1985, ousting Stalinist and Brezhnevite doctrines, were those which had been developed within the Soviet intellectual community during the 1950s and 1960s. The fate of Soviet Marxism demonstrates that, although ideas can be controlled, manipulated and used by those in power, they will fail to be effective and meaningful if they lose touch with the reality they purport to be able to explain.

Notes

1 Opinions vary on the exact extent of Stalin's 'contribution' to this chapter. It undoubtedly carries the hallmark of Stalin's own writing style. In all probability he substantially reworked and amended an early draft provided by Yaroslavsky.
2 This is an interesting example of the way in which the regime, even though it controlled intellectual life, continued to take ideas seriously. The implication of a disjuncture between the ideology and the practice was considered to be too dangerous in undermining the legitimacy of the CPSU to be ignored.
3 Stalin's intervention actually served a useful purpose in freeing linguistic studies in the USSR from the grip of Marr's bizarre ideals. The same cannot be said however of genetics, with Stalin's support for Lysenko doing untold harm to Soviet genetics.
4 There are a number of unresolved problems with Stalin's position. In particular, it is unclear how exactly a socialist system would ensure that the socialist economy was designed to meet human needs when it was subject to 'objective' economic laws.
5 Details can be found in a number of texts. See for instance Lewin (1975).
6 For those who wish to pursue this topic in more depth, there have been a number of key texts and thinkers. See for example Bahro (1978); Rakowski (1978); Vajda (1981).

References and further reading

Bahro, R. (1978) *The Alternative in Eastern Europe*. London: NLB.
Bottomore, T., L. Harris, V.G. Kiernan and R. Miliband (1983) *A Dictionary of Marxist Thought*. Oxford: Blackwell.
Central Committee of the Communist Party of the Soviet Union (CC of CPSU) (1939) *History of the Communist Party of the Soviet Union (Bolsheviks): Short Course*. Moscow: Foreign Languages Publishing House.

Central Committee of the Communist Party of the Soviet Union (CC of CPSU) (1961) *The Road to Communism*. Moscow: Foreign Languages Publishing House.

Evans, A. (1993) *Soviet Marxism–Leninism. The Decline of an Ideology*. Westport, CT: Praeger.

Kolakowski, L. (1978) *Main Currents of Marxism*, volume 3. Oxford: Oxford University Press.

Kusin, V. (1971) *The Intellectual Origins of the Prague Spring*. Cambridge: Cambridge University Press.

Lewin, M. (1975) *Political Undercurrents in Soviet Economic Debates*. London: Pluto

McLellan, D. (1979) *Marxism after Marx*. Basingstoke: Macmillan.

Marcuse, H. (1958) *Soviet Marxism*. London: Routledge and Kegan Paul.

Markovic, M. and R.S. Cohen (1975) *The Rise and Fall of Socialist Humanism*. Nottingham: Spokesman.

Meiklejohn Terry, S. (ed.) (1984) *Soviet Policy in Eastern Europe*. New Haven, CT: Yale University Press.

Rakovski, M. (1978) *Towards an East European Marxism*. London: Allison & Busby.

Sandle, M. (1997) 'The Final Word: The Draft Party Programme of July/August 1991', *Europe–Asia Studies*, 48: 1131–50.

Sandle, M. (1999) *A Short History of Soviet Socialism*. London: UCL Press

Scanlan, J. (1985) *Marxism in the USSR*. Ithaca, NY: Cornell University Press.

Stalin, J.V. (1947) *Problems of Leninism*. Moscow: Foreign Languages Publishing House.

Stalin, J.V. (1950) *Marxism and Problems of Linguistics*. Moscow: Foreign Languages Publishing House.

Stalin, J.V. (1952) *Economic Problems of Socialism in the USSR*. Moscow: Foreign Languages Publishing House.

Stalin, J.V. (1976) *The Foundations of Leninism*. Peking: Foreign Languages Publishing House.

Vajda, M. (1981) *The State and Socialism*. New York: St. Martin's.

Waller, M. (1988) 'What is to Count as Ideology in Soviet Politics?' in S. White and A. Pravda (eds), *Ideology and Soviet Politics*. Basingstoke: Macmillan.

Part II

5 Eurocommunism

Rick Simon

The late 1960s and 1970s were characterised by profound economic and political instability which put into question the certainties of the post-war period. Against this background, the communist movement itself began to unravel, reevaluating its traditions, strategy and goals, and giving rise to the phenomenon commonly referred to as 'Eurocommunism'.

The development of Eurocommunism, a term usually credited to the Yugoslav journalist Frane Barbieri, who used it in an article in June 1975, centred on the three largest Western European communist parties, the Italian (PCI), the French (PCF) and the Spanish (PCE), but other smaller parties, for example in Sweden, Belgium and Britain, were also affected. The communist parties themselves were reluctant to adopt the Eurocommunist label and, at the June 1976 World Conference of Communist and Workers' Parties, PCE leader Santiago Carrillo said that 'the term is most unfortunate . . . There is no such thing as Eurocommunism' (quoted in Preston, 1981: 36). Carrillo's denial of the very existence of Eurocommunism suggests how problematic the term was.

If we accept that such a phenomenon as Eurocommunism existed then it is in recognition of the fact that a number of communist parties adopted apparently similar political positions concerning crucial aspects of their strategy and ideology: first, a critical attitude towards the Soviet Union and the Soviet model of socialism; second, an emphasis on the national specificity of each path to socialism; third, an acceptance that a socialist society should be democratic and safeguard human and civil rights; fourth, a belief that progressive political change and the achievement of socialism could and should occur through the institutions of the liberal democratic state.

In the sum of its positions, Eurocommunism sought to provide an alternative, a 'third way', to both Soviet-style socialism and Western European social democracy. Its major failing was, however, that, in its emphasis on strategy, alliances and national peculiarities, it failed to generate an enduring theoretical framework. Its coherence, such as it was, derived from a temporary coincidence in the evolution of national parties, much as an eclipse produces a transitory alignment of celestial bodies whose trajectories are radically different. Although Carrillo was one of the few influential communists to try and provide a theoretical underpinning, his reluctance and that of other communist party leaders to accept the existence of Eurocommunism was precisely because the term assumed the emergence of a common model at a time when such a notion was being abandoned in favour of an emphasis on national conditions and specificities. Moreover, Eurocommunism proved an inaccurate expression for the following reasons. First, similar changes occurred in parties outside of Europe, especially the Japanese. As Lange correctly observed, Eurocommunism was a phenomenon 'associated not so much with Europe as with advanced industrial democracy' (Lange, 1981: 3). Second, it affected Western European parties, being rejected by even the most autonomous of the Eastern Europeans: the Yugoslavs and Romanians. Third, it gave the impression of an homogeneous and finished product rather than a transitory phase in the evolution of world communism.

Lack of theoretical justification for the changes in policy combined with a general scepticism on the part of some commentators led at the time to a questioning of the communist parties' sincerity: was this a genuine change of direction or simply a new attempt by the communist parties to disguise their real subversive intent under the rhetoric of reformism and respect for democratic institutions? Communism's evolution during the final quarter of the twentieth century, and especially the collapse of the regimes in Eastern Europe and the Soviet Union itself, makes it possible to assess more accurately the historical significance of Eurocommunism as a phase in the development of the communist parties' relationship to the USSR on the one hand, and to the capitalist state on the other.

Eurocommunism and the USSR

If Eurocommunism can be given a date of birth then it would be 11 July 1975, when a statement of principles was signed by the leaders of the PCI (Enrico Berlinguer) and PCE (Santiago Carrillo) at Leghorn in Italy (Levi, 1979: 13). Like all births, however, the emergence of Eurocommunism cannot be attributed to a single event but was the culmination of a long gestation period. Ernest Mandel, who was sharply critical of Eurocommunism from the left, argued that its threads 'were woven into the future of the world communist movement from the very moment the theory of "socialism in one country" was adopted' (Mandel, 1978: 16), thus tracing its beginnings to the original sin of Stalinism. Such a broad statement does not explain, however, why only some parties suffered Eurocommunist complications when all had been infected by the Stalinist virus. An answer must be sought in the way specific national experiences interacted with the relationship to the Soviet Union and the precepts of Stalinist ideology.

The world communist movement, embodied in the Communist International (Comintern), was created on the crest of the revolutionary wave following the 1917 Russian Revolution. All communist parties had to adhere to 21 conditions of membership of the Comintern, which established a strongly centralised organisation, and the need to follow up the Bolsheviks' example as rapidly as possible left little room for discussion of the specificities of each party's national situation. Within five years of the Comintern's foundation, however, the revolutionary tide had ebbed, the Soviet Union was isolated and Lenin was dead. Such conditions provided the backdrop to the rise of Stalinism, whose ideological linchpin, the theory of 'socialism in one country', postulated, contrary to the classical Marxist tradition, that it was possible to construct a socialist society within the boundaries of a single state (and a comparatively backward one at that). At the same time, the Comintern was turned from an instrument of world revolution into an organisation which subordinated the activities of all communist parties to the defence of the Soviet Union's state interests.

Thus, until Stalin's death in March 1953, the relationship to the USSR was the dominant factor in determining the strategy, cohesion and *raison d'être* of individual communist parties. As well as the primacy of the interests of the Soviet state, the Soviet model of 'socialism', with its one-party state and ruthless suppression of any opposition, became the only one permissible. As long as communist parties kept within these constraints, however, actual strategy and tactics could vary considerably between countries and over time. Western European parties experienced a variety of tactical turns, from extreme sectarianism towards social democracy in the early 1930s to its diametrical opposite, the Popular Front, which encouraged collaboration with any forces claiming to be anti-fascist. During the Second World War, communist parties played prominent roles alongside other anti-fascist groups in the resistance to Nazi occupation but the post-war division of Europe into pro-Western and pro-Soviet spheres of influence meant that Western European communist parties were encouraged not to disrupt this balance by pursuing too radical a strategy.

The period after the Second World War witnessed the dramatic expansion of Soviet influence, creating the paradox of a more secure Soviet Union as a state while sowing the seeds for the fragmentation of global communism. On the one hand, Soviet security was enhanced, first by expansion into Eastern and Central Europe and second by the revolutions in Yugoslavia and China. In the former case, 'socialism in one country' was broadened into 'socialism in one bloc' through a process completely controlled by the Soviet leadership and in which any potential opposition was ruthlessly suppressed. The comparatively autonomous revolutions in Yugoslavia and China, however, served to promote centrifugal tendencies in the communist movement. Soviet efforts to keep the communist movement subordinated to Moscow were not helped by the fact that, in 1943, Stalin had unilaterally dissolved the Comintern in order to facilitate negotiations with Roosevelt and Churchill (Claudin, 1975: 18). Although it was not obvious at the time, as the Soviet leadership continued to exercise some control over national communist parties, especially through financial levers, the dissolution of the Comintern allowed national parties in theory to become 'wholly independent and without any links between them', an important factor when considering the future emergence of Eurocommunism (Claudin, 1975: 15).

The twists and turns of Soviet interests had in any case produced parties with substantially different national strategies and leaderships. The PCI had been subjected to fascist repression during the 1920s and 1930s, was a small party during the war, but grew exponentially as a result of its resistance role and post-war activity to an organisation with a membership of around 2.6 million in 1951. As early as 1944, the PCI leader Palmiro Togliatti had expressed, in the so-called 'Salerno turn', rejection of a revolutionary seizure of power and a vision of co-operation with Social Democrats, Christian Democrats and even monarchists who favoured 'progressive democracy' in Italy after the defeat of fascism. As a consequence of this strategy the PCI played a crucial role in reforging the Italian state after 1945 until it was expelled from government with the onset of the Cold War. Even such a seemingly radical strategy fully accorded, however, with Soviet interests in Western Europe at that time and had been sanctioned by the Kremlin. Nevertheless, the PCI was never fully 'stalinised' and its huge membership and electoral support made it susceptible to domestic pressures.

The same could not be said of the PCF, which, despite an important resistance role, possessed a leadership which had slavishly followed the Soviet line through the 1930s and 1940s, had its own 'personality cult' around Maurice Thorez, and went so far in its replication of Soviet actions that it conducted its own purges in the early 1950s (McInnes, 1979: 53). Jean Elleinstein claims that Thorez began to reject Stalinism as early as 1946 by expressing the idea of separate, national roads to socialism (Ellenstein, 1976: 205). Such an assertion should be taken with a rather large pinch of salt. As in Italy, such a line would not necessarily have conflicted with Moscow's, and the Soviet model still represented the socialist goal. Given their generally close relationship to Moscow, it is not surprising that the PCF demonstrated a rather shaky commitment to Eurocommunist positions and ultimately retreated from them. Lange suggests that the PCF

> often seemed more a free rider than an innovator, less a convinced eurocommunist than a seconder of the initiatives of others. The French party . . . was more willing than the others to try to capitalize on the conjuncture without developing broader analyses or drawing more general theoretical and strategic conclusions.
>
> (Lange, 1981: 4)

Even in countries subject to authoritarian regimes through to the mid-1970s, the communist parties evolved in quite different ways. Under Franco, the PCE became staunchly Eurocommunist and yet its next-door neighbour, the Portuguese Communist Party (PCP), which had endured similar conditions under Salazar and Caetano, remained an essentially Stalinist organisation. Amongst smaller parties, the Communist Party of Great Britain (CPGB) pursued an explicitly parliamentary road to socialism after 1951, but again this fitted in with Soviet strategy and was sanctioned by Stalin himself (Beckett, 1995: 121–3).

While Stalin was alive Moscow strove to maintain the monolithic character of the communist movement. The troublesome but comparatively insignificant Yugoslavs were excommunicated if not brought to heel and the Chinese, despite having seized power against Stalin's wishes, were intent on following his precepts regarding industrialisation and collectivisation. Stalin's death in 1953, however, brought in its train a fundamental transformation of world communism. The new

Soviet leadership, for its own reasons of self-preservation and consolidation, decided that Stalin's regime of unpredictability and terror was no longer appropriate. Internationally, maintaining Soviet 'hegemony' meant a certain distancing from the Stalin era and a relaxation of controls over other communist regimes and the world communist movement itself. Ideologically, the emphasis was now placed on 'peaceful coexistence' and economic rather than military competition with capitalism.

Destalinisation, coupled with capitalism's unprecedented stability and the high degree of legitimacy seemingly enjoyed by liberal democratic institutions, provided the impetus for the PCI, which enjoyed the support of a substantial and growing part of the electorate but without any prospect of involvement in government, to transform its strategy. The question was increasingly posed of how far the USSR continued to represent a viable, attractive and appropriate model of socialism in the advanced capitalist states.

Following Khrushchev's 'Secret Speech', which revealed many of Stalin's crimes and denounced the so-called 'cult of Stalin's personality', Togliatti developed the concept of 'polycentrism': all communist parties should have complete autonomy to follow their own national traditions in formulating their political strategy; socialist states should be free from interference in their internal affairs; there should be no return to centralised relations between communist parties; and the Soviet model of socialist construction, although appropriate to Soviet conditions, 'cannot provide a ready-made solution [or] contain directives for resolving all the questions which might present themselves today' (Lange and Vannicelli, 1981: 219). Nevertheless, while distancing itself strategically from Moscow on the one hand, the PCI de facto still acknowledged Soviet authority in Eastern Europe, and the USSR as the defender of the interests of socialism, accepting the need for Soviet intervention to suppress the Hungarian revolution in the same year.

The PCI's estrangement from Moscow gathered momentum during the 1960s. It expressed concern at the rift between Moscow and Beijing. Although the PCI had no sympathy for the Chinese position it considered Soviet efforts to subordinate them inimical to its own interests. Following Togliatti's death in 1964, the new PCI leadership published his 'testament of Yalta' which was sharply critical of Stalin, Khrushchev and the Soviet system. Three years later, the PCI leader Luigi Longo emphasised the need for communists to collaborate with socialists, Social Democrats and even 'progressive' Christian Democrats. Indeed, according to Russo, the PCI's growing contact with the German Social Democrats in the late 1960s laid the groundwork for the latter's Ostpolitik, through which West Germany established more friendly relations with the communist bloc (Russo, 1979: 91).

The PCI's distancing from the Soviet camp was theoretically the most sophisticated but other parties also clashed with Moscow. The Soviet Union's geopolitical interests, especially the Soviet Union's desire to disrupt the harmony of the Western alliance and of the emergent European Economic Community (EEC), proved increasingly detrimental to the communist parties' domestic appeal. In 1965, the

PCF supported the presidential candidature of the socialist François Mitterrand against de Gaulle despite Moscow's support for the latter because of his independent stance within NATO. Nevertheless, the PCF leadership was generally much more dependent on Moscow for political and financial support so there was a limit to such implied criticism. Perhaps the starkest conflict emerged between Moscow and the PCE, where Soviet wooing of the Franco regime in an effort to weaken its links with the United States was severely at odds with the PCE's strategy of leading the struggle to overthrow the regime.

Such disputes concerning Soviet realpolitik helped to foster a more independent and critical stance amongst Western European communist parties, which was further encouraged by the emergence of more independent currents inside the Soviet bloc itself. The turning point was the Prague Spring in 1968 and its suppression through the Warsaw Pact invasion in August of that year, which brought considerable protest from Western European parties, who saw it as an attempt to reassert Soviet hegemony and a monolithic conception of socialism.

The reaction of Western communist parties to the invasion was not, however, completely uniform. The PCI and PCF sent a joint delegation to Moscow shortly before the invasion, warning of the consequences of armed intervention, and the PCE also formulated a similar position (Schapiro, 1983: 49). Moscow's action was thus taken in the full knowledge of its potential impact on relations with the major Western European communist parties but the reaffirmation of Soviet control in Eastern Europe was paramount. The PCI subsequently expressed its 'grave dissent' at the intervention, which undermined party autonomy and state independence, and called for a rapid withdrawal of Warsaw Pact forces so that the reform process could continue (Lange and Vannicelli, 1981: 213–4). The PCF, on the other hand, merely expressed its 'disapproval' (Lange and Vannicelli, 1981: 236). Its ambivalence toward Soviet action was further demonstrated when it approved the post-invasion 'normalisation' process in Czechoslovakia, which effectively purged pro-reform elements from the party. Opposition to the invasion was particularly important if the communist parties were to retain some sort of appeal to younger people, following on as it did from the student revolts earlier in 1968. For the PCI especially, it also represented an extension of its previously enunciated polycentrist line concerning the autonomy of individual parties to pursue their own paths to socialism.

The invasion of Czechoslovakia brought to an end, at least until Gorbachev in 1985, any prospect of 'reform' communism in the Soviet bloc whereby the party itself could undertake a democratisation of the system. In the 1970s the terrain of change shifted to dissident and opposition movements of varying types. In this new context, the PCI argued against the repression of dissent and pledged its support for Charter 77 in Czechoslovakia and the various manifestations of worker opposition in Poland, which culminated in 1980 in the formation of Solidarity, the first genuinely autonomous and mass workers' organisation in the Soviet bloc. Indeed, the introduction of martial law in Poland in December 1981 and the suppression of Solidarity led the PCI formally to break its ties with Moscow.

Throughout the 1970s the three leading Eurocommunist parties utilised forums of the international communist movement to express their positions, particularly on the autonomy of national parties. While party leaders usually kept their criticisms fraternally muted at such gatherings, they frequently encountered a hostile reception from the Soviet leadership, which cold-shouldered those who had made overtly critical comments. Such practices served to widen the distance between Moscow and the Eurocommunist parties.

Criticism of the Soviet Union itself became possible for two basic reasons: first, détente relaxed tensions between American and Soviet camps and relieved the communist parties of the need to adhere dogmatically to the Soviet model; and, second, new opportunities were appearing because of the crisis in the global capitalist economy, which required considerable tactical flexibility and reduced ideological baggage. As well as an insistence on organisational autonomy, the gradual estrangement of communist parties from Moscow began to assume a more theoretical character involving reassessments of the Russian Revolution, the rise of Stalin and the character of the Soviet political system. In the most sophisticated Eurocommunist analysis of Stalinism, the PCF's Jean Elleinstein sought to go beyond what he considered the inadequate analysis of the Stalin period, embodied in Khrushchev's 'Secret Speech', which focused on the 'cult of the personality' and individual aberrations. Elleinstein was, however, caught in essentially the same dilemma as Khrushchev in attempting to justify the fundamental character of the Soviet Union as a socialist system while decrying its Stalinist excesses:

> Though it cannot and must not be taken as a model, Soviet Socialism nevertheless constitutes the first and most important socialist experiment in history. However tragic the Stalin phenomenon was, it remains limited in terms of time and place.
>
> (Ellenstein, 1976: 218)

By emphasising the historical specificity of Stalinism, Elleinstein was striving to justify the need for individual communist parties to pursue their own strategies.

Despite the unprecedented nature of Elleinstein's critique of the Soviet Union, Santiago Carrillo went much further, arguing that the Soviet Union was 'evidently not a bourgeois State, but neither is it as yet the proletariat organised as the ruling class, or a genuine workers' democracy' (Carrillo, 1977: 157). Furthermore, under Stalin it possessed 'a series of formal characteristics similar to those of the fascist dictatorships' (Carrillo, 1977: 157). In a characterisation reminiscent of Trotsky's *The Revolution Betrayed* but not acknowledged as such, Carrillo talked of the existence of a bureaucratic stratum in the Soviet Union which 'wields excessive and almost uncontrolled political power. It takes decisions and settles questions over the heads of the working class, and even of the party, which, taken as a whole, finds itself subjected to that bureaucratic stratum' (Carrillo, 1977: 164). Such a situation derived from the Soviet Union's isolation and 'the impossibility of building complete socialism in a single country without socialism also triumphing in a series of developed countries' (Carrillo, 1977: 166). In this respect, Carrillo argues, movements towards socialism in advanced capitalist countries assist the development of socialism in the Soviet Union (Carrillo, 1977: 172). Unlike Trotsky, however, Carrillo's concept of the movement towards socialism no longer centred on the seizure of power by the revolutionary party.

Eurocommunism and the capitalist state

By the late 1960s the identity of Western European communist parties, what made them distinctive from other parties, was being called increasingly into question. The underpinning of that identity – the psychological and ideological commitment to the Soviet Union and the Soviet model of socialism – was deteriorating while, at the same time, integration into their own political systems was producing greater acceptance of the existing liberal democratic institutions, thus challenging the notion that these parties in any way represented a radical alternative to capitalism.

The unattractiveness of the traditional left parties for many young people was dramatically demonstrated in France during the events of May 1968 and in Italy during the 'hot autumn' of 1969. Across Western and, to a certain extent, Eastern Europe, a generalised student revolt erupted against the backdrop of the Vietnam War and the huge expansion of higher education. In addition, the rank and file of the workers' movement militantly pursued higher wages and better working conditions, demanding also an increased commitment to democratic practices both domestically and in the Soviet bloc. Such movements developed outside of party control and pointed to an emergent social crisis.

The latter was reinforced in the early 1970s by the end of the post-war economic boom and the oil crisis of 1973–74, which plunged global capitalism into its deepest recession since the 1930s. The existence of an economic and political crisis has traditionally been viewed by communist parties as an opportunity to promote a revolutionary alternative to the existing capitalist order. This was not, however, the response of the Eurocommunist parties: the deeper the crisis, the more profoundly wedded to the institutions of liberal capitalism they became. In Italy, the PCI developed the strategy of the so-called 'historic compromise' designed to produce a governing coalition between itself and the dominant Christian Democrats. After the 1976 parliamentary election, the PCI became part of the pro-government majority, having gained more than 34 per cent of the vote, and advocated the introduction of a 'constructive austerity' policy. In Spain, the PCE pursued the strategy of the 'Pact of Liberty', which promoted a broad coalition against the Franco regime, and then, in return for recognition as a legal political party, agreed to the Moncloa Pact, which consolidated democratic institutions in the aftermath of Franco's death while limiting workers' demands. The partial exception to this strategy of alliances with overtly bourgeois forces was the PCF, which pursued an electoral alliance with the Socialist Party (the so-called 'Union of the Left'). Why did communist parties pursue such a cautious strategy and how did they justify it to their memberships?

Although little theoretical foundation was provided for Eurocommunism's innovations, the ideological environment of a communist party demanded that some lip-service be paid to the Marxist tradition in order to justify the adoption of new positions. In the case of Eurocommunism, these can be broken down into the following (although they are completely interrelated): the nature of the capitalist state, the strategy for socialist transformation, and the applicability of the Soviet model of socialism.

It has become a Marxist cliché that Marx himself never developed a thorough analysis of the state and shied away from speculating about the contours of the future socialist society. Nevertheless, Marx (and Engels) did refer to the state as the 'executive committee of the bourgeoisie' in *The Communist Manifesto* and utilised the expression 'the dictatorship of the proletariat' when discussing the Paris Commune in 1871. It was left to Lenin to develop this theme on the eve of the Russian Revolution. In *The State and Revolution*, Lenin characterised the state as the mechanism through which the ruling class in any given society exercises its dictatorship. This dictatorship might be softened by the presence of democratic mechanisms but it remained ultimately a coercive arrangement designed to ensure the reproduction of the prevailing relations of production. The apparatus of the capitalist state could not be utilised by the proletariat to usher in a socialist society but had to be overthrown and replaced with a new state structure, based on soviets, appropriate to the dictatorship of the proletariat. For Lenin, therefore, the key point in any revolution was the seizure of state power by the revolutionary party. There could be no talk of a gradual capture of state power over a long period of time – revolutions were the outcome of a generally short-lived crisis in which the forces of the old ruling class were pitted against those of the insurgent proletariat in a violent conflict.

Rather ironically, the theoretical underpinning of the Eurocommunist concept of the state derived from the dominant analysis of the current phase of capitalist development promulgated by Soviet and Eastern European ideologists: state monopoly capitalism. According to this theory the capitalist state was increasingly becoming the representative of certain dominant monopolistic firms, and was also exercising greater control over economic activity as a whole. Thus, in accordance with these precepts, Carrillo stated that 'free competition . . . is totally disappearing. The fabulous growth of technology has killed it' (Carrillo, 1977: 21). For Carrillo the state's assumption of a leviathan-like domination of the entire capitalist system meant that it was increasingly representative of only a comparatively small group of monopolistic capitalists. Whereas the state had previously taken the form of an arbiter mediating between opposing classes, it now confronted not only the proletariat but also broader strata including part of the bourgeoisie (Carrillo, 1977: 24). This notion that the state represents some kind of arbiter, suggesting a degree of neutral mediation between classes, is clearly at variance with the classical Marxist view of the state and would seem to have more in common with classical liberal theory. Nevertheless, Carrillo was saying that now the state did indeed represent the interests of a small minority. Thus, the Marxist theory of the state as established in *The Communist Manifesto* continued to be relevant and, 'even in countries where there are most liberties, the State is the organised power of one class for oppressing another' (Carrillo, 1977: 146). The nature of this polarisation between state and society meant that the struggle over the state became the dominant struggle within society, provoking a crisis within the state itself. Moreover, workers had to achieve state power in order to transform society but:

> The question is to decide whether *this is possible* without breaking the rules of democracy, while changing the content of traditional democratic institutions, complementing them with new forms which expand and establish political democracy still more firmly. We Spanish communists and other parties in the developed capitalist countries declare that this is possible.
>
> (Carrillo, 1977: 149, emphasis in the original)

With the expansion of the state apparatus, which comprised mainly people from less privileged backgrounds, it was possible to infiltrate and transform the state by winning these strata over to the side of the proletariat and its allies (Carrillo, 1977: 25–6). Capitalism's development also meant that the distinction between classes was also much more blurred so that, 'while the proletariat continues to be the main revolutionary class, *it is no longer the only one*' (Carrillo, 1977: 44, my emphasis). Workers therefore had to make alliances with other strata if they were to be victorious.

Carrillo was writing at a time when liberal democratic institutions were being consolidated in Spain. Nevertheless, his comments can be taken as typical of the Eurocommunist position. In Italy, the PCI developed analogous positions. The advantage for the PCI leadership was that, unlike other Western European communist parties, they could appeal to their own theoretician for support in their reevaluation of the state and the struggle for socialism: Antonio Gramsci. The PCI claimed that Gramsci's theory of hegemony, and his clear demarcation between Eastern European and advanced capitalist countries, meant that Lenin's theory of the state and its revolutionary overthrow could not be applied in Italy and legitimised the gradualist strategy they had adopted. The achievement of working-class hegemony was only possible over a protracted period and through alliances with other strata.

Fairly clearly, if socialism could be achieved through democratic means, utilising the institutions of the capitalist state, the concept of the 'dictatorship of the proletariat' had also become redundant. All Eurocommunist parties removed the achievement of the dictatorship of the proletariat from their programmes during the 1970s, claiming that any notion of dictatorship was unacceptable to people brought up with universal suffrage and regular elections. The fact of regular elections also meant that communists could not hang on to power indefinitely if they were victorious at the ballot box. They would have to accept the will of the people and voluntarily cede power if the electorate voted them out.

Ironically, the adoption of positions in favour of a democratic road to socialism was undertaken by leaderships generally resistant to too much democracy within their own parties. 'Democratic centralism' was still employed as the mechanism through which the leadership imposed its will on the wider membership, stifling debate and, where necessary, expelling opponents.

Eurocommunism, post-communism and social democracy

By the early 1980s, Eurocommunism as an identifiable current had ceased to exist. In Italy, the 'historic compromise' of an alliance between the PCI and Christian Democracy had failed to the detriment of the PCI, which suffered persistent electoral failure throughout the 1980s. In France, the PCF's 'Union of the Left' with the Socialists had disintegrated in September 1977. Subsequently, the PCF re-established less critical relations with the USSR, became more nationalist in its domestic politics, and suffered a severe decline in its electoral support. In Willie Thompson's opinion, 'Eurocommunist strategy achieved no success anywhere, or at most one so paltry as to be negligible, and which was soon erased' (Thompson, 1998: 170). If this is the case, what is Eurocommunism's significance?

Eurocommunism represented a departure from the communist parties' ideology and political practice of the 1950s and 1960s. It was not, however, a sudden rupture but an evolution that had its roots in the ideology of Soviet communism. This evolution was prompted by the very real problems confronted by the communist movement in the advanced capitalist countries during a period of economic expansion and the implementation of social democratic welfare programmes. In trying to make sense of these developments and to elaborate an adequate strategy, communist parties were pulled in different directions by their relationship to the USSR on the one hand, and their appeal to a mass electorate on the other. Unfortunately, the changes in orientation which came to be known as Eurocommunism were never adequately theorised by the parties themselves. This was partly due to traditional political practice in which the leadership proposed and the membership disposed, frequently leading to the undemocratic removal of critics from the party, as well as to the exigencies of political strategy and tactics. In its focus on political institutions at the expense of an analysis of socio-economic factors, Eurocommunism revised Marxist theory in the following areas: the nature of the state; the character of capitalism and the nature of capitalist crisis; the character of the transition to socialism, the class forces involved and the alliances required to achieve progress.

The PCI took this evolution to its furthest point, rejecting its communist heritage by transforming itself into the Democratic Party of the Left (PDS) soon after the fall of the Berlin Wall, and joining the Socialist International. This was possible in Italy because no social democratic rival to the PDS existed and, with the collapse of Christian Democracy, a huge political vacuum opened which the PDS sought to fill by moving to the centre. In 1996, the PDS in alliance with a number of other parties, including remnants of the discredited and disintegrated Christian Democrats (the 'historic compromise' writ small?), formed a left-of-centre government for the first time since 1947. In government, however, the PDS-led coalition pursued policies of austerity, cutbacks in welfare expenditure, and further integration into the EU through joining the single currency. In this respect it has evolved to such an extent that it is indistinguishable from the 'new realist' orthodoxy of traditional West European social democratic parties. A minority of the former PCI in the organisation Communist Refoundation has opposed this trajectory and attempted to reassess the communist tradition in Italy from a more Marxist perspective while making itself more open to dialogue with other currents on the Marxist left.

In other countries, the rightward evolution of former Eurocommunist currents has not been so clearcut. In France, the retrenchment of the PCF in the early 1980s and the existence of a large social democratic party has blocked its evolution in a thoroughly social democratic direction. Although it retains some vestiges of its communist past, including its name, in order to promote a distinctive image, the collapse of communism in the USSR and Eastern Europe has done irreparable damage to its prospects, although this has not prevented it from participating in coalition governments with the Socialist Party. The PCF's inability to address its past in a critical manner, and its adoption of frankly reactionary positions for example on immigration, has led to a considerable haemorrhaging of electoral support and membership. In Spain, the PCE has also declined in influence but became the central force behind the United Left electoral front. Again, the existence of a strong social democratic party has prevented the PCE from following completely in the footsteps of the PCI and it has striven to retain its communist identity.

In historical perspective, therefore, Eurocommunism represented a phase in the crisis of world communism and in the transition of Western European communist parties away from orthodox Marxism. Indeed, Boggs argues that probably the closest historical analogy to Eurocommunism is Kautsky's strategy of democratic transformation, and thus 'classical' social democracy. The former departs from the latter, however, in its rejection of economic collapse and social upheaval as the detonator of transition (Boggs, 1980: 431–2). Unsurprisingly, this interpretation was disputed by the Eurocommunists themselves. In 1977, Carrillo stated that 'we are just as communist as we were in the past. We are not trying to "hold out our hands" to decadent imperialist capitalism, but to speed up its abolition; we are not going over to the camp of social democracy, which we continue to combat ideologically' (Carrillo, 1977: 19). For Carrillo, it was a question of circumstances changing and of the party having to adapt but without losing its fundamental ideology. That ideology had, however, already been undermined by the revisions perpetrated by the Soviet leadership under Stalin, beginning in the 1920s and reinforced in subsequent decades, even during the process of destalinisation. The most significant of these revisions concerned the sanctification of purely national roads to socialism. What is not in question is that different states have different national peculiarities necessitating different tactics but that, in the classical Marxist tradition, nation states refract global processes. Ultimately, socialism can only be constructed on a global scale. By emphasising national distinctiveness to the detriment of the global dimension, Eurocommunism could only follow a reformist path.

References

Beckett, F. (1995) *Enemy Within: The Rise and Fall of the British Communist Party*. London: John Murray.

Boggs, C. (1980) 'The Democratic Road: New Departures and Old Problems' in C. Boggs and D. Plotke (eds), *The Politics of Eurocommunism: Socialism in Transition*. Montreal: Black Rose Books.

Carrillo, S. (1977) *'Eurocommunism' and the State*. London: Lawrence & Wishart.

Claudin, F. (1975) *The Communist Movement: From Comintern to Cominform*. Harmondsworth: Penguin.

Elleinstein, J. (1976) *The Stalin Phenomenon*. London: Lawrence & Wishart.

Lange, P. (1981) 'Dilemmas of Change: Eurocommunism and National Parties in Postwar Perspective' in P. Lange and M. Vannicelli (eds), *The Communist Parties of Italy, France and Spain: Postwar Change and Continuity. A Casebook*. London: George Allen & Unwin.

Lange, P. and M. Vannicelli (eds) (1981) *The Communist Parties of Italy, France and Spain: Postwar Change and Continuity. A Casebook*. London: George Allen & Unwin.

Levi, A. (1979) 'Eurocommunism: Myth or Reality?' in P.F. della Torre, E. Mortimer and J. Story (eds), *Eurocommunism: Myth or Reality?* Harmondsworth: Penguin.

Mandel, E. (1978) *From Stalinism to Eurocommunism: The Bitter Fruits of 'Socialism in One Country'*. London: New Left Books.

McInnes, N. (1979) 'From Comintern to Polycentrism: The First Fifty Years of West European Communism' in P.F. della Torre, E. Mortimer and J. Story (eds), *Eurocommunism: Myth or Reality?* Harmondsworth: Penguin.

Preston, P. (1981) 'The PCE's Long Road to Democracy' in R. Kindersley (ed.), *In Search of Eurocommunism*. London: Macmillan.

Russo, G. (1979) 'Il Compromesso Storico: The Italian Communist Party from 1968 to 1978' in P.F. della Torre, E. Mortimer and J. Story (eds), *Eurocommunism: Myth or Reality?* Harmondsworth: Penguin.

Schapiro, L. (1983) 'Soviet Attitudes to National Communism in Western Europe' in H. Machin (ed.), *National Communism in Western Europe: A Third Way for Socialism?* London: Methuen.

Thompson, W. (1998) *The Communist Movement Since 1945*. Oxford: Blackwell.

Further reading

The major exposition of Eurocommunist thought by a leading party member was Santiago Carrillo, *Eurocommunism and the State*, London: Lawrence & Wishart, 1977, but see also Giorgio Amendola, 'The Italian Road to Socialism', *New Left Review*, 106: 39–50, 1977, and Fernando Claudin, *Eurocommunism and Socialism*, London: New Left Books, 1978. In addition, see the very valuable collection of documents which traces the evolution of the PCI, PCF and PCE through to the 1970s: Peter Lange and Maurizio Vannicelli (eds), *The Communist Parties of Italy, France and Spain: Postwar Change and Continuity. A Casebook*, London: George Allen & Unwin, 1981.

The most detailed critique of the Soviet Union from a Eurocommunist perspective is Jean Elleinstein, *The Stalin Phenomenon*, London: Lawrence & Wishart, 1976, and there are a number of analyses of Eurocommunism mainly produced in the late 1970s/early 1980s: Ernest Mandel, *From Stalinism to Eurocommunism: The Bitter Fruits of 'Socialism in One Country'*, London: New Left Books, 1978, is a critique of Eurocommunism from a Trotskyist perspective. Keith Middlemas, *Power and the Party: Changing Faces of Communism in Western Europe*, London: Andre Deutsch, 1980, is a detailed examination of the post-war evolution of the PCI, PCF, PCE and PCP. Texts which bring the evolution of Western communism more up to date are the following: Willie Thompson, *The Communist Movement Since 1945*, Oxford: Blackwell, 1998; Martin J. Bull and Paul Heywood (eds), *West European Communist Parties after the Revolutions of 1989*, Basingstoke: Macmillan, 1994.

6   Western Marxism

Joseph Femia

The term 'Western Marxism' is somewhat puzzling, since it was never meant to refer to the geographic origins or location of its practitioners. Nor did it necessarily mean Marxism appropriate to the West, as opposed to the Marxism of the USSR or China. All Marxists, needless to say, consider their own interpretation of the doctrine to be universally applicable. What, then, was the differentia specifica of Western Marxism – a style of thought that lasted (approximately) from 1920 to 1970? It was, above all, a repudiation of the orthodox form of Marxism known as 'dialectical materialism', or 'diamat' – a theoretical system devised, after Marx's death, by his friend and collaborator, Friedrich Engels, with important contributions from Karl Kautsky and Georgi Plekhanov. In a nutshell, 'diamat' was a variant of naturalistic determinism, which assumed that unalterable economic laws, dialectical in structure, were the driving forces of history and that consciousness was but a reflection of physical and social reality. Society was described in the language of the natural sciences, in terms of mechanical causality. There was, on this conception, no need to consider the explanatory role of human intentions or purposes, for these were themselves objects to be explained by underlying material causes. And so the progression from one historical phase to the next, culminating in communism, was seen as a matter of natural necessity. Capitalism was therefore doomed by its internal contradictions, which would cause (not simply predispose) the proletarian class to rise as one against their oppressive conditions.

By the end of the First World War, this set of assumptions was already becoming hard to sustain. The patriotism displayed by the workers of the belligerent nations rather destroyed the notion that there was something 'natural' about proletarian solidarity, or something essentially 'bourgeois' about love of country. Even Marxism's great success, the Russian Revolution of 1917, appeared to defy the Marxist idea of historical progression, which assumed that communism would issue from the contradictions inherent in a developed capitalist society, and not from the collapsing power structure of a decaying, semi-feudal autocracy. Antonio Gramsci (1891–1937), one of the great 'Western Marxists', went so far as to hail the communist rise to power in 1917 as a 'revolution against *Capital*', by which he meant that it had been a triumph of human will over the kind of histori-cal determinism defended by Marx in his master-work.

Nevertheless, neither Gramsci nor any other 'Western' Marxist ever conceded that they were radically transforming Marx's doctrines; on the contrary, they typi-cally claimed to be rescuing the 'true' Marxism from the distortions of determin-ism and reductive materialism. Only rarely did they hint that Marx himself may have been responsible for these alleged distortions. But, in fact, both orthodox and so-called Western forms of Marxism could find sustenance in his ambiguous legacy.

We may distinguish two principal, and possibly contradictory, motifs in Marx's thought. The first, the romantic or moralistic motif, condemns capitalism for its destruction of human creativity and for its dissolution of 'organic' ties and loyal-ties. These objections are epitomised in Marx's famous and multi-faceted concept of 'alienation', which, for all its complexity, can be reduced to one simple idea; that in all spheres of life human beings have forfeited what is essential to their nature – to be in control of their activities – to 'external' forces of their own mak-ing: vengeful gods, pitiless economic 'laws', repressive and fraudulent states. The subjugation of the collectivity to its own products also entails the mutual isolation of individuals. 'Man', having alienated himself from his creative essence, loses all sense of what it means to be human. Spiritual values disappear as social relations are transformed into purely instrumental or contractual relations.

Marx inherited his notion of alienation from Hegel (1770–1831), the German idealist philosopher, for whom history was the progressive unfolding of the col-lective human Spirit or Mind (*Geist* in German), searching for reconciliation with itself and with the world. Hegel grounds this remarkable claim on two central propositions. First, there is the idealist insistence that all things – Gods, numbers, men, mice, stones – are aspects of a single reality whose nature is spiritual or mind-like. The second proposition is that *Geist* is an activity or process whose goal is that of self-knowledge. From this it follows that *Geist* (and therefore mankind) only realises its aim, self-knowledge, when it appreciates that it is the whole of reality. It must 'recognise itself in everything in heaven and on earth' and see that there is no 'out and out other' besides itself (Hegel, 1969: 2). Alienation therefore ceases as reality is deprived of its objective, hostile character. The object, the 'other' in whatever guise it may appear, is taken up into rational subjectivity and is, in this sense, one with it. The hidden truth of history is the unity of thought and being – and this truth is revealed through a dialectic of negativity which opens up new horizons at every historical stage. The final stage arrives when 'man', abstractly conceived, assimilates and ratifies the world as his own truth.

According to Marx, Hegel asked the right questions, but arrived at the wrong answers. For he mistakenly assumed that human existence is centred in the head, thereby reducing history to a process of thought. Marx instead focused on 'earthly reality'. In his estimation, man is a practical being whose thought processes are governed by material needs: if he feels his life to be empty and meaningless, the origins of his distress must be sought in objective reality rather than in any false conceptions he might have about his existential condition. The transcendence of alienation is brought about by communism – the goal of history, a total transformation of human existence, the recovery by man of his natural 'essence'. Communism does away with private property in the means of production, as well as all the evils that flow from it: religion, crime, inequality, class conflict and state repression. Men and women, living under a system of communal property, will no longer feel estranged from their fellow citizens or from anonymous sources of power. We 'humanise' the world not by thinking about it in the 'right' way, à la Hegel, but by making it into one whose contents bear our stamp and reflect back to us our own scale of values. In such a world, previously repressed individuals, treated as mere objects in the capitalist order, will be encouraged to realise their full creative potential.

The ideas outlined above were all advanced in Marx's early writings, in particular the Paris Manuscripts of 1844, which remained unpublished until the 1930s. Before long, however, he developed the second motif in his oeuvre, that of scientific determinism. Marx often spoke of the 'laws' of social life, operating in the same way as the laws of nature. By this he meant that they impose themselves on people with the same inexorable necessity as an earthquake or a typhoon. It is for objective scientific thought to study these laws as a naturalist does, without sentiment or prejudice. In Marx's well-known words, 'Marxism does not preach morality at all'. The normative concepts of alienation, freedom, and self-realisation faded from view as Marx increasingly portrayed himself as a scientific analyst of socio-historical processes, 'working with iron necessity towards inevitable results'. Although he never repudiated his early ideas in so many words, and a case can be made for the thesis that these ideas remained implicit in his later works, the Hegelian and humanistic concerns of his youth sit uneasily alongside the kind of determinism that sees individuals as 'personifications of economic categories' and historical evolution 'as a process of natural history' (Marx in Feuer, 1959: 135–7). The role of human agency is explicitly dismissed by the older Marx, who describes 'the process of thinking' as nothing but a reflexive reaction to an underlying material reality: 'With me, . . . the ideal is nothing else than the material world reflected by the human mind and translated into forms of thought' (Marx in Feuer, 1959: 145).

Marx's rich and contradictory body of theory, with its contrasting strains of humanism and scientism, voluntarism and determinism, gave his interpreters considerable latitude. The initiators of Western Marxism were all neo-idealists, steeped in Hegel or Hegelian thought, and anxious to restore Marx's humanist anthropology in its radical opposition to the hated 'diamat'. Georg Lukács (1885–1971), for example, owed much to the romantic idealism that was prominent in Germany a century ago, while Gramsci adopted the terminology and preoccupations of Benedetto Croce, Italy's leading liberal and neo-Hegelian philosopher. An almost promiscuous desire to 'borrow' from 'bourgeois' thought is another distinguishing characteristic of Western Marxism. The collective work of the Frankfurt School – to take another example – was permeated from the 1930s onwards with the concepts and principles of Freud's psychoanalysis. Herbert Marcuse's (1898–1979) major study, *Eros and Civilization* (1955), was constructed around the Freudian vocabulary of 'repression' and 'sublimation', 'reality principle' and 'performance principle', 'Eros' (love) and 'Thanatos' (death). Jean-Paul Sartre (1905–80), who became a Marxist after establishing himself as the most eminent existentialist philosopher in France, insisted that concepts derived from Heidegger, such as 'authenticity' and 'angst', could rescue Marxism from its sclerotic dogmatism.

From what has been said so far, humanism – a quasi-idealist emphasis on human subjectivity – might be deemed one of the defining features of Western Marxism. Louis Althusser (1918–90) was a spectacular exception, however. His theoretical system, worked out during the 1960s, was hostile to humanism and all things Hegelian, and used the newly fashionable doctrine of structuralism to show that Marxism could provide a scientific method of investigation from which human choice and historical continuity were consciously excluded. Structuralism, which originated as a method of linguistics, was indifferent to what Marx called 'the evolution of the economic formation of society' (Marx in Feuer, 1959: 137), but Althusser did not allow this inconvenient detail to stand in the way of his novel interpretation of Marxist science. In a sense, then, he was similar to the humanists he censured.

All the main thinkers of Western Marxism had recourse to non-Marxist philosophers in order to legitimise, explicate, or supplement the philosophy of Marx himself. On the face of it, this eclecticism was an odd phenomenon. Marxism is not a doctrine we would associate with locutions such as 'on the one hand, this . . . on the other hand, that'. Its adherents, whatever their other virtues, have never been renowned for their tolerance or receptiveness to contrary ideas. Marxist thought, while not being a model of clarity, 'always gives the impression of saying to anyone who approaches it, with a certain bravado, "you are either for me or against me"' (Bobbio, 1988: 169). Yet history is littered with attempts to reinvigorate Marxism by forcing it into 'strange shotgun marriages' with apparently antithetical philosophies (Bobbio, 1988: 169).

The puzzle may be solved if we acknowledge that the Western Marxists were not 'good' Marxists in the sense of resolute, steadfast, loyal. Some observers have plausibly questioned whether – in a few cases at least – they can be considered Marxists at all. Their equivocations can perhaps be explained by historical circumstances. Perry Anderson has argued that the 'hidden hallmark of Western Marxism' is that 'it is a product of defeat' (Anderson, 1976: 42). Although the word 'defeat' is clumsy and misleading in this context, Anderson's substantive point, as he explains it, is a valid one: the various expressions of Western Marxism all reflected a crisis of confidence, spawned by the evident gap between theory and practice. We have already seen how, by 1918, events had called Marxist categories into question. Worse was to come. In Anderson's words, the 'failure of the socialist revolution to spread outside Russia, cause and consequence of its corruption inside Russia, is the common background to the entire theoretical tradition of this period' (Anderson, 1976: 42). Post-war uprisings in Germany, Italy and Hungary were all crushed or neutralised. Russia, rather than becoming a 'workers' paradise', descended into chaos and oppression. The victory of fascism, though explicable in Marxist terms, was a catastrophic blow to morale, mainly because it happened in countries thought ripe for revolution. Gramsci composed his famous *Notebooks* while in prison during the early 1930s, surrounded by dejected inmates who were once dynamic revolutionaries. This was also the time of the Great Depression – a disaster that superficially vindicated Marxist predictions but in reality demonstrated that the workers were unlikely to make revolution even in the most propitious circumstances. Following the Second World War, the situation became even more depressing for Marxists. Stalin's incredible brutality, increasingly hard to deny, made virulent anti-communism respectable in all Western countries. Moreover, the massive economic boom of the 1950s and 1960s, which ushered in the 'consumer society', made it difficult to convince the workers that they had – in Marx's ringing phrase – 'nothing to lose but your chains'.

The duller comrades could explain away these setbacks as the natural vagaries of the historical dialectic, but intellectuals of the calibre of Lukács or Gramsci understood that something was deeply wrong with the conventional Marxist scheme. The diagnosis that emerged pointed to a paradox. Just like their 'bourgeois' liberal enemies, orthodox Marxists had reduced the individual to *Homo economicus*, seeing men and women as mere units of production and consumption, without any cultural reference points. Vast areas of human experience were dismissed as epiphenomenal to underlying economic reality. Burdened by a mechanical and utilitarian conception of social interaction, the orthodox Marxists could neither make sense of the historical process nor provide a convincing description of human liberation. So said the Western Marxists. Their own tendency to ignore economics and focus instead on cultural or psychological needs was encouraged by the fact that they were, on the whole, professional academics rather than political activists. This represented a departure from the classical heritage, which assumed that individual Marxists would actually embody the unity of theory and practice. Largely insulated from the practical demands of the working class, Western Marxists could let their minds roam freely. Even Gramsci, who was Secretary General of the Italian Communist Party at the time of his arrest, made his main theoretical contribution to Marxism during his incarceration, with his cell being the functional equivalent of an 'ivory tower'.

Having explained the context, I am now in a position to examine the main ideas advanced by the Western Marxists. In the interests of exegetical simplicity, I shall concentrate on the various 'schools' of thought as well as on the most distinguished and representative figures. To the degree that it is possible, my discussion will proceed in chronological order.

Hegelian Marxism

Writing in the aftermath of the Russian Revolution, the Hegelian Marxists concluded that the realisation of Marxism's revolutionary 'essence' required abandonment of the fatalistic determinism that had encouraged Marxists to view socialism as 'manna from heaven', or, more accurately, 'History', in no way dependent on free human choice. When it came to making or preparing for revolution, many Marxists were seized by an overwhelming lethargy, a feeling that the forces of history were impervious to the efforts of mere individuals. The Bolshevik revolution apparently proved otherwise. Lenin and his colleagues demonstrated, by their actions, that human willpower could overcome supposedly objective laws of development – a point that Gramsci hammered home with particular force. This attack on the passivity of orthodox Marxism involved a recovery of Hegelian idealism, with its emphasis on consciousness or subjectivity. But the main architects of the new synthesis did not want to repeat the Hegelian error of interpreting human action solely in terms of Mind or Spirit. For them, the great contribution of Marx's philosophy lay in its perfect fusion of human creativity and socio-economic materiality. Although men and women operate within structurally determined limits, they retain a capacity for autonomy.

Lukács and Gramsci were the best known Hegelian Marxists, but the contribution of Karl Korsch (1886–1961) should not be ignored. Although the three men were almost exact contemporaries, Lukács was the first to make a philosophical impact, with the publication of *History and Class Consciousness* in 1923. At the time Gramsci was an active politician in his native Italy. His philosophical themes were not really developed until the early 1930s when – surveying the world from a fascist gaol near Bari – he compiled his *Prison Notebooks*, which remained unpublished until after the Second World War. Lukács and Korsch, for all their acclaimed philosophical sophistication, also had political ambitions, with the former actually becoming Commissar of Education during the ill-fated Hungarian Soviet Republic of 1919. Exiled in Austria throughout the 1920s, he was a leading member of the Hungarian Communist Party, briefly becoming General Secretary in 1928 – this despite being attacked as a 'revisionist' by the more orthodox types in the movement. Korsch, for his part, was one of the founders (in 1920) of the German Communist Party – but he was also a professor of philosophy at Jena University, a post he occupied until Hitler's accession to power. In 1923 he published his most important work, *Marxism and Philosophy*, whose idealist perspective earned a rebuke from none other than Stalin himself. Korsch, a harsh critic of Bolshevik repression, was expelled from the Party in 1926, after which he wrote and spoke as an independent, 'professorial' (and thus properly 'Western') Marxist.

Given their shared stress on 'man the creator', the acting subject, the Hegelian Marxists rejected naturalistic materialism as 'bourgeois' and un-Marxist. 'Man' was not simply an object in nature; nor – on their reading – did Marx ever conceive him as such. Marx's materialism did predicate the priority of 'being' over 'thought', but 'being' was, in his view, not synonymous with matter. Rather, 'being' referred to the productive organisation of society, which of course embodied human subjectivity. So far from accepting the 'diamat' assumption that human history was a particular application of the general laws of nature, the Hegelian Marxists conceived nature, as we know it, as an extension of man. Orthodox Marxism operated with a 'contemplative' conception of knowledge. The cognitive act – irrespective of the stimuli that provoked it, or of how the accuracy of its content was determined – was the 'passive' assimilation of a ready-made universe. The Hegelian Marxists were scornful of this epistemology – even in the case of the natural sciences. Nature, they insisted, is not wholly external to us; it is not independent of human design. Natural circumstances affect our lives not directly but through the intermediary of productive forces and thus present themselves to us as social and historical phenomena. Whereas scientific theories may allow us to make precise predictions about the behaviour of natural forces, the 'laws' we 'discover' are, to a degree, reflections of our own social activities and preoccupations.

But Marxism was particularly concerned with knowledge of the social universe, and here exact prediction was impossible, not least because human beings – unlike, say, a falling stone – exercised free will. The Hegelian Marxists contemptuously dismissed the positivist notion, notably advanced by Engels and Lenin, that the concepts and techniques derived from physics or chemistry could be applied to the study of society. One cannot forecast revolution in the way that one forecasts the weather, as if human intervention were irrelevant to the outcome. Therefore, Marxism is not a 'science' as understood by the positivists. It does not reflect some pre-existent reality or offer an 'objective' account of empirical facts. Rather, it is the intellectual expression of the class struggle of the proletariat. Like all theories of society, it is an integral part of the reality it seeks to understand and reflects the needs and aspirations of a particular social group. The Hegelian Marxists, believing as they did that reality is partly constituted by our cognitive and evaluative structures, refused to posit a strict separation between subject and object. I 'access' the world through the categories in my mind; only God could see the world 'as it is'. This explains why the Hegelian Marxists saw consciousness, not material developments, as decisive in history. For them (and they attributed this view to Marx as well), there could be no practical action in the absence of theory, even if the theory was only implicit. The 'vulgar materialists', with their one-way causal sequences, with their tendency to move directly from economic cause to political or cultural effect, were once again distorting Marx's intentions. In keeping with their emphasis on human creativity, the Hegelian Marxists saw Marxism as a humanistic philosophy, aiming for a cultural renaissance in which freedom, self-development and solidarity would be the birthright of all. Man could never achieve this noble status if he were encouraged to view himself as a passive plaything of material forces.

Notwithstanding these shared ideas, Hegelian Marxism was no monolith – a point that can be effectively illustrated if we highlight the differences between Lukács and Gramsci, who were the acknowledged 'heavyweights' of this school of thought. The former, while rejecting mechanical determinism, did not see the future as open-ended. For he followed Hegel in arguing that history manifested an 'inner logic' (Lukács, 1971: 15) which would propel the human race towards its 'essential', predetermined goal of (for Lukács) the victory of communism. Because of the intrinsic needs and propensities of the human spirit, history was fated to have a happy ending. Gramsci, in contrast, rejected Hegelian teleology and denied that all events – past, present and future – fit into some foreordained pattern. The social world, according to him, was a fluid process, characterised by infinite variety and multiplicity. History possessed no inherent meaning, immanent in human nature. The historical process was susceptible to different kinds of resolutions.

Another difference between Gramsci and Lukács concerned their vision of the future society. In common with the orthodox Marxists, the Italian was a 'productivist', who wanted to order the factors of production in accordance with the principle of optimality, where this meant the rationalisation and mechanisation of the productive process. He had no opportunity to read Marx's (posthumously published) Manuscripts of 1844, and some of the ideas expressed there might have struck him as unacceptably heterodox. For he never used the language of 'alienation' or 'human essence', language he associated with conventional idealism, and he therefore focused on improved industrial output as the key to human emancipation.

On this issue, he and Lukács could not have disagreed more. The latter's hostility to the capitalist labour process and its detrimental effects on the wider society is summed up in his concept of 'reification', whose similarity to Marx's doctrine of alienation is remarkable, given that the 1844 Manuscripts did not become available until a decade after the publication of *History and Class Consciousness*. Put simply, 'reification' denotes a process whereby men and women become passive spectators of the social forces that structure their lives. The origins of this passivity lie in capitalism's dehumanisation of the worker, who is reduced to a marketable commodity, a 'thing', to be bought in the market, just like any other instrument of production or consumption. Since, in the quest for profit, technical efficiency is all that matters, work is fragmented in order to achieve maximum output. Workers are consequently confined to narrow, repetitive tasks, which transform them from spiritual beings, with individual talents and ideas, to mere appendages of the productive machine, robbed of initiative and programmed for the maximisation of profit. Eventually, the principles of factory organisation spread to other spheres of life: the factory becomes a microcosm of the whole structure of capitalist society. All aspects of social interaction are specialised, standardised, and subsumed under formal, calculable rules. In every domain, human beings are spiritually crippled, confined to a narrow range of skills and subjected to the deadening effects of instrumental rationality. The quality of imagination gradually disappears as everyone, not just manual workers, sinks into a state of mechanical passivity. The world around us – the product of our own creativity – comes to be experienced as alien and hostile, a system of independent 'things', ruling us through apparently unbreakable laws. Capitalism thus persists because it (temporarily) subdues our essential humanity through a barrage of 'rational' rules and procedures.

Gramsci's explanation for the persistence of a system so rife with internal contradictions was rather different. For him, Marx's epigones, by reducing thought to a 'reflex' of the productive process, had underestimated the power of myths and ideas. It was common for Marxists (though not Lukács) to assume that bourgeois society was held together by pure force or at least the threat of it. Even the Hungarian, by pinpointing the passivity of the masses, denied that they might actively embrace bourgeois ideology. According to Gramsci, however, the cohesion of the modern capitalist order stemmed primarily from the 'hegemony', the spiritual and cultural supremacy, of the ruling classes, who – through manipulation of the mechanisms of socialisation, such as the media, the churches, the schools – had managed to foist their own values and beliefs on an unsuspecting populace. In such a setting, revolution presupposed a transformation of mass consciousness, effected through a protracted 'battle of ideas', or 'war of position' (Gramsci was fond of military metaphors). With its stress on gradual subversion, on persuasion and consent, his proposed strategy undoubtedly differed from the straightforward insurrectionary approach advocated by Lenin. To Gramsci, this approach would work only in backward societies, where consent counted for little. Yet he opposed the 'parliamentary road' to socialism, and saw the war of position as a prelude to, rather than a substitute for, a paramilitary assault on the state. His novel analysis and prescriptions struck a responsive chord in the 1960s and 1970s, when the traditional communist shibboleths no longer seemed to make contact with reality. Depressed by the bureaucratic degeneration of Soviet communism, and by the stubborn refusal of Western workers to see the light, many Marxists exalted Grasmsci as a prophet of 'alternative' communism.

Unlike his Italian contemporary, Lukács never descended from the Olympian heights of abstraction to devise any kind of political strategy. All we learn is that the revolution will occur when the proletariat, or its representatives, grasp the 'totality'. If reification equates to a process of alienation and fragmentation, the solution lies in an apocalyptic moment when the universal class comes to see the social/historical universe as a single, dynamic whole which determines and gives meaning to its constituent parts. The essence of the Marxist method of analysis, Lukács maintains, is not economic determinism but the idea of 'totality' – understanding the part in relation to the whole. However, the totality does not merely refer to a way of perceiving or describing reality, for it is also the mainspring of social revolution, an active constituent of the social reality to which it is applied as a method. Understanding and changing reality are not two separate processes but one and the same phenomenon. Knowledge and action, theory and practice, subject and object are united as the historical process reaches its predetermined conclusion – abolition of the class society with its division of social life into objective processes, outside human control.

Lukács never properly explains how we come to an understanding of the 'totality'. It cannot be reconstructed by accumulating facts, since, in his eyes, facts do not interpret themselves: their meaning is only revealed in relation to the whole, which must be known in advance and is thus logically prior to the facts. He simply rests content in the assumption that the proletariat, by virtue of its social situation, enjoys privileged insight. If the totality is the expression of history ripening towards the final transformation, then it is also the theoretical consciousness of the social agent, namely the proletariat, by which that transformation is to be brought about. In this sense, the proletariat is, like Hegel's Spirit, 'the identical subject–object of history', the historical demiurge that abolishes all 'otherness' (Lukács, 1971: 197). There seems to be a paradox in Lukács's theory: the proletariat is spiritually crippled by capitalist reification, yet only the proletarian perspective can (and does) apprehend history in its totality. The apparent paradox is resolved when we look at Lukács' conception of working-class consciousness. This consciousness is 'neither the sum nor the average of what is thought or felt by the single individuals who make up the class'; it is, on the contrary, an 'ideal-type', the rational expression of their 'true' interests, as defined by the Communist Party (Lukács, 1971: 51). So it turns out that the truth of the totality is identical to Marxism itself. But why is Marxism correct? Because it is the 'true' self-knowledge of the proletariat, whose particular interests coincide with those of humanity. Through this process of circular reasoning, Lukács attempted to solve a problem that bedevils Hegelian Marxism. If no theory is true in itself in the sense of 'reflecting' the world accurately, if philosophy and theories of society are nothing more than the intellectual projection of practical social movements and interests, the question of 'truth' in the ordinary sense appears to be meaningless. Such epistemological relativism hardly provides a convincing basis for the radical restructuring of society.

Although Gramsci faced the same dilemma, he refrained from offering a transparently bogus solution, in the manner of Lukács. Instead, the Italian offered no solution at all. He was adamant that Marxism was a form of 'historicism' in as much as it held that the 'truth' of philosophy or science is truth in a socially pragmatic sense, in terms of its functions and origins rather than its intrinsic properties. For there can exist no 'extra-historical and extra-human objectivity' (Gramsci, 1971: 445). All knowing is bound up with doing, and everything we know is filtered through a framework of human values. It follows that Marxism, like any other doctrine or philosophy, proves its rationality and 'truth' to the extent that it articulates the needs of its time and wins 'mass adhesion' (Gramsci, 1971: 341). But can this relativisation of Marxism sustain a revolutionary stance? Is Gramsci being consistent? For example, he often writes as if it is self-evidently true that an active, self-autonomous, theoretically self-conscious human being is superior to a passive, uncritical and obedient one. But does this evaluation not rely on universal human values – on an unacknowledged, non-historical factor belonging to the permanent, unchanging idea of humanity? Would a consistent historicist be moved to revolutionary outrage? Implicit in Gramsci's thinking, the argument runs, is an 'Archimedean point', outside history, on which his critique of bourgeois society is based. Nevertheless, Gramsci's explicit commitment to historicism did incline him towards a healthy scepticism. Like the pragmatists, whose theory of truth resembled his own, Gramsci expressed opposition to a number of inveterate and unattractive Marxist habits: a priori reasoning, a craving for absolutes, and the pretence of finality in truth.

The Frankfurt School

The term 'Frankfurt School' denotes a school of Marxist (or neo-Marxist) thinkers associated with the Frankfurt Institute for Social Research, an academic centre founded in 1923. The abundant output of the Institute covered many areas of humanistic studies: philosophy, empirical sociology, musicology, social psychology, law, economics. Its approach to Marxism was far from dogmatic, especially in the early years. Deliberately remaining aloof from the titanic struggle between communism and social democracy, it accommodated scholars of significantly varying political persuasion. Indeed, its members always emphasised the independence and autonomy of theory and opposed its absorption by all-embracing practice, though they were – without exception – anxious to criticise society with a view to transforming it. In 1930, Max Horkheimer (1895–1973) became Director of the Institute and set about using the appointments procedure to create a 'school' of humanistic Marxism, whose reflections came to be known as 'critical theory'. The most impressive of the young intellectuals who joined the institute around this time were Herbert Marcuse and Theodor Adorno (1903–69). The former had only loose ties with the organised workers' movement; the latter, like Horkheimer himself, had no personal links whatsoever to socialist political life. When the Nazis came to power in 1933, the Institute could no longer function in Germany. Horkheimer managed to arrange its formal transfer to the United States in 1934, where it was affiliated to Columbia University in New York. Enticed by the promise of chairs for its leading members, the Institute returned to Frankfurt in 1949–50, though some of its key thinkers, including Marcuse, remained in America, taking up prestigious posts in a succession of eminent universities. The Frankfurt School is largely responsible for the stereotype of Western Marxism as pure theory, divorced from practical political activity. Its members became an international clique of tenured professors, highly paid, protected from the ravages of the market, feted by the academic establishment, and increasingly contemptuous of the proletariat whose cause they were presumed to support.

Continuing the tradition of Lukács, whom they greatly admired, the prominent thinkers of the Frankfurt School showed little interest in the idea of historical materialism as a 'science'. Marx was, in their opinion, essentially a philosopher of human freedom, condemning the alienation and reification of bourgeois society. They injected into Marxism a strong dose of *Kulturkritik*, an ill-disguised animus against modern civilisation, with its reliance on science and technology and its addiction to 'mass' forms of production and communication. Although they did not deny the existence of capitalist exploitation, neither did they dwell on it or regard it as the source of all evil. Their main theme was the threat posed by technological progress and its indifference to spiritual needs. This nostalgic romanticism, inherited from Lukács, was massively reinforced in 1932, when Marx's Paris Manuscripts were finally published. The pervasive moralism of these writings encouraged the critical theorists to develop a new dimension of Marxist critique. Whereas conventional Marxists condemned capitalism for producing poverty, the principal grievance of Horkheimer and his colleagues was that capitalism engendered abundance and satisfied a multiplicity of artificial needs. In contradistinction to orthodox Marxism, with its stress on efficient material production, the Frankfurt thinkers gave pride of place to the quality of life, to the liberation of our distinctively human potentialities. They were convinced that 'man' possesses a hidden 'essence' which tells us not only what he empirically is but also what he would be if he fully realised his own nature. Recall that Lukács derived the 'essential' aim of mankind from a historical teleology which posited the proletariat, rather than the Hegelian Spirit, as the personification of this a priori norm. Critical theory, on the other hand, relinquished the Hegelian metaphysics of the subject and with it the myth of the revolutionary proletariat. It could detect no 'logic' of history, no 'necessary' outcomes, no universal agent or transcendent subject. Accordingly, its proponents refused to identify with the proletarian movement and generally eschewed class analysis altogether, instead concentrating on a sweeping indictment of modern culture as a betrayal of reason. If this was Marxism at all, it was Marxism without the proletariat.

Adorno's and Horkheimer's *Dialectic of Enlightenment*, published in 1947, became the first gospel of critical theory. Written towards the end of the Second World War, the book was dominated by the question of Nazism, which the authors saw as a drastic manifestation of the universal barbarism into which humanity was falling. They attributed this decline to the very same values, ideals and rules that had once lifted mankind out of barbarism, and that were summed up in the concept of 'enlightenment'. The 'dialectic' consisted in the fact that the movement which aimed to conquer nature and emancipate humanity from the shackles of dogma had by its own inner logic turned into its opposite. It had created a 'scientistic', utilitarian ideology, reducing the world to its purely quantitative aspects, destroying customary meanings and natural human attachments, degrading the arts, and increasingly subjecting mankind to the tyranny of what Marx called 'commodity fetishism'. How did this come to pass? Enlightenment, in seeking to liberate men from the oppressive sense of mystery in the world, simply declared that what was mysterious or intangible did not exist. Using natural science as its paradigm, it sought to reduce all qualities to a common measure: 'In the anticipated identification of the wholly . . . mathematicized world with truth, enlightenment intends to secure itself against the return of the mythic. It confounds thought and mathematics' (Adorno and Horkheimer, 1973: 24–5). Individual things and human beings alike are turned into mathematical abstractions, to be manipulated and exploited for the purpose of rational control. For example, the natural human propensity to make artefacts, to create, becomes a commodity, measured in units of abstract labour-time. Individuality and spirituality, being unquantifiable, are seen as barriers to instrumental efficiency. Culture itself is transmuted into a commodity, degraded by the commercial values of the market. Commodity fetishism prevails in every sphere of life; the assimilation of human characteristics to interchangeable commodities is the totalitarian idea latent in enlightenment thought.

This critique of enlightenment rationalism could easily degenerate into a form of nihilism, and this is arguably what happened in Adorno's *Negative Dialectics* (1973), one of the seminal texts of twentieth-century philosophy, notwithstanding the obscurity of its style and argumentation. Here Adorno explicitly negates all metaphysics and epistemology as attempts to confine the world within arbitrary principles. The idea of immutable truth or of an absolute starting point is dismissed as a delusion. Thus philosophy, as normally conceived, is an exercise in futility. But he also rejects the Marxist 'primary of practice' in which theory is dissolved and loses its autonomy. Lukács, then, was wrong to identify 'truth' with the proletarian perspective. But if theory is autonomous, what does it discover? Attempts to embrace the 'whole' are pointless since they presuppose a metaphysical faith in the ultimate identity of everything. According to Adorno, Marxists wrongly treat the dialectic as a schema that can explain the universe in all its minute particulars. Strictly speaking, however, the dialectic is neither a method nor a description of the world but an act of repeated opposition to all existing descriptive schemata and all methods pretending to universality. The dialectic is essentially negative since it denies that any system can capture an inherently contradictory and constantly changing reality.

Given his 'deconstruction' of traditional philosophical techniques and claims, Adorno would appear to fit into the honourable tradition of scepticism. But, as Kolakowski points out, Adorno is not a sceptic (Kolakowski, 1978: 366–7). He is a romantic anti-capitalist who attacks the whole mechanism of bourgeois society for reducing all qualitative differences to the common denominator of money and for condemning human beings to an all-embracing process of 'reification'. Implicit here is some criterion of truth. However, in rejecting the 'fetishes' of 'bourgeois' logic and empirical science, as well as all abstract categories, he deprives his normative preferences (or aversions) of any kind of rational grounding. They are nothing more than a series of ex cathedra pronouncements that are never explained or justified.

Adorno's hostility to system building owes more to Nietzsche than to Marx. Adorno (and Horkheimer) also departs from Marx in rejecting the theory of progress and historical necessity and the idea of the proletariat as the standard bearer of a new society. Stripped of these Marxist ingredients, their critique of science, technology and commodity production seems more reactionary than revolutionary, calling to mind the aristocratic rants against emergent capitalism. This impression is reinforced by their complaint that mass-produced culture kills creativity or any possibility of transcending the present. In what is almost a parody of the traditional conservative contempt for the masses, they tell us that the accessibility of art inevitably means its degradation, and that jazz and rock music exemplify the destruction of civilisation. Ironically, a romantic disdain for 'the age of the common man' is precisely what motivated the inventors of fascism and Nazism. For the critical theorists to interpret this political deformation as a logical outcome of enlightenment rationalism rather than a complete negation of it is historically absurd.

Yet Adorno and Horkheimer did manage to articulate an uncomfortable truth about the triumph of rationalism and the type of society it breeds. We have come to see the world in terms of problems and solutions, ends and means. These are all terms postulating the self as an abstract agent, detached from any traditional world of meanings and therefore ripe for manipulation in accordance with bureaucratic criteria. Everything and everybody must be fitted into a system and subjected to regulation in pursuit of stipulated aims or objectives. During the 1950s and 1960s, many students and intellectuals came to agree with the critical theorists in their assumption that the spread of 'instrumental rationality', not the exploitation of the workers, was the chief malady of 'the affluent society'. However, the speculative and almost wilfully obscure writings of Adorno and Horkheimer were unlikely to capture the imagination of the reading public. Critical theory found its most effective spokesman in the person of Marcuse, whose works were accessible enough to make him the 'guru' of the New Left.

While other critical theorists resorted to arcane philosophical speculation, he squarely confronted the practical problem faced by Marxists during the post-war boom years. Marx had been convinced that the objective conditions of capitalist society were driving towards the conclusion of a classless society. The free market, he argued, would generate increasing dysfunctions, such as falling profit rates and class polarisation. Ground down by poverty and insecurity, the proletariat would eventually overthrow the capitalist order and replace it with a (socialist) system more attuned to the requirements of efficient production. But this scenario never materialised. Capitalism had apparently 'solved' its 'internal contradictions'; the technology of advanced industrial society was now producing enough wealth to assimilate the proletariat and neutralise their negative potential. How, then, was it still possible to urge the necessity of liberation from a relatively well-functioning and affluent society?

In *Eros and Civilisation*, Marcuse attempted to shift the argument from the sphere of political economy to that of metapsychology. He took as his starting point Freud's philosophy of civilisation. In Freud's view, the history of man is the history of his repression. Since there is an eternal clash between civilised values and the demands of human instincts, all civilisation is based on the permanent subjugation of instinctive desires and their deflection to socially useful activities. Freud describes this as the transformation from the 'pleasure principle' to the 'reality principle'. Marcuse revises this theory by arguing that the repression so far characteristic of all human civilisations arises from the need to master nature in the struggle against scarcity. But if this is so, then the repressive organisation of instinctive life does not arise from any law of biology or history which requires this to be so forever. In other words, the reality principle is not universal; it is culturally specific to an economy of scarcity. Once technology made it possible to remove the obstacle of scarcity, repression increasingly became 'surplus repression' – repression in excess of that necessary for maintaining civilisation. On this ground, Marcuse suggests that instrumental reason, and hence a society whose guiding principle is technical efficiency, is potentially self-undermining, for there is no longer any intrinsic necessity, in terms of the struggle for existence, for civilisation to be repressive. The possibility of utopia is inherent in the technology of advanced industrial societies. The instincts that would no longer be devoted to ungratifying work would become free to create a libidinous civilisation in which 'Eros', the 'pleasure principle', would reign supreme.

Some may wonder why a book which substitutes 'instinctual repression' for 'economic exploitation' and contains no class analysis should be considered 'Marxist'. Others may fail to see why economic abundance should obviate the need for suppression of instincts. What about natural human aggression, or the 'death instincts' (Thanatos) in Freud's idiom? Still others may question Marcuse's assumption that pursuit of the pleasure principle would cause people to reject, and not actively embrace, the consumer society. Marcuse himself soon developed grave doubts about this assumption. In *Eros and Civilisation*, he argues that a high level or instrumental rationality is the precondition for liberation. But in *One Dimensional Man* (written in 1964), his most famous work, he claims that it is this same development of the productive forces that is the effective basis for stifling potential rebellion or liberation. He swings from hope to despair, informing us that technology 'serves to institute new, more effective, and more pleasant forms of social control'. Technology can no longer be considered 'neutral'. Since its 'overwhelming ... efficiency' satisfies all reasonable material desires, it has removed the obvious reasons for dissent or protest and created 'a system of domination' (Marcuse, 1972: 177). Under the impact of sustained and expanding affluence, the working classes have been transformed into passive, acquiescent instruments of the established order.

Marx, as Marcuse notes, expected a proletarian revolution because the labouring masses, in their misery, represented the absolute negation of bourgeois society. But in a world where workers own cars, houses, televisions, household appliances etc., the standard Marxist doctrine of class conflict is inapplicable. A suffocating consumer fetishism unites all classes: the inhabitants of the affluent society find their identity in their material possessions and not in their personal qualities. The very instinctual structure of individuals is moulded to suit the requirements of the system. It is not simply that people's ideas are distorted by consumerism; their personalities are changed, as they become sheep-like creatures, without minds of their own and bound to their consumer lifestyles at the deepest psychic level.

One-dimensional thought and behaviour is reinforced, according to Marcuse, by the triumph of scientific and technological rationality in all areas of life. Here he repeats the point made by other critical theorists that such rationality reduces everything to observable and measurable quantities. Because questions of value cannot be resolved by calculation or sense perception, they are ignored or else dismissed as inconsequential matters of subjective preference. The victory of the scientific method thus spells the defeat of critical imagination. What is more, this method, because it involves a manipulative and instrumental attitude towards the world of nature, encourages a manipulative and instrumental attitude towards the human world. People come to be viewed as things, pushed hither and thither in the interests of 'rational' organisation.

That the citizens of the affluent society see themselves as free only highlights their one-dimensionality. Freedom, says Marcuse, is not determined by 'the range of choice open to the individual' but by 'what can be chosen and what is chosen by the individual' (Marcuse, 1972: 21). Giving a slave a choice between two different masters does not make him any less a slave. In a society driven by consumption, where all are ensnared within a system of false values and false needs, the existence of 'choice' becomes another form of social control.

It seems, then, that the status quo defies all transcendence. It is possible, Marcuse allows, that society's marginalised groups – the ethnic or racial minorities, dropouts, the long-term unemployed – might take to the streets and shake the system at its foundations. But pessimism remained his keynote.

Marcuse's criticism of consumer fetishism found a sympathetic audience among alienated middle-class rebels who deemed the categories of orthodox

Marxism dated and implausible in the Western context. The student movement of the 1960s was very much inspired by Marcuse's works, and its offshoot – the Green movement – has obviously carried forward its critique of rampant technology and the relentless pursuit of wealth.

Up to a point, most people could agree with Marcuse. It is not just non-conformists or revolutionaries who are disturbed by the uncontrollable greed of modern capitalist society. As a Marxist philosopher, however, he leaves a lot to be desired. How exactly does he know that 'the prevailing needs to relax, to have fun, to behave and consume in accordance with the advertisements, to love and hate what others love and hate, belong to [the] category of false needs . . .' (Marcuse, 1972: 19)? Since he scorns 'the abstractions of formal logic and of transcendental philosophy', as well as 'the concreteness of immediate experience', he is forced to rely on a Hegelian notion of 'dialectical logic' which is never adequately defined. This higher reason will supposedly allow us, in some mysterious way, to intuit normative 'essences', including the true essence of humanity itself (Marcuse, 1972: 116–17). But, as Kolakowski asks, how can we know that this essence is revealed by one particular intuition rather than another (Kolakowski, 1978: 416)? Marcuse himself barely gets beyond tautology. The 'essence' of man, he tells us, aims at the realisation of qualities that are 'typically human' (Marcuse, 1972: 169), or at the 'free development of human needs and faculties' (Marcuse, 1972: 174). Those readers in need of further instruction can find a passage where we learn that 'freedom from toil is preferable to toil, and an intelligent life is preferable to a stupid life' (Marcuse, 1972: 106). Well, yes. Historical experience teaches us that 'human nature' comprises a welter of often contradictory needs, propensities and faculties. Why some should be singled out as 'essential' and others considered 'non-essential' remains unclear. In any case, it is far from self-evident that such an exercise could ever provide determinate criteria for the organisation of society. For example, an obvious human need is respect or recognition from one's fellows. Surely, one way of achieving this is the acquisition of high-quality material goods. In this light, the desire to accumulate and consume hardly corresponds to a 'false need'. There are of course other, perhaps more admirable, ways of gaining respect and satisfaction. It does not follow, however, that those who pursue the paths of altruism or creativity are more 'human' than their acquisitive neighbours. 'Human nature' furnishes no standard for distinguishing between good or bad modes of life.

It may be unfair of Kolakowski to label Marcuse 'the ideologist of obscurantism' (Kolakowski, 1978: 420), but it must be said that his popularity has been attained at the expense of academic rigour. Also, in his pessimism, his contempt for science and technology, his fondness for abstract essences, and his dismissal of the revolutionary potential of the industrial proletariat, he has shown himself to have very little in common with the Marxist tradition. With friends like Marcuse, Marxism has no need of enemies.

Existentialist Marxism

After the Second World War, the major innovation within the Marxist milieu was the attempt, in France, to restore Marxism as a philosophy of subjectivity and freedom by integrating it with the existentialism that had become fashionable during the Nazi occupation. The key figure, by far, was Jean-Paul Sartre, a playwright and novelist as well as a philosopher, who found it difficult to confine his revolutionary outlook within the rigid categories of orthodox Marxism. Sartre never joined the Communist Party but refrained from attacking it until the suppression of the Hungarian revolt in 1956. Thereafter he developed his ideas outside of any organisational frame of reference. At the same time he became more emphatic in his identification with Marxism. In *Critique de la raison dialectique* (1960) he attempted to find room within Marxism for the existentialist concepts of 'creativity' and spontaneity, while still preserving the social significance of human behaviour. Whether this synthesis was logical or coherent is a moot point.

Central to existentialism, as understood by Sartre, is the conviction that 'man is condemned to be free'. Freedom, in this sense, comprises three elements. First, unlike inert nature, human behaviour is not governed by causal laws. Why? Because, in contrast to stones or trees, human beings possess imagination, an ability to transcend our immediate situation in unpredictable ways. The second element of existential freedom is that there are no universal traits of human nature, no innate dispositions to adopt certain attitudes and forms of conduct rather than others. Third, freedom, according to Sartre, means that there are no absolute moral laws, binding on all human beings and dictated by some infallible source – be it scripture or abstract 'Reason' or 'History'. We are free to choose our own values, because the universe is inherently meaningless or – in Sartre's terminology – 'absurd'.

Since there are no universal ethical norms, no unbreakable social or historical laws, no fixed traits of human nature, each individual is totally responsible for everything he or she does. The result is angst, anxiety, dread. Brought face to face with their own freedom, men and women wilt under so vast a burden of responsibility. Small wonder, then, that we try to avoid this anguish by seeking refuge in 'bad faith' or self-deception, whereby we pretend that things are inevitable or self-evidently true when they are not. Most people lead inauthentic lives, forever making excuses or hiding behind 'infallible' guides (God, history, social convention), in order to deny the void at the centre of human existence.

Existentialism, it can be seen, insists on free will, individuality and the essential meaninglessness of life. These are not qualities that are normally associated with Marxism, which – in its classical form – preaches determinism and collectivism, and attributes an intrinsic coherence and purpose to history. How could Sartre fuse these two opposing philosophies? He begins by distinguishing Marx from later 'lazy Marxists', with their mechanical modes of analysis and their vulgar reduction of human beings to the status of material objects. Orthodox Marxists, we are told by Sartre, forgot Marx's own contention that 'man makes his own history', that human beings are capable of choice and autonomy: they are not the passive tools of some irresistible dialectic. Contrary to Marx's intentions, historical materialism has become a dogmatic, a priori formula, forcing everything that happens into a preconceived mould: 'Marxism has reabsorbed man into the idea, and existentialism seeks him everywhere where he is, at his work, in his home, in the street' (Sartre, 1963: 28). Existentialism, by encouraging Marxists to recognise free will, as well as the uniqueness of particular individuals and particular situations, could therefore revive Marxism – or so Sartre and his numerous admirers said.

If we limit our gaze to the humanistic strain in Marxist thought, there are indeed similarities between the two philosophies. Both believe that human beings have surrendered individual freedom to false idols of their own making; both pour scorn on capitalist oppression and bourgeois hypocrisy; both want to remove the means of production from the hands of a single class and place them at the disposal of the entire collectivity. Yet it is hard to see how a consistent Marxist could agree with existentialism's gloomy diagnosis of the human condition. Unlike Marx, Sartre assumes that alienation in the sense of 'otherness' is inescapable. Every man is a project of alienating objectification for every other. The permanence of this subject–object duality is bound up with the permanence of scarcity. For Sartre, it is the struggle against scarcity that generates violence, exploitation and class conflict. In the prosecution of this struggle, the world is organised into 'serial' collectivities, inhuman aggregations of individuals who eye one another with suspicion and anxiety. Their formal antithesis is the 'fused group' in which all persons are united in a fraternal enterprise to achieve a common goal. The best example of a fused group is a mass movement at the apocalyptic moment of a successful revolutionary uprising. But to maintain itself in existence, such a group must endow itself with functional specialisation, thus losing its fraternal connections and becoming conservative and hierarchical. The state is the ultimate outcome – and its invariable structure involves bureaucratic manipulation and repressive 'terror'. What was once a fused group is degraded into serial passivity. In the Marxist context, the state tries to abolish the inevitable alienation that accompanies this process through devices aimed at the suppression of multiplicity in the name of absolute unity. But such unity is chimerical in a climate of scarcity, where 'others' take on the appearance of cruel predators. Hence the classical Marxist notion of the 'dictatorship of the proletariat' is a contradiction in terms. Unless we reduce it to the status of a theoretical concept, a 'class' cannot rule, as it is a compound of competing interests and needs, not an organic unity.

Sartre clearly did not share the conventional ('lazy') Marxist conviction that 'history is on our side'. For him, the defining theme in human development was the intractable problem of scarcity, and he ridiculed the tendency of Marxists to assume that this problem had either been solved already or else would be at some predictable point in the foreseeable future. The burden of scarcity, he concluded, was 'a fundamental determination of man' (Sartre, 1976: 138–9). Perhaps at the end of a long dialectical process, a society without scarcity, without struggles and conflicts, will emerge – but a society of this kind is beyond our experience and comprehension. For us, it is literally inconceivable.

In many respects, the *Critique of Dialectical Reason* reads like a critique of Marxism itself. Some commentators are convinced that Sartre was flying under Marx's banner only because it was fashionable at the time. Indeed, he departed from Marxism at the most fundamental ontological level, accusing its adherents of treating collectives as 'things', as real entities, with an organic or metaphysical composition of their own, apart from the individuals who make them up at any given time and place. To him, a collective is always constituted, never constitutive, and the only constitutive organism in the socio-political world is the individual. This is in tune with existentialism, but it means that there can be no Totalising Subject of history, no standpoint transcendent to the historical process itself. If this is so, it implies that we are not entitled to speak of the 'essence' of history, of what history 'really' is, or of history as a closed and fixed entity. Since Sartre also rejects the idea of a human essence or nature, the philosophical justification for his 'Marxism' remains opaque. The only generalisation he makes about human beings is that our inherent singularity prevents us from fusing into totalised totalities. But why, then, should any individual abdicate his judgment in the interest of collective solidarity, Marxism's be-all-and-end-all? Would this not be an example of 'bad faith', of inauthenticity? Curiously, however, Sartre adopted a strikingly authoritarian political stance, championing 'Maoism' and even defending state terror as a way of preserving communal commitment in the face of individual subjectivity. Maybe his contempt for the cowardly majority who led inauthentic lives caused him to concur with Rousseau's paradoxical conclusion: the people must be 'forced to be free', i.e. forced to shed the bourgeois falsehoods that prevent the attainment of 'authenticity'. In Sartre we see an unfortunate illustration of how Marxism's theoretical concern for human liberation could translate into a practical demand for political conformity.

Structuralist Marxism

In the 1960s, orthodox Marxist materialism came under attack from another maverick French philosopher, Louis Althusser, a 'semi-detached' member of the French Communist Party, who offered an intriguing and temporarily influential synthesis of Marxism and structuralism. The latter had its origins in the linguistic studies of Ferdinand de Saussure (1857–1913), which investigated the universal structure underlying human language. Years later, Claude Levi-Strauss used the concept of structure to illuminate primitive myths and kinship systems. By 'decoding' these, he found that the activities of diverse tribal communities followed invariant logical patterns or structures, of which participants were unaware. His conclusion was that all societies unconsciously adopt a combination of timeless structural components, independent of human intentions.

Structuralism enabled Althusser to develop a theoretical perspective equidistant from humanistic Marxism, on the one hand, and orthodox Marxism, on the other. Against thinkers like Gramsci and Sartre, he insisted that history is a 'process without subjects', which must be analysed in terms of objective and autonomous structures. Our behaviour, in other words, is reactive, not active or freely chosen;

it is subject to deep structural determinants. But if human purposes and choices are merely the products of objective forces, beyond our control, then notions dear to Marxist humanists – authenticity, self-realisation, self-determination – are so much idealistic nonsense. Humanists, said Althusser, paid too much attention to Marx's early writings, which were still heavily indebted to Hegelian categories and assumptions. There is an 'epistemological break' (Althusser, 1970: 34), no continuity whatsoever, between the young, 'pre-Marxist' Marx, and the older, 'true' Marx, who inaugurated a scientific revolution in social thought. That is to say, he moved from myth to reality, illusion to truth. In reducing truth to changing historical conditions, the Hegelian Marxists had belittled the special dignity and objectivity of science in general and Marxist science in particular.

Althusser, despite his desire to restore the scientific rigour of Marxism, strongly objected to the mechanistic materialism of the orthodox Marxists. For one thing, he rejected their simplistic model of base and superstructure. The economy, he maintained, is just one structure among others: the political, the scientific and the ideological. Society is best described as a 'structure of structures', a 'decentred totality' of four autonomous structures interacting one with another. Each structure determines, and is determined by, the global structure, as well as all the others. Social determination is therefore complex. This is what Althusser labels the 'law of overdetermination' (Althusser, 1970: ch. 3). At first glance, this 'law' might seem a radical deviation from the principles of historical materialism, but he preserves his Marxist credentials by saying that the autonomy of so-called superstructures is relative as opposed to absolute; economic practice is determinant 'in the last instance' (Althusser, 1970: 111), because it determines the respective degrees of autonomy of the other practices, or structures. On this model, causality is understood in structural rather than linear or mechanical terms. It is not that A causes B, where A and B are isolated phenomena, but that A and B require each other. The focus is on co-existential regularities, not on causal laws in the classical Marxist sense. Because social change is the result of interacting structures, exerting a multitude of reciprocal influences and burdened by a bewildering variety of contradictions, there is no logical or inevitable dynamic to the process, and historical prediction – even historical generalisation – becomes impossible. Insofar as Marx himself and subsequent Marxists attempted to impose a grand design on history, they fell victim, Althusser argued, to the insidious influence of Hegelian teleology, with its mystical premise that human behaviour expressed some 'higher', 'rational' purpose.

For a time, Althusser enjoyed the status of an honoured prophet. His avoidance of reductive generalisations inspired a number of disciples, most notably Nicos Poulantzas (1936–79), to refine and develop the Marxist theory of the state, hitherto confined, in orthodox circles, to a few simple-minded propositions (e.g. 'the state is a tool of the capitalist class.'). In addition, Althusser's attempt to defend Marxism's scientific standing was attractive to those who resented the 'infection' of Marxism by a succession of 'idealistic' intellectual fashions. Certainly he reminded us that the Marxist humanists were remarkably selective in their approach to Marx.

Nevertheless, the brand of Marxism developed by Althusser was ultimately sterile and unappealing. His emphasis on the irreducible complexity of social causation seemed to render his scientific pretensions otiose. If everything interacts with everything else in empirically diverse and unpredictable ways, how can we discover impersonal laws of social development? And is a science of society possible in the absence of such laws? Althusser had an eccentric view of science as a purely theoretical enterprise, unbounded by any 'external' criteria of truth, such as empirical evidence. Observation and verification/falsification played no obvious role. He also failed to appreciate that his conception of the self as a passive bearer of impersonal forces undermined the moral case for communism. The humanists, for all their inconsistencies and limitations, at least recognised that the Marxist utopia had to be justified in terms of human needs and capacities. The 'liberation' promised by Marxism surely presupposes the existence of human agency, of individuals who are not merely social ciphers.

Conclusion

If the point of revolutionary theory is to change the world, then Western Marxism must be judged a failure. It has inspired no social upheavals of the kind Marx would have recognised, and few of its leading figures bothered to involve themselves in the struggles of the working class. As a varied body of theory, however, Western Marxism can boast some achievements. It gradually freed itself from the mythology of the infallible proletariat and the belief that Marx's categories were absolute truth. It made Marxism seem relevant to the changing realities of modern life. It also contributed to the critique of scientistic philosophy, by drawing attention to the absurdities and latent normative assumptions of positivist social science. And (Althusser excepted) it revealed the tension between human emancipation and orthodox Marxism's deterministic conception of human behaviour.

Still, attempts to rescue Marxism by divesting it of its most distinctive features ultimately served to create confusion and highlight the doctrine's shortcomings. To concede that Marxism, as conventionally understood, is too reductive, too deterministic, too narrow in its view of the human condition, is – in effect – to say that Marxism must be transcended. The various forms of 'hyphenated Marxism' constituted an implicit critique of the Marxist project, though those who devised these strange hybrids thought they were doing something constructive, not something destructive. This lack of self-awareness helps to account for the bewildering contradictions we find in the thought of just about all Western Marxists. It is not surprising, then, that in the latter part of the twentieth century those who were meant to carry the torch of Western Marxism began to think of themselves as 'post-Marxists'. The discrediting of communism as a viable alternative to liberal capitalism has meant that the most interesting radical thinkers no longer feel the need to identify themselves with Marxism of any sort. A case in point is the leading philosopher in the second generation of the Frankfurt School, Jurgen Habermas, who was once considered a Marxist. He has evolved a philosophy that is less indebted to Marx than to hermeneutic and linguistic philosophy. For him, social reproduction cannot be reduced to the simple division of labour, as Marx had reduced it in his theoretical writings. Rather, in addition to the activity of dominating nature, the practice of communicative interaction must be regarded as an equally fundamental dimension of historical development. The species evolves, in part, through liberation from the constraints that inhibit rational communication, and distorted communication cannot be fully explained in terms of relations stemming from human labour. This is precisely the type of left-wing idealism that Marx came to abhor. Apart from hostility to the status quo, it contains nothing that can be called 'Marxist'. Western Marxism involved combinations of Marxism plus 'something else'. Nowadays, radical thinkers seem more interested in developing the something else, while paying only ritualistic respects to a great thinker who is no longer taken as gospel.

References and further reading

Adorno, T.W. (1973) (translated by E.B. Ashton) *Negative Dialectics*. London: Routledge.

Adorno, T.W. and M. Horkheimer (1973) (translated by J. Cumming) *Dialectic of Enlightenment*. London: Allen Lane.

Althusser, L. (1970) (translated by B. Brewster) *For Marx*. New York: Vintage Books.

Anderson, P. (1976) *Considerations on Western Marxism*. London: New Left Books.

Bellamy, R. and D. Schecter (1993) *Gramsci and the Italian State*. Manchester: Manchester University Press.

Bobbio, N. (1988) (translated by R. Griffin and edited by R. Bellamy) *Which Socialism?* Oxford: Polity Press.

Callinicos, A. (1976) *Althusser's Marxism*. London: Pluto Press.

Connerton, P. (1980) *The Tragedy of Enlightenment: An Essay on the Frankfurt School*. Cambridge: Cambridge University Press.

Femia, J.V. (1981) *Gramsci's Political Thought*. Paperback edition in 1987. Oxford: Oxford University Press.

Feuer, L. (ed.) (1959) *Marx and Engels: Basic Writings on Politics and Philosophy*. New York: Doubleday.

Finocchiaro, M. (1988) *Gramsci and the History of Dialectical Thought*. Cambridge: Cambridge University Press.

Gramsci, A. (1971) (edited and translated by Q. Hoare and G. Nowell Smith) *Selections from the Prison Notebooks*. London: Lawrence and Wishart.

Hegel, G.W.F. (1969) (translated by W. Wallace and A.V. Miller) *The Philosophy of Mind*. Oxford: Oxford University Press.

Held, D. (1980) *Introduction to Critical Theory*. London: Hutchinson.

Jacoby, R. (1981) *Dialectic of Defeat: Contours of Western Marxism*. Cambridge: Cambridge University Press.

Kolakowski, L. (1978) (translated by P.S. Falla) *Main Currents of Marxism*, volume III: *The Breakdown*. Oxford: Clarendon Press.

Korsch, K. (1970) (translated by F. Halliday) *Marxism and Philosophy*. London: New Left.

Lukács, G. (1971) (translated by R. Livingstone) *History and Class Consciousness*. London: The Merlin Press.

McBride, W.L. (1991) *Sartre's Political Theory*. Indianapolis, IN: Indiana University Press.

MacIntyre, A. (1970) *Marcuse*. London: Fontana/Collins.

Marcuse, H. (1955) *Eros and Civilisation*. Boston, MA: Beacon Press.

Marcuse, H. (1972) *One Dimensional Man*. London: Abacus.

Merquior, J.G. (1986) *Western Marxism*. London: Paladin.

New Left Review (ed.) (1977) *Western Marxism: a Critical Reader*. London: New Left/ Verso. The essays on Althusser – one by N. Geras and the other by A. Glucksmann – are especially worth reading.

Parkinson, G.H.R. (1977) *Georg Lukács*. London: Routledge & Kegan Paul.

Poulantzas, N. (1973) *Political Power and Social Classes*. London: New Left Books.

Sartre, J.P. (1963) (translated by H. Barnes) *The Problem of Method*. London: Methuen.

Sartre, J.P. (1976) (translated by A. Sheridan Smith) *Critique of Dialectical Reason*. London: New Left Books.

Warnock, M. (1965) *The Philosophy of Sartre*. London: Hutchinson.

7 African Marxism's moment

Daryl Glaser

Was there a distinctive African contribution to Marxist thought? Curiously, many of Africa's Marxist leaders answered this question emphatically in the negative. Following an initial wave of what was dubbed 'African socialism' in the early post-independence years, a new cohort of Marxist–Leninist leaders coming to power mainly in the 1970s insisted on their orthodoxy. If African socialists had sought a path to socialism that appealed to African specificity, the later cohort insisted that there could be no specifically African socialism or Marxism, that there was just one universal Leninist Marxism, albeit one that needed to be fitted to local conditions in Africa as everywhere else it was employed. The new cohort positioned themselves relative to the African socialists much as Marx and Engels did vis-à-vis the utopian socialists, contrasting the scientific character of their approach with the eclecticism, romanticism and naïveté of the African socialists.[1] Yet the story of Marxism in Africa was not entirely bereft of original contributions. In the first place, Marxists, as bearers of a doctrine concerned with revolution under advanced capitalism, had to innovate theoretically to explain Marxism's relevance to the European colonial realm – and sub-Saharan Africa represented an acute instance of a region that was definitely not economically developed or even, outside South Africa, subject to the sort of 'combined and uneven' development that marked, say, Imperial Russia. Secondly, the African socialism narrative is not quite as sharply distinguishable from the 'Afro-Marxist' one as some of the later and more orthodox Marxists insisted: at least two of the most prominent African socialist leaders, Sékou Touré and Kwame Nkrumah, viewed Marxism as a part of their theoretical lineage, and Nkrumah became explicitly Marxist after being thrown out of power.[2] We can therefore choose to view African socialism as itself contributing – and as imparting originality – to African Marxism. Finally, and pro-fessions of conformity notwithstanding, some of the orthodox Marxist–Leninists themselves made distinctive practical and theoretical contributions to Marxism.

'African socialism'

In respect of both African socialism and later orthodox Marxism, Africa was an object of socialist theorizing before it became a source of it. The movement of thinkers *about* Africa that most directly stimulated first-wave African socialism was Pan-Africanism, whose most prominent early intellectual figures – W.E.B. Du Bois and George Padmore – belonged to the African diaspora. Their guiding concerns were to free Africa of European domination and to unify the continent on a socialist basis. Their activity centered on Pan-Africanist congresses held in 1919, 1921, 1923, 1927 and, most influentially, 1945 (Nelkin, 1964: 72–3; Padmore, 1964). Marxism was an element in Pan-Africanist discourse, but its role varied between thinkers and across time. Padmore started out as a communist but later broke from the party and sought thereafter to defend a non-dogmatic application of Marxist theory. Du Bois, by contrast, was a long-time non-Marxist socialist who became increasingly pro-Soviet in his later years.[3]

Pan-Africanism influenced African socialism directly through the person of Nkrumah, who helped to organize the fifth Pan-African Congress and led Ghana to independence in 1957 (Nkrumah, 1963: 134–40). In power, Nkrumah and other radical African socialist leaders continued to pursue African unification. The controversy aroused by this quest exposed a division between radical and conservative independent African states (Nelkin, 1964: 73–6).

The ideology of African socialism was woven of a number of themes. These included the belief that precolonial African society was essentially communalistic and that its spirit could be invoked by those building postcolonial societies. Africa's early communal experience (the theory went) qualified new African states to advance to socialism without passing through the period of capitalist development and class conflict that, according to Marxist orthodoxy, was supposed to precede it. Further, leaders could appeal to an essential African-ness (what Léopold Senghor called 'Negritude') in their efforts to mobilize popular energy behind a project of development whose aim was to give economic substance to formal political independence.[4] If these were 'utopian' socialists, they were not rustics: Nkrumah and successive governments in Algeria wanted to establish modern states to promote industrialization.[5] Nor did they think that African society was primed for socialism: the spirit of African communalism would have to be actively revived and, indeed, a socialist 'new man' forged through exhortation and public education.[6] For this purpose African socialists sought inspirational party leadership: but because they believed that Africa could attain socialism without class struggle, they organized mass parties rather than Leninist revolutionary vanguards. Nkrumah's Convention People's Party at one stage claimed a membership of 2 million in a total population of 4.7 million (Nkrumah, 1964a: 105; Ottoway and Ottoway, 1986: 15, 20). Guinea's Sékou Touré 'experimented with an enormous variety of institutions in his painful search for an overall system which would embody his vision of socialism' (Ottoway and Ottoway, 1986: 55). His ruling Parti Démocratique du Guinée started life as a mass organization, morphed into a vanguard party, re-emerged as a party for all the people, and finally reinvented itself as a 'party state'. In this last permutation it sought literally to dissolve the state by absorbing society into the party (Ottoway and Ottoway, 1986: 52–9).

The mass party idea suited the voluntarist, humanistic style with which the African socialists set out.[7] It was a style that did not survive the test of reality:

confronted by peasants who appeared far less keen on socialism than the theory of African communalism had supposed them to be, Sékou Touré and Tanzania's Julius Nyerere coerced them into villages (Ottoway and Ottoway, 1986: 45–59). It would be wrong, though, to suppose that African socialism was all theory and no practice. The more committed African socialist governments initiated programmes of nationalization, rural cooperative-building and popular mobilization that look pretty radical by today's lights.

When first-wave socialism came unstuck – toppled by coup in Ghana, ground down by economic failure in Guinea, Tanzania and Zambia – some of its disillusioned apostles turned on their earlier faith in African egalitarianism. Radicalized by his overthrow in 1966, the later Nkrumah scorned the notion of 'an idyllic, African classless society . . . enjoying a drugged serenity' (Nkrumah, 1973: 79) and insisted that socialism could only be attained through class struggle waged under the leadership of a vanguard party (Nkrumah, 1973; Ottoway and Ottoway, 1986: 19–22). In positing the necessity of struggle and warning of betrayal by the African elite, Nkrumah was picking up a line of thought established by another African socialist revolutionary: Algeria's Franz Fanon (Fanon, 1967: 140; Cohen, 1986: 48). As late as the 1980s, 'ideological socialists' in Tanzania, the star of African socialism following Nyerere's 1967 Arusha declaration, were blaming their country's woes on an insufficiently 'scientific' socialism (McHenry, 1994: 22–3). The Ghanaian leader's Marxist interventions, like those of Fanon before and the Tanzanian 'ideological socialists' later, straddled the divide between first-wave African socialism and the succeeding wave of orthodox 'Afro-communism'.

Marxist theory about Africa

As is well known, Marx and Engels expected the proletarian revolution to break out, and socialism to be established, in advanced capitalist societies. They did consider the possibility that certain societies with recently strong communal traditions (notably Russia) might be able to skip capitalism, but they never developed this thought into a theory (Marx, 1881; Cox, 1966: 47–8). Trotsky and Lenin took a different route to justify revolution in largely agrarian Russia: they argued that Russia had too weak a liberal bourgeoisie to establish a successful bourgeois-democratic order, yet just enough of capitalism and a working class to enable workers and peasants to stage a revolution under the leadership of a proletarian vanguard party. The nature of that revolution remained for long unclear, but Lenin came increasingly round to Trotsky's view that it would be socialist rather than bourgeois-democratic (Liebman, 1975: 62–83, 180–9). Although they believed Russia ripe for revolution, both Lenin and Trotsky thought that the post-revolutionary state's survival, and certainly its flourishing, would depend on supportive proletarian revolutions breaking out in more advanced capitalist societies. It was the failure of these to materialize, and the prospect of an isolated socialist Russia, that prompted communists to turn their attention to fostering anticolonial revolution (Padmore, 1964: 225; Drew 2000: 95). Some began to think that the world capitalist system might be sooner and more successfully attacked at its weak colonial link than in its metropolitan heartland. During the 1920s the Moscow-led Communist International threw its weight behind the aspiration of colonized people for national independence.

In the decades after the Second World War the Soviet Union and international communist movement faced an exciting new circumstance: a decolonizing Africa and Asia falling to postcolonial leaders often determined to build socialism. The Soviets remained orthodox enough Marxists to doubt whether the newly independent countries were ready to embark on socialist construction. They nevertheless adapted their theory sufficiently to enable them to take advantage of new opportunities to project Moscow's influence abroad (Keller, 1987: 5–6). Soviet theorists began to argue in the 1950s that a 'non-capitalist' path of development had been opened for Third World countries by the presence of an international socialist bloc led by a relatively advanced Soviet Union. In effect, the USSR and its allies could provide the support to postcolonial countries that the Bolsheviks had hoped to find in advanced-capitalist Europe after 1917. This support would, viewed another way, play the role for African Marxists that Africa's supposed indigenous communalism was meant to do for first-wave socialists: supply the magic ingredient that would enable poor and dependent societies to bypass capitalist development on their way to socialism. Later Soviet theorists posited the possibility of 'societies of socialist orientation'. While this theoretical refinement rationalized close ties with Marxist–Leninist regimes in Africa, its formulators remained somewhat doubtful about the prospects for socialism, as opposed to Moscow-friendly regimes, in Africa.[8] Naturally the Soviet Union's proud Marxist–Leninist allies in Africa did not share their scepticism (Somerville, 1986: 194–6).

Marxism's missionaries

How did a European-hewed doctrine like Marxism make its way to Africa? A part of the answer carries some irony: via colonialism. Activists in the colonies acquired a fair proportion of their Marxism through contact with communist and labour movements based in colonial metropoles. The contact occurred when African students studied in European capitals, notably in Lisbon in the case of the Partido Africano de Independéncia de Guine e Cabo Verde (PAIGC) and the Movimento popular de libertação de Angola (MPLA); and it occurred when European socialist and communist parties and trade union federations – especially French federations – established branches in the colonies. Sékou Touré, for example, started out as an organizer in the communist-dominated Confédération Générale du Travail. Much earlier, the British labour movement had closely influenced the beginnings of South African Marxism. The colonial powers also implanted settlers whose numbers included a leftist fringe, for example anti-Salazarists amongst the Portuguese settlers in Angola. Once implanted in Africa, Marxist ideas often jumped from one African state to another, with Algeria's Front de Libération Nationale (FLN), the long-established Sudanese Communist Party and the PAIGC's Amilcar Cabral serving as particularly important local transmitters.[9] In all this there is a parallel with Christianity: a universalistic European doctrine, projected into the less 'civilized' colonies, where its egalitarian message inspired and found recruits amongst an indigenous population who turned its precepts against their colonial masters. (One difference, of course, is that Christianity was also recruited to serve colonialism; but then the European communist left was itself not consistently anticolonialist.)

A second route that Marxism took to Africa passed via class, racial, ethnic and cultural outsiders living in African urban centres like Brazzaville, Luanda, Bissau and the Witwatersrand. These included educated sectors, notably students and teachers, sometimes civil servants; relatively privileged African *assimilados* in Lusophone Africa; mixed-race *mestiços* in Angola and Mozambique and 'coloureds' in South Africa; and immigrants who were in important senses culturally different from both black indigenes and white settlers, namely Indians in South Africa and the Portuguese colonies (many of the latter Goans) and Jewish immigrants from the Russian Empire who settled in, again, South Africa.[10] These were groups that were educated enough to read Marxist texts and enjoyed cultural connections with a wider world. From their ranks, not surprisingly, sprang a university-centred academic Marxism, plugged into metropolitan Marxist theory, that tried to comprehend the post-colonial state, centre–periphery economic relationships and, in South Africa, the class basis of apartheid. Its key bases were the University of Dar es Salaam and various universities in South Africa (Turok, 1986: 59–60; Bozzoli and Delius, 1990; Glaser, 2001). For *assimilados*, Marxism offered a formula for anticolonial struggle that kept faith with Western modernity. White, Indian and *mestiço* leftists found in Marxism's prioritization of class over race an analysis that did not associate them indelibly with the system of oppression or exclude them from exercising active influence in radical politics. Many Jewish immigrants, for their part, belonged to a cohort that had escaped the parochialism of the *shtetl* and come to identify with the larger Russian labour movement, whose ideals they brought to the new country.[11]

These groups, along with organized workers (Allen, 1989: 62, 68–9; Radu and Somerville, 1989: 160), formed Marxist milieux in the capital cities of African states. These were to be found not only in African countries that went Marxist, but in many that did not (Turok, 1986). The component groups of the radical milieux interacted dynamically with Marxists in power, cooperating with them in some cases, in others competing, sometimes violently (Keller, 1988: 177, 218–19, 199–200; Allen, 1989: 31–2, 68–9). The milieux also threw up a variety of 'left oppositions'.[12]

The anchorage of Marxist regimes in the radical, racially mixed milieux of capital cities goes some way to account for the distrust felt towards them among three groups: rural Africans, Africans located in the cities but outside the milieux, and inhabitants of regions beyond capital city hinterlands. Thus, in Angola, Unita appealed with some success to the resentments of African peasants, especially those located outside the MPLA's Kimbundu heartland, while the government's leftist opponents found an audience in Luanda's slum-dwellers. In Mozambique the Marxist southerners who dominated the Front for the Liberation of Mozambique (Frelimo) contended with the suspicions of both northern Makonde traditionalists and Africanist leaders from the central regions.[13] The submersion of Marxist regimes in metropolitan milieux helps, further, to explain their modernist zeal. Marxist rulers were hostile to traditional authorities, religions and practices while favouring rapid industrialization, high technology and large-scale mechanized farming.[14]

The radical milieux were themselves often internally fractious. Organizational and ideological rivalries were common. These were played out most viciously between the Ethiopian People's Liberation Party (EPRP) and the All-Ethiopian Socialist Movement (MEISON) in Addis Ababa in 1977–78 (Ottoway and Ottoway, 1986: 134–7; Clapham, 1988: 66–7; Ayele, 1990: 17, 20–1). The milieux were fissured also by ethnic and racial rivalries. Thus, while radicals drawn from rival African ethnic groups jostled for influence in Benin, Congo and Ethiopia,[15] the leftist milieux of Mozambique and Angola were riven by tensions between Africans on the one side, whites, *mestiços* and Indians on the other. Regarding the latter, it is noteworthy that the shift to economic liberalization in Angola and Mozambique in the mid-1980s was accompanied by the marginalization of non-African leftists.[16] A similar trend may be under way in South Africa now. Black Africans who lose faith in socialism can fall back on Africanism; *mestiços*, Indians and whites cannot.

The third route of Marxism's transmission to Africa ran via the international communist bloc, especially the USSR, the German Democratic Republic (GDR) and Cuba. China – and Maoism – was an early contender, but fell by the wayside.[17] Obviously, Eastern bloc military aid gave its suppliers significant leverage, especially with movements or regimes (most obviously the MPLA and Ethiopia's ruling Provisional Military Administrative Council, known as the Derg) who were fighting desperate wars for survival. There is also no doubt that the Soviets reinforced Leninist orthodoxy – for example by encouraging the Ethiopian and Somali military governments to set up vanguard parties, offering political and technical education courses in the USSR and supplying teachers versed in dialectical materialism to universities and ideological schools in Africa.[18] Yet it would be wrong to suppose that Africa's Marxist movements adopted Marxist policies in order to secure Soviet arms or Cuban troops. Their Marxism usually preceded the relationship with the Eastern bloc or developed independently of it. Tension occasionally broke out between Marxist governments and the Soviets (for example when the MPLA leadership suspected Moscow's hand in a 1977 coup attempt) (Ottoway and Ottoway, 1986: 5–10, 34; Keller, 1988: 237, 268–70; Ciment, 1997:163–4). Marxist governments in Mozambique, Guinea-Bissau and Benin kept lines of communication open with the West in order to offset dependence on the Soviets, while others, like Angola, invited Western capitalists to help them develop extractive industries – much as African socialist Guinea had done.[19] Nor, contra Saul and others (Saul, 1985: 28, 138, 145–6; Ottoway and Ottoway, 1986: 80–1; Saul, 1993a: 73), can the authoritarian tendencies of African Marxist regimes be ascribed in any substantial measure to Eastern bloc influence: they were largely the home-grown product of African Leninism.

Yet, if the Soviet Union did not cause Africans to adopt Marxism, it is nevertheless the case that the USSR's economic weakness and withdrawal from the African scene beginning in the mid-1980s forced African governments to turn to the West, and that economic liberalization was part of the price they paid for International Monetary Fund (IMF) and World Bank support. The Eastern bloc did not cause Africans to be Marxist, but (at least in some cases) it made it possible for them to be.

Coup d'état versus people's war

The prominence of the military in African Marxism stirred controversy both within civilian radical milieux and amongst academic commentators. Marxism–Leninism came to power by military *coup d'état* in Congo-Brazzaville (1963), Mali (1968), Dahomey (1972), which was later renamed Benin, Somalia (1969), Ethiopia (1974), Madagascar (1975) and Upper Volta (1983), later renamed Burkina Faso. Obviously enough, Marxist military takeover was not envisaged in the Marxist classics; nor did it acquire, like guerilla war, a subsequent iconic status in Marxist revolutionary theory. Problematically, it involved armed forces delivering revolution from on high rather than the people securing it from below. Critics saw soldiers as more likely to erect militaristic and regimented political systems than to fulfil popular hopes for participatory democracy. The superficiality of the military's acquaintance with Marxism, its weak popular roots and its preoccupation with power certainly made soldiers improbable bearers of socialist deliverance (Halliday and Molyneux, 1981: 35–8; Giorgis, 1990: 54). Perhaps not surprisingly, quite a few academic observers concluded that these regimes were not really Marxist. They were thus denied recognition of their leftist authenticity in the same way that earlier African socialists had been.[20] In my own judgement these critics underestimated the Marxist–Leninist commitments of military leaders, just as many had earlier underestimated the seriousness of the radical African socialists. There are no grounds for thinking that the military regimes were more authoritarian, or less authentically Marxist, than those established by guerilla war. These regimes *were* authoritarian, acted pragmatically rather than ideologically in certain instances, were vulnerable to coups and warlordism and spent a lot on the military. But the same could be said of, for example, Angola's ruling MPLA in the 1980s. Somalia set aside ideological affinity to invade Ethiopia – but so, to use non-African examples, did China invade Vietnam and Vietnam Cambodia (products all of guerilla war).

The fact is that officers, especially in junior ranks, were often highly radicalized. Some, like Captain Thomas Sankara of Burkina Faso, were politicized in advance of the revolutionary process whereas others, like Benin's Lieutenant-Colonel Mathieu Kérékou, swung left in the course of it.[21] In Congo, Ethiopia and Madagascar, arguably also Benin, the military came to power as part of a popular movement.[22] Once in power they cooperated or competed with civilian leftists on matters ideological, generally with radicalizing effect (Covell, 1987: 6; Keller, 1988: 192, 196; Ayele, 1990: 16–17). Military leaders issued symbolically important Marxist–Leninist pronouncements, notably the Derg's Programme for the

National Democratic Revolution, Madagascar's Revolutionary Charter, Sankara's Political Orientation Speech and General Siad Barre's Blue-and-White-Book.[23] Aware that military rule violated the canons of Leninism, military governments also constructed Marxist–Leninist parties. Although in Congo and Somalia the transition from military to civilian party rule was a façade, in Benin and Madagascar it marked a genuine if incomplete process of civilianization.[24] Finally – the proof of the Leninist pudding, some might say – military governments instituted central planning, widespread nationalization and serious efforts to improve health, education and literacy.[25] Where the military–civilian government in Madagascar deviated from the Leninist script it was in order to preside over the most pluralistic Marxist regime in Africa.

The other route to power for African Marxists was guerilla warfare. Armed struggle broke out in countries where intransigent regimes – colonial and African, white and black – refused to relinquish colonies (Portugal, Morocco, South Africa), grant regional autonomy (Ethiopia, Sudan), abandon minority rule (Rhodesia, South Africa) or stem human rights violations and ethnic favouritism (Uganda). Guerilla war brought to power the MPLA in Angola (1975), PAIGC in Guinea-Bissau and Cape Verde (1975), Frelimo in Mozambique (1975), the Zimbabwe African National Union (ZANU) in Zimbabwe (1980), the South West African People's Organisation (SWAPO) in Namibia (1990) and the Eritrean People's Liberation Front (EPLF) in Eritrea (1991) and played some part in the victory of the ANC in South Africa (1994). It also enabled the Tigray People's Liberation Front (TPLF) to achieve dominance in Ethiopia at the head of a multinational Ethiopian People's Revolutionary Democratic Front (EPRDF) (1991) and the National Resistance Movement (NRM) to gain power in Uganda (1986). Of these formations only MPLA and Frelimo set up Marxist regimes; several others were definitely Marxist at some point before achieving power (PAIGC, EPLF, TPLF) or harboured Marxist tendencies (ZANU, SWAPO and the NRM); and the African National Congress (ANC) won office in the 1994 elections in alliance with the South African Communist Party, albeit with the latter by then definitely the junior partner. Originally Marxist-orientated guerilla movements are still contending for power (though currently only diplomatically) in Western Sahara (the Popular Front for the Liberation of the Saguia el Hamra and Rio de Oro, or Polisario) and southern Sudan (the Sudanese People's Liberation Movement, or SPLM). With the arguable exception of the ANC in the early 1960s, these movements opted for a variant of the sort of people's war developed by Mao Zedong, General Giap and others in Asia, rather than for the more elitist and militaristic *foco* style of warfare associated with guerilla movements in Cuba and South America (Munslow, 1986: 8–9; Young, 1997: 33). Among the features of people's war were extensive political preparation amongst the peasantry, who supplied the physical force behind armed struggle, the privileging of political leadership over military command and the establishment of 'liberated zones' in which movements could establish rear bases and build embryonic socialist orders. Frelimo and PAIGC were most successful in securing liberated zones; other groups achieved more brittle or fleeting successes.[26]

For their admirers in the 1970s and early 1980s, the movements that had engaged in people's war were definitely to be taken more seriously as Marxists than
either the reformist first wave of African socialists or the later Marxist military
regimes (Ethiopia perhaps excepted). According to some commentators, Frelimo,
MPLA and PAIGC in particular were beneficiaries of a 'logic of protracted struggle' that inculcated democratic habits and socially transformative zeal. Because
these movements depended on peasant support, they understood the value of
popular participation; and because their leaders had to fight so long and hard,
honing their politics along the way in rivalry with reformist or reactionary elements, they were likely to be theoretically more astute and committed. In contrast
to the African socialists, they were genuinely radical; in contrast to the military
Marxists, they were, at least potentially, authentically democratic. Having already
roused the population from its passivity they were moreover likely to be beneficiaries, post-revolution, of a release of popular energy.[27]

The Marxist who did most to theorize this type of warfare in an African context
was Amilcar Cabral. A product of exposure to radical politics in Lisbon, Cabral
became the founder, chief publicist and a major strategist of the PAIGC and its
long struggle to evict Portugal from Guinea-Bissau and Cape Verde. Cabral's influence derived partly from the PAIGC's military success, partly from his efforts
to unify the Lusophone liberation movements and partly from the role of Guinea-
Bissau's armed resistance in triggering the April 1974 coup against Portugal's
neo-fascist regime – a coup that in turn hastened in a successful conclusion to
the armed struggles of PAIGC, Frelimo and MPLA. Cabral never witnessed these
victories over the shared Portuguese foe: he was assassinated in 1973.

Cabral argued that the colonized could regain control of their economic desti-
nies only if they mounted a revolutionary challenge to neocolonial capitalism as
well as colonialism. The success of this challenge depended on the willingness
of the petite bourgeoisie to offer revolutionary leadership to the peasantry, committing 'class suicide' in the process. Given Portuguese colonial intransigence,
liberation also necessitated armed struggle. Instead of seeking in Guinea-Bissau
the sort of popular front established by Frelimo and MPLA, Cabral wanted from
the outset a party of struggle-tested cadres to lead an alliance of the peasantry, the
nascent proletariat and the progressive middle sectors. The peasantry were central
to Cabral's thinking. First, they were the repository of an indigenous culture that
had resisted colonization, and 'returning to the source' – going amongst the them
– was a necessary part of the Africanization of alienated urban petit bourgeois.
Second, the peasant masses could provide the foot soldiers of armed resistance,
and mobilizing them was the only way to defeat better armed colonialists. Party
cadres were obliged to be honest with the peasantry, sharing with them the results of hard-headed analyses of the state of struggle ('tell no lies, claim no easy
victories'), living amongst them and involving them in discussion. At the same
time, Cabral argued, the party should transform rural culture along progressive,
modernist lines. Properly reworked, national culture could serve as a powerful
force for liberation.[28]

How convincing are the positive claims that were made for 'protracted struggle' and 'people's war'? Viewed retrospectively, the answer must be: not very. It is not clear, for example, that the guerilla movements were less militaristic than the military Marxist regimes. It may be no coincidence that Africa's most successful anticolonial guerilla army, PAIGC's Forças Armadas Revolucionárias do Povo (FARP), provided a base for opposition to the first postcolonial government, that of Cabral's brother Luís, which it overthrew in 1980 (Dhada, 1993: 138); or that the leader then installed, Joao Vieira, was himself deposed in the course of a bloody civil war in 1999. The MPLA, for its part, assigned substantial areas of Angola to military control in the 1980s, spent an estimated 70 per cent of government revenue on its armed forces and was besieged by recurrent warlordism both in opposition and power (Somerville, 1986: 65; Ciment, 1997: 130, 160). It is also striking how little the experience of liberated zones did to entrench post-independence democratic practice or to cement a lastingly sympathetic relationship between Marxist governments and the peasants they earlier depended upon. Frelimo, for example, discarded the participatory priorities and pro-peasant orientation of its guerilla-war days to set up, post-1975, a centralized pro-industrial regime willing to employ coercion against its rural subjects. It is a moot point whether the liberated zones were anyway ideal incubators of future democratic practice. The exigencies of warfare were as likely to inculcate habits of military command as they were to cultivate democratic instincts. And finally, there is no evidence that Marxists honed by protracted struggle stuck to their socialist commitments any more tenaciously than military Marxist or even African socialist regimes when confronted by economic crises in the 1980s and the hard bargaining of international lending agencies.

Exceptional cases: South Africa and Ethiopia

Amongst Africa's actual and would-be revolutions, two have seemed exceptional. Whereas most Marxist movements in Africa contended with European colonialism or recently decolonized states and with embryonic African class structures, in South Africa and Ethiopia they confronted well-developed indigenous class systems, capitalist in the first case, feudal in the second.

Already by the turn of the twentieth century Transvaal's gold mining industry had drawn to South Africa a substantial skilled working population from Britain, Australia and elsewhere. Radicals amongst them implanted Marxism and syndicalism in sub-Saharan Africa, but in accordance with a template that had not been adapted to colonial conditions. Early socialists organized almost exclusively the white working class, which was well established and, until its historic defeat in the 1922 'Rand Revolt', frequently militant. While the South African Labour Party (formed 1910) openly aligned itself with white workers, even radicals initially assumed that whites would constitute the proletarian vanguard in a country where the African working class was still tiny, unskilled and tied to the land. In time, however, the left grew disillusioned with the racism and, after 1922, the passivity of white labour. The Communist Party of South Africa (CPSA), established in 1921, actively recruited Africans from 1924 (Bunting, 1975: 17–42; Ellis and

Sechaba, 1992: 15; Drew, 2000: 20–40 and ch. 4). Despite this, it came as a huge shock to much of the party's leadership when in 1928 the sixth Congress of the Comintern demanded that South African Communists set aside the cherished goal of proletarian revolution and devote their energies to establishing an 'independent native republic' in South Africa (Drew, 2000: 97–101). After years of internal ructions (Bunting, 1975: 61–74; Ellis and Sechaba, 1992: 19–22; Drew, 2000: 102–108), the CPSA, later renamed the South African Communist Party (SACP), aligned itself closely with the ANC. Yet South Africa's large settled white population, early independence (1910) and relatively developed economy always made it distinctive in African terms. Throughout the (post-1920s) twentieth century there were left-wing critics who insisted that the Communists had travelled too far down the nationalist road, and that South Africa, far from being a colonial realm (subject to a 'special type' of internal colonialism, according to the SACP), was a dynamic capitalist society whose expanding black proletariat was increasingly capable of making a social revoluton. But the draw of nationalism proved irresistible even to most Trotskyists and (by the mid-1980s) many union-based workerists who, like the Communists, forged alliances with nationalist movements in the hope of tapping into the legitimacy that the latter enjoyed amongst the African masses (Glaser, 1998). The SACP pursued its alliance strategy with stunning success: the party virtually took over the ANC at the end of the 1960s (Ellis and Sechaba, 1992: 10, 52–62, 150–1, 201). Ironically, it found itself marginalized just when, in the early 1990s, the ANC stood on the cusp of power – a demotion that signalled exactly the subordination of socialism to nationalism that the class-emphasizing left had long warned about.

If South Africa's colonial status was dubious, Ethiopia fitted the colonial bill not at all: with the exception of a brief period of Italian occupation, it had never been a European colony. Ethiopia was different in another way: its traditional ruling class was feudal in a fashion that bore comparison with the *ancien régime* in Europe, complete with exploitative landlords and centralized royal authority. The coup that overthrew Emperor Haile Selassie in 1974 was at first glance an elite affair, similar to other African coups that had issued in leftist military dictatorship. On the other hand, the Derg brought to a conclusion a popular urban-centred uprising and, once in power, overhauled the feudal order. These facts, coupled with the assassination of the monarch, reminded some observers of the two paradigmatic revolutions of the preceding decades and centuries: those of France in 1789 and, even more so, Russia in 1917. Halliday and Molyneux influentially insisted that this was a genuine socialist revolution, albeit a 'revolution from above' (Halliday and Molyneux, 1981: 25–31).

Revolutionary Ethiopia resembled Russia in another way: it inherited what amounted to a multinational empire and, from the outset, confronted autonomist and secessionist demands from various ethnic groups. Indeed, the national question in Ethiopia addressed itself not to a European empire but a homegrown African one. It arose from the desire of nationalities within the country to escape what they perceived to be an oppressive state dominated by one group, the Amhara. Like the Bolsheviks and subsequently the Communist Party of the Soviet Union, the new regime attempted to assuage this nationalism by speaking a Leninist language of respect for national self-determination. Unlike Russia, it was not able to fend off national demands and stabilize the state, and it collapsed more or less simultaneously with its Soviet patron largely for this reason, albeit after a much shorter life. Even so, the Ethiopian revolution's features set it apart from – or assured it a special place within – the general discussion of Marxist military rule, indeed of Marxist government, in Africa (Lefort, 1983; Munslow, 1986: 7; Ayele, 1990: 11–12).

Was there a distinctive African Marxism?

Africa's Marxist leaders and thinkers applied a single template to the continent. Though eager socialists, they acknowledged that Africa was not immediately capable of achieving full socialism, let alone communism. The initial phase of revolution was 'national democratic' and would yield what Marxist ideologues termed people's democracy or 'people's democratic dictatorship'. People's democracy would eliminate feudal vestiges and, bypassing the capitalist stage of development, lay the basis for socialism and the dictatorship of the proletariat.[29] Political leadership during this stage would fall to a vanguard party representing an alliance of workers, peasants and the progressive petit bourgeois. Workers would be the leading element in the alliance but, in the absence of a substantial proletariat, their leading role would be exercised by proxy through the party. This core class alliance might cooperate with other social elements where tactically necessary, but it would struggle against any existing or aspirant classes that blocked progress to socialism (Somerville, 1986: 99). Such was, roughly speaking, the path that all 'societies of socialist orientation' were expected to ply according to a Marxist discourse shaped over decades by Lenin's theories of imperialism and national self-determination, the experience of popular-front politics in the 1930s through to mid-1940s, and post-war Soviet theory. In this respect African Marxists had little distinctive to offer: they considered that the above represented a universal formula, albeit one that required local adjustments. It was the formula African Marxist governments were applying when they converted popular fronts or military juntas into vanguard parties, and it informed their programmes of nationalization, state-steered development and mass mobilization.

It would be wrong, though, to suggest that there was no original contribution from Africa's Marxist movements and regimes. Perhaps the most idiosyncratic was General Mohammed Siad Barre's attempt to synthesize Marxism and Islam (Samatar, 1988: 108–9; Library of Congress, 2005). The only other significant movement I know to attempt something similar is the People's Mojahedin (Mojahein-e-Khalq) in Iran. The philisophico-theological innovations of Siad Barre and the People's Mojahedin echo, though within an explicitly Marxist discourse, the earlier efforts of Algeria's Ben Bella and his successor Boumedienne to develop an 'Arabo-Islamic' socialism (Humbaraci, 1966: 90, 109, 237, 244, 249–50, 253, 269–70). Whereas these amounted to explicit syntheses, most socialist and Marxist movements operating in Muslim-majority societies felt compelled to accommodate Islam to one degree or another. Notwithstanding his confrontation with the Muslim Brotherhood, Egypt's Nasser benefited from the theological support of the *ulema*, the country's official religious leaders (Woodward, 1992: 35). And Islam remained the official religion, taught in schools, of the People's Democratic Republic of Yemen (Lackner, 1985: 109–10).

The EPLF and TPLF made an interesting addition to Marxist thinking on the national question. The EPLF insisted that nations had a right to secession even from socialist states, while the TPLF proposed that African states should recognize national differences and constitute themselves where necessary on a multinational basis. In both cases the movements were invoking Leninist norms, but these were at best inconsistently applied in the USSR and were positively frowned upon in post-independence Africa, with its insistence on ethnicity-transcending nation-building and aversion to the rearrangement of existing state boundaries. The EPLF and TPLF took these ideas very seriously, as the former showed when it brought about Eritrean secession, the latter in its governing practice at the head of Ethiopia's ruling EPRDF (Pool, 1979: 56–71; Young, 1997: 214).

On a practical level, I have already mentioned Sékou Touré's experimentation with mass-party forms; another instance of institutional innovation worth noting is that of Madagascar. There a military–civilian regime, in a formula possibly unique in the world, permitted a competitive multi-party democracy limited to socialist and Marxist parties. To qualify for admission to electoral politics, parties had to subscribe to a founding revolutionary document, the Charter of Malagasy Revolution. Although the regime established its own party, the Avant-Garde of the Malagasy Revolution (Arema), it joined its cooperative competitors in a National Front for the Defence of the Revolution (Covell, 1987: 1–2, 60–2, 119). This pluralism-within-the-left arrangement resembles the sort of politics that some libertarian leftists advocated from time to time in the last century. Malagasy Marxism was more generally eclectic; in the early 1980s, for example, it sought a philosophical rapprochement with Christianity, which in Madagascar had developed along fairly progressive lines. Malagasy Marxists never turned their pluralistic formula into a theory: indeed many were Leninists who saw their political system as a temporary and rather unsatisfactory compromise dictated by circumstances (Covell, 1987: 60–1). Even so it represented, by comparison with other more rigid African Marxisms of the time, a not wholly unattractive accident.

Decline and fall

The life of African Marxism was pretty short. Most of the Marxist regimes were set in place in the mid-1970s, and most had begun to liberalize economically by the mid-1980s. During 1990–91 almost all of them renounced Marxism and embraced liberal representative democracy (Waterhouse, 1996: 11; Hall and Young, 1997: 202–19; Hodges, 2001: 50–9, 70–102). African socialism's commencement dated back further – to the later 1950s, in fact – but it followed a similar trajectory of decline and fall in the later 1980s and early 1990s. The overwhelming consensus amongst participants and observers was that both Marxist and African socialist experiments had failed. None of the socialist economies had escaped underdevelopment; some ended the 1980s amongst the world's very poorest countries. Formerly Marxist or Marxist-influenced movements that came to power in the 1980s and 1990s – the NRM, SWAPO, EPLF, the TPLF – did not even attempt to institute socialist experiments; nor did the communist-allied ANC. Curiously, a fair number of former Marxist parties and leaders remained politically viable into the 1990s and in some cases beyond, having adapted well to the new world of electoral competition and pro-capitalist politics. At the time of writing MPLA and Frelimo remain in power in Angola and Mozambique, and PAIGC is still a contender in Guinea-Bissau. Former president Didier Ratsiraka returned to office by election in Madagascar in 1996, having reinvented himself as an ecological humanist; he was finally ousted in an uprising in 2001–2. Sankara's ideologically eclectic successor, Captain Blaise Compaoré, was re-elected in 1998. In Benin, Kérékou won elections in 1996 and 2001. Congo's Colonel Sassou-Nguesso was reelected in 2002. Of the explicitly Marxist systems (as opposed to individual leaders), only those of Mali, Somalia and Ethiopia were physically overthrown; the last two were also the most tyrannical. Meanwhile former ruling elites have flourished in a new climate of 'raw' or 'predatory' capitalism, making money in doubtful and often corrupt ways even as their societies grew increasingly un-equal.[30]

So what happened to the attempt to build socialism in Africa? And does its abandonment offer lessons for attempts in the current (unpropitious) time to advance a left-social democratic project, in Africa or elsewhere?

What makes African socialism and Afro-Marxism's failure especially difficult to diagnose is that it lay at the intersection of two larger failures: of Marxist governance globally, and of African governance irrespective of ruling ideology. For any given formerly Marxist African country it is, in other words, difficult to separate out the effects of Marxism's inadequacies and of Africa's malaise. Nevertheless it is possible to identify a range of factors that subverted what started out as a hopeful experiment.

Some of these fit the classic 'scarcity plus encirclement' scenario that sympathizers often use to explain the difficulties faced by leftist governments. Socialist governments in Africa inherited undeveloped agrarian economies in which growth had centred on a few enclaves. The colonial education system generated scandalously few skilled people, and the number of the latter were further depleted when settlers and expatriates in Guinea-Conakry, Mozambique and Angola fled after independence. The Derg inherited a long history of land degradation in the Ethiopian highlands – a factor at least contributory to the devasting famine of 1983–86 in which a million people died (Ottoway, 1990: 4; Kebbede, 1992). The MPLA and Frelimo faced extremely costly, externally backed armed insurgencies that wrecked promising social programmes. Ethiopia was invaded by (Marxist though US-backed) Somalia in 1977 and challenged from within by armed secessionists; the Somali regime and the Derg were both finally toppled by insurgents in 1991. Angola and the Horn of Africa became Cold War battlegrounds while apartheid South Africa practiced 'destabilization' successfully across much of southern Africa. Though commentators from the late 1980s began properly to underline the extent to which socialist governments brought their difficulties upon themselves

(Saul, 1993b; Kaure, 1999: 2–3), inherited underdevelopment and military pressure were enough on their own to render economic reconstruction formidably difficult under any ideological rubric.

Endogenous failings were nevertheless many. One was a radical impatience that led African socialists and Marxists to require too much too soon of states that were hampered by insufficient skilled personnel and other resources.[31] Overconfident socialist rulers did not hesitate to vest in the hands of flimsy state systems the task of centrally planning entire economies. They also overestimated the capacity of their societies to industrialize rapidly from a low base in a context of capital and skill shortages and limited economies of scale. The fallout of this over-ambition included bureaucratic paralysis, loss-making urban and rural enterprises and, in several cases, high levels of debt. Given what we know now about the necessity for some sort of market under feasible socialism, it would have been more prudent for these governments to provide space for private enterprise while developing the state's capacity to collect revenue, supply social benefits, redistribute wealth and engage in overall economic steering. And given the costs and uncertainty attending large-scale, capital-intensive projects, it would have been more sensible not to take on external debt to finance them. Rapid debt accumulation was the undoing of socialism in Benin and Madagascar (Covell, 1987: 63–8; Allen, 1989).

In keeping with their radical ambition, socialist governments overestimated the ripeness of the countryside for fast-track socialism or indeed rapid modernization. Socialist incumbents tried, understandably, to rearrange rural life to facilitate welfare provision, higher productivity, egalitarian land distribution and social cooperation – and in Ethiopia, in the mid-1980s, simply to avoid mass starvation (Kebbede, 1992: 79–84). The methods they chose to achieve these objectives were generally resented by rural populations. It is not that the peasants were pro-capitalist: they did not, for the most part, want a free market in land and opposed attempts by the TPLF and Frelimo to introduce one in the 1990s; they mostly welcomed redistribution of land from state holdings and big landowners (Ottoway and Ottoway, 1986: 139–42; Waterhouse, 1996: 23; Young, 1997: 198–9). At the same time, peasants did not usually wish to work on cooperatives or collective farms or, in Ethiopia, to be relocated to supposedly more fertile land hundreds of miles away. Faced with peasant reluctance to join such arrangements, Marxist governments, like some of their African socialist predecessors, turned to force.[32] Peasant agriculture suffered from a range of factors that were not fully under state control, from drought and war to shortages of capacity, but the use of coercion against peasants must be counted as a deliberate and reckless forfeiture of goodwill. Many peasants also resented the way urban-based leaders disparaged entrenched animist beliefs and sidelined traditional leaders, often coercively. If there is a clear message from countries like Mozambique, but also, say, Afghanistan under the Soviets, it is that urban elites need to treat the countryside and its ways with care, employing methods of consultation and persuasion wherever possible rather than force in realizing modern values. Alienation of peasants directly fuelled armed opposition in Mozambique, Angola and Ethiopia and passive non-cooperation in other cases.

It is generally striking how ready Marxist regimes were, on first coming to power, to gratuitously alienate whole swathes of the societies they intended to govern. Until the mid-1980s the governments of Mozambique and (to a lesser degree) Angola harrassed already suspicious Christian churches, guaranteeing their outright hostility (Marcum, 1987: 74; Ciment, 1997: 172, 185; Hall and Young, 1997: 85–7). Although foreign capital was courted, domestic capital seemed often to face an undifferentiating animus. The honing of vanguard parties for its part required systematic purges that isolated party elites from society (Somerville, 1986: 56–7, 90, 92–5; Radu and Somerville, 1989: 172–3; Hodges, 2001: 48). Ethnic identity was demeaned, for example by denial of indigenous language rights, while ethnic out-groups were under-represented in state bodies.[33] Eritrean demands for independence were ignored by a Derg determined to transform the Ethiopian empire into an effectively unitary state with only limited concessions to national groups (Keller, 1988: 202–3, 240; Ottoway, 1990: 607; Iyob, 1995: 118–9). Clearly, socialist governments were convinced that, in imposing modernization, history was on their side; they also felt compelled to prosecute struggles against often determined class and ideological enemies. When things went wrong, they needed scapegoats. Nor should we forget how different, and more left-sympathetic, was the temper of the 1960s and 1970s – a temper conducive to what Saul called 'cockiness' (Saul, 1993a: 72–3). But whatever the explanation, the politics seem desperately inept.

Most problematic of all was the theory and practice of democracy. Socialist movements and regimes considered popular participation necessary to the realization of democratic values and to the canalization of popular energies into development tasks. Their democratic idealism impressed not a few observers, as did the neighbourhood committees, workplace councils, peasant associations and sectoral mass organizations established in liberated zones and within the jurisdiction of the new socialist states.[34] Some observers thought that this participatory democracy more than compensated for the absence of representative democratic institutions. Yet it is clear, now, that this democracy was a sham. In the playing out of the dialectic between leadership and mass action referred to by Saul and others, a commandist concept of leadership seemed relatively quickly to win out once socialists were in power. The result was a downgrading of participatory democracy (Ottoway and Ottoway, 1986: 200–7; Saul, 1990: 55; Hall and Young, 1997: 74–6). In many cases its demotion was prompted by the fact that factional opponents of the government or military – youth-wing militants in Congo, oppositionists in Benin's Committees for the Defence of the Revolution, leftist conspirators in Luanda's *poder popular*, the EPRP in Ethiopia's neighbourhood *kebeles* – had established bases in the participatory organs. In other, less dramatic cases, participatory organs, like the *grupos dinamizadores* in Mozambique and workers' self-management bodies in Algeria, Angola and Mozambique, were sacrificed to governments' search for discipline and centralized coordination.[35]

More important, those organs were part of a misconceived model of democracy in the first place. When African socialist and Marxist regimes spoke of participation they meant mobilization of the population to realize collective ends defined by the ruling party. To be sure, this might require popular input through discussion and criticism, and such input might influence the choice between regime-vetted candidates, the technical details of policies, even the clauses of constitutions.[36] But participants were not meant to, nor could they, challenge the ruling party or its ideological direction. For the regime, participatory bodies served primarily as venues to explain already decided policies; alternatively, as mechanisms for co-opting dissent and subjecting the population to surveillance (Ciment, 1997: 145). The so-called 'mass organisations' of youth, workers, women and others were designed for their part to function as transmission belts between the regime and population.[37] With a few exceptions, no autonomous associational realm was allowed to develop outside them.[38] Nor were there other, compensating checks on the concentration of power. Elected national representative assemblies served as rubber stamps.[39] Leninist democratic centralism eviscerated internal party democracy (Saul, 1985: 78–9; Radu and Somerville, 1989: 192–3; Giorgis, 1990: 62–3). Ruling parties were anyway invariably subordinated to powerful presidencies or (in Congo and Somalia) to military cabals.[40]

A deeper democratic philosophy informed the operation of the participatory bodies. The democracy the socialist regimes put in place was teleological rather than representative. Its architects sought a state structured around the singular goal of building socialism rather than one enabling citizens to choose among diverse collective projects. If the system 'represented' anyone it was not actual but an ideal or higher people: that is, the people as they would think and act if they were free of false consciousness and able to apprehend their real interests or the real good of society. In this sense, Africa's socialist regimes made a Rousseauian distinction between the will of all and the general will, with the party embodying the latter through its scientific grasp and farsightedness. During the transition to socialism and communism, strictly speaking, the regime would represent the higher will only of the proletariat and its class allies – though they in turn served as intimations and forebears of a still-to-come classless people.

The theory and practice of democracy in African Marxist states (Madagascar apart) differed in no significant way from that operative in the generality of Marxist–Leninist regimes extant until 1989–91. It can properly be described as the Leninist approach to democracy, legitimized by the particular interpretation that the Bolsheviks and subsequently the CPSU gave to the often ambiguous work of Marx and Engels, generalized globally by the Comintern (Glaser, 1999). In the end this conception was not sustainable, because it failed to take account of irreducible social diversity, whether of values or interests; and because it left regimes open to delegitimation by enemies – Western governments, local insurgents – who could plausibly portray them as oppressive dictatorships. In the early 1990s the (ex-)socialist governments discarded the teleological democratic model in favour of a more open-ended representative one. Citizens can now, at least in principle, choose amongst competing collective projects embodied in rival programmes and parties. This is the framework, bereft of guarantees of power, in which socialist or social-democratic parties of the future will have to seek office. It means governing only with the revocable consent of actual, empirical peoples.

I said in principle: in practice African states of all stripes, depleted by decades of economic failure, have been subjected to a form of 'recolonization' (Saul 1993b) that has closely limited their real options. Much of the authority in these states now rests with the IMF and World Bank and, on the domestic stage, with international non-governmental organizations.[41] What the international lending agencies required, at least until recently, was a one-size-fits-all policy of privatization, deregulation, devaluation and spending cuts that imposed great social hardship, sharpened inequality and unleashed venality.[42] Although the turn to representative democracy (at least where it is not rigged or a facade) gives citizens the right to scrutinize leaders and evict tyrants, crooks and incompetents – rights not to be belittled – it will take a reordering of international relationships to bring about a situation in which they have real ideological choices. What is clear is that the new capitalism is not the elixir its champions expected it to be. The task for socialists and social democrats is to navigate a path that avoids the pitfalls of neoliberalism in its various versions but also fully takes on board the many negative lessons of Africa's experience with socialism and Marxism. It falls to them to find, this time within the framework of formal democracy, new ways to limit social inequality, deepen democracy and generate sustainable economic growth. In their search they may yet need to consult Marxism, if not to devise a new political order, then at least to provide a clear-sighted analysis of the new pattern of class inequality that has formed on the ruins of discarded socialisms.

Notes

1 Nkrumah, 1973: 77, 79, 82; Adamolekun, 1976: 35; Ottoway and Ottoway, 1986: 1, 25–30; Keller, 1987: 3, 7–8, 11; Clapham, 1988: 66; Radu and Somerville, 1989: 173, 187; Hall and Young, 1997: 61.
2 Nkrumah, 1963: 129; 1964a: 79, 89–90, 103; 1973: 83; Cox, 1966: 83; Rivière, 1977: 86–7; Munslow, 1986: 27; Ottoway and Ottoway, 1986: 18–24; Keller, 1987: 1.
3 Nelkin, 1964: 63–72; Padmore, 1964: 227, 230; Cohen, 1986: 42–3.
4 Friedland and Rosberg, 1964: 4–9; Nyerere, 1964: 239–43, 246; Nkrumah, 1963: 107; 1964a: 78–9, 106; 1964b: 263; Senghor, 1964: 264–6; Ottoway and Ottoway, 1986: 13–17.
5 Nkrumah, 1963: 110, 119; 1964b: 260–2; Senghor, 1964: 264; Ottoway and Ottoway, 1986: 59–65.
6 Nyerere, 1964: 242; Dia, 1964: 249; Nkrumah, 1963: 124, 130; 1964b: 263.
7 Nkrumah, 1964a: 78–9, 95, 98, 106; Nyerere, 1964: 246–7; Dia, 1964: 248; Ottoway and Ottoway, 1986: 16–17.
8 Ottoway, 1978; Halliday and Molyneux, 1981: 273–83; Ottoway and Ottoway, 1986: 32–3; Somerville, 1986: 194–5; Turok, 1986: 65.
9 Marcum, 1969: 17–18, 37–41, 69–70; De Andrade, 1979: xx–xxvi; Ottoway and Ottoway, 1986: 31–2, 53–4; Somerville, 1986: 23–4, 187; Keller, 1987: 1; 1988: 176–7; Radu and Somerville, 1989: 160; Iyob, 1995: 99; Ciment, 1997: 11, 163, 175–6; Drew, 2000: 20–40.
10 Marcum, 1969: 37–41; De Andrade, 1979: xxiii; Marcum, 1987: 69; Ottoway and Ottoway, 1986: 69; Lewis, 1987; Clapham, 1988: 65; Keller, 1988: 176–7; Baxter and Somerville, 1989: 247; Radu and Somerville, 1989: 160; Allen, 1989: 62; Ciment, 1997: 11, 123, 128; Hall and Young, 1997: 83–4; Kaure, 1999: 29.

11 De Andrade, 1979: xxiii–xxiv; Ottoway and Ottoway, 1986: 101; Ciment, 1997: 38; Hall and Young, 1997: 64–6, 73–4; Drew, 2000: 24.
12 Ottoway and Ottoway, 1986: 134–7, 201; Somerville, 1986: 48–53; Covell, 1987: 124–7; Clapham, 1988: 66–8; Allen, 1989: 33–3, 47; Radu and Somerville, 1989: 172; Ayele, 1990: 19–21; Young, 1997: 106–12.
13 Somerville, 1986: 102; Marcum, 1987: 75; Ciment, 1997: 126–7, 140–1, 143; Hall and Young, 1997: 83.
14 Davidson, 1981: 73–4; Samatar, 1988: 107–8; Allen, 1989: 65–6; Saul, 1993a: 61, 64–5; Waterhouse, 1996: 56–7; Hall and Young, 1997: 83–7; Ciment, 1997: 63, 66, 160–1, 168–9, 172; Kaure, 1999: 24–5, 30–1.
15 Keller, 1988: 239; Radu and Somerville, 1989: 170–1; Iyob, 1995: 132; Young, 1997: 87, 98, 100–117, 171.
16 Marcum, 1987: 75; Hanlon, 1990: 208; Hall and Young, 1997: 199; Hodges, 2001: 47.
17 De Andrade, 1979: xxix; Munslow, 1986: 8–9; Ottoway and Ottoway, 1986: 34; Keller, 1988: 195; Radu and Somerville, 1989: 172; Ciment, 1997: 42; Hall and Young, 1997: 62–3; Young, 1997: 33, 77, 80, 84.
18 Saul, 1985: 28, 138, 145–6; Ottoway and Ottoway, 1986: 6–10, 34, 80–1, 154–5; Somerville, 1986: 26; Clapham, 1988: 67–8, 84; Keller, 1988: 266–7; Samatar, 1988: 111; Saul, 1993a: 73; Ciment, 1997: 11, 128, 162; Hall and Young, 1997: 62–3.
19 Adamolekun, 1976: 13; Ottoway and Ottoway, 1986: 52–9, 118–19; Marcum, 1987: 78; Allen, 1989: 116, 129; Hanlon, 1990: 234–6, 178–9; Davidson, 1992: 305; Ciment, 1997: 168; Kaure, 1999: 37–8.
20 Covell, 1987: 4–5, 158, 162; Clapham, 1988: 81; Keller, 1988: 191; Harbeson, 1990.
21 Allen, 1989: 31–2, 62; Baxter and Somerville, 1989: 248; Radu and Somerville, 1989: 173; Ayele, 1990: 15.
22 Halliday and Molyneux, 1981: 11–50; Ottoway and Ottoway, 1986: 128; Covell, 1987: 1–2, 161; Keller, 1988: 173; Allen, 1989: 31–2; Radu and Somerville, 1989: 164–5; Ayele, 1990: 15.
23 Covell, 1987: 97–100, 158; Clapham, 1988: 66; Keller, 1988: 197–8; Allen, 1989: 50–1; Baxter and Somerville, 1989: 249; Library of Congress Country Studies, 2005.
24 Covell, 1987: 115–19; Clapham, 1988: 96; Samatar, 1988: 110–13, 152–3; Allen, 1989: 70–1, 121; Radu and Somerville, 1989: 174–8, 200.
25 Ottoway and Ottoway, 1986: 151–2; Covell, 1987: 100; Keller, 1988: 219–23; Samatar, 1988: 87–9, 98, 100–104; Allen, 1989: 37; Baxter and Somerville, 1989: 250; Radu and Somerville, 1989: 189–90, 229.
26 Chaliand, 1980: 51; Houtart, 1980: 99–107; Ottoway and Ottoway, 1986: 71–2; Dhada, 1993: 136–7.
27 Machel, 1980: 199; Davidson, 1981: 97–9; 1992: 296–308; Saul, 1985: 9–10; Munslow, 1986: 8–11.
28 Cabral, 1969: 71–2, 83–93; 1973: 59–64, 67–9; 1979: 44–6, 57–60, 85, 94–7, 143–53; Davidson, 1979: xi; Cohen, 1986: 50.
29 Ottoway and Ottoway, 1986: 77–8; Somerville, 1986: 54, 82–3, 98; Clapham, 1988: 66; Keller, 1988: 197–8; Radu and Somerville, 1989: 190; Iyob, 1995: 127–9; Young, 1997: 80–4, 99–100.
30 Saul, 1993a: 75–6; Waterhouse, 1996: 19, 31, 42–3; Ciment, 1997: 182–3; Hall and Young, 1997: 227–9; Hodges, 2001: 5, 34, 39–40, 115–22, 169–71.
31 Somerville, 1986: 108; Keller, 1988: 214–15, 263; Ottoway, 1990: 3; Hall and Young, 1997: 80–2; Hodges, 2001: 46.
32 Keller, 1988: 225–7; Giorgis, 1990: 64–6; Kebbede, 1992: 6, 79–84, 90; Waterhouse, 1996: 30–1; Ciment, 1997: 63; Young, 1997: 29, 145, 169–70.
33 Somerville, 1986: 102; Marcum, 1987: 75; Keller, 1988: 239; Hall and Young, 1997: 212.

34 Houtart, 1980: 106; Saul, 1985: 80–1; Ottoway and Ottoway, 1986: 56, 71–2, 82, 104; Somerville, 1986: 115–22; Covell, 1987: 54, 57, 61–2, 94–5, 111–13; Keller, 1988: 196, 232–5; Allen, 1989: 35–7, 54; Baxter and Somerville, 1989: 249, 255; Radu and Somerville, 1989: 165; Iyob, 1995: 130; Waterhouse, 1996: 61; Young, 1997: 104.

35 Ottoway and Ottoway, 1986: 60–1, 75, 81–2, 86–92, 108–9, 113–20, 149–51, 227–8; Somerville, 1986: 115–22; Keller, 1988: 232–4; Allen, 1989: 38–9, 53; Radu and Somerville, 1989: 165–8; Ciment, 1997: 66–7; Hall and Young, 1997: 74–6.

36 Saul, 1985: 92–3; Keller, 1988: 239; Allen, 1989: 42; Hanlon, 1990: 204; Waterhouse, 1996: 23.

37 Saul, 1985: 81–2, 96–7; Somerville, 1986: 115–22; Keller, 1988: 218–19; Samatar, 1988: 112–13; Allen, 1989: 54, 68–9; Radu and Somerville, 1989: 166

38 Marcum, 1987: 72–3; Allen, 1989: 71–3, 122; Waterhouse, 1996: 9, 61; Ciment, 1997: 127.

39 Ottoway and Ottoway, 1986: 83; Clapham, 1988: 94–5; Allen, 1989: 46–7; Dhada, 1993: 136–8; Ciment, 1997: 177; Hall and Young, 1997: 71–2, 77–8.

40 Somerville, 1986: 92; Covell, 1987: 101; Clapham, 1988: 79–81; Keller, 1988: 240; Samatar, 1988: 110–13, 152–3; Allen, 1989: 51–2; Giorgis, 1990: 55–67; Hall and Young, 1997: 70–3, 77; Hodges, 2001: 48–51.

41 Waterhouse, 1996: 11, 34, 42–3, 54, 61; Ciment, 1997: 169; Hall and Young, 1997: 196–9, 225–6; Young, 1997: 201–13; Hodges, 2001: 77–82, 103–8.

42 Saul, 1993a: 75–7; Waterhouse, 1996: 19, 31, 42–3; Ciment, 1997: 130–1, 169–70, 182–3; Hall and Young, 1997: 201, 227–9; Hodges, 2001: 36–7, 40–1.

References

Adamolekun, L. (1976) *Sékou Touré's Guinea: An Experiment in Nation Building*. London: Methuen.

Allen, C. (1989) 'Benin' in C. Allen, M.S. Radu, K. Somerville and J. Baxter, *Benin, The Congo, Burkina Faso: Economics, Politics and Society*. London: Pinter Publishers.

Ayele, N. (1990) 'The Ethiopian Revolution: Political Aspects of the Transition from PMAC to PDRE' in M. Ottoway (ed.), *The Political Economy of Ethiopia*. New York: Praeger.

Baxter, J. and K. Somerville (1989) 'Burkina Faso' in C. Allen, M.S. Radu, K. Somerville and J. Baxter, *Benin, The Congo, Burkina Faso: Economics, Politics and Society*. London: Pinter Publishers.

Bozzoli, B. and P. Delius (1990) 'Radical History and South African Society', *Radical History Review*, 46 (7): 13–45.

Bunting, B. (1975) *Moses Kotane: South African Revolutionary*. London: Inkululeko Publications.

Cabral, A. (1969) *Revolution in Guinea: Selected Texts by Amilcar Cabral*. Redhill, Surrey: Love and Malcolmson.

Cabral, A. (1973) *Return to the Source: Selected Speeches by Amilcar Cabral*. New York: Monthly Review Press.

Cabral, A. (1979) *Unity and Struggle: Speeches and Writings*. New York: Monthly Review Press.

Chaliand, G. (1980) 'The Guerilla Struggle' in B. Davidson, L. Cliffe and B.H. Selassie (eds), *Behind the War in Eritrea*. Nottingham: Spokesman.

Ciment, J. (1997) *Angola and Mozambique: Postcolonial Wars in Southern Africa*. New York: Facts on File.

Clapham, C. (1988) *Transformation and Continuity in Revolutionary Ethiopia*. Cambridge: Cambridge University Press.

Cohen, R. (1986) 'Marxism in Africa: The Grounding of a Tradition' in B. Munslow (ed.), *Africa: Problems in the Transition to Socialism*. London: Zed Books.

Covell, M. (1987) *Madagascar: Politics, Economics and Society*. London: Frances Pinter.

Cox, I. (1966) *Socialist Ideas in Africa*. London: Lawrence and Wishart.

Davidson, B. (1979) 'Introduction' in A. Cabral, *Unity and Struggle: Speeches and Writings*. New York: Monthly Review Press.

Davidson, B. (1981) [1969] *No Fist is Big Enough to Hide the Sky: The Liberation of Guinea and Cape Verde*. London: Zed Press.

Davidson, B. (1992) *The Black Man's Burden: Africa and the Curse of the Nation-State*. London: James Currey.

De Andrade, M. (1979) 'Biographical Notes' in A. Cabral, *Unity and Struggle: Speeches and Writings*. New York: Monthly Review Press.

Dhada, M. (1993) *Warriors at Work: How Guinea Was Really Set Free*. Niwot, CO: University Press of Colorado.

Dia, M. (1964) 'African Socialism' in W.H. Friedland and C.G. Rosberg (eds), *African Socialism*. Stanford, CA: Stanford University Press.

Drew, A. (2000) *Discordant Comrades: Identities and Loyalties on the South African Left*. Aldershot: Ashgate.

Ellis, S. and T. Sechaba (1992) *Comrades against Apartheid: The ANC and the South African Communist Party in Exile*. London: James Currey.

Fanon, F. (1967) *The Wretched of the Earth*. Harmondsworth: Penguin.

Friedland, W.H. and C.G. Rosberg (1964) 'The Anatomy of African Socialism' in W.H. Friedland and C.G. Rosberg (eds), *African Socialism*. Stanford, CA: Stanford University Press.

Giorgis, D.W. (1990) 'The Power of Decision-making in Post-Revolutionary Ethiopia' in M. Ottoway (ed.), *The Political Economy of Ethiopia*. New York: Praeger.

Glaser, D. (1998) 'Changing Discourses of Democracy and Socialism in South Africa' in D. Howarth and A.J. Norval (eds), *South Africa in Transition*. Basingstoke: Macmillan.

Glaser, D. (1999) 'Marxism and Democracy' in A. Gamble, D. Marsh and T. Tant (eds), *Marxism and Social Science*. Basingstoke: Macmillan.

Glaser, D. (2001) *Politics and Society in South Africa*. London: Sage.

Hall, M. and T. Young (1997) *Confronting Leviathan: Mozambique since Independence*. London: Hurst and Company.

Halliday, F. and M. Molyneux (1981) *The Ethiopian Revolution*. London: New Left Books.

Hanlon, J. (1990) [1984] *Mozambique: The Revolution under Fire*. London: Zed Books.

Harbeson, J.W. (1990) 'State and Social Transformation in Modern Ethiopia' in M. Ottoway (ed.), *The Political Economy of Ethiopia*. New York: Praeger.

Hodges, T. (2001) *Angola: From Afro-Stalinism to Petro-Diamond Capitalism*. Oxford: The Fridtjof Nansen Institute and the International African Institute, with James Currey.

Houtart, F. (1980) 'The Social Revoluion in Eritrea' in B. Davidson, L. Cliffe and B.H. Selassie (eds), *Behind the War in Eritrea*. Nottingham: Spokesman.

Humbaraci, A. (1966) *Algeria: A Revolution that Failed: A Political History since 1954*. London: Pall Mall Press.

Iyob, R. (1995) *The Eritrean Struggle for Independence: Domination, Resistance, Nationalism, 1941–1993*. Cambridge: Cambridge University Press.

Kaure, A.T. (1999) *Angola: From Socialism to Liberal Reforms*. Harare: Sapes Books.

Kebbede, G. (1992) *The State and Development in Ethiopia*. Atlantic Highlands, NJ: Humanities Press.

Keller, E.J. (1987) 'Afro-Marxist Regimes' in E.J. Keller and D. Rothchild (eds), *Afro-Marxist Regimes: Ideology and Public Policy*. Boulder, CO: Lynne Rienner Publishers.

Keller, E.J. (1988) *Revolutionary Ethiopia: From Empire to People's Republic*. Bloomington, IN: Indiana University Press.

Lackner, H. (1985) *P.D.R. Yemen: Outpost of Socialist Development in Arabia*. London: Ithaca Press.

Lefort, R. (1983) *Ethiopia: A Heretical Revolution?* London: Zed Press.

Lewis, G. (1987) *Between the Wire and the Wall: A History of South African 'Coloured' Politics*. Cape Town: David Philip.

Library of Congress (2005) *Somalia*, Country Studies, available at: www.country-studies.com/somalia/.

Liebman, M. (1975) *Leninism under Lenin*. London: Merlin Press.

Machel, S. (1980) 'His Struggle was the People's Struggle' in B. Turok (ed.), *Revolutionary Thought in the Twentieth Century*. London: Zed Press.

McHenry, D.E. (1994) *Limited Choices: The Political Struggle for Socialism in Tanzania*. Boulder, CO: Lynne Rienner Publishers.

Marcum, J. (1969) *The Angolan Revolution*, volume 1: *The Anatonomy of an Explosion (1950–1962)*. Cambridge, MA: MIT Press.

Marcum, J. (1987) 'The People's Republic of Angola: A Radical Vison Frustrated' in E.J. Keller and D. Rothchild (eds), *Afro-Marxist Regimes: Ideology and Public Policy*. Boulder, CO: Lynne Rienner Publishers.

Marx, K. (1881) *First Draft of Letter to Vera Zasulich*, available at: www.marxists.org/archive/marx/works/.

Munslow, B. (1986) 'Introduction' in B. Munslow (ed.), *Africa: Problems in the Transition to Socialism*. London: Zed Books.

Nelkin, D. (1964) 'Socialist Sources of Pan-African Ideology' in W.H. Friedland and C.G. Rosberg (eds), *African Socialism*. Stanford, CA: Stanford University Press.

Nkrumah, K. (1963) *Africa Must Unite*. London: Panaf.

Nkrumah, K. (1964a) *Consciencism: Philosophy an Ideology for Decolonization*. London: Panaf.

Nkrumah, K. (1964b) 'Some Aspects of Socialism in Africa' in W.H. Friedland and C.G. Rosberg (eds), *African Socialism*. Stanford, CA: Stanford University Press.

Nkrumah, K. (1973) *The Struggle Continues*. London: Panaf.

Nyerere, J. K. 1964, 'Ujamaa: The Basis of African Socialism' in W.H. Friedland and C.G. Rosberg (eds), *African Socialism*. Stanford, CA: Stanford University Press.

Ottoway, M. (1978) 'Soviet Marxism and African Socialism', *Journal of Southern African Studies*, 16 (3): 477–85.

Ottoway, M. (1990) 'Introduction: The Crisis of the Ethiopian State and Economy' in M. Ottoway (ed.), *The Political Economy of Ethiopia*. New York: Praeger.

Ottoway, M. and D. Ottoway (1986) *Afrocommunism*, second edition. New York: Africana.

Padmore, G. (1964) 'A Guide to Pan-African Socialism' in W.H. Friedland and C.G. Rosberg (eds), *African Socialism*. Stanford, CA: Stanford University Press.

Pool, D. (1979) *Eritrea – Africa's Longest War*. Anti-Slavery Human Rights Series, Report No. 3.

Radu, M.S. and K. Somerville (1989) 'The Congo' in C. Allen, M.S. Radu, K. Somerville and J. Baxter, *Benin, The Congo, Burkina Faso: Economics, Politics and Society*. London: Pinter Publishers.

Riviére, C. (1977) *Guinea: The Mobilization of a People*. Ithaca, NY: Cornell University Press.

Samatar, A.I. (1988) *Socialist Somalia: Rhetoric and Reality*. London: Zed Books.

Saul, J. (ed.) (1985) *A Difficult Road: The Transition to Socialism in Mozambique*. New York: Monthly Review Press.

Saul, J. (1990) *Socialist Ideology and the Struggle for Southern Africa*. Trenton, NJ: Africa World Press.

Saul, J. (1993a) 'The Frelimo State: From Revolution to Recolonization' in J. Saul (ed.), *Recolonization and Resistance in Southern Africa in the 1990s*. Trenton, NJ: Africa World Press.

Saul, J. (1993b) 'Introduction' in J. Saul (ed.), *Recolonization and Resistance in Southern Africa in the 1990s*. Trenton, NJ: Africa World Press.

Senghor, L. (1964) 'African-Style Socialism' in W.H. Friedland and C.G. Rosberg (eds), *African Socialism*. Stanford, CA: Stanford University Press.

Somerville, K. (1986) *Angola: Politics, Economics and Society*. Boulder, CO: Lynne Rienner Publishers.

Turok, B. (1986) 'The Left in Africa Today' in B. Munslow (ed.), *Africa: Problems in the Transition to Socialism*. London: Zed Books.

Waterhouse, R. (1996) *Mozambique: Rising from the Ashes*. Oxford: Oxfam.

Woodward, P. (1992) *Nasser*. London: Longman.

Young, J. (1997) *Peasant Revolution in Ethiopia: The Tigray People's Liberation Front*. Cambridge: Cambridge University Press.

8 Applying Marxism to Asian conditions

Mao Zedong, Ho Chi Minh and the 'universality' of Marxism

Nick Knight

Marxists in Asia confronted numerous theoretical and practical difficulties applying Marxism to the problems of revolution and socialist construction in the varied social contexts of Asia. These social contexts were so different from the European context analysed by Marx in the mid- to late nineteenth century that it would appear, at first glance, that Marx's ideas could have had little relevance to aspiring revolutionaries in Asia during the first half of the twentieth century. Yet it is one of the great ironies in the history of the Marxist tradition that Marxism has had a greater political impact in Asia than any other region of the globe, including Europe itself. In parts of Asia as diverse as Russia, China, North Korea, Vietnam, Cambodia and Laos, political parties claiming an ideological allegiance to Marxism have formed governments after successful revolutions or wars of national liberation. In other parts of Asia – Indonesia, Malaysia, Japan, India, the Philippines – Marxist parties and movements have had a very significant impact on the political and intellectual history of their countries, but without being able to form national government. Marxism's impact in Asia has been profound. It is therefore quite impossible to understand the history of the region without an understanding of how the ideas of a German intellectual who lived entirely in the nineteenth century could have attracted and mobilized countless millions of people in Asia. But to understand this connection – between the ideas of Marx and the thought and policies of Marxists in Asia – is no easy matter. To do so requires a consideration of how Marxists in Asia were able to extract apparently relevant forms of social analysis and revolutionary strategies from Marx's voluminous and not always consistent writings. It requires too an appreciation that, for many Marxists in Asia, the ideas of Marx contained a kernel of truth that had universal relevance, and which transcended the historical period and social context in which Marx himself lived and which he studied. What might this universal element of Marx's thought be, and how did influential Marxists in Asia, such as China's Mao Zedong and Vietnam's Ho Chi Minh, employ it to advance revolution and socialist construction in their own countries?

Marx and Europe, Marxism in Asia

Karl Marx (1818–83) was in many respects a quintessentially European intellectual, one profoundly influenced not only by the European historical context in which he lived but also by the intellectual and philosophical tradition of Europe going back to the ancient Greeks. Marx believed, despite some occasional ambivalence (Avineri, 1968: 151–2), that his critique of earlier European thinkers, such as Georg Hegel, Adam Smith and David Ricardo, and his analysis of contemporary capitalism had created a theory of history and social change that had universal relevance (Marx, 1971: 20–2). In other words, his theory had revealed the laws of historical development, not just of European societies, but of all societies, regardless of their specific historical characteristics.

In what sense can Marx's theory of history be regarded as universal, and therefore of relevance to revolutionaries in places as diverse as China, Vietnam and Indonesia? The answer lies in his historical method, and in his critique of capitalism. Marx's historical method, the 'materialist conception of history', stressed the primacy of production in shaping society. Production, for Marx, included not only the technology of production (the instruments of labour) but the relationship between classes and the struggle between them. This materialist perspective could equally be applied to the rest of the world as to Europe. Similarly, his critique of capitalism had worldwide implications given the global dominance of the capitalist system. His conception of a socialist future was premised on the widespread development of capitalist industrialization, which would pave the way for the eventual overthrow of capitalism as class tensions – between capitalist and worker – grew in response to the exploitation of the working class. Marx's theory of history thus provided a credible theory of revolution, premised as it was on the international potential of capitalism as an economic system and the universal phenomenon of class struggle, which emerged under capitalism in its most extreme form.

It was precisely these ideas – industrialization, class struggle, socialism – that revolutionaries in Asia found so attractive in Marxism. What was required, however, was a development of Marx's theory in order to make it relevant to Asia, much of which was, by the beginning of the twentieth century, still largely feudal, with very little modern industry. Much of Asia was also either under direct European colonial rule (Vietnam, Cambodia, Laos, Indonesia, the Philippines, Malaya, India, Burma) or suffering the interference of the colonial powers (China and Thailand). Lenin, the Marxist leader of the Russian Revolution of 1917, provided just the theoretical development that Marxism required to make it relevant to Asian revolutionaries. Lenin articulated a theory of imperialism that gave to anti-colonial revolutions an important role in the world revolution. Lenin believed that capitalism in Europe had reached the stage at which, in order to keep expanding, it required access to new sources of cheap labour and raw materials, and new sites for investment and markets. These could be provided only through the acquisition of colonies by the European nations. The scramble for colonies in the latter half of the nineteenth century was part of this process of capitalist expansion. Lenin believed that the expansion and economic success of European imperialism were important reasons why the industrial working class in Europe had not risen in revolution, as Marx had suggested it would. By using the profits extracted from the colonies, European capitalism had been able to 'buy off' its working class, to improve its living standards and thus defuse its potential for socialist revolution (Lenin, 1969; Knight, 1985).

According to Lenin, if imperialism was an international economic system, any revolutionary uprising in the colonies that weakened it by reducing or eliminating the flow of profits from the colonies to Europe, and thus increased the possibility of revolution there, was part of the international anti-imperialist struggle. It was the task of Marxist–Leninist revolutionaries in the colonies to channel nationalist revolutions in a socialist direction and, where possible, to gain leadership of them (Lenin, 1967; Carrèrre d'Encausse and Schram, 1969: 149–86; Pantsov, 2000).

It was this strong anti-imperialist theme in Lenin's writings that so attracted revolutionaries like Ho Chi Minh and Mao Zedong, for Lenin's ideas sanctioned not only social revolution, but national revolution as well. This fusion of nationalism and social revolution made Marxism relevant to colonial or semicolonial contexts, as different as these were from the industrialized European context that Marx had analysed in the mid-nineteenth century. Far from being parochial and localized nationalist struggles, anticolonial revolutions could now, on the basis of Lenin's analysis, be perceived as part of a world revolution. This sense of being part of an international movement against imperialism was one which many radical nationalist leaders in the colonies found ideologically satisfying, and it increased their identification with Marxism (Lenin, 1969; Knight, 1985).

The ideas of Marx and Lenin that appealed to revolutionaries in Asia were thus built on analysis and critique of European capitalism and the international system of European imperialism. Ironically, Marx's extensive writings on the 'Asiatic mode of production' and its position in the development of world history have been largely ignored by Asian Marxists (Marx, 1964). There are two reasons for this. First, Marx's analysis appeared to depict 'Asiatic' societies as stagnating, and lacking any internal mechanism for change. This in turn suggested an external force, such as European imperialism, would be required to dislodge 'Asiatic' societies from their historical rut and bring them into the mainstream of world history. Imperialism, from this perspective, could be seen as playing a positive role in Asian societies, but this was not a perspective welcomed by Asian revolutionaries who resented the oppressive and exploitative behaviour of the imperialist powers. Second, Stalin made the decision, following his rise to power in the Soviet Union in the late 1920s, that the 'Asiatic mode of production' had no place in the historical schema of orthodox Marxism. He asserted that the European historical experience represented the pattern of world historical development, and anticipated its future (Sawer, 1977; Dunn, 1982). To avoid losing the recognition and support of the Soviet Union, Marxist political parties in Asia were consequently obliged to reject or ignore Marx's writings on Asia. Moreover, Marxists in Asia aspired to be part of the mainstream of world history, to share the experiences and benefits of industrialization and modernization, and to participate in a future of socialism and communism. They thus willingly forsook the temptation to regard Asian societies as unique, as having an historical logic substantially different from the pattern of European history. Consequently, they accepted that the laws of history and social change formulated by Marx on the basis of his analysis of European history were relevant to Asia, and began to grapple with the theoretical and practical problems of using these laws to gain an understanding of their own societies.

One of the most successful in this project was the leader of the Chinese revolution, Mao Zedong, who not only successfully led the Chinese revolution to victory in 1949, but then attempted, with less apparent success, the Herculean task of constructing socialism in China. His interpretation of Marxism and his revolutionary strategy have, at one time or another, been widely emulated by Marxist revolutionaries in Asia, in countries such as Nepal, Vietnam, the Philippines, Cambodia, India and Indonesia (Dirlik *et al.*, 1997). Mao's Marxism, often referred to as Mao Zedong Thought, thus represents a very significant strand of Marxism in Asia, for he adapted Marxism to the concrete conditions of a largely feudal Asian country experiencing imperialist oppression, conditions widely shared throughout Asia during much of the twentieth century.

Mao Zedong and the Sinification of Marxism

> A communist is a Marxist internationalist, but Marxism must take on a national form before it can be applied. There is no such thing as abstract Marxism, but only concrete Marxism. What we call Marxism is Marxism that has taken on a national form, that is Marxism applied to the concrete struggle in the concrete conditions prevailing in China, and not Marxism abstractly used. If a Chinese communist, who is a part of the great Chinese people, bound to his people by his very flesh and blood, talks of Marxism apart from Chinese peculiarities, this Marxism is merely an empty abstraction. Consequently, the Sinification of Marxism – that is to say, making certain that in all of its manifestations it is imbued with Chinese peculiarities – becomes a problem that must be understood and solved by the whole party without delay.
>
> (Mao in Schram, 1969: 172)

This passage, written in 1938, sums up much of Mao's view of Marxism. He stressed the need to understand Chinese conditions, while at the same time insisting on the importance of Marxism as a theoretical guide to action. This insistence on comprehending China's 'actual situation', including its class structure and level of class struggle, led Mao to recognize the revolutionary potential of China's huge peasant population and to formulate a strategy for revolution appropriate to China's rural conditions. Rather than bemoaning the low level of China's capitalist industrialization and the consequent lack of a working-class base for his revolution, Mao actively organized among the peasants. He recruited them into the Red Army, formed in 1927, and developed an astute approach to guerrilla warfare that recognized the strategic superiority of his enemy while exploiting its weaknesses tactically. The peasants and the feudal rural conditions within which they lived thus became central to Mao's ultimately highly successful revolutionary model.

But in what sense can such an approach to revolution be considered Marxist? After all, the conventional interpretation of Marx's writings suggests a rather dismissive attitude towards the peasantry and the 'idiocy of rural life' (Marx, 1973: 71), and an insistence that the industrial proletariat, situated in the cities and large towns, would both lead and prosecute a socialist revolution. One can discern, in Mao's response to this dilemma, the way in which he understood the concept of the Sinification of Marxism.

First, Mao derived from Marx the idea that societies are divided into classes, and that the economic inequality between them generates struggle and thus change and development. This concept – of class and class struggle – became central to Mao's thought, and he regarded it as one of the universal historical laws of Marxism. After all, if all societies are made up of classes, it follows that class analysis is fundamental to the way in which a Marxist revolutionary understands his or her society. However, class analysis was, for Mao, a methodology; it was a way of discovering the structure of economic inequality within Chinese society, and the extent to which inequality generated a potential to political action, whether revolutionary or not. Class analysis did not signify, as it did to some of his comrades, a particular conception of class structure within China, one that conformed to Marx's analysis of European capitalist societies in which the working class was becoming the largest and most revolutionary class. Mao believed that, if a class analysis of Chinese society revealed both the overwhelming size and revolutionary potential of the peasantry, a Marxist had no option but to act on that information and devise strategies that could exploit the peasants' capacity for revolution.

Second, and related to the previous point, while Mao recognized the importance of the peasantry to China's revolution, he never retreated from the belief that the peasants required working-class leadership. Some commentators have viewed Mao's reliance on the peasants as evidence that he was little more than a peasant revolutionary, and consequently a very unorthodox Marxist if one at all.[1] However, these views totally ignore Mao's constant reference, from 1927 to 1934, to the importance of providing the peasants with working-class leadership (Knight, 1997–98), and he was under no illusion that the peasants, left to their own devices, were capable of conceiving and fighting for the modernizing and socialist goals of the Chinese revolution. The political demands of the peasants were limited, Mao thought, to 'honest officials and a good emperor' (Schram, 1994: 171). Moreover, the peasants lacked the organizational skills of the working class, and Mao frequently complained that the problems of the Party and the Red Army were a result of the large numbers of peasants recruited, through force of necessity, into those institutions. Thus, despite its small numbers, the working class retained a pivotal role in Mao's conception of the Chinese revolution, and it is evident that his confidence in the working class derived from Marxism. Mao believed this to be an aspect of the universal dimension of Marxism. No matter what alliance of classes was mobilized in a revolution with modernizing and socialist objectives, that alliance had to be led by the working class.

Third, Mao derived from Marxism a vision of the future that had a powerful impact on his thought and policies. The prediction that all societies will move through the same historical stages towards communism, and that political action can facilitate and accelerate this process, provided Mao with a profound sense of certainty in the direction in which he was taking the revolution and, after 1949, socialist construction in China. However, once again, Mao applied Marx's theory of history in the attempt to understand China's particular stage of historical development. Thus, whereas Marxism supplied a vision of the direction of change, what was required to move China in that direction was strategies and tactics founded on an intimate knowledge of China's own specific characteristics. In particular, Mao recognized that capitalism was quite undeveloped in China, and that it therefore made no sense to speak, in the 1930s, of a socialist revolution. Rather, China was undergoing a 'bourgeois-democratic revolution', the leadership of which had passed, in 1921, from the bourgeoisie to the proletariat and its vanguard party, the Chinese Communist Party. During this era of 'New Democracy', the objectives of the revolution were anti-feudal and anti-imperialist, and the proletariat thus had to seek class alliances with other revolutionary or potentially revolutionary classes, particularly the peasantry, but also the petite bourgeoisie and the bourgeoisie. However, the proletariat could not lose sight of the fact that the victory of the New Democratic revolution would allow China to proceed to the socialist revolution, during which the class allies in the current phase of revolution could well become the target of class struggle (Knight, 1991).

Fourth, while Mao accepted and endorsed the internationalism of Marxism, he was also quite overtly a Chinese nationalist. He reconciled the contradiction between these apparently conflicting themes by invoking Lenin's insistence that anti-imperialist revolutions were part of the world revolution that would see the ultimate destruction of capitalism and the establishment of a socialist world order. Chinese Marxists were internationalists, Mao insisted, but their most pressing task was the ejection of imperialism from China and the establishment of an independent Chinese nation-state. Only when this had been achieved could China make a significant contribution to socialism on an international scale. The following passage, written in 1938 when the very survival of China was threatened by Japanese imperialism, is typical of Mao's position on the relationship between nationalism and internationalism:

> Can a Communist, who is an internationalist, at the same time be a patriot? We hold that he not only can be but must be . . . Chinese communists therefore must combine patriotism with internationalism. We are at once internationalists and patriots and our slogan is, 'Fight to defend the motherland against the aggressors.' For us defeatism is a crime and to strive for victory in the War of resistance is an inescapable duty. For only by fighting in defence of the motherland can we defeat the aggressor and achieve national liberation. And only by achieving national liberation will it be possible for the proletariat and other working people to achieve their own emancipation. The victory of China and the defeat of the invading imperialists will help the

people of other countries. Thus in wars of national liberation patriotism is applied internationalism.

(Mao, 1965: 196)

We will see, shortly, that the issues of nationalism and internationalism were also central to Ho Chin Minh's Marxism. It is, indeed, instructive that these two influential Asian Marxists perceived no ultimate conflict between their nationalist and internationalist objectives, and were able to reconcile the apparent tensions between these two themes by drawing on the logic of Marxism–Leninism. However, the behaviour of the Chinese state under Mao and the Vietnamese state under Ho suggests that their resolution of the tension between nationalism and internationalism may have been more apparent than real. Both of these Marxists, once in power, frequently perceived the interests of their own nations as paramount, and indeed were sometimes in conflict with other socialist nations, including each other's. Moreover the split between China and the Soviet Union in the early 1960s signalled the end of the internationalist unity of the Soviet-led communist camp and the emergence of Chinese hostility towards those socialist nations that had remained loyal to the Soviet Union. This hostility sometimes led to armed conflict.

Finally, one can discern in Mao's deep interest in the Marxist philosophy of dialectical materialism an acceptance that Marxism provided the natural laws and concepts through which reality, whether natural or social, could be known. In 1936–37, during a lull in his revolutionary activities, Mao closely studied and annotated a number of Soviet texts on Marxist philosophy (Knight, 1990). He then proceeded to write a number of philosophical essays (*On Contradiction* and *On Practice*) which, while clearly revealing the influence of Soviet philosophy of the 1930s, demonstrate his intention to use Marxist philosophy to gain an accurate perception of China's social reality (Knight, 1997). In particular, Mao used the philosophical idea – that all things consist of contradictions between which there is struggle – to analyse the contradictions of Chinese society, and to construct political and military strategies that would help resolve those contradictions in ways that would aid the revolutionary cause (Mao, 1975: 311–47). Similarly, Mao derived from Marxist philosophy an epistemology (a theory of knowledge) that reinforced his own inclination to investigate 'facts', rather than relying on the classics of Marxism in a dogmatic fashion (Mao, 1975: 295–309).

Mao therefore perceived in Marxism a philosophy and a theory of history that, while emerging from a European context, were relevant to China's history and society. European and Chinese history shared certain fundamental characteristics, such as class, and similar successive historical stages, that pointed to a uniformity in world history. However, Mao recognized, perhaps more than many of his comrades, that China was different to Europe in terms of particular characteristics, and it was these he was so concerned to discover, for a detailed knowledge of China allowed the formulation of correct strategies for revolution and socialist construction. The distinctive character of Chinese Marxism – the stress on the peasants in rural revolution, organizational tactics such as the 'mass line', the mobilization of the masses in often violent and disruptive mass campaigns such as the Great Leap Forward and the Cultural Revolution – grew out of Mao's insistence on adapting Marxism to China's specific characteristics. However, he never abandoned the view that Marxism represented a universal theory of history. His apparently successful adaptation of it to the Chinese revolution could not, he believed, be automatically applied in other Third World contexts. Chinese experience, he warned visiting revolutionaries from Latin America, could not be transplanted mechanically. Rather, 'the experience of any foreign country can serve only for reference and must not be regarded as dogma. The universal truth of Marxism–Leninism and the concrete condition of your countries – the two must be integrated' (Mao, 1977: 326).

Ho Chi Minh and Vietnam's revolution: patriotism and proletarian internationalism

Vietnam's Ho Chi Minh (1890–1969), like Mao, had no reservations about the truth of Marxism–Leninism, although, again like Mao and perhaps even more so, he was strongly driven by nationalism. Ho's attraction to Marxism–Leninism was founded on the importance of achieving Vietnam's independence from colonialism and imperialism, and it was to this end that he devoted his considerable political talents and energies. For this reason, he was less concerned than was Mao with a detailed study and elaboration of the theoretical dimensions of Marxism–Leninism. However, the numerous references to Marxism, and particularly to Leninism, in his writings indicate an unwavering commitment to the general theoretical principles of Marxism–Leninism. Although less a theorist than Mao, he was no less insistent on the need to adapt and apply these principles to the requirements of Vietnam's revolutionary struggle, particularly its struggle against colonialism and imperialism. Importantly, Ho accepted that Vietnam's oppression was a manifestation of an international imperialist system, one incisively explained by Lenin on the basis of Marx's critique of capitalism. Marxism–Leninism was thus, for Ho, a theory of universal significance; the problem was how to adapt this theory to Vietnamese conditions in the cause of revolution and national liberation.

It was in the context of French colonialism with its policy of assimilation – the belief that colonial subjects should absorb French values and culture, and learn the French language – and Vietnamese resistance to it that Ho Chi Minh commenced his career as a revolutionary and Vietnamese patriot. Living for some time, in the late 1910s and early 1920s, in first France and then the Soviet Union, he was influenced in turn by the French Communist Party and by Soviet Marxism, becoming a committed activist and agent for the Comintern. Particularly influenced by Lenin's view of imperialism, Ho came to see the international significance of the struggle against French colonialism in Vietnam, for the struggle would aid the struggle of anticolonial movements elsewhere. Lenin's ideas exerted a profound influence on Ho precisely because they endorsed the fusion of the two ideals that were so important to him: nationalism and communism (Lacoutre, 1967).

Eventually returning to Vietnam after a long absence, Ho formed the Vietminh (the Revolutionary League for the Independence of Vietnam) in 1941, which appealed successfully to various classes and groups in Vietnamese society – peasants, the middle class, intellectuals, nationalist organizations and mass associations – to support the struggle for national independence and economic justice. The Vietminh was, however, dominated by the Indochinese Communist Party (McAlister, 1969). Ho's strategy of establishing and then gaining leadership of a broad coalition of disparate social and political forces mirrored the Leninist view that colonialism impacted on the classes and social groups of a colonized country in different ways, although for the most part negatively. For their different reasons, these classes and groups would rally to the nationalist cause. Ho perceived his task as being to create a united front against colonialism, and then gain leadership of it in order to lead the anticolonial struggle in the eventual direction of a socialist revolution

On 2 September 1945, following Japan's defeat by the Allies, Ho established the Democratic Republic of Vietnam (DRV) with himself as its president. France, refusing to accept Ho's independent Vietnam, sought to reassert its authority through military force. This led to the First Indochina War, which culminated in the battle of Dien Bien Phu in 1954, at which the French were decisively defeated militarily. However, while the Geneva peace settlement of July 1954 ended French colonialism in Vietnam, it divided Vietnam into North and South Vietnam, supposedly to be reunited following general elections. The fact that these elections were never held, largely because the US knew that Ho would be victorious and thus resisted them, was to lead to the Second Indochina War, in which the US was the major imperialist power. The division of his country thus thwarted Ho's dream of an independent and united Vietnam, although he continued to struggle for the achievement of that goal until his death in 1969.

It is clear, then, that a major motivation for Ho's political thought and actions was nationalism. However, like Mao, Ho perceived no contradiction between nationalism and his internationalist Marxist–Leninist beliefs. Ho explained this fusion of nationalism and socialist internationalism in typical Leninist terms:

> There should be a close association of patriotism and proletarian internationalism in both the national liberation revolution and the socialist revolution. In our time, the national liberation revolution is an inseparable part of the world proletarian revolution; the national liberation revolution must develop into the socialist revolution if it is to achieve complete victory.
>
> (Ho, 1979: 184)

Ho, like Mao, also accepted the Marxist conception of class as central to social analysis and the development of revolutionary strategies. Although Ho's was an inclusive nationalism, and he was dedicated to building a 'broad front' of the various patriotic classes of Vietnamese society, he was, again like Mao, insistent that the working class lead any coalition of class forces. Moreover, Ho believed that the working class itself had to be led by a 'genuine revolutionary party' which 'knows how to apply Marxism–Leninism creatively to the specific conditions' of Vietnam (ibid.: 183). This revolutionary party had to 'organize the systematic study of Marxism–Leninism in order to raise the cultural and political level of Party members' (Ho, 1979: 66).

The policies of Ho's government in North Vietnam after 1954 also demonstrate that he was not purely a nationalist, for he was concerned to restructure Vietnamese society along socialist lines. The most dramatic example was the programme of land reform and rural collectivization carried out in stages throughout the 1950s. The first stage was underpinned by class struggle directed at rich peasants and landlords, and the creation of mutual-aid teams in which control was vested in the hands of the poor and middle peasants. By 1958, most of North Vietnam's agricultural land was collectivized (Wolf, 1971: 190–2; Fall, 1967: 304–6). In its foreign policy, too, Ho's government clearly aligned itself with the socialist camp headed by the Soviet Union, and it received aid from both the Soviet Union and China (Fall, 1967: 295). Finally, despite his victory against French colonialism, Ho did not relinquish his ideological belief in Marxism–Leninism. As he pointed out in 1957, Marxism–Leninism 'elaborated a just and complete theory of anti-imperialist national revolution', one which was of great significance to Vietnam and its own revolution (Fall, 1967: 330).

Applying Marxism to Asian conditions: critical evaluation

Although Marxism originated in Europe in the nineteenth century as a critique of capitalism, it was in the context of feudal and colonial Asia in the twentieth century that it was to have the most dramatic impact. Revolutionaries in Asia enthusiastically adopted Marxism, for they perceived in it an explanation of and a solution to the serious problems of class oppression and colonial exploitation from which they suffered. Marxism provided, at a general level, a philosophy of history and a theory of social change that made eminent sense to them. However, the general principles of Marxism had to be applied to specific Asian contexts in order to generate revolutionary strategies that would work. Probably the most successful revolutionary leader in Asia to achieve this was Mao Zedong, who asserted on many occasions that Marxism had to be applied to the particular characteristics and needs of the Chinese revolution. He argued that the integration of Marxism's universal principles with China's concrete reality would create a Sinified Marxism, one that was both genuinely Marxist and Chinese. Similarly, Vietnam's Ho Chi Minh adopted a Marxist–Leninist solution to Vietnam's colonial oppression and feudal backwardness. He recognised that Vietnam, albeit of great importance to himself as a Vietnamese nationalist, was not unique in terms of its social composition, its pattern of historical progression or, importantly, its fate as a colony. Only by perceiving Vietnam's problems in the context of imperialism as an international stage in the development of capitalism could appropriate strategies be formulated that would be effective for Vietnam itself.

However, whereas both Mao and Ho were quite evidently successful in leading revolutions in their respective countries, their attempts to establish socialism in a context of underdevelopment – a project on which Marx was largely silent – were not as successful. Both Mao and Ho pursued socialism largely through conventional Soviet strategies of agricultural cooperativization, socialization of industry and centralized economic planning. In China, these strategies were modified by Mao's belief in the large-scale mobilization of the Chinese masses in pursuit of political and economic objectives. In particular, Mao believed that the enthusiasm of the masses could, at least in part, substitute for scarce material resources needed for China's industrialization. This sometimes led to disastrous consequences, as in the Great Leap Forward of 1958–60, during which China's peasants were organized into huge communes and diverted into poorly conceived attempts at industrialization such as the backyard steel furnaces. This wildly ambitious mass campaign led to enormous economic and social dislocation, and resulted in one of the worst famines in human history, with up to 30 million people perishing.

Nevertheless, despite the absence of many of the appropriate conditions, both Mao and Ho did make significant progress in establishing a socialist and industrialized society in their respective countries. However, following their deaths, and particularly following the restructuring and then collapse of the Soviet Union, the leaders of both China and Vietnam have aggressively pursued a form of economic development closer to capitalism than socialism. While the Chinese and Vietnamese communist parties have retained a tight grip on political power, both have opened their economies to capitalist foreign investment and trade, and have introduced wide-ranging reforms – the sale of many state-owned enterprises, dismantling the communes, the establishment of stock markets, encouragement of the profit motive – which have had the effect of undermining and then transforming their previous socialist economies.

Indeed, the post-Mao and post-Ho economic reforms in China and Vietnam raise the question of whether Marxism – a theory of European origin but which claimed universal validity – was ever really applicable to the feudal and colonial contexts of Asia. We might tentatively conclude that, as a theory of revolution, Marxism was relevant to the aspirations of revolutionaries in China, Vietnam and elsewhere in Asia. Both Mao and Ho accepted Marxism and developed successful military and political strategies based on its basic premises. However, the picture is much less clear – and much less positive – when China and Vietnam's record of socialist construction is considered. Neither country possessed what Marx appeared to suggest was essential for a successful transition to socialism: a highly developed capitalist economy, widespread industrialization, and a large and politically conscious working class. In the absence of these preconditions, Mao's China and Ho's Vietnam attempted to create them politically, with some success it is true, but resulting in large bureaucratic states that frequently behaved in an oppressive and elitist manner.

It was, then, as a theory of revolution, rather than of socialist construction, that Marxism has had its greatest impact in Asia. Marxism provided a theory of history and social change that encouraged Marxists in Asia to overthrow their feudal economies and political systems and to challenge colonial domination of their countries. It was their urgent desire for national liberation, modernisation and socialism that motivated Asian Marxists to accept Marxism's claim to universality and to apply its principles to the cause of revolution. The success of the revolutions in China and Vietnam, and Mao and Ho's leadership of them, attest to the power of this mixture of Marxist theory and revolutionary practice.

Note

1　One scholar (Schwartz, 1951: 76–7) has argued that 'Mao demonstrated his readiness to turn his back on the industrial proletariat in the face of all theoretical considerations in order to take full advantage of the elemental forces which he found in the village.' Another (Meisner, 1982: 99, 138, 225) suggests that Mao 'distrusted the revolutionary capacities of the urban proletariat' and believed that the peasantry was the 'true revolutionary class'.

References

Avineri, Shlomo (1968) *The Social and Political Thought of Karl Marx*. Cambridge: Cambridge University Press.

Carrèrre d'Encausse, Hélène and Stuart R. Schram (1969) *Marxism and Asia: An Introduction with Readings*. London: Allen Lane The Penguin Press.

Dirlik, Arif, Healy, Paul and Knight, Nick (eds) (1997) *Critical Perspectives on Mao Zedong's Thought*. Atlantic Highlands, NJ: Humanities Press.

Dunn, Stephen P. (1982) *The Fall and Rise of the Asiatic Mode of Production*. London: Routledge & Kegan Paul.

Fall, Bernard B. (ed.) (1967) *Ho Chi Minh – On Revolution: Selected Writings, 1920–66*. New York: Frederick A. Praeger.

Ho Chi Minh (1979) *Patriotism and Proletarian Internationalism*. Hanoi: Foreign Languages Publishing House.

Knight, Nick (1985) 'Leninism, Stalinism and the Comintern' in Colin Mackerras and Nick Knight (eds), *Marxism in Asia*. London and Sydney: Croom Helm.

Knight, Nick (1990) (ed.) *Mao Zedong on Dialectical Materialism: Writings on Philosophy, 1937*. Armonk, NY: M.E. Sharpe.

Knight, Nick (1991) 'Politics and Vision: Historical Time and the Future in Mao Zedong's Thought, 1936–1945', *Journal of Oriental Studies*, 29 (2): 139–71.

Knight, Nick (1997) 'The Laws of Dialectical Materialism in Mao Zedong's Thought: The Question of "Orthodoxy"' in Arif Dirlik, Paul Healy and Nick Knight (eds), *Critical Perspectives on Mao Zedong's Thought*. Atlantic Highlands, NJ: Humanities Press.

Knight, Nick (1997–98) 'Mao Zedong and Working Class Leadership of the Chinese Revolution, 1927–1930', *China Information*, 12 (3): 28–45.

Lacoutre, Jean (1967) *Ho Chi Minh*. Harmondsworth: Penguin Books.

Lenin, V.I. (1967) *Lenin on the National and Colonial Questions: Three Articles*. Peking: Foreign Languages Press.

Lenin, V.I. (1969) *Imperialism, The Highest Stage of Capitalism: A Popular Outline*. Peking: Foreign Languages Press.

McAlister, John T. Jr (1969) *Vietnam: The Origins of Revolution*. New York: Alfred A. Knopf.

Mao Tse-tung (1965) *Selected Works of Mao Tse-tung*, volume II. Peking: Foreign Languages Press.

Mao Tse-tung (1975) *Selected Works of Mao Tse-tung*, volume I. Peking: Foreign Languages Press.

Mao Zedong (1977) *Selected Works of Mao Tse-tung*, volume V. Peking: Foreign Languages Press.

Marx, Karl (1964) (edited and with an introduction by E.J. Hobsbawm) *Pre-Capitalist Economic Formations*. London: Lawrence and Wishart.

Marx, Karl (1971) *A Contribution to the Critique of Political Economy*. London: Lawrence and Wishart.

óMarx, Karl (1973) (edited and introduced by David Fernbach) *The Revolutions of 1848: Political Writings*, volume 1. Harmondsworth: Penguin Books.

Meisner, Maurice (1982) *Marxism, Maoism and Utopianism*. Madison, WI: University of Wisconsin Press.

Pantsov, Alexander (2000) *The Bolsheviks and the Chinese Revolution, 1919–1927*. Richmond: Curzon Press.

Sawer, Marian (1977) *Marxism and the Asiatic Mode of Production*. The Hague: Martinus Nijhoff.

Schram, Stuart R. (1969) *The Political Thought of Mao Tse-tung*. Harmondsworth: Penguin Books.

Schram, Stuart R. (ed.) (1994) *Mao's Road to Power: Revolutionary Writings, 1912–1949*, volume II: *National Revolution and Social Revolution, December 1920–June 1927*. Armonk, NY: M.E. Sharpe.

Schwartz, Benjamin I. (1951) *Chinese Communism and the Rise of Mao*. New York: Harper and Row.

Snow, Edgar (1972) *Red Star over China*. Harmondsworth: Penguin Books.

Wolf, Eric R. (1971) *Peasant Wars of the Twentieth Century*. London: Faber and Faber.

9 Marxism in Latin America/ Latin American Marxism?

Ronaldo Munck

Latin American Marxisms have always been in a 'liminal' situation, part European but also, arguably, distinctly American, and it is thus no coincidence that the concept of hybridity has had great resonance in Latin America. However, the original Marxist engagement with Latin America was anything but felicitous, with Karl Marx having a singular misencounter with the continent as we shall see. Marxism did, however, take roots and produced, for example, Latin America's equivalent to Antonio Gramsci, the Peruvian thinker and activist José Carlos Mariátegui (1894–1930). We trace these early developments and then sketch in the trajectory from the Stalin-led official Marxists through to Fidel Castro. A subsequent section deals with the recent renewal (*renovación*) of Marxism, particularly in Chile and the other distinctly 'new' current, the Zapatistas of Mexico. The intellectual contribution of Marxism in relation to dependency theory and conceptions of the national-popular is considered next, and a final section considers the future prospects of Marxism, in its various forms, in the Latin America of the new century. Whether there is, in fact, a distinctive 'Latin American Marxism' is an issue we consider but, ultimately, leave open.

Marx in Latin America

In 1873, Raymond Wilmart, a leader of the First International based in Argentina, advised Karl Marx that there could be little progress made there without a further wave of European immigrants because the locals were 'unable to do anything but ride on horseback' (quoted in Falcón, 1980: 37). Marx's correspondent in Argentina displayed a total inability to engage with the complex social and political struggles of the post-independence period in Latin America. Underlying this was an innate confidence in the development of capitalism in the New World, a confidence Wilmart shared with thousands of other immigrants. Unfortunately, Marx did not achieve in regard to Latin America the break from evolutionism and Eurocentrism he made in relation to Ireland and Russia in his later writings. This led to the commentary by Marx and Engels being somewhat of an embarrassment to Marxists in the region. Who, for example, could stand behind the throwaway remark of Engels in 1847 that: 'We have witnessed the conquest of Mexico and have rejoiced at it . . . It is to the interests of its own development that Mexico will in the future be placed under the tutelage of the United States' (Marx and Engels, 1976: 527)? Engels (and one assumes Marx) stood with 'splendid California' against the 'lazy Mexicans' (Marx and Engels, 1977: 365).

Perhaps more significant than Marx's openly evolutionist statements on Latin America is his explicit attempt to engage with Simón Bolívar, hero of the South American independence movement, for an entry in *The New American Cyclopaedia* in 1858 (Marx and Engels, 1982). Marx concentrated on Bolívar's authoritarianism rather than his role in the national independence movement. Bolívar's penchant for pomp and ceremony, the declamatory proclamations and incipient personality cult, led Marx to catalogue the *Libertador* (Liberator) as a minor Latin American reflection of France's Napoleon III. What is most remarkable is the total absence of any 'Marxist' analysis of Bolívar's historical role, the situation of the indigenous peoples, the roles of the different social classes in the independence struggles and so on. It would seem that Marx here followed Hegel's view of America as an empty territory where events were but an echo or a pale reflection of what happened in Europe. Marx's understanding of how the nation-state had been formed in Europe at the very least blurred his vision in the Americas, and his conception of politics ill equipped him to understand, let alone empathise with, the particular Latin American route to modernity.

What Marx had to say about India also guided his attitude towards Latin America: 'India has no history at all, at least no known history, what we call its history is but the history of successive intruders' (quoted in Avineri, 1969: 132). This preconception – Eurocentric and colonialist to its core – lies behind Marx's engagement with Latin America. It led Marx, for example, to view the continent merely as a brake on the Spanish revolution and as a hinterland of Bonapartist expansion. Marx was even blinded to Bolívar's progressive pan-American project and his concern to prevent the Balkanisation of South America, an orientation he and Engels sympathised with in Europe of course. For Marx as for Hegel, José Aricó argues, 'America only exists in Europe' or to be precise 'Latin America was only considered in its exteriority, in its condition of reflection of Europe, because its interiority was incomprehensible, and as such non-existent' (Aricó, 1982: 100). Not only was Marx blind to the particular route of nation-state formation in Latin America but his categories seemed unable to grasp the economic, political and racial particularities of development there. Marxism would have to go through a process of 'nationalisation' before historical materialism could prove a fruitful tool for analysis and guide to action for revolutionaries in Latin America. Its Eurocentrism would remain a contested element right up to the 1970s.

Marx's thought was taken up in Latin America by a generation of immigrant, or European educated, socialist thinkers and activists. Perhaps emblematic was Juán B. Justo (1865–1928) from Argentina. Justo was prominent amongst the intellectuals who sought to 'Latinamericanise' Marx, seeking to adapt his thinking to a land he seemed to have understood so little. In 1895 Justo not only completed the first Spanish translation of Marx's *Capital* but also helped found the Socialist Party of Argentina. Although he claimed his inspiration from Marx, the main mentors in Justo's evolution were the 'revisionist' socialist Eduard Bernstein, the French socialist thinker Jean Jaurès and, above all, the evolutionist early sociology of Herbert Spencer. His 'Latin American' Marxism would be thoroughly marked by evolutionist thinking. In essence, he read Marx as an evolutionist, which would be, indeed, a plausible reading for a Latin American of that expansionist nation-creating era. He liked Marx's general vision of history as he read it but had no great feeling for the then developing theory of imperialism. Against fellow Socialist Party members like Manuel Ugarte, who warned eloquently of domination or even absorption by the United States, Justo believed that foreign capital was necessary for development, that it would accelerate the continent's evolutionary process and would lay the foundation for the eventual (though never clear when to be achieved) socialisation of the means of production.

From the turn of the century onwards Marxism in Latin America would reflect, albeit in hybridised forms at times, the movements, splits and transformations in Europe. Social democracy, lead by Justo and his co-thinkers across the continent, settled into a parliamentary routine which sometimes chalked up significant achievements. They established a discourse and a practice which has endured to this day, even enjoying a significant revival in the 1970s. Their positivist socialism tied in well with the immigrant aspirations of workers and later the immigrant industrialists. They helped force the agrarian oligarchy to concede basic political and social rights, contributing to the 'civilising' of the New World. This evolutionary tendency was disrupted by the Russian Revolution of 1917, whose repercussions crossed Latin America like a tidal wave. Its more apocalyptic tone and its messianic message had a great impact. Although not at the forefront of Leninist thinking and the successive turns of the Communist International, Latin America was fertile territory for Bolshevism, in its organisational commitment, its revolutionary fervour and the undoubted quality of its activists. The Comintern came to dominate the story of Marxism in Latin America, at least until the Cuban revolution of 1959. Of its thinkers none stand out as much as José Carlos Mariátegui, dubbed, with not too much exaggeration, the continent's Gramsci.

Mariátegui and 'national Marxism'

Mariátegui, the Peruvian socialist thinker and leader, may or may not have met Antonio Gramsci during his exile years in Europe but there are uncanny parallels between their thought. If Gramsci was the author of an article dubbing October as the 'revolution against *Capital*' (Gramsci, 1977), Mariátegui was also the promoter of a Latin American revolution which could be seen as 'against the Comintern'. His was an open, fluid Marxism, quite alien to the twists and turns of dogmatic Comintern doctrine. Much as Gramsci did, he admired the work of Italian philosopher Benedeto Croce, which gave rise to a certain 'idealism' in his thinking, a tendency towards 'Marxist humanism' perhaps. He did not conceive of Marxism as a finished or closed system of thinking but rather as a non-dogmatic, fluid and creative guide to a critical analysis of social reality. Mariátegui was particularly attuned to the changing cultural context in which political strategies have to be applied. The Marxism of Mariátegui was 'a method based wholly on reality, on facts. It is not, as some erroneously believe, a body of principles with rigid consequences, the same in all historical climates and all social latitudes' (Mariátegui, 1969a: 112). In his stress on its subjective factor, Mariátegui rejected all determinisms and argued that where Marxism 'has shown itself to be revolutionary, [it] has never observed a passive, rigid determinism' (Mariátegui, 1969b: 65).

There is today a prolific Mariátegui myth industry and his memory is claimed by such disparate forces as reformist Peruvian generals and the fundamentalist guerrillas of *Sendero Luminoso* (Shining Path). Yet most are agreed that Mariátegui's is a 'national Marxism'. For Mariátegui the socialist party 'adapts its praxis to the concrete situation of the country' (Mariátegui, 1969a: 153). A whole generation of Marxists in the colonial world – Amilcar Cabral comes to mind – would later stress the national, culturally specific roots of their Marxism. In a similar way for Gramsci, the universality of Marxism (or to be precise Leninism) consisted in its ability to better comprehend a reality other than the one where it originated and, furthermore, in its capacity to operate in that new reality as an original force (Gramsci, 1977). So, for Mariátegui, Marxism was not a universal truth to be 'applied' in Peru but rather needed to become a true expression of Peruvian social reality. Mariátegui is sometimes (like Gramsci) accused of eclecticism, for example in his admiration of George Sorel's revolutionary syndicalism. Certainly, Mariátegui seems to have maintained a conflictual relation with certain elements of what one could call 'actually existing Marxism', but his multifaceted and active engagement with Peruvian reality and construction of a flexible and viable political practice can be seen to be in the best traditions of Marx himself.

If there is one key contribution by Mariátegui to Marxist thinking in Latin America it is in what the Comintern dubbed the 'indigenous question'. As José Aricó notes, 'the confluence, or aleatory relationship, between indigenism and socialism' lies at the heart of Mariátegui's analysis of the history and problems of Peru (Aricó, 1980: x). Mariátegui read the indigenous questions in terms of the land question but also from a broad culturalist optic. He envisioned the establishment of an Indo-American socialism in Peru based on the communal values of the Inca empire. In the absence of a sizeable industrial proletariat in Peru, Mariátegui turned naturally towards the indigenous and peasant masses. Yet Mariátegui's belief in an 'indigenous renaissance' went further than a translation of the orthodox worker–peasant alliance into national Peruvian terms. His links with the indigenous movement allowed Mariátegui to connect with the 'real' or 'hidden' Peru as he saw it. It is perhaps no coincidence that it was around this time that Mao Zedong in China was elaborating not dissimilar ideas and lines of action around the centrality of peasants and the issue of land reform in the colonial and semicolonial world.

Mariátegui, national Marxist and theorist of indigenous socialism though he was, was also a pioneer of internationalism in Latin America. His was not a narrow nativist nationalism and he always acknowledged his formative European experiences (he attended the 1921 founding congress of the Italian communists at Livorno for example). His journal *Amauta* ('teacher' in Quechua) promoted solidarity with the Cuban and Nicaraguan revolutionary movements and the incipient revolutionary Russian state. In his famous essay *Internationalism and Nationalism* (Mariátegui, 1973), Mariátegui not only articulates classical Marxist internationalism but also presages current concerns with the globalised network society.

> Communications are the nervous system of internationalism and human solidarity. One of the characteristics of our epoch is the rapidity, the velocity, with which ideas spread, with which currents of thought and culture are transmitted. A new idea that blossoms in Britain is not a British idea except for the time that it takes for it to be printed. Once launched into space by the press, this idea, if it expresses some universal truth, can be instantaneously transformed into an international idea.
>
> (quoted in Waterman, 1998: 257–8)

Mariátegui's was not an abstract internationalism but one grounded in national realities. He believed simply that capitalism had internationalised human life and that, consequently, internationalism had become a historical reality.

A thinker and leader of such potential and such independence as Mariátegui was bound to run foul of the 'official' Marxists in the Communist International. There were many issues at stake, including Mariátegui's emphasis on the peasantry and his *Indigenismo*. After his death, the Comintern in Latin America was to fight the 'populist' deviation of 'Mariáteguismo'. At the 1929 Conference of Latin American Communist Parties, Mariátegui was censured for calling his party 'socialist' rather than 'communist'. Much ink has been spent on debating the significance of this controversy, and to what extent Mariátegui was actually departing from Leninism, but it seems symptomatic simply of his constant emphasis on adapting Marxism to concrete national realities. It may simply have been a decision based on the legitimacy of the term 'socialist' as against 'communist', but it does also seem to be a symbol of Mariátegui's independence from dogmatic centralised doctrinal organisation. The Comintern and its loyal Peruvian followers responded with the accusation of 'populist', second only to that of 'Trotskyist' in the lexicon of deviation from true communism. Much later the thought of Mariátegui would find organic (though not always recognised) expression in the Cuban revolution of 1959 and the Sandinista uprising in Nicaragua in 1979.

From Stalin to Castro

After its summary dealing with the 'Mariátegui issue' at the 1929 Conference of Latin American Communist Parties, Comintern practice in Latin America proceeded to mirror the twists and turns of policy in Russia and Europe. Symptomatic of this ideological dependency was the Conference's reduction of the complex 'indigenous question' to the more formulaic 'national question', which led to quite a few Latin American delegates complaining about an unthinking application of

European schemes to the recalcitrant reality of their continent. The Comintern's 'class against class' Third Period (1929–35) led to a disastrous peasant insurrection in El Salvador in 1932 and the rather more grounded Cuban revolt of 1933 which saw the formation of 'soviets' amongst the sugar workers. The nationalist struggle against the US occupation of Nicaragua (1926–34) led by Augusto César Sandino was dismissed by the Comintern on the completely false basis that 'the struggle ended by the capitulation of Sandino and his passage over to the side of the counter-revolution' (Aguilar, 1968: 199). Prior to 1935 there was still some independent Marxist thought in communist circles, and a certain congruence or 'fit' between a revolutionary historical phase and the prevailing Comintern line. After 1935, with the inauguration of the Popular Front line which lasted until 1945, the definitive impoverishment of 'official' Marxist thought set in and the memories of Mariátegui, the Cuban radical Marxist leader Julio Antonio Mella (1903–29) and the Chilean workers' leader Luis Emilio Recabarren (1895–1924) were in the dim and distant past.

The Popular Front strategy was applied most consistently in Chile, where it had the effect of fostering a tradition of democratic, parliamentary-based reformism that culminated in the Popular Unity victory of 1970. Marxism became a new 'common sense' for a whole layer of trade union and community activists, and inspired the work of artists such as the great poet Pablo Neruda. But while in Chile there was a certain 'nationalisation' of Marxism, in Argentina a historical divorce between Marxism and revolutionary nationalism was caused by the Comintern's ideological centralism. The post-1941 'fascism versus democracy' line of Soviet Communists led official Marxists in Argentina (along with the British embassy) to oppose the populist-nationalist General Peron and his trade union supporters as 'fascists'. The resulting isolation of most Marxists from an expanding and confident labour movement meant that right up until the 1970s in Argentina the term 'Marxism' had reactionary connotations in popular circles. More creative Marxist writers (including some Trotskyists) did engage with the national-popular labourist tradition of Peronism and produced some original analysis. The point is that, whether it worked in some way (Chile) or not (Argentina), the imposition of Marxism from the outside was not the best way to create a revolutionary symbiosis in the colonial or semicolonial world.

The slumbers of dogmatic Marxists were to be rudely awakened by the Cuban revolution of 1959 and Castro's declaration in 1961 that he was, indeed, a Marxist. Notwithstanding the late-in-the-day participation of Cuba's official Marxists in this revolution, it was in all respects a revolution 'against Marxism' or as Cuban thinkers put it, a 'revolution in the revolution'. It was a watershed in the history of Marxism in Latin America, the effects of which were to last for twenty years or more. By its sheer example of overcoming all the odds, the solidarity it awakened across Latin America in many political circles, and its audacity in 'exporting the revolution', the Cuban version gradually came to dominate over official Marxism. In doing so, however, it arguably became absorbed and enmeshed by Soviet state interests to the extent that today Castro appears as a voice for orthodoxy in the wilderness. But throughout the 1960s and much of the 1970s the Cuban revolution helped create a sturdy new Marxist hybrid in Latin America. Castroism or Guevarism brought a healthy dose of voluntarism into the stale dogma Marxism had become. The Trotskyist notion of a permanent revolution seemed to have been given a new lease of life in Latin America as the dusty textbooks of revolution 'by stages' disappeared in the vortex created by a quasi-messianic belief in the effectiveness of armed struggle.

The Cuban hybrid took root and the 1967 OLAS (Latin American Solidarity Organization) declaration concluded categorically that 'the lesson of the Cuban Revolution shows that guerrilla warfare as a genuine expression of the people's armed struggle is the most effective and most adequate form of waging and developing revolutionary war in our countries, and, subsequently, on a continental scale' (OLAS, 1967: 58). The death of Che Guevara in Bolivia that very year may not have stopped the discourse of armed struggle (which very much took on a life of its own) but the writing was on the wall. As these 'lessons' were sometimes unthinkingly applied in the streets of Brazil and Argentina with disastrous consequences for a whole generation of activists, so the shortcomings of the guerrilla war strategy became apparent. At first the 'auto critiques' of the proponents of armed struggle were half-hearted, criticising only the particular mode of applying the strategy but, gradually, the very basis of a moralistic and militaristic politics was drawn into question. As we shall see in subsequent sections, Marxists (even critical ones) began to revalorise democracy, and politics (rather than physical force) began to come to the fore again. In retrospect it was the impoverished Marxism of the official communism which had created the space for the Cuban hybrid to flourish.

With the successful uprising of the Sandinistas in 1979, it seemed that another revolutionary wave akin to that inaugurated by Cuba in 1959 was to commence. The international balance of forces seemed more favourable and a new phase of hope, realignment, rearming and resolve seemed to be opening up. Yet ten years later the official communist experience worldwide was at an end and the Sandinistas were voted out of office a year later. There is probably still much to learn from the Sandinista experience concerning amongst other things the economic difficulties confronting a democratic socialist regime and the complexities of dealing democratically with an indigenous population. The Sandinista experience offers lessons also about the dangers of militarism, 'personalism' and sexism. The main point, though, is that Sandinismo was the swansong of a national-popular type of Marxism in Latin America and not the start of a new wave. Sandinismo never really had much impact outside the particular situation of Central America, and in Chile (see next section) a very different political dynamic was occurring within Marxist circles. What the collapse of Sandinismo also signalled was the end of the 'armed road' as a viable strategy for the left. Notwithstanding a continuing 'traditional' communist insurgency in Colombia, the peace processes unfolding in El Salvador and Guatemala in the 1990s were to be much more typical of the post-Cold War political period.

Renovadores and Zapatistas

The overthrow of the Popular Unity government in Chile by General Pinochet in 1973 was another event that was to have far-reaching political ramifications. While a few Trotskyists believed that it proved that the 'only road' was the 'armed road', for most Marxists in Chile it inaugurated a period of profound rethinking of socialism and democracy. From this process emerged the *renovadores* (renewalists) who today predominate in the Chilean left and are a guiding force in the post-Pinochet political dispensation. They criticised the teleological dimension of the classical Marxist paradigm in Latin America and articulated a new, more democratic, more processual vision. They sought to move the locus of revolutionary activity from a frontal assault on state power to the reconstruction of civil society and a new democratic hegemony. They treated the rule of law as an unqualified human good, and not a crafty bourgeois ruse. The distinction between 'formal' and 'real' democracy, as argued by most Marxists, made little sense under the Pinochet dictatorship. Above all, against previous all-or-nothing zero-sum conceptions of politics (e.g. *Patria o Muerte*: Country or Death) the *renovadores* began to raise the once taboo question of class compromise and the need to enter a stable democratic pact with a whole range of 'bourgeois' political parties in order to move beyond the dictatorship.

The *renovadores* did not just advocate a tactical retreat or cosmetic redesign of their ideological image. What emerged was a watershed in Marxist thinking which affected not only the Southern Cone but also Central America and elsewhere. Traditionally, Marxists in Latin America were sceptical of political pluralism and the whole notion of accommodation or compromise. Politics was conceived in an essentially Manichean way and was often seen as an extension of the warfare which prevailed between social classes. This messianic concept of politics was confronted by a call in the 1980s to 'desacralise' politics. Democracy was revalorised and politics was brought to the fore with the demilitarisation of the revolutionary mindset. Revolution was no longer the simple articulating axis of Marxist politics in Latin America as democracy and civil society came to the fore. As the Chilean political scientist Manuel Antonio Garretón explains the new perspective, 'There is no socialist model only a socialist process ... Socialism cannot be defined as a model for society that is established once and for all ... Socialism is a principle of social transformation, of the elimination of various kinds of alienation, oppression and exploitation ... It is based on the ideas of social emancipation and popular empowerment' (Garretón, 1989: 26).

The renewal of Latin American Marxism cannot be understood in isolation from the remarkable influence which the ideas of Antonio Gramsci had in the region from the late 1960s onwards. Although Latin America was not the Occident neither was it the Orient, and Gramsci's subtle analysis of Italy in the 1920s had great resonance. Whereas the new Cuban Marxism preached 'socialism or fascism' as stark alternatives, Gramsci's influence allowed for the introduction of the concept of hegemony and the possibility of a very different, more open, democratic socialist politics. The open Marxism of Gramsci encouraged a vigorous strand of analysis of Latin American reality centred around concepts such as hegemony, civil society and 'transformism'. The Marxist understanding of the state became far more nuanced than mere repressive apparatus, and the concept of the historical bloc pointed towards a new strategy for advancement by the subaltern classes. Class reductionism and economism became less common, and politics became less essentialist. The new axis for revolutionary strategy was to be constructed by the group which could achieve hegemony in the construction of a transitional pro-gramme articulating the needs of the people (pueblo). There is a hidden history of Gramsci's entry into Latin American Marxist theory and practice (see Portantiero, 1983, and Aricó, 1988) that provides the key hinge between the old and the new left politics.

The 1994 uprising of the Zapatistas in Mexico – and the international ramifica-tions of it – could be seen to run counter to the Gramscian *renovador* tendency in the region. Once more it seemed possible to 'storm the heavens' and that armed struggle could be effective. As has often happened in Latin America, the cause of the Zapatistas has been taken up abroad in a somewhat simplified manner. The im-age of ski-masked indigenous insurgents in the jungle posting their proclamations on the Internet was certainly striking. However, the social and political reality of Zapatismo is both more prosaic and more complex. Some of its activists come from the Maoist groups which took up arms after the student massacre of 1968. Its outlook contains elements of a 'long war' strategy and accumulation of forces not dissimilar to the approach taken by *Sendero Luminoso* in Peru. But then, as with the Sandinistas, there is a much more Gramscian (and Mariáteguista) tone to their discourse and a pragmatic non-dogmatic aspect to their political practice. The complexity of the indigenous politics of the Lacandón region cannot be gone into here (see Harvey, 1998) but their projects and demands are as much about participation in the fruits of development as about 'identity'; indeed, in the past ethnic identity has in fact divided different indigenous communities from one another. So, what have the Zapatistas achieved?

Manuel Castells has dubbed the Zapatistas the 'first informational guerrilla movement' (Castells, 1997: 79). While armed struggle was deployed it was done so politically and was designed to make a political statement, not win a war. A relatively weak insurgent movement was able to use modern communication methods to capture the imagination of the Mexican people and of a dynamic in-ternational solidarity movement. The relationship between political leaders and the social movement of Chiapas is more in keeping with the ethos of the new social movements than the top-down pyramid model of the Comintern and its 'radical' successors. The Zapatistas have articulated a particular local response to the ravages of globalisation. Yet it is also well to recall that they act as Mexican patriots and democrats demanding that the government respect its own constitu-tion. Their resonance within wider layers of Mexican society reflects their ability to tap into a revolutionary nationalist-popular tradition, symbolised in the claim to the memory of Emiliano Zapata. As with Latin American politics as a whole, the Zapatistas reflect the mixed temporalities of the continent, from 'premodern' to 'postmodern', its uneven and combined development, its 'liminal' nature betwixt and between the West and the rest. Yet it is well to bear in mind that the far less attractive (from a radical democratic perspective) *Sendero Luminoso* in Peru also reflected this perverse postmodern condition (see Munck, 2000) and it is not plausible to claim the one while seeking to bury the other.

Intellectual contributions

It must be said that Latin American Marxism tends to be 'consumed' in the developed countries as a series of icons, from Che Guevara to the Zapatistas. While Europeans theorise, it is left to Latin Americans to act. Yet the intellectual contributions of Latin American Marxism are considerable. Even Che Guevara, romantic icon of action, can be seen to have had an original economic analysis which made a contribution to the critical understanding of the transition to socialism (see Lowy, 1973). If one were to seek a short-list of Latin America contributions it would include:

1 dependency theory;
2 theories of the 'national-popular';
3 theories of radical democracy.

The various Latin American theories of development and underdevelopment, clustered around the concept of 'dependency', represent some of the most influential moments of Marxism and radical thinking in the region. Long before it became popularised in the West by André Gunder Frank, Latin American Marxists were developing Lenin's throwaway term of 'dependency', describing those nation-states which were politically independent yet economically dominated by imperialism, with considerably more sophistication and nuances. Not only did it pose the necessary relationship between the development of one part of the globe and the underdevelopment of another, but it also explored the social and political basis of this essentially economic relationship. In a neglected survey Cristóbal Kay examines in detail the various strands of the dependency school and concludes that, today, after the exhaustion of the once omnipotent neo-liberal revolution, this critical perspective on development may yet regain some influence (Kay, 1989; Munck, 1999). It is significant that the Marxist dependency theory emerged as a conscious reaction to the perceived failure of the Leninist theory of imperialism to address directly the problems and the prospects of the developing countries. Classical Marxist theories of imperialism were concerned with the world system and the West, not the development problems of the colonial and postcolonial worlds. The excesses of dependency theory can often be traced back to its simplified diffusion in the West. Indeed, to date, this perspective provides some of the most sophisticated structural/historical readings of Latin American history. Concerns with class and ethnic relations, the role of the state and the issues of 'cultural dependency' are all current in the era of globalisation. One sub-set of the dependency debate was around the issue of 'marginality', that floating population in the shanty-towns of Latin America which could not be reduced to Marx's 'reserve army of labour'. A close reading of current debates on 'social exclusion' from a non-Eurocentric point of view would show that many of its themes were prefigured in the 1970s Latin American debates on marginality.

The category of the 'national-popular', for its part, entered the political lexicon of Latin America's politics as part of the critique of orthodox Marxism, but it also represents a major contribution by the continent's Gramscian movement (if it can be called that). In the dependent capitalist social formations, the Gramscians argue, the class consciousness of the subaltern masses takes a primarily national-popular form. Against all types of class reductionism and manipulative party forms, the notion of the national-popular represents a break with orthodoxy. Class readings of populism have proven mechanical whereas new approaches direct attention to the crucial discursive domain. Certainly, mechanical schemata based on Marx's own sketchy analysis of social classes have little purchase in societies such as those of Latin America. Here there emerged no pristine proletariat but 'popular classes' more in tune with the analysis of Mariátegui and Gramsci. As to the national dimension – that great blind-spot for orthodox Marxism – this could hardly not come to the fore in Latin America. It was the Gramscian theme of a 'national-popular will' which provided the basis for a democratic struggle against the dictatorships and helped to forge a democratic alternative. These are concepts which have since been applied fruitfully in relation to the struggle in South Africa (see Norval, 1996), the former state-socialist states and authoritarian development states in the Third World.

In relating classical Marxism to what has become known as post-Marxism the influence of the Argentinian political theorist Ernesto Laclau has been significant. In his work not only do we detect a very 'Latin American' influence of Gramsci, but also an enduring engagement with the national-popular discourse of Peronism. The widely influential conception of 'radical democracy' (Laclau and Mouffe, 1985) can in this way be seen to have distinctively Latin American roots. Laclau's break with orthodox Marxism can be seen in his argument, now widely accepted, that 'socialism is no longer a blueprint for society, and comes to be part of a radical democratisation of social organization' (Laclau, 1990: xv). Clearly, demands for emancipation are diversifying in today's world and their unification around any 'big break' seems unlikely. Struggles by new social movements and by Third World peoples for self-determination can, however, be linked by what Laclau calls 'a chain of democratic equivalences' (Laclau, 1990: 228). These perspectives have given rise to a wide-ranging and ongoing international debate. Our only point here is to signal their Latin American origins. As Laclau notes in an autobiographical political interview: 'When I began to read Gramsci and Althusser systematically in the mid-1960s . . . my interpretation was essentially political and non-dogmatic because I could relate it directly to my Argentinian experience' (Laclau, 1990: 199). European Marxism looks different from Latin America, to put it in subjective and/or spatial terms.

In conclusion we need, perhaps, to ask whether there is such an entity as 'Latin American Marxism' comparable to 'Chinese Marxism' for example. My basic conclusion is that attempts to 'nationalise' Marxism in Latin America have not led to a fundamentally new hybrid. Where hybridisation has happened, as in Argentina with the meeting of Marxism and Peronism, the nationalist discourse has tended to prevail. So, what we have in Latin America is a plurality of Marxisms, from the most dogmatic to the most creative. Though not well known outside the Spanish-speaking world, Marta Harnecker's Althusserian primer *Conceptos Elementales del Materialismo Histórico* (Elementary Concepts of Historical Materialism; 1975) sold some three quarters of a million copies in a region with high illiteracy rates. The surprising popularity of an oversimplified Althusserianism is a remarkable element in the diffusion of Marxist ideas in Latin America. Harnecker's schematism and impoverishment of Marxism reached new depths in *La Revolución Social: Lenin y América Latina* (The Social Revolution: Lenin and Latin America; 1986), a bizarre attempt to read Latin America through a literal Russian Revolution lens. At the other end of the spectrum, a host of Latin American cultural theorists have reinvigorated a creative Marxism, none more so than Nestor García Canclini, whose *Culturas Hibridas* of 1992 (*Hybrid Cultures*; 1995) has had considerable impact across disciplines and has been lauded by First World Marxist intellectuals such as Frederic Jameson (Jameson, 1998: 66). The cultural turn both within Marxism and further afield could be truly said to have Latin American roots.

Reinventing revolution

There are two diametrically opposite scenarios on the prospects for Marxism in Latin America (or Latin American Marxism): either that it is defunct and best forgotten or that it is experiencing a magnificent revival. Many erstwhile true believers have now become fervent advocates of neo-liberalism and have taken the motto TINA (There Is No Alternative) to heart. This is a reaction akin to those ex-communists in the 1930s who berated the 'God that failed' (Koestler *et al.*, 2001 [1949]), a response which is understandable but not particularly fruitful. Ex-guerrilla *comandantes* have sometimes enthusiastically embraced the cause of the new world order. Ex-leaders of social movements have entered government in Chile and continued with essentially Pinochetista policies. Fernando Henrique Cardoso, father or perhaps grandfather of the radical dependency theory, presided over a deeply anti-popular government in Brazil between 1994 and 2002. Even so, a simple recitation of these apostasies misses some of the nuances of the current conjuncture and risks a lapse into moralistic critique. Perhaps a better way of looking at left prospects in Latin America is to see the world historical events of 1989 as an opportunity rather than a closure. In many ways the collapse of communism has freed up Marxists in Latin America; they no longer need to defend the indefensible (or endlessly debate their precise critique of Soviet socialism) and can give freer rein to the undoubted reserve of creativity and energy still present on the Latin American left.

From the 'repentant' Marxists we pass to the 'revivalists' such as James Petras for whom a wonderful new dawn has come for the left. For Petras 'The Left in Latin America is staging a major comeback . . . a vast movement of opposition is growing that in time could challenge the dominance of the whole free market power structure' (Petras, 1999: 13). He points to the landless movement in Brazil, the cocaleros (coca-growers) of Colombia, the Communist Party of Chile and, of course, sub-*comandante* Marcos of the Zapatistas as harbingers of the new true Marxism. For Petras 'two dynamic forces are in an increasingly confrontational mode: peasants versus the US empire' (Petras, 1999: 49). This new dynamic, re-playing the 1960s binary opposition of 'socialism or fascism', is only thwarted, according to Petras, by the post-Marxists who have ensconced themselves in the NGOs doing research shaped by an imperialist agenda. It is true that a new wave of popular struggle seems to have begun in the mid-1990s, and it is also true that many *renovadores* have turned their backs on the popular movements they once sought to lead to socialism. However, it is hard to see how this emotive and uncritical harking back to the thinking of the 1960s can lead to a credible critical Marxist alternative for the next century. As a strategy for progressive transforma-tion – as against a Sartrean endorsement of the most oppressed groups in society – it lacks purchase and is redolent of colonialist noble savage myths.

The more sober voices of Latin American Marxism are now committed to a se-rious reappraisal of past practices and a desacralised look to the future. Above all, as against the Petras problematic, they realise it is incumbent on them to provide a viable political economy to replace the diminishing return of the neo-liberal pre-scriptions. Jorge Castañeda (privileged recipient of Petras's scorn) is an exemplar of this tendency with his widely read book *Utopia Unarmed* (Castañeda, 1993). For Castañeda, nationalism in Latin America could once again – as it did in the 1930s and 1940s – become a force for social inclusion. There is much need across Latin America for a national strategy for industrial growth including a revitalised welfare state. The old-fashioned triangle of nation, industrialisation and welfare state is a reformist project but also a national-popular one. If this does not mate-rialise, more *Senderos Luminosos* will do so instead, according to Castañeda, re-flecting as they do the social disintegration of the country, in the same way as the violence of Rio de Janeiro or the drugs industry of Colombia. The resonance that Castañeda has achieved across Latin America is due not to widespread reform-ist deviation but to his readiness to address the need for a democratic, equitable and sustainable alternative to the status quo. This is a task which critical Marxist thinkers have not been too quick to engage in, having so badly misjudged things in the 1970s.

Marxism in Latin America is more diversified than it ever has been before. There is not only a wide spectrum of political beliefs lurking under the same general label, but political practice has diversified into manifold arenas and forms. As Canclini puts it, the task now facing the new left is the cultural reorganisa-tion of power: 'to analyse what political consequences result from the shift away from a vertical and bipolar conception of socio-political relations, to one which is decentred and multidetermined' (García Canclini, 1995: 323). There are many new forms of radical thinking emerging in the social, cultural and local domains (see Alvarez *et al.*, 1998), that cannot be reduced to idle post-Marxist musings that do nothing to challenge the US empire. It is just that, while the old paradigm is definitely buried, the new ones are still taking shape, as Gramsci would have put it.

What chance is there then of 'reinventing revolution' in Latin America? Much will depend on the post-Castro outcome in Cuba and the ability of the left to challenge the PRI (Institutional Revolutionary Party) in Mexico. Breakthroughs for a renewal or democratic Marxism in these countries would have a dramatic effect. For Ramiro Abreú of the International Relations Department of the Cuban Communist Party Central Committee, 'The Latin American left is facing a very difficult moment. Seldom has the left had such a clear picture of the inability of capitalism to solve our problems and such prospects for power. But the left is facing many moral, political, social, ideological and psychological problems' (quoted in McCaughan, 1997: 9). The Latin American left's crisis of identity has much wider roots than the collapse of the state-socialist reference point after 1989. The armed struggle has left a heavy legacy, as has repression of course. To be radical without being fundamentalist has never been easy for Latin America's Marxists. There is also a symptomatic lack of interaction with the feminist movement which has done so much to transform the left in other latitudes. When Richard Harris argues that 'Marxist theory, with certain revisions' (Harris, 1992: 3), can still be a guide to action in Latin America I would argue that these 'revisions' must amount to a reinvention if they are to achieve their objective.

Prospects

Even a few years after the above sections were written, events had moved fast in Latin America (as elsewhere) but in a way that once again placed socialism, or at least social transformation, on the agenda. According to Perry Anderson in Latin America, 'here and only here, the resistance to neoliberalism and to neo-imperialism welds the cultural with the social and national' (Anderson, 2004: 42). This verdict is certainly congruent with our own historical sketch of Marxism in Latin America, which shows the overwhelming weight of the national questions and the way the political is always social and cultural at the same time. Anderson also stresses the continuous revolutionary history of Latin America, from the Mexican Revolution nearly one hundred years ago, until today. Although this continuity and its revolutionary nature might be contested, Anderson's third distinctive point is quite persuasive: 'here and only here, do we find coalitions of governments and movements in a broad front of resistance to the new world-wide hegemony' (Anderson, 2004: 43). Latin America has seen the birth of the World Social Forum in Porto Alegre, but also of the G-22 group of powerful semi-peripheral countries set up in Cancún.

The World Social Forum started its influential trajectory in Porto Alegre, Brazil, in 2001 in conditions that were as much as regionally and nationally determined as they were global. The Workers Party (PT) control of the state of Rio Grande do Sul and the municipality of Porto Alegre – with its exemplary participative budget experience – were key factors in the dynamic of a movement with a global ambition. The notion that 'another world is possible' reflects its Latin American origins. Likewise, the PT loss of power in the state of Rio Grande do Sul, and then in Porto Alegre, greatly complicated the organisation of the 2005 World Social Forum. This Latin American dynamic or cycle of radical impetus and conservative backlash is, to some extent, reflected in the World Social Forum itself, whose *raison d'être* after 2005 became less clear or transparent. Was it now necessary to construct a more durable organisation and offer concrete political strategies? Or was it sufficient to construct a moral alternative to the global neo-liberal order and reject the classic Marxist or Leninist conceptions of the state, party and power?

In terms of theorising the new challenges to neo-liberal globalisation, its obligatory point of reference is Hardt and Negri's *Empire* (Hardt and Negri, 2000). Its reception in Latin America was quite different from the celebratory tone it awoke in wide sectors of the global left. Although none of its Latin American critics doubted the political integrity of the Negri project (Borón, 2005) they were fiercely critical of its broadly optimistic vision of globalisation and its inherent Eurocentrism. The very notion of 'Empire' as a decentred and deterritorialised apparatus looks peculiarly abstract from a Latin American perspective, as does the notion that the era of imperialism has now closed insofar as no one nation can be hegemonic, as was the case under classic European imperialism. But what critics such as Nestor Kohan find 'one of the most scandalous and provocative theses of *Empire*' (Kohan, 2002: 69) is the anti-dependency notion of Hardt and Negri, that regions such as Latin America are not different in kind from the capitalist production and circulation regimes prevailing in the USA, but rather show only differences of degree.

Another attempt to recast traditional Marxist understandings of capitalism and revolution is John Holloway's *Change the World without Taking Power* (Holloway, 2005). This is a publication whose intellectual roots go back to 1970s enthusiasm, in parts of the British left, for Italian *autonomist* Marxism. Thus, it is not unrelated to Negri's bold foray into counter-globalisation politics and strategy. But Holloway's intellectual/political enterprise is in fact inseparable from the rise of and reflection on Zapatismo. It is exaggerating but outlandish to suggest a relationship similar to that of Regis Debray's *Revolution in the Revolution* (Debray, 1970) as a mirror, but also very partial reading, of the Cuban revolution. Holloway's basic message is quite simple in essence: we must distinguish between 'power over' (characteristic of private property, under capitalism) and 'power to' (which needs to be appropriated by those seeking to transform the world). In Argentina after the 2001 crisis this thinking gained some followers but in general the pressures of power politics, the reality of party politics and the lack of a truly developed civil society have left this political message somewhat marginalised in practice.

Countering the autonomist radicalism of Negri and Holloway, there is a counter-move towards reasserting traditional Marxist categories by some intellectuals. Thus, Petras and Veltmeyer in reviewing the post-2000 rise of centre-left government across Latin America are scathing about any local development or reformist options. Quite simply, for these authors: 'Electoral politics binds any party to the system, turning it towards neoliberalism – towards forces that govern the system ... the "moment" of state power as it were ... was lost' (Petras and Veltmeyer,

2005: 233). And the way to move towards state power was not through local politics or alternative development strategies (as promoted by the World Bank to divert popular energies) but rather through 'constituting a critical mass of insurgent forces, and mobilising them into a movement that could potentially bring down the . . . government, but also change the course of . . . history' (Petras and Veltmeyer, 2005: 217). In this world-view, it is almost as if we were back in the 1980s when traditional Marxist–Leninist conceptions of class, state and power had some resonance in the real world of politics. These views will persist, though, insofar as the reformist alternative will not deliver either sustainable development or a decent living standard for all.

It is very easy to paint an optimistic picture of the 'forward march of history' in Latin America, in the current period. By 2006 there were left or leftist governments in many countries: 'Lula' and the PT (Workers Party) in Brazil, Hugo Chávez in Venezuela, Lucio Gutierrez in Ecuador, Evo Morales in Bolivia, and across the Southern Cone: Silvia Bachelet in Chile, Nestor Kirchner in Argentina and Tabaré Vazquez of the Frenti Amplio (Broad Front) in Uruguay. The US dream of a free trade zone across the Americas lay in tatters as regionalism and nationalism once again held sway. Social movements – above all the indigenous movement in the Andean countries – were once again active in articulating their demands and presenting visions of an alternative future. Only Colombia stood out as a country torn between an authoritarian government and an old-style communist insurgency, with little likelihood of a progressive outcome. In general democracy was being deepened, the forces of reaction were in disarray and neo-liberal hegemony was everywhere contested. It did seem that a reformist – if not quite revolutionary – wave was crossing the continent.

However, it is also possible to take a more critical view of recent politics in Latin America that does not provide such comforting revolutionary thoughts for the international left. In first place we would need to mention the trajectory of the PT (Workers Party) under Lula, in which a whole generation of Brazilian socialists had pinned their hopes. Petras and Veltmeyer write bitterly that 'To demonstrate that the PT was an acceptable interlocutor with Brazilian big business, it dumped its Marxist and socialist identity early on' (Petras and Veltmeyer, 2005: 134). Whether or not this transformation of the most successful socialist party in Latin America was due to the inevitable compromises with neo-liberal globalisation when in power is as yet unclear. In 2006 the PT was engulfed in a corruption scandal (money for votes) that tarnished its image even further. Although Lula himself has emerged to some extent unscathed from this process, Latin America's first 'worker-president' can no longer be seen as the fresh face of a democratic non-Stalinist, non-statist, social movement-based Marxist movement.

Venezuela and its current president Hugo Chávez is another poignant and important case in defining the meaning of socialism and social transformation in contemporary Latin America. As was the case with Cuba, Nicaragua and most recently the Zapatistas, there are many international commentators (see Gott, 2005) who see Chávez in quite messianic terms. At the World Social Forum of 2005 in Porto Alegre, Hugo Chávez filled the huge Gigantinho stadium to capacity.

He thus effectively became a leader of the anti-neo-liberal anti-neo-imperialism movement in Latin America. The 2006 Regional Social Forum was thus, not surprisingly, held in Caracas. But this was not without opposition from more anti-statist and feminist forces on the left who saw the 'big man' syndrome in Latin American politics repeating itself. Chávez has also taken on quite ambitious regional aspirations with political bargaining accruing from Venezuela's oil wealth. Time will tell whether Chávez is close to Perón (my own position) or indeed represents a bold new leader for the whole of the Latin American left. Uncritical support would not, however, be a sensible socialist strategy.

To some extent we are still witnessing a conflict between an old and a new left, and the always unfulfilled promise of theoretical renewal. There are many Marxists and socialists across the continent who still hold fairly orthodox views on the class struggle as the 'motor of history', the perils of liberal democracy and the inevitability of the 'dictatorship of the proletariat'. For many others, the path since the 1970s has seen a steady accommodation with liberal democracy and even the inevitability of neo-liberal so-called reforms of the economy. More recently, there has been an engagement with the broad alter-globalisation movement that has been productive, but also potentially divisive. To put it at its simplest, the World Social Forum 'looks' different and has a different political significance in Latin America from that which it has as a global signifier for an alternative world order. The brutal reality of global uneven development and the persistence of imperialism beyond its more obvious manifestations mean that in Latin America the confrontation with the neo-liberal global world order will take different forms from in the advanced industrial or post-industrial societies.

This is the place where I might once have placed my thoughts on 'the way forward'. However, today no such intellectual or political arrogance is persuasive. The truth is that Latin America, as always, is at a crossroads and its political future is both complex and uncertain. We have seen how political opinions tend to divide into binary oppositions, either 'for' or 'against' Chávez, for recognition of indigenous rights versus a 'return' to the class struggle. Must we really choose between a path seeking to 'conquer' state power and one where we believe we can change the world without seizing the state? In the real world of politics on the ground such dilemmas have little purchase. The left in Latin America is undergoing a constant process of renewal, and the meaning of Marxist politics is being constantly reinvented. Beyond optimistic and pessimistic scenarios, we can posit a continued role for left/socialist/Marxist thinking and political action in Latin America. We can also confidently predict that this thinking and praxis will have a global effect.

References

Aguilar, L. (ed.) (1968) *Marxism in Latin America*. New York: Alfred Knopf.

Alvarez, S., E. Dagnino and A. Escobar (eds) (1998) *Cultures of Politics: Politics of Cultures – Re-visioning Latin American Social Movements*. Boulder, CO: Westview Press.

Anderson, P. (2004) *The Role of Ideas in the Construction of Alternatives*. Los Angeles: UCLA (mimeo).

Aricó, J. (1980) 'Introducción' in J. Aricó (ed.), *Mariátegui y los Orígenes del Marxismo Latinamericano.* Mexico City: Siglo XXI.

Aricó, J. (1982) *Marx y América Latina.* Mexico City: Alianza Editorial.

Aricó, J. (1988) *La cola del diablo. Itinerario de Gramsci en América Latina.* Buenos Aires: Puntosur.

Avineri, S. (ed.) (1969) *Karl Marx on Colonialism and Modernization.* New York: Anchor Books.

Borón, A. (2005) *Empire and Imperialism: A Critical Reading of Michael Hardt and Antonio Negri.* London: Zed Books.

Castañeda, J. (1993) *La Utopia desarmada. Intrigas, dilemas y promesa de la izquierda en America Latina.* Buenos Aires: Ariel.

Castells, M. (1997) *The Information Age,* volume II: *The Power of Identity.* Oxford: Blackwell.

Debray, R. (1970) *Revolution in the Revolution.* London: Penguin Books.

Falcón, R. (1980) *La Primera Internacional y Origenes del Movimiento Obrero en Argentina (1857–1879).* Paris: CEUSAL.

García Canclini, N. (1995) *Hybrid Cultures: Strategies for Entering and Leaving Modernity.* Minneapolis, MN: Minnesota University Press

Garretón, M.A. (1989) 'The Ideas of Socialist Renovation in Chile', *Rethinking Marxism,* 2 (Summer): 8–39.

Gott, R (2005) *Hugo Chavez: The Bolívarian Revolution in Venezuela.* London: Verso

Gramsci, A. (1977) 'The Revolution against *Capital*' in A. Gramsci, *Selections from Political Writings (1919–1920).* London: Lawrence and Wishart.

Hardt, M. and A. Negri (2000) *Empire.* Cambridge, MA: Harvard University Press

Harnecker, M. (1975) *Los Conceptos Elementales del Materialismo Historico.* Mexico City: Siglo XXI.

Harnecker, M. (1986) *La Revolución Social: Lenin y America Latina.* Mexico City: Siglo XXI.

Harris, R. (1992) *Marxism, Socialism and Democracy in Latin America.* Boulder, CO: Westview Press.

Harvey, N. (1998) *The Chiapas Rebellion: The Struggle for Land and Democracy.* Durham, NC: Duke University Press.

Holloway, J. (2005) *Change the World without Taking Power: The Meaning of Revolution Today.* London: Pluto.

Jameson, F. (1998) 'Notes on Globalization as a Philosophical Issue' in F. Jameson and M. Miyoshi (eds), *The Cultures of Globalization.* Durham, NC: Duke University Press.

Kay, C. (1989) *Latin American Theories of Development and Underdevelopment.* London: Routledge.

Koestler, A., I. Silone and A. Gide (2001 [1949]) *The God that Failed.* New York: Columbia University Press.

Kohan, N (2002) *Toni Negri y los desafíos de Imperio.* Madrid: Campos de Ideas.

Laclau, E. (1990) *New Reflections on the Revolution of our Time.* London: Verso.

Laclau, E. and C. Mouffe (1985) *Hegemony and Socialist Strategy.* London: Verso.

Lowy, M. (1973) *The Marxism of Che Guevara: Philosophy, Economics and Revolutionary Warfare.* New York: Monthly Review Press.

McCaughan, E. (1997) *Reinventing Revolution: The Renovation of Left Discourse in Cuba and Mexico.* Boulder, CO: Westview Press.

Mariátegui, J.C. (1969a) *Ideologia y Politica.* Lima: Amauta.

Mariátegui, J.C. (1969b) *Defensa del Marxismo.* Lima: Amauta.

Mariátegui, J.C. (1973) *Internacionalismo y nacionalismo in Historia de la Crisis Mundial*. Lima: Amauta.

Marx, K. and F. Engels (1976) *Collected Works*, volume 7. London: Lawrence and Wishart.

Marx, K. and F. Engels (1977) *Collected Works*, volume 8. London: Lawrence and Wishart.

Marx, K. and F. Engels (1982) *Collected Works*, volume 9. London: Lawrence and Wishart.

Munck, R. (1999) 'Dependency and Imperialism in Latin America: New Horizons' in R. Chilcote (ed.), *The Political Economy of Imperialism: Critical Appraisals*. New York: Kluwer Academic Press.

Munck, R. (2000) 'Culture, Politics and Postmodernism in Latin America' in A. Jones and R. Munck (eds), *Cultural Politics in Latin America*. London: Macmillan.

Norval, A. (1996) *Deconstructing Apartheid Discourse*. London: Verso.

OLAS (1967) 'General Declaration', *International Socialist Review*, 28, 6 (November–December).

Petras, J. (1999) *The Left Strikes Back: Class Conflict in Latin America in the Age of Neoliberalism*. Boulder, CO: Westview Press.

Petras, J. and H. Veltmeyer (2005) *Social Movements and State Power: Argentina, Brazil, Bolivia, Ecuador*. London: Pluto Press.

Portantiero, J.C. (1983) *Los usos de Gramsci*. Buenos Aires: Folios Editor.

Waterman, P. (1998) *Globalization, Social Movements and the New Internationalisms*. London and Washington: Mansell.

Further reading

Becker, M. (1993) *Mariátegui and Latin American Marxist Theory*. Ohio: Ohio University Center for International Studies.

Caballero, M. (1996) *Latin America and the Comintern, 1919–1943*. Cambridge: Cambridge University Press.

Carr, B. and S. Ellner (eds) (1993) *The Latin American Left: From the Fall of Allende to Perestroika*. Boulder, CO: Westview Press.

Castañeda, J. (1993) *Utopia Unarmed: The Latin American Left after the Cold War*. New York: Random House.

Debray, R. (1977) *A Critique of Arms*, volume 1. Harmondsworth: Penguin.

Dietz, M. and G. Shildo (eds) (1998) *Urban Elections in Democratic Latin America*. Delaware: SR Books.

Gramsci, A. (1971) 'Against Byzantism' in A. Gramsci, *Selections from the Prison Notebooks*. London: Lawrence and Wishart.

Hodges, D.C. (1974) *The Latin American Revolution: Politics and Strategy from Apro-Marxism to Guevarism*. New York: William Morrow.

Keck, M. (1992) *The Workers' Party and Democratization in Brazil*. New Haven, CT: Yale University Press.

Lander, E. (2003) 'Hacia el Foro Social Mundial Caracas 2006' in J. Seoane (ed.), *Movimientos sociales y conflicto en America Latina*, Buenos Aires: CLACSO.

Liss, S. (1984) *Marxist Thought in Latin America*. Berkeley, CA: University of California Press.

Lowy, M. (ed.) (1992) *Marxism in Latin America from 1909 to the Present: An Anthology*. London: Humanities Press International.

Munck, R. (1984) *Revolutionary Trends in Latin America.* Montreal: McGill University.

Roberts, K. (1998) *Deepening Democracy? The Modern Left and Social Movements in Chile and Peru.* Stanford, CA: Stanford University Press.

Vanden, H. (1986) *National Marxism in Latin America: Jose Carlos Mariategui's Thought and Politics.* Boulder, CO: Lynne Rienner Publishers.

Part III

10 Marxism and socialism

Howard Chodos

The subject explored in this chapter is the relationship between Marxism, as a body of theory, and the attempts that were made in the course of the twentieth century to utilize its insights to replace capitalism with socialism. It would clearly be impossible in the framework of a single chapter to provide a detailed examination of the diverse experiences that constitute the historical record of Marxist-inspired socialism in the twentieth century. Three broad historical facts, however, serve to inform what follows.

First, the fact that the vision that inspired the creation of historical communism did not survive the twentieth century intact. The main states that were built in the name of Marxism either collapsed, as in the case of the former Soviet Union and its allied People's Democracies, or have been so thoroughly transformed as a result of a series of economic reforms, as in the case of China, as to be unrecognizable. There are, of course, a number of exceptions to this rule, such as Cuba and North Korea, but it would not seem fitting to draw broad conclusions based on such exceptions. Second, the fact that serious violations of human rights, not to say outright criminal behaviour, have repeatedly occurred in states purporting to implement the Marxian vision, under a sufficiently wide array of circumstances to constitute a prima facie case that there was something amiss at the heart of the twentieth-century socialist project. And finally, the fact that historical communist[1] regimes were never able to live up to the standard that they themselves established as the criterion by which they should ultimately be judged, that is, they never did surpass capitalist liberal democracies either in terms of their ability to sustain economic growth, or in terms of meeting the material needs of their citizens.

For anyone concerned with the future of the socialist project, it would be hard to overstate either the significance or the complexity of the debate over the relationship between Marxism and socialism. Many difficult and unresolved issues converge and overlap, raising questions of political and economic theory, as well as sociological and historical analysis. Still, the combined effect of this experience can legitimately be said to call into question the validity of the Marxist project itself. Even those who are sympathetic to the goals and ideals articulated by the Marxist tradition must recognize the gravity of the legacy of twentieth-century Marxist-inspired socialism. So the question that animates this chapter is the extent to which the historical record can be said to challenge the central theoretical propositions about capitalism and socialism that constitute the distinctive contributions of the Marxian approach.

Marxist-inspired socialist projects in the twentieth century are located at the point of intersection between theory and practice. The attempt to bring into being the classless society envisaged by Marx and Engels figures without doubt amongst the most significant projects of theoretically driven social engineering ever undertaken. The goal was, ostensibly, a noble one. Marxism envisaged the possibility of a successor system to capitalism that would not only be more just in the way that it distributed the fruits of society's labour, but also enable more of the goods and services that people actually needed to be produced than capitalism ever could. Justice, freedom, equality would reign, as all forms of oppression and exploitation would be consigned to the dustbin of history.

One of the attractive features of the Marxian synthesis was that it came as a total package. Its cogent analysis of the gross inequality of wealth and power that characterized nineteenth-century capitalism situated the development of capitalism as a mode of production in the framework of an epochal trajectory of social systems. This enabled Marxism to propose a way forward that drew on its understanding of capitalism not only to define the broad contours of its successor, but also to locate within capitalism itself the human agents who, while being the pure products of capitalism, were also, in Marx and Engels' celebrated image, its gravediggers. But it is precisely the coherence of the classical Marxian synthesis that makes it vulnerable to being challenged *in toto* in the wake of the shortcomings of historical communism.

Of course, any attempt to discuss the relationship between Marxism as a body of theory and the subsequent practice of those who claimed to be drawing inspiration and guidance from it immediately confronts the difficulty that there is not a single Marxism but many Marxisms. In what follows I will not try to adduce definitive arguments about what Marx really meant, or seek to define the true elements of the Marxist doctrine with regard to socialism. Rather, I accept that there are numerous plausible interpretations of what Marx wrote.[2] These Marxisms derive not only from the diversity of the interpreters, but also from the limitations of Marx's own work. There are many elements in Marx that he left undeveloped, with the theory of the state and of socialism being amongst the most notable of these, and certainly the most relevant to this chapter (see Van den Berg, 1988; Barrow, 2000; O'Hagan, 1981). However, it is only necessary for our present purposes to look at the relationship between certain types of practice that were typical of twentieth-century attempts to build socialism and key propositions that formed a recognizable part of the Marxian corpus.

Marx and socialism as working-class power

Marx's argument was, on the surface at least, a reasonably consistent and coherent one, and it is important to begin by briefly summarizing a few key elements. For Marx, the struggle between classes – groups whose existence is rooted in the production of the material necessities of life – to preserve their privilege or to secure better conditions for themselves was the engine that drove social evolution. The state itself emerges in the course of this process and becomes the main institution for regulating the class struggle. Under 'normal' circumstances, the state serves as an instrument for securing the domination of one class over the others.

However, Marx also believed that the epoch of class societies was coming to an end, and that capitalism was the last social order that would be characterized by pervasive class antagonisms. The task of accomplishing this great historic mission fell to the class that occupied the subordinate position under capitalism, the working class or proletariat. In struggling to better its own position under capitalism, and ultimately by overthrowing the capitalist order, the working class would not only end its own exploitation and oppression but usher in the first truly free society in the annals of human history. The working class could not free itself without simultaneously liberating all of humanity from the ravages of class society as such.

However, the emergence of a truly classless society required a transitional phase of class rule (called by Marx the dictatorship of the proletariat) in which the working class itself would become the ruling class. Although this proletarian state was still a state in which one class held the reins of political power, it would be a state unlike any previous class state. Its goal would not be the consolidation and preservation of the dominance of one class over others, as had been the case in all recorded history till then, but rather the elimination of classes. Marx thus argued that capitalism produces not only its own gravediggers, but also the agents of destruction of all forms of class rule.

The economic strategy that Marx and Engels envisaged would accompany this political transition entailed bringing the process of production and distribution of goods and services under the conscious control of the collectivity. This meant socializing the means of production and finding a way to coordinate economic activity so that production was driven by the goal of meeting the needs of the people and not that of capital. Thus Marx wrote in the third volume of *Capital* that:

> socialized mankind, the associated producers, will regulate their interchange with nature rationally, bring it under their common control, instead of being ruled by it as by some blind power
>
> (in Tucker, 1978: 441)

while Engels[3] indicated that:

> The seizure of the means of production by society eliminates commodity production and with it the domination of the product over the producer. The anarchy within social production is replaced by consciously planned organization.
>
> (Engels, 1975: 97)

Marxism and revolution

In the course of the twentieth century, movements and organizations inspired by revolutionary Marxism succeeded in taking state power in the largest and most populous countries in the world, and it is easy to forget that for much of the century they appeared to constitute a serious threat to the dominance of global capitalism. An examination of the relationship between Marxism and socialism must therefore first ask to what extent it is possible to attribute the initial success of Marxist-inspired revolutions to the theoretical guidance of Marxism. From Marx onwards, the insights provided by the doctrine were hypothesized not only as providing a way of understanding the world, but also as offering a practical guide to the kinds of action needed to transform it. Starting in Russia in 1917, numerous regimes have successfully taken power under the banner of revolutionary Marxism, and there can be no doubt that those involved perceived their commitment to Marxism as being instrumental in enabling them to elaborate appropriate strategies and tactics for overthrowing the old social order. Of course, not all movements that claimed Marxism as their guide were successful. Most notably, nowhere did a Marxist-inspired indigenous revolution occur in the most capitalistically developed countries that the doctrine itself had originally argued were most ripe for the transition to socialism.

The reasons behind the success or failure of any specific revolutionary movement, inspired by Marxism or not, are many and complex. It is well beyond the scope of this chapter to offer even elements of the kind of historical investigation that would be needed in order to explain why certain efforts triumphed while others did not. What is possible, however, is to reflect briefly on the significance of the fact that Marxist-inspired revolutions are not the only ones to have succeeded in the twentieth century. The list of other types of ideological motivation that have served as the basis around which revolutionary movements have coalesced is a long one and includes varieties of nationalism, populism, national liberation, anti-imperialism and anti-fascism, as well as a variety of religions. Most significantly, I would argue that it is not possible to locate anything that is fundamentally unique to Marxist-inspired revolutions with regard to their approaches to strategy, tactics or organization. Even the much-vaunted Leninist-type party cannot lay claim to exclusive ownership of its various features, whether it be democratic centralism (shared by any parliamentary government that enforces a practice of cabinet solidarity), a strong ideological outlook and a reliance on political agitation and propaganda (shared by most religiously inspired movements) or organization in small cells of professional revolutionaries (shared by terrorist organizations of whatever persuasion).

What this suggests is that a revolutionary movement requires the cohesion that is fostered by an ideological outlook, but that there are many ideologies that can respond to this requirement. Of course, movements must be able to adapt their programme and tactics to the specific context they confront, and the outcome in any given situation will therefore be a highly contingent matter that will very much depend on the actual relationship of forces that prevails and on the skill of the participants on both sides of the conflict. Nonetheless, an ideological under-pinning is a key ingredient that contributes to generating the capacity the revo-lutionary group requires in order to intervene. It helps to draw people together and provides them with the motivation and determination to pursue what can be a very difficult and dangerous struggle. It can help to inspire broader support amongst the target population and to offer people the hope of a brighter future. However, the fact that a similar role can be played by religious fundamentalism, narrow nationalism or revolutionary Marxism strongly suggests that this function is, at least to a very significant degree, independent of the specific content of the motivating ideology.

The implication of this brief analysis is that it is not possible to draw general, all-encompassing conclusions about the impact of any specific ideology on the success or failure of attempts at revolution. One cannot say, for example, that *only* Marxism can help inspire and guide the revolutionary overthrow of a specific type of regime. Rather, it is necessary to conduct a detailed historical examination of each specific instance in order to decipher the impact of the various political, ideological, economic and other factors that yielded a given outcome. However, the situation with regard to the building of a new social order on the ruins of an old one is not the same. Here, if there is a consistent attempt to use a particular model as the starting point for constructing a new state structure, it should be possible to identify those elements that derive from a particular outlook or ideology, and to the extent that there are enough examples to compare, to draw some conclusions with regard to the success or failure of that model.

Assessing the Soviet experience

Much of the debate about the record of historical communism has focused, rightly, on the country that was the first to attempt to build socialism in the twentieth century, the Soviet Union. In many ways the USSR provided the template that all subsequent variants sought to adapt to their particular circumstances. It would be impossible even to summarize the complex history of Soviet Russia through its numerous phases in the space here available. Nonetheless, given the centrality of the Soviet experience to the debate over the relationship between Marxism and socialism it is essential to identify the key features of its social organization. Part of the difficulty in attempting this is that the nature and characteristics of the Soviet social order are highly contested, as much within the Marxist tradition (broadly defined) as outside it.

Figure 10.1 summarizes the broad spectrum of positions that have been advanced within the Marxist tradition concerning the nature of historical com-munism. There are four qualitatively different positions that can be discerned, although these overlap and shade into one another, so that individual commenta-tors may advance positions that contain a mixture of elements. A fifth position – that any attempt to apply Marxism leads inexorably to 'totalitarianism' – has also been included as an additional reference point, although it is obvious that

Figure 10.1 Marxist positions on the nature of historical communism.

such a stance would be defended by people who situate themselves outside the Marxist tradition.

Working from left to right in the diagram, the first position (comprising the first three boxes) holds that the regimes typified by the Soviet Union were indeed 'socialist' to a sufficient degree to allow them to be qualitatively differentiated from capitalist regimes. Defenders of this kind of position do not necessarily attempt to argue that these regimes were perfect, or that, prior to their implosion, they had completed the long and arduous transition to mature (and presumably) classless socialist societies. They also often point to the relatively 'backward' nature of the countries that undertook the transition to socialism, both economically and politically, and to the constant harassment from the considerably richer and more developed capitalist world, as key factors in explaining both the defects of historical communist regimes and their ultimate collapse. Nonetheless, they view historical communist regimes as having been, on the whole, faithful to the model laid out by classical Marxism and qualitatively superior in practice to their capitalist competitors in fostering social justice and equality.[4]

The second broad position (fourth box), articulated almost exclusively by the Trotskyist tradition within orthodox Marxism (starting with Trotsky himself), argues that a powerful bureaucracy took over political control of the socialist regimes after these had been created by genuine popular revolutions. Once it had gained political ascendancy, this bureaucratic stratum utilized the institutional framework (grounded in the nationalization of the means of production) to further its own narrow interests, leading to a kind of hybrid state in which the economic infrastructure remained fundamentally socialist, but the political superstructure was no longer under the control of the working class. These states were deemed 'degenerate workers' states'. Supporters of this view generally defended these 'degenerate workers' states' insofar as they opposed international capitalism, but also insisted that they were ripe for a new political revolution so that power could be wrenched away from the bureaucracy and genuine socialism restored (Bellis, 1979).[5]

With the third position along the continuum (box five) the argument becomes that the historical communist states cannot be considered to be socialist in any meaningful sense. It is argued that the ruling elite in control of the state not only deprived the people of any say in political decision-making, but also ran the economy primarily to serve its own private interests and, in essence, continued to exploit the working class, just as do capitalist regimes. There are a number of variants of this view (Cliff, 1974; Bettelheim, 1976; Resnick and Wolff, 2002), but proponents tend to argue that, contrary to the ideals articulated by traditional Marxism, ordinary working people neither controlled the historical communist regimes nor benefited from the wealth they created. On this view, the ruling elite that seized power continued to exploit and oppress the majority of the population, and these regimes must therefore still be thought of as variants of capitalism. Proponents of this position do not necessarily agree on whether the Soviet regime ever actually succeeded in breaking with capitalism, nor do those who believe that there was indeed a period during which genuine socialist construction was begun necessarily locate the moment of the restoration of capitalism at the same point in time. The Maoist version[6] of this position went so far as to argue that these 'social imperialist' (socialist in name, imperialist in deed) regimes were a more significant danger to world peace than the leading capitalist states, such as the United States.

The next position (boxes six and seven) agrees that the historical communist regimes bear little or no resemblance to the socialism envisaged by the Marxist tradition, but does not believe that it is accurate to characterize them as a variant of capitalism. Rather, proponents of this view argue that historical communism represented a new type of regime that arose as a result of the overthrow of capitalism, and is characterized by novel ways of organizing wealth generation and surplus appropriation. The distinctive features of this new social order are usually said to include the highly centralized political control maintained by the single ruling party, extensive nationalization of the means of production, and reliance on central planning rather than markets to allocate resources and distribute goods (Sweezy, 1980).[7]

Finally, there are those who see historical communist regimes as the necessary and logical totalitarian consequence of any attempt at utopian social engineering (Pipes, 2001). Although the term totalitarian is used in different ways, the general thrust of this argument is that those who were at the pinnacle of the historical communist state apparatus wielded total control over all aspects of social, political and economic life, and did so in a highly authoritarian, and often criminal, manner. No respect for the rule of law or for the well-being of the population was shown, with the predictable result that the most horrific suffering was perpetrated.

All too often, the debate over the nature of the Soviet Union on the left has been marked by political infighting and sectarianism amongst advocates of particular versions of socialism. It is indeed obvious that one's understanding of the very meaning of the terms 'capitalism' and 'socialism' play a central role in deciding which position one finds congenial, and that, conversely, how one reads the history of the Soviet Union will condition one's view of what a future socialism might look like. Unfortunately, exploring competing definitions of capitalism and socialism is yet another topic whose full elucidation is far beyond the scope of the present chapter. What is possible is to attempt a very cursory assessment of the balance sheet of the Soviet experience, in order that we may draw some provisional conclusions. There are two key questions. First, was the Soviet experiment, on balance, a success or a failure? And, second, can we identify the structural elements in the model of social organization represented by the Soviet Union that contributed to the historical outcome?

Table 10.1 presents a very rough summary of some of the key points raised by both critics and defenders of the Soviet regime. Presented in this way, it might seem as if each negative is more or less balanced by a positive. That it is possible to view the historical balance sheet in this way may also help explain why many well-meaning people chose to support the USSR, despite also being prepared to acknowledge its many 'shortcomings'. To think this, however, would in my view represent a serious underestimation of the scope and scale of the negative features

Table 10.1 Assessing the Soviet legacy

Defenders insist that the USSR:	Critics say that the USSR:
Demonstrated the possibility of successfully overthrowing capitalism	Discredited anti-capitalist alternatives by its failure to surpass capitalism
Survived for almost 80 years in the face of hostility and invasion, marked by the heroic efforts of the population to build and defend the regime	Collapsed ignominiously amidst a complete absence of visible signs of popular support
Intermittently displayed examples of mass democracy	Was a highly repressive and undemocratic regime, to the point of criminally causing millions of innocent deaths
Allowed the working class to secure some real advantages, such as job security	Had working-class rule in name only
Rapidly industrialized and maintained higher rates of growth than Western economies during its initial phases	Suffered from economic stagnation and inefficiency during its 'mature' phases
Provided relatively egalitarian access to health care and education	Treated people unequally, based on their degree of political loyalty to the ruling elite
Led the world with some of its scientific and technological achievements (military, space)	Was unable to match broadly based Western technological and scientific progress
Narrowed the gap between rich and poor	Produced poor-quality consumer goods that were always in short supply
Made a decisive contribution to the war against fascism and supported numerous progressive causes worldwide	Subordinated the interests of foreign revolutionary and progressive movements to the state interests of the USSR

compared to the positive ones. Moreover, when judged against the objectives it set for itself (and that were inscribed in the original Marxian vision of what socialism would be), it should be clear that the Soviet experiment constitutes a massive failure. A few simple examples will illustrate why.

That some leaders of the Soviet Union and of other Soviet-style regimes can legitimately be considered amongst the biggest mass murderers of the twentieth century stands as an indictment of the socialist project that cannot be ignored. The exact figures may still be in dispute (Courtois *et al.*, 1997),[8] but there are sufficient examples of horrendous crimes committed in the name of socialism to give pause to anyone seeking to pursue the path of revolutionary socialism in the twenty-first century. Although Stalin's Gulag and the Killing Fields of Kampuchea may stand out on account of their premeditated and cold-blooded nature, the many examples of policy-induced famine (from the Ukraine in the 1930s, to China in the 1950s, to North Korea still today) that also took the lives of millions must, as well, be counted amongst the inexcusable consequences of attempts to realize Marxist-inspired socialism.

Nor can the extent to which historical communism made a mockery of the predictions that socialism would eliminate the waste that was seen as endemic to, and characteristic of, profit-seeking capitalism be underestimated. From the production of goods that were unwanted or unusable, to the ways in which the central plan encouraged production based on artificial criteria, waste was rampant. In the USSR, imports would sit untouched in warehouses and crops would be left to rot in the fields because they could not be brought to market. Socialism was supposed to lead to production for need and to avoid the disregard for the environment that often characterizes the profit-driven capitalist economies. However, the rush to industrialize in the absence of any checks and balances from civil society led to environmental catastrophes, from the drying up of the Aral Sea to Chernobyl (Silber, 1994: 139–41).

The preponderance of the negative over the positive features is sealed by the decline and unexpected collapse of the Soviet Union during the final fifteen years of its existence. The most compelling explanation of why this came about in the way that it did, and which also helps to situate the initial successes of the Soviet model, locates the nub of the problem in the inability of the Soviet Union to manage the transition from an extensive mode of development to an intensive one (Castells, 1998: 4–69). Extensive development relies mainly on the deployment of previously unused resources, be they human or natural, whereas intensive development yields higher output by improving the efficiency with which these resources are employed. So, although the Soviet Union was able to make important strides in its initial industrialization, it proved incapable of sustaining this growth over time. It is not hard to think of reasons why this was so, in a society where the exchange of knowledge and information was so strictly controlled that the use of photocopy machines was severely restricted.

How should these regimes be characterized then? A key insight from historical materialism is relevant here. For Marxism, modes of production were defined essentially by the way in which they structured, organized and utilized the social surplus that they were able to generate. One does not have to subscribe to the theory of history that Marxists, beginning with Marx, built upon the foundation of this notion of differing modes of production in order to accept that there is a great deal of value in interrogating the structure of social accumulation, and even in using the variations in the way different social orders approach this task as a means of comparing them.

In this spirit, it is possible to identify two key features of the way in which historical communism organized surplus production that are part of its *differentia specifica* as a social order. In the first place, the central role played by the Communist Party in these regimes clearly stands out as a defining feature. Both ardent defenders of Marxist-inspired socialism as well as its most strenuous critics share this view of the centrality of the party to the nature of the regime. Some see the Marxist-inspired vanguard party as the single most significant element in defining the dynamics that are particular to these societies (Lebowitz, 2000). The second feature of historical communism that defines a unique form of social organization involves what could be called the fusion of the economic and political spheres. In my view, it is important to distinguish this as a separate element, rather than to see the fusion of the economic and political as simply being a consequence of the functioning of the vanguard party itself. This is because there is no reason, in principle, that an authoritarian and politically centralized state could not allow for a much greater degree of autonomous economic activity than was the case under historical communism.[9]

It is the combination of an ideologically driven, centralized, authoritarian political leadership with the control of all key economic levers by the state apparatus that was at the Party's disposal that produces the dynamics of surplus production and control over wealth that are characteristic of historical communism. Since all of the Marxist-inspired socialist states that emerged in the twentieth century can be characterized in this fashion, it is therefore not surprising that similar dynamics prevailed across the board.

Marxism and socialism

We now need to try to unravel the connection between the Marxian conception of socialism as working-class power and the actual practice of historical communism. One's understanding of the nature of this relationship obviously depends to a large extent on the assessment one makes of the historical record of Marxist-inspired socialism. Rendering a negative judgment in this regard does not automatically entail a wholesale rejection of the Marxian theory that helped to define historical communism in the twentieth century. In fact, there is no shortage of modalities for absolving Marxism of responsibility, in whole or in part, even for those events whose instigators proclaimed their fealty to the tradition. Before attempting my own explanation, it is worth a brief look at some of these. Figure 10.2 presents a schematic overview of a similar continuum of arguments to those that were already considered with regard to the nature of the USSR. Although there is much overlap between the two series of argument, as would be expected, a few comments on some in this second set are in order.

It seems to me that the historical record confronts arguments two through four on this continuum (the 'misinterpretation', 'betrayal' and 'no blueprint' hypotheses) with a serious challenge. The problem with the 'no blueprint' hypothesis is that, even if one accepts for the sake of argument that the formula for socialist construction was never spelled out by the founding fathers of Marxism, one still has to explain the actual experience of Marxist-inspired socialism if one wishes to have any hope of persuading people to engage in another attempt at replacing capitalism with socialism. If the absence of a 'blueprint' produced failure, then it is hardly inspiring simply to insist that it will be possible to succeed in the future guided by the same lack of a blueprint.

The 'misinterpretation' and 'betrayal' hypotheses suffer from a similar defect. They implicitly posit a 'correct' Marxism that needs to be 'rediscovered' in order to avoid the setbacks incurred throughout the twentieth century. Even if one assumes this to be the case, however, a question that would still need to be answered is how to explain the fact that the theory was so consistently misinterpreted and/or betrayed. Asserting that one can explain how it is that the hundreds of millions of people who engaged in projects of socialist construction all got it wrong, simply by referring back to the same texts that were used by these 'misinterpreters' and

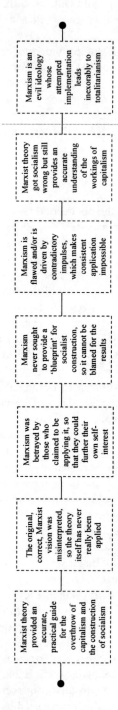

Marxist theory provided an accurate, practical guide for the overthrow of capitalism and the construction of socialism

The original, correct, Marxist vision was misinterpreted, so the theory itself has never really been applied

Marxism was betrayed by those who claimed to be applying it, so that they could further their own self-interest

Marxism never sought to provide a 'blueprint' for socialist construction, so it cannot be blamed for the results

Marxism is flawed and/or is driven by contradictory impulses, which makes consistent application impossible

Marxist theory got socialism wrong but still provides an accurate understanding of the workings of capitalism

Marxism is an evil ideology whose attempted implementation leads inexorably to totalitarianism

Figure 10.2 Explaining the relationship between Marxism and historical communism.

'betrayers' in the course of their efforts, is as unpersuasive as the idea that a new version of socialism will simply crystallize in the course of working to bring it into being, as advocates of the 'no blueprint' hypothesis would have one believe.

So, how should one approach understanding the relationship between Marxism as theory and historical communism as practice? First, it is important to acknowledge that the very way that Marxism understood the nature of the successor society to capitalism is marked by a teleological view of the course of human history. No matter how it is formulated, the idea that 'socialism equals working-class power' contains within it the view that the working class, as it is constituted under capitalism, is somehow predestined to both defeat capitalism and bring into being a new form of social organization, socialism. One can try to discount the more egregiously teleological statements that occur in Marx himself,[10] but the reality is that this teleology is embedded in the most basic approach to socialism propagated by the tradition.

However, it is equally important to recognize that this kind of teleology, in and of itself, does not lead straight towards the abyss of Stalinism, any more than a belief in the Holy Trinity automatically leads to the Inquisition. Many people – probably the majority of humanity – believe that there is a direction to human history, and many also are convinced that it is possible for us to decipher at least the broad implications of this basic fact for how we should conduct our lives. In this, those who were persuaded over the past century that the inevitability of socialism was inscribed in the pattern of human social development are no different. Moreover, a broad teleological view of this sort can be the basis for justifying any approach that yields the desired results, and does not necessarily specify the exact means that are required. Either ecumenism or the Inquisition can be championed as the road to the Kingdom of Heaven on earth. That is, different means can be advocated by people who share a common conviction that certain kinds of ends are desirable, and perhaps even inevitable. In this respect, those who argued that the technological development of capitalism would produce a working-class majority that could bring socialism into being via the electoral process could also be said to have held a teleological view of history, yet would have been quite unlikely to endorse the type of one-party rule that characterized historical communism.

More is therefore needed to get us from a belief that the working class is destined to liberate humanity from the evils of exploitation and oppression to the realities of twentieth-century historical communism. Belief in the scientific character of the Marxist doctrine provided another linchpin. It was argued that, as with any science, Marxism enabled its adherents to acquire objective knowledge. Those who were able to master the science could understand the laws that govern social evolution (just as natural science teaches us about the laws governing the physical universe) and become capable of using this knowledge for practical purposes. Here is how the classic text of the Stalinist period, the *History of the Communist Party of the Soviet Union (Bolsheviks)*, put it:

> if the world is knowable and our knowledge of the laws of the development of nature is authentic knowledge, having the validity of objective truth, it

follows that social life, the development of society, is also knowable, and that the data of science regarding the laws of development of society are authentic data having the validity of objective truths.

(CC of CPSU, 1939: 114)

It does not require much effort to get from the idea that the knowledge acquired through a careful study of Marxism has an objective character to the conclusion that it should be possible, under any given set of circumstances, to decipher the unique way forward towards the desired goal of replacing capitalism with socialism. The argument does not have to be that there is a single, unchanging template that can be applied universally. Clearly, that would be a highly rigid and sterile form of dogmatism that would have had little appeal, and even less practical success. Rather, the belief in the ability to acquire objective knowledge about social laws provides a strong basis for the belief that there is but one way to facilitate the realization of the desired end. It is then possible to add on a second component to the argument that assigns to a select group of people the mission and the capacity to discover what this effective strategy is, and to take a leading role in implementing it.

But even this is not yet enough. A further element that is required to produce the framework in which the Marxist-inspired doctrine of socialism can be converted into the reality of historical communism is a Manichean understanding of the struggle that is driving social evolution forward. Socialism is seen as possible only if the working class triumphs in a life-and-death battle with the forces aligned with capital. The dictatorship of the bourgeoisie must be replaced by the dictatorship of the proletariat, and this entails a ruthless struggle against the class enemy directly, and against all those who side with the class enemy. Moreover, the objective is often seen to be nothing less than a total transformation of social life.

And finally there is the question of capacity. The concentration of enormous political and economic power in the hands of a small elite at the pinnacle of the state apparatus, largely unaccountable to the population at large, with very few external constraints imposed by non-state institutions, creates the optimum conditions for the realization of the worst tendencies fostered by the Marxian paradigm of social transformation. Although one should avoid a determinist reading (i.e. that the experience of historical communism was the inevitable result of adopting Marx's analysis of capitalism), the fact that these tendencies were indeed realized under a wide variety of circumstances indicates the potency of the brew.

Marxism and socialism in the twenty-first century

Could a successor system to capitalist liberal democracies avoid the defects of this form of social organization? Although a much fuller inquiry would be necessary to even venture a positive response to this question, our analysis does provide initial guidelines for defining some of the contours of a feasible post-capitalism.

It is first important to ask whether the experience of twentieth-century Marxist-inspired socialism sheds any light on the appropriate general attitude to be adopted towards the relationship between existing capitalism and a future socialism. To borrow a phrase from Marshall Berman (1999: 97), I would argue that it points to the need to start from the recognition that both the good and the bad come from the same place. If one is to argue that the flaws in the capitalist system can be traced to structural defects that define the particular dynamics of capitalism, then there are strong logical grounds for assuming that the positive attributes of capitalism (that is, unless one denies that there are any) should also be similarly linked to the workings of the system itself.

Adopting such an attitude means that one must not treat any positive developments that have taken place under the watch of capitalist liberal democracies as simply accidental occurrences, divorced from the underlying structure of the system, and/or as purely the result of the struggles of the oppressed for their legitimate rights. Measures taken by ruling elites that may have been primarily designed to consolidate their pre-eminence, but that nonetheless contributed to enhancing the living conditions and freedoms of subaltern groups, must be analysed in all their complexity, and not treated as simply being a trap designed to deviate the oppressed classes from their true path to liberation. In this same vein, accepting that there are features of the old social order that must be integrated into any successor system implies that a transition away from capitalism does not require the complete refashioning of the human personality, or a fundamental revision of moral standards, or a total overhaul of all social practices.

More specifically, at a macro level I would contend that the history of Marxist-inspired socialism in the twentieth century points to the importance of avoiding the fusion of the economic and political spheres that was one of its characteristic features. There must not be a 're-feudalization' of the state[11] in the sense that the economy and polity become inextricably bound together and in which, in the name of popular control over the economy, all key economic decisions are centralized within the state structure. Rejecting the historical communist model does not mean that a new relationship between economics and politics under socialism is necessarily inconceivable or undesirable. There are, indeed, many important debates to be had concerning such crucial dimensions of social organization as the relationship between market-based activities and state intervention in the economy; forms of ownership and control of economic resources; distribution and redistribution of economic wealth. What I am asserting, however, is that it is critical that these debates take as a starting point a negative assessment of the re-feudalized state that was typical of historical communism and a recognition that the disembedding of the economy from the polity that was accomplished under capitalist liberal democracies represents one of its positive legacies. A re-feudalized state, no matter the specifics of its constitution, concentrates and centralizes power in the hands of the elite that controls the state in a way that is not conducive either to democratic flourishing or to economic prosperity.

Achieving greater collective self-determination was certainly one of the core objectives of Marxist-inspired socialism, and such a goal clearly requires that there be in place genuinely democratic mechanisms for constituting and asserting the popular will. However, the single-party state characteristic of historical communism did not promote the achievement of this objective. Political competition involving multiple parties and the open expression of diverging views, including on the most fundamental societal issues, must therefore figure in the plans for a successor system to capitalist liberal democracies. For this competition to give genuine expression to the will of the people, there can be no a priori limits set on the issues to be debated or on the possible outcomes of the political contest.

This means that progress in building the yet-to-be-defined socialism of the twenty-first century will, as a matter of principle, have to be both 'open' and 'reversible'. One clear lesson from the experience of historical communism in the twentieth century is that, no matter how ringing the declaration of irreversibility on paper, the key guarantor of social change is not its entrenchment in a constitution. What is required is ongoing popular support. If socialism (however it is defined) is to become 'irreversible' it will do so on the grounds that it is demonstrably more successful than available alternatives. Legislative and/or constitutional means will no doubt have to be deployed to achieve this success, but they are the means to an end, not the end in itself. In fact, socialists have nothing to gain by insisting that, once the transition away from capitalism has begun, nothing will be allowed to stop it. In all likelihood, given the experience of historical communism, such an insistence on the irreversibility of the process is more likely to discourage support for a socialist option than to rally people behind its banner. Rather, socialists have everything to gain by embracing 'reversibility', as it alone can provide the basis for democratic legitimacy.

At the same time, there must be a commitment to the inherent sanctity of human rights and freedoms. Never again must leaders who have proclaimed their allegiance to the ideal of socialism stand accused of violations of fundamental human rights, to say nothing of crimes against humanity. To say that universal rights have inherent value does not deny their contingent character, and, in particular, the recognition that these rights have been secured through much struggle and spilling of blood. Furthermore, since they are at best partially respected throughout the liberal democratic world, it is to be expected that popular vigilance will be required to ensure their consistent application. Nonetheless, existing achievements with regard to the protection of human rights are the starting point for future progress, and their defence must not be made subordinate to the realization of the objectives of any single party, class or group. Thus, the idea that respect for human rights is secondary to the implementation of socialism, no matter how construed, is to miscast the problem. Rather, socialism, if it is to be worth it, must allow a fuller and more extensive respect for universal human rights than is possible under capitalism.

It is important to stress that, framed as conditions for an eventual socialism, these commitments are general and do not go very far in specifying the substance of what that socialism could look like. This is something to be worked out over time, and there is no reason to preclude many different variations that can be adapted to the particular circumstances and histories of individual countries. The key will be to focus efforts on identifying and changing the core dynamics that are characteristic of capitalism, and the richness of the Marxist tradition in this area remains an invaluable resource.

It is worth noting that this way of thinking about the transition from capitalism to socialism does not imply that only a slow process of reform remains as a viable strategy for change. The idea that not everything about capitalism must change in order to create a more just and equitable society is not, per se, an intervention in the reform versus revolution debate that is one of the defining features of the boundary between the two great currents of twentieth-century socialism, social democracy and communism. Fundamental, qualitative change depends on altering the core dynamics of the capitalist system, that which defines its characteristic pattern of accumulation. Until there is a broad consensus on exactly what is in fact central to capitalism, it will be impossible to specify in advance an appropriate transformative strategy. Nonetheless, the Marxist vision of enhancing the degree of popular control over wealth that is socially produced could provide the kind of reference point that is needed to distinguish fundamental change from superficial reform.

Finally, and perhaps most controversially from the perspective of traditional approaches to Marxism, the analysis presented in this chapter strongly suggests that a key flaw in the basic Marxist-inspired strategy is its insistence that socialism represents the realization of working-class power. The idea that the path to a classless society passes through a period of overt class rule by the working class cannot be assumed to be the only approach that is consistent with the key commitments of the Marxist tradition. Rejecting socialism as the realization of working-class power does not have to mean abandoning the goal of a classless society, which is at the heart of the Marxian vision of social transformation. Neither does it mean that class analysis as a tool for understanding the structure and dynamics of all class-based systems, including capitalism, is no longer relevant. And it most definitely does not mean that the struggle to improve the situation of countless millions of people whose lives are blighted by one form or another of class oppression and exploitation must be abandoned.

What it does mean is that the relationship between the struggle by the subordinate classes for a better life under capitalism and the struggle to transform the capitalist system itself must be entirely rethought.[12] Clearly, this is no simple task. However, the empirical evidence is clear – attempts to build a successor society to capitalism on the grounds of the explicit assumption of power by the working class have been a failure. At a theoretical level, I believe I have shown that it is plausible to hold that at least some of the key deficiencies of historical communism can be linked to the idea that socialism should be defined as the working class in power. This implies that, if there is to be a future for Marxist-inspired socialism, a way must be found to initiate the transition to classlessness without the intermediate phase of working-class power. In other words, can the core Marxist idea of a classless future be separated from the strategy to implement it that was adopted by Marxists throughout the twentieth century? How this question is answered will, in my view, decide the fate of Marxist-inspired socialism in the twenty-first century.

Notes

1   Throughout this text I will use two terms interchangeably to refer in general to the states that were created in the attempt to put into practice the theoretical propositions (broadly defined) of classical Marxism. These are 'Marxist-inspired socialism' and 'historical communism.'

2   One could also say that the content of the present volume itself also attests to this fact.

3   The question of the degree of harmony between Marx and Engels is not really relevant here. This is because the vast majority of twentieth-century Marxists, and especially those who were responsible for actually building historical communism, saw them as jointly responsible for the theory of socialism.

4   For example, this is still the position of what remains of the Communist Parties in both Canada and the US.

5   The most prominent post-Trotsky defender of this position was the late Ernest Mandel.

6   In the period following Stalin's death in 1953 and his denunciation by his successors led by Khrushchev, the leadership of the Chinese Communist Party, which had won power in 1949 under Mao Zedong took an increasingly critical view of the nature of the Soviet regime, first deeming it 'revisionist' and then proclaiming in a series of fierce polemics that it had restored capitalism in the Soviet Union. Despite these profound disagreements over the nature of socialism, it remains logically consistent to include the Chinese regime under the umbrella designation of historical communism since it based its attempts to differentiate itself from its Soviet counterpart on its fealty to the orthodox Marxian vision of socialism and communism.

7   There are versions of this argument that claimed the USSR was a form of 'bureaucratic collectivism' that date back to debates within the Trotskyist movement in the post-Second World War period, as well as more recent variants, such as Paul Sweezy's essay 'Is There a Ruling Class in the USSR' (Sweezy, 1980).

8   *The Black Book of Communism* puts the total for all historical communist regimes at close to 100 million killed (Courtois, 1997: 14).

9   It is thus possible that the current regime in China is incubating a significantly different type of mode of production. One could also think of the coexistence of authoritarian political regimes, including full-blown fascist and military dictatorships, and capitalism as another illustration of the fact that the political and economic spheres can coexist in many different ways.

10   One example is the passage, referred to earlier, that concludes the opening section of the *Communist Manifesto*: 'The development of Modern Industry, therefore, cuts from under its feet the very foundation on which the bourgeoisie produces and appropriates products. What the bourgeoisie, therefore, produces, above all, is its own grave-diggers. Its fall and the victory of the proletariat are equally inevitable.'

11   Those who think that using the term 're-feudalized' to describe the historical communist state is an exaggeration might want to think of the transfer of power from Kim Il Sung to his son Kim Jong Il in North Korea. Although hereditary rule was not the norm in historical communist states, the North Korean example does serve to illustrate the short distance that separates a 'socialist' feudal state from the hereditary rule that is characteristic of classic feudal states. The parallel that is often made between the Russian Tsars and the Stalinist regime also draws its plausibility from this structural similarity.

12   Moishe Postone has drawn a similar conclusion from his reinterpretation of Marx's theory of value. In *Time Labor and Social Domination* (1993: 324), he writes that 'Marx's presentation . . . implicitly contravenes the notion that the relation between the capitalist class and the working class is parallel to that between capitalism and socialism, that the possible transition to socialism is effected by the victory of the

proletariat in class struggle (in the sense of its self-affirmation as a working class), and that socialism involves the realization of the proletariat.' However, this aspect of Postone's reading of Marx was contested by a number of the contributors to a symposium on his work published in *Historical Materialism*, Vol. 12, No. 3 (2004).

References and further reading

Barrow, Clyde W. (2000) 'The Marx Problem in Marxian State Theory', *Science & Society*, 64 (1): pp.

Bellis, Paul (1979) *Marxism and the USSR*. Atlantic Highlands, NJ: Humanities Press.

Berman, Marshall (1999) *Adventures in Marxism*. London: Verso.

Bettelheim, Charles (1976) *Class Struggles in the USSR, 1917–1923*. New York: Monthly Review Press.

Castells, Manuel (1998) *End of Millennium*. Oxford: Blackwell.

Central Committee of the Communist Party of the Soviet Union (CC of CPSU) (1939) *History of the Communist Party of the Soviet Union (Bolsheviks)*. Toronto: Francis White Publishers.

Cliff, Tony (1974) *State Capitalism in Russia*, London: Pluto Press.

Courtois, Stéphane, Nicolas Werth, Jean-Louis Pammé, Andrzej Paczkowski, Karel Bartos`ek and Jean-Louis Margolin (1999) *The Black Book of Communism*. Cambridge, MA: Harvard University Press.

Engels, Frederick (1975) *Socialism: Utopian and Scientific*. Beijing: Foreign Languages Press.

Hoffman, David L. (ed.) (2003) *Stalinism*. Oxford: Blackwell.

Michael A. Lebowitz (2000) 'Kornai and the Vanguard Mode of Production', *Cambridge Journal of Economics*, 24 (3): 377–392.

O'Hagan, Timothy (1981) 'On the "Withering-Away" of the Superstructures', in John Mepham and D.-H. Ruben (eds), *Issues in Marxist Philosophy*, volume 4. Brighton: Harvester Press.

Pipes, Richard (2001) *Communism: A History*. New York: Modern Library.

Postone, Moishe (1993) *Time Labor and Social Domination*. Cambridge: Cambridge University Press.

Resnick, Stephen A. and Richard D. Wolff. (2002) *Class Theory and History: Capitalism and Communism in the USSR*. New York: Routledge.

Silber, Irwin (1994) *Socialism: What Went Wrong?* London: Pluto Press.

Sweezy, Paul (1980) 'Is There a Ruling Class in the USSR', in (ed.) *Post-Revolutionary Society*. New York: Monthly Review Press.

Tucker, Robert C. (1978) *The Marx-Engels Reader*, second edition. New York: W. W. Norton.

Van den Berg, Axel (1988) *The Immanent Utopia: From Marxism on the State to the State of Marxism*. Princeton, NJ: Princeton University Press.

11 Marxist theory, Marxist practice

Daryl Glaser

Having been expelled from history, at least for now, Marxism has no choice but to stand back and think about the preconditions of historical re-entry. Implicit already in this opening sentence are several of what would once have been considered heterodoxies: history is not itself bearing Marxism to victory; we have real choices; action is not everything (if by action is meant practical activism). I wish to add another (for Marxists) unorthodox notion: we should not assume a priori that Marxism's historical re-entry is desirable. That it is so needs demonstrating. Professed Marxists have done enormous harm in power. The minimum we have to be sure of before sending Marxism back into the fray is that it will do no harm next time around. But of course, if we are Marxists, we want something more positive than that: grounds for thinking that Marxist praxis will significantly benefit humanity, and in distinctive ways that other doctrines do not.

This paper is an exercise in Marxist metatheory. Its main concern is to identify some of the preconditions of defensible and successful Marxist intervention in the world. It focuses on a nexus crucial to Marx: that between theory and practice. Marxism is in the first instance a body of theory; but in order to advance the values impelling it, it must translate into practice, and Marxists from Marx onwards have attached great importance to its application and verification in practical struggles for social change. The focus here is on the metatheoretical background of Marxist theory and action rather than on the content of a viable Marxist theory, methodology, analysis or programme.

Part of what I will argue is that good Marxist practice involves more than getting the substantive Marxist analysis right: it requires that Marxists operate certain theory–practice translation rules. These rules assume that epistemological relativism is wrong, but also that truth claims are uncertain.

I will, secondly, argue that Marxism as an activity devolves into three roles, interpreter, politico and Legislator, each of which requires its own operating principles. These rules and roles in turn require that Marxists be procedural democrats.

Finally, I will argue that a useful Marxism has to advance substantive theoretical positions that are recognizably Marxist even if not orthodox: that doing so is both a prerequisite of Marxism being worthwhile and (provided the above-mentioned rules and roles are respected) compatible with democratic and pluralistic intervention.

The question of whether Marxism's substantive propositions are correct falls largely outside this metatheoretical examination; but some reasons to think certain of them plausible or useful will be offered in the course of 'fleshing out' the roles of politico and Legislator.

Marxism, democracy, epistemology

Marxists need to pause to reflect on the desirability of their project for many reasons. One reason is that putatively socialist economies failed to deliver high levels of material well-being in the East and South. Another, of more immediate concern here, arises from the record of Marxist ('Marxist'?) movements and regimes in the field of democracy and human rights. That record included, at its worst, slavery, genocide and the forced resettlement of populations in countries such as the Soviet Union, China and Kampuchea. It routinely included detention without charge, torture, show trials, surveillance, censorship, incarceration of dissidents in mental institutions and, of course, the absence of any semblance of democratic government.[1] A good number of Marxists have denied that this record has anything to do with what is an essentially democratic and humane doctrine. Exponents of this position have to explain why so many self-labelled and theory-versed Marxists were implicated in large-scale repression; they also have either to uphold the Marxist demotion of 'bourgeois' rights and liberties or to make the case that Marxism, contrary to widespread perception, championed them. Neither of these latter positions seems defensible or plausible to me

Most critics of Marxism argue, by contrast and more plausibly, that Marxist theory has historically been either negligent or actively faulty when it comes to theorizing human rights and democracy, and point for support to its amoralism, objectivism, scientism, teleological determinism, utopianism and class-reductionism.[2] Many also tend to see the connection between Marxist theory and totalitarian practice as necessary and unbreakable. In this latter they are, I will argue, mistaken. Whereas the earlier-cited record of economic failure under 'actual socialism' may be less ethically pressing, it is also more difficult to see a way beyond. Happily, a way out of the connection between Marxist theory and anti-democratic practice is much easier to discern. It does, however, require that aspects of Marxist epistemology and politics be rethought. Rethinking them is the task of the rest of this section. Fortunately for Marxism, it does not require that all aspects of its theory be reworked, and in fact aspects of it condemned as anti-democratic by some critics turn out, on my account, to be democracy-compatible.

One line of post- and anti-Marxist criticism holds that Marxism's link to totalitarianism is inscribed in its commitment to a variant of scientific epistemology (whether this is understood as positivist or realist) and to metanarration: i.e. producing comprehensive theories of society and history that relativize other systems of thought.[3] Whatever the merits of social science as an approach to understanding reality, it is not, I would argue, inherently politically anti-democratic in its effects. Conceived in a particular way it is indeed democracy-friendly and perhaps (I'm less certain of this) necessary for democracy. Compared with relativism, scientific epistemology is pro-democratic to the extent it invites us to take each other seriously (that is, to assume that others are engaged in truth-seeking rather than tale-telling) and entitles us to stand our ground on points of principle and conviction (so that not just 'anything goes'). It also allows room for theories that accord democracy an epistemic value: which postulate that it (over the long run) facilitates understanding (and hence mastery) of adverse external realities. Whereas relativism might be suited to societies of individualists, it seems less so to societies in which a common language is needed to guide effective collective action or shape binding rules; and although it might be adequate for self-sufficient, hermetic or ascetic communities, it seems less appropriate to societies in which people have to come together (themselves, and with other communities) to address serious challenges and advance collective goals.

At the other 'extreme', certain forms of naïve positivism and realism are certainly democracy-hostile. The main problem with them (in terms of democracy) is that they encourage the view that truth can only be accessed by scientific elites (justifying technocratic or revolutionary vanguardism) and underwrite an unwarranted confidence in the capacity of certain theories (and hence theorists) truly to 'know' the external world (thus justifying the imposition of 'true' beliefs coercively on unbelievers as well as dangerous social engineering). But there is a middle range of epistemologies – including both falsificationist positivism and critical realism – which eschews notions of scientific, value-free, empirically verifiable certainties while hewing to the idea that there is an external reality which we can come to know better via good theory and research.[4] Here lie epistemologies too uncertain of the truth to provide justification for scientific authoritarianism or reckless social experiments, too alert to the role of values to think that human purposes and priorities can be scientifically ordered. Although there is no invariant relationship between an actor's epistemology and politics, it is these middle-range theories that sit most comfortably with an idea of democracy as collective, participatory, governed by reasoned discussion, and instrumentally effective.

Whatever else Marxism is, it is not relativist.[5] The democratically dangerous things it might be are naïvely positivist (whether inductive or deductive) and what might be termed metaphysical-realist. Both naïve positivists and metaphysical realists believe that there are objective, value-free truths, indisputably superior scientific rules and systems, and privileged (because scientifically trained) knowledge-bearers. Whereas the former believe that science has direct access to reality through observation, the latter believe we only ever directly know concepts and whether they logically cohere. These positions correspond, within Marxism, roughly to the orthodox and Althusserian positions, both of which have claimed for Marxism the status of an objective, value-free science and (I would argue) encourage the view that Marxists should serve as a societal vanguard, overriding (where necessary) the subjective, ideology-bound wills of ordinary people. It follows that democratic Marxism fits most comfortably with middle-range epistemologies, both because relativism (which is conceivably democracy-friendly) is non-Marxist and because naïve positivism and metaphysical realism (though they might be Marxist) are too risky as starting points for democratic thought and action.

Two rules

The first theory–practice translation rule that Marxists must adopt will, accordingly, appeal most readily to Marxists of mid-range epistemology. It requires them to accept that nothing can be known to be certainly true. A rule framed in these terms does not require that Marxists adopt relativism, cease to harbour convictions about the true nature of things, or even that they cease to think of Marxism as (in some sense) scientific. It demands only that Marxists accept the provisionality of knowledge and the political-normative implication of this: that Marxists cannot force people to be free. If we could be certain of a people's best interests, we might actually be *obliged* to force upon it policies we believe correspond to those interests. But given that we may be wrong, we are then risking imposing on peoples policies that will do them harm. If absolute conviction is implicated in countless crimes, these are liable to multiply in the hands of true believers motivated by ambitiously transformative goals. The more radical the alteration envisaged to any status quo, the more necessary it is to proceed with caution about the truth.

Yet we cannot leave matters there. The first rule in isolation warrants at best the confinement of Marxist practice to the task of debate-promotion and critique, at worst a kind of political quietism. If Marxist theories are correct and capable of being beneficial, the prescriptions which flow from them do need to be imposed on people in a certain sense: they need to be implemented as policies, whether of movements or governments. Policies are embodied, in turn, in laws, rules and orders that bind people within certain jurisdictions. As democratic theorists have long known, this can only be done non-coercively in the presence of unanimity-based voting rules or authentically consensual deliberation. If, as much theory and experience suggests, these modalities are impractical in large, complex or diverse societies, then some form of coercive imposition is unavoidable. According to the second translation rule, a legitimately binding decision can only be one which, in some credible sense, enjoys the freely given consent of the majority (or large plurality) of those bound by it, or of their freely chosen representatives, in circumstances where individual votes count equally. This is not because such consent will overcome epistemic uncertainty; there is no guarantee that democratic decisions will be 'right' or 'true' (although there is evidence that democracy does result in better decision-making over time). What consent permits is decision-making that is legitimate and thus less likely to require unacceptable violence to implement. It also gives expression to the principle that, where there is no guarantee against error, people should be entitled to make their own mistakes. In the absence of certainty on the part of the paternalistic guardian, the value of individual self-determination reasserts itself (and this is a value that, after all, Marxists support; which, arguably, they seek communism in order to maximize[6]).

Marxists should, in other words, respect the precepts of procedural democracy.[7] If they wish to implement a programme they must acquire a mandate to do so via open-ended procedural decision-making rules; and they must do so on a renewable basis. (In these terms, revolution is permissible only to overthrow undemocratic states or insofar as it denotes sustained radical reform implemented by democratic mandate.)

Although some Marxists will (with reason) find these rules politically restrictive – they do render radical change less likely – it is important to underline the sense in which they are permissive or enabling for Marxism. Many critics of Marxism would have it junk every theoretical commitment that can be linked in any way to anti-democratic practice. They would, for example, want it to dispense with a structuralist account of human agency, historical laws of motion and theories of ideology and 'false consciousness'. These positions, critics often argue, feed into the demotion of normative or ethical discussion (by reducing the scope of human moral choice), justify the subordination of individual interests to supposed historical imperatives and rationalize the dictatorship of the Enlightened.

Such arguments do, I accept, expose real anti-democratic possibilities in Marxist thought. Even so, there are good reasons not to pursue the democratic purification of Marxism too zealously *at the level of its substantive precepts and theories*. Taken too far, such a process would void it of a distinctive content. That matters for Marxists. But there would also, I believe, be a cost in this zealotry to democracy itself, conceived as a political project. For Marxism does have useful and distinctive insights to contribute to democratic theory and these are dialectically linked to structuralism, economic determinism, sociological realism and other potentially undemocratic attributes of Marxism. Thus, while Marxism dangerously demotes ethical discourse, individual rights and democratic procedure, it also usefully directs our attention to the contradictions between democracy and capitalism and to the limits of legalistic formalism. The risk is that in jettisoning Marxism's democracy-unfriendly features we might abandon also its robustly democracy-promoting ones.

And if my translation rules are well-founded, this jettisoning is unnecessary for democracy. So long as they observe the translation rules, Marxists are free to offer teleological, determinist and structuralist theories. They might legitimately, for example, argue that the proletariat is immersed in false consciousness and that only Marxists correctly grasp the class's true interests. So long as Marxists do not profess certainty about this, and so long as they follow through the political and moral logic of their uncertainty, the proletariat will be protected from the coercive imposition of Marxist-derived 'truths'. Marxists will, if they wish to carry out their programme, then have to persuade the proletariat itself (and the wider public) that Marxist analysis is right and that existing dominant beliefs are false.

One does not wish to make this seem simpler than it is. There is obviously a tension between, say, structuralism and democratic concepts of human agency and choice. The translation rules themselves stand in a paradoxical relationship with Marxism since, if Marxism is true, the translation rules must be a diversion that serves the interests of the bourgeoisie. They codify doubt about the very theory they are being attached to. This links to a second complication. The translation rules are exogenous to Marxism. They are required by democratic Marxists and can be coherently introduced into Marxist practice; but they do not derive *from* Marxism. That is what I meant by my earlier reference to metatheory: the argument here is not so much Marxist as *about* and *for* Marxism. Metatheoretical reflection of this kind could be equally undertaken by non-Marxists, and indeed the translation rules ought to be respected by advocates of all theoretical systems claiming truth and aiming to change the world. (Authoritarian social engineering can issue from religion, nationalism, fascism, even liberalism.) Does this non-Marxist provenance matter? Only if one proceeds from an assumption that the domain of the Marxist explanandum covers all aspects of human thought and life. The metatheorizing here posits a domain of autonomous normative reflection.

Three hats

But let us return to the implications of these translation rules for Marxism itself. What the foregoing suggests is the necessity for a Marxist role differentiation. When Marx wrote '[t]he philosophers have only interpreted the world . . . the point is to change it', he intimated two Marxist roles, those of interpreter and of actor in the world. Within the second category I suggest we further distinguish the roles of politico and constitution-giving founder or Legislator. Marxists in effect wear three hats, and the democratically proper method of connecting theory and practice differs according to which hat Marxists are wearing. The following role depiction is normative, describing not actual Marxist actors but the proper conduct of each role according to the translation rules.

As *interpreters* Marxists are free to pursue large theoretical ambitions. By this I mean that they are *democratically* entitled to advance holistic theories of history and society and to justify far-reaching changes in human arrangements. They are permitted, that is, to engage in the form of theoretical activity that some critics would deem 'totalizing'. Comprehensive and radical theorizing carries risks for political practice, and the way to accommodate these is by observing the translation rules. The alternative risk management strategy – self-denyingly to suppress radical thoughts – would forgo potential epistemic and human-welfare advances (since some radical theories might be substantively true), remove a stimulus to human creativity and unreasonably narrow the range of ideological competitors in the democratic arena. It would further hand permanent advantages to those who guard an existing, apparently 'natural' state of affairs and who thus have nothing to gain from critical reflection upon the way the world works. The status quo may have its theorists, but is less in need of them than are social critics and reformers. Theoretical ideation is needed to fill the gap between what is and what could be.

And if futuristic theory is permissible, something else follows: that theorists are entitled to (because logically they must) posit the possibility that they are (as it were) ahead of the game, discovering possibilities of which others are unaware. Theoretical activity, at least of the radical sort, is necessarily a form of vanguardism. The populist in radical thinkers may genuflect to the coal-face knowledge or common sense of the masses. But although they might accord popular insight a place in their theoretical scheme, radical intellectuals cannot follow the people and still be radical intellectuals (or at any rate ones who add value to processes of radical change). Radical theorizing is a labour of the forward-looking if not invariably the far-sighted. Its goals may be democratic, but it is never particularly democratic in itself.

As *politicos* Marxists seek to persuade others of the veracity of their world-view and, having won popular support, mobilize people against specific injustices or for social-system transformation. Here Marxists wear their activist hat, whether as oppositionists or governors; they seek to implement and at the same time, through practice, to test and modify their theories. Though committed to operating within procedural-democratic channels that are open to multiple political pos-sibilities, Marxist politocos themselves pursue a particular vision and programme, the implementation of which requires that they gain power. Procedural democracy is not always available for this purpose, of course; they may be up against dicta-torship. When Marxists face a clearly undemocratic system, they are permitted to use force, if necessary with less than majority backing, to establish a formal democracy. Where formal democracy does exist Marxist politicos campaign for governmental power by consent. By the same token, as principled proceduralists, they are obliged to surrender governmental office when they lose popular support. While in office they legitimately use the democratic coercive power of the state to secure social change, provided that in their actions they respect liberties internal to democracy, as well as other vital liberties.

Marxist politicos are not required, of course, to focus all energy on the state. In civil society too they are entitled (and as Marxists perhaps obliged) to campaign to secure or defend social gains, whether or not socialists are in governmental office. Though principled supporters of procedural democracy, Marxist politicos would still be open, if they ignored civil society, to a variant of the old charge of 'parliamentary cretinism'. A radical politics is conducted in multiple arenas, and indeed an additional reason to support democratic proceduralism is that it requires, intrinsically, the sorts of free assembly and association that civil society instantiates. The principle difference between state and civil society actors, from a proceduralist point of view, is that the latter lack the mandate to impose social changes on non-associates. But they can do much else that radical democrats, including Marxist politicos, admire: agitate for political change, fight local injus-tices, initiate participatory self-government within civil associations, attempt to shape popular culture, convey intensities of public feeling insufficiently conveyed by the ballot box. Marxist politicos engage in the politics of both party and move-ment.

As *Legislators* Marxists in power contribute to designing institutions appropri-ate to democratic government. The term 'Legislator' is borrowed from Rousseau, but the analogy with the Rosseauian Legislator is rough; the Marxian counterpart is neither an individual nor possessed of superior qualities (though of course radi-cal politics will throw up its charismatic leaders, especially at times of transition and constitutional flux). Marxists as Legislators find themselves in a position to design a constitution, perhaps having inherited power after the overthrow of a dictatorship, or having secured a popular mandate for constitutional reform. What is important here, and follows from the translation rules, is that Marxists qua constitution-givers set out to design, not institutions of a 'socialist democracy', but formal democratic institutions in which socialists can compete with their political rivals for influence and office on a reasonably even playing field. Marxist Legislators behave as good liberal democrats. As will be explained more fully later, this does not mean they leave their Marxism behind them. Marxist Legislators will use the insights of Marxist democratic theory to expose the limits of a conservative understanding of liberal democracy, and attempt to show that the logic of liberal democracy itself requires, or must allow for, constitutional features left out of actually existing parliamentary orders.

Marxist Legislators would not, in this spirit, constitutionally entrench socialism. To do that would be to ignore the first translation rule requiring recognition of uncertainty. Marxists can never be so sure of the rightness of socialism that they become entitled (or feel obliged) to build it into the constitution or codify it as a societal *telos*. In any case the legal entrenchment of socialism would vest too much of the responsibility for defending it in judges and lawyers. Social-system goals should be determined in the democratic arena. Marxist Legislators *would* refuse a provision in the bill of rights protecting productive property from public ownership or prescribing orthodox macro-economic policy constraints; would also want to allow, perhaps even demand, that the rules of electoral democracy apply to the government of enterprises; would sympathetically consider entrenching constitutional rules restricting private campaign finance, guaranteeing rival parties access to public media, and perhaps granting newspapers and parties public subsidies. The specific list does not matter here; its inclusions and exclusions can be debated. The point is that whatever the Legislator does must be defensible on egalitarian and universalistic grounds and protect a reasonable maximum of pluralism. It must appeal to the same meta-principles that Marxists of the sort depicted here share with all procedural democrats.

What is the relationship between the interpreter, the politico and the Legislator? A first important point: the three roles can in principle be united in a single person. That is why I talk of hat-wearing: a single individual can, according to this popular metaphor, wear different hats in different contexts. What is important is that Marxists recognize which hat they ought to be wearing in a particular situation and follow the prescriptions/proscriptions of that role. Many of Marxism's historical disasters are traceable to the failure to observe this role differentiation. The Marxist theorist of false consciousness who authorizes coercive vanguardist rule and the constitution designer who, guided by a theory of the inevitability of socialism, sets up a socialist constitutional order: these are just two examples of role conflation that yield authoritarian or totalitarian outcomes. But it is not only anti-democratic rule that role differentiation protects against: it also guards against forms of reformist retreat that are not democratically required. The proceduralist who concludes that radical social goals should be abandoned as incompatible with pluralism and openness, the constitution-giver who refuses to consider the extension of democracy to the economy because doing so violates ideological neutrality: both of these are examples of a conflation that unnecessarily blocks transformative possibilities. If the first set of examples involves the collapse of the procedural into the politically substantive, the latter illegitimately constricts the contestation of societal goals in the name of proceduralism.

It is interesting and significant that Marxism classically failed to recognize the role of Legislator at all. It is not that Marxists eschew constitution-making; it is rather that they have considered it an inherently secondary moment, a moment concerned with the adjustment of the politico-legal superstructure to the imperatives of the economic base and to the requirements of the historical juncture (indeed, forged in the crucible of revolution). Since orthodox Marxism failed to accord an independent weight and value to political institutions and mediations, it could hardly recognize the Legislator as distinctive; the Legislator's job was to do the bidding of the revolutionary movement in its pursuit of substantive historical goals, as when Lenin abolished Russia's freely elected Constituent Assembly in January 1918. Even those, like Kautsky, who thought that socialists should use parliament to gain power and govern, short-circuited hard questions about proceduralism and the Legislator by assuming what we know to be false: that the growing numerical strength of the working class renders socialism inevitable.

It seems, though, that an understanding of the role of the Legislator has gradually registered among Marxists. It figured, implicitly, in the theoretical stance of the Eurocommunists, who envisaged deepening democracy within proceduralist constraints. The Sandinistas, perhaps in spite of themselves, acted as founders of Nicaragua's constitutional democracy. It probably informed the role that Mexico's Zapatistas intended to play as they agitated for constitutional reform. The African National Congress, supported by the South African Communist Party, established a liberal democracy in South Africa too but in this case, one suspects, because they lost faith in radical transformation, rather than to provide an arena in which it could be pursued. (A few in the ANC and SACP ranks still hanker after the older, neo-Stalinist model.) Many one-time socialists are to be found at this juncture of proceduralist advance and neo-liberal retreat. The coupling of socialist radicalism and principled proceduralism: that is the intriguing possibility – I'm tempted to say 'holy grail' – allowed by the translation rules yet too rarely explored in practice (at least in Marxist practice; depending on the yardstick of radicalism, some social democracies may be adjudged to have been there). This combination (which itself can be variable in its detailed content) is the only democratic way forward for Marxist socialism.

Theoretical stocks

So far the content of Marxist theory has been discussed only passingly, and more needs to be said about where it fits into the picture. Marxists, I propose, will draw upon different bodies of substantive theoretical work according to which hat they are wearing. The concern in this section will be with politicos and Legislators, for the simple reason that Marxists qua interpreters generate and draw upon the whole of Marxist theory: they develop the theory that the other two roles differentially draw upon. Politicos and Legislators by contrast draw on *particular* theoretical stocks. Politicos will be interested in theory that informs successful political mobilization and socialist governance; Legislators will take account of Marxist analyses of the relationship between formal rules/procedures and substantive power relations. In describing the relationship between roles and theoretical stocks I will be hoping to substantiate two claims and to table a third. The first is that there is a difference between the (wide range of) Marxist theory that interests the politico and the (rather narrower) body of theoretical work that informs the Legislator. The second is that the preceding metatheory allows Marxists to adopt distinctively Marxist, even orthodox, theoretical postures without violating democratic requirements. (It of course does not require that Marxists be orthodox: the point is one about permissiveness.) The third is that Marxist theory can usefully inform a democratic and progressive politics. This last claim is advanced here only tentatively and largely by implication; to develop it anything like adequately would require a separate paper (indeed several papers). The validity of my argument about rule and role differentiation in no way hinges upon the truth of anything that I shall now say about the usefulness of particular Marxist theories.

The politico will need to draw on a wide swathe of Marxist theory. Qua politico, Marxists will be less interested in the scholastic aspects of Marxism (at least until their practical utility is clarified). Their main interest will be in theory that has a direct bearing on political action, in the sense of either pointing towards specific choices or providing a general orientation. There is a vast amount of Marxist theory that might be cited in this connection. For illustrative purposes I will focus on just two bodies of theoretical Marxism: class analysis and theories of socialism.

Of obvious interest to the politico is the way Marxism analyses social forces in order to distinguish potential supporters and opponents of socialist change. Classically Marxism has located the proletariat at the centre of the transformative project. Much neo-Marxist theory of the past couple of decades has been devoted to announcing the termination of the proletariat's mission (perhaps even of the proletariat) and the rise of new agents of social change such as the women's and environmental movements.[8] This new Marxism does not necessarily involve abandoning class analysis, since it is anchored in part in a recognition of the rising importance of new middle classes in the capitalist heartland; but it certainly involves a relegation of the working class.

Whatever the merits of this turn (I think there are some), it should be made clear that it is not necessitated by *democratic* considerations. That is to say, although Marxists might have good reasons to embrace the new social forces and movements – because they believe in *all* kinds of equality, because they want to save the planet, because they want more popular support – they are not required to do so in order to demonstrate democratic credentials. Class-based movements can be democratic, functioning as legitimate sectional interest groups bidding for popular recognition of their concerns. Workerists might find it more difficult to win support than more socially inclusive forces; they may or may not have the best policies on, say, gender and ecology. But so long as they observe procedural rules – do not impose their will on others undemocratically – they constitute no inherent democratic threat (indeed cross-class alliances can pose a larger one, sucking more political life into a single movement). Whatever reasons there might be to demote the working class politically, the imperatives of pluralism are not among them.

The elevation of the proletariat in Marxist thought is linked to its prioritization of socialism as a goal. For some 'new social movement' critics, the focus on socialism is itself undemocratically exclusive, downgrading other progressive goals. Yet, politically speaking, Marxism has little that is distinctive to offer except as a theory of socialist transformation. Nor need it be undemocratic because it is that. Socialism is a particular desideratum; it does not cover the whole field of progressive desiderata, in which are to be found also ecological sustainability, appropriate recognition of legitimate cultural identities and of course many equalities including of race, ethnicity and gender. What socialism is concerned about, in the first instance, is the collective management of economic life and the advancement of material equality. As long as socialism in this sense is still deemed feasible and desirable, it makes sense to seek out the social forces that have a present or future interest in it. Whether or not the proletariat turns out to be the central social force having that interest (there are other candidates in the professional strata and voluntary and public sectors, as well as among the marginal poor), it seems likely that the array of social groups interested in socialism will not coincide exactly with the constituency of the new movements, whatever the overlap. There thus remains a specific task for Marxists in identifying actually and potentially pro-socialist forces and in understanding the possible tensions between these and new social movement supporters.

In any case, the expansion of the field of progressive forces to encompass new movements need not conflict with advocacy of a more prominent political role for the working class and poor in alliances for change. Here indeed a more positive (as opposed to negatively permissive) case can be made for the Marxist's interest in class. Political parties directly connected to new social forces have rarely won the support of more than 8–10 per cent of voters in the longer-established capitalist societies. The primary party-political division remains left–right and anchored in class differentiation, even if electoral dynamics encourage a centrist clustering. The new movements need a wider support base, and their natural ally is to be found in the 'older' labour movements. At the moment the alliance between the two, where it functions, is mediated primarily through the agency of new middle classes prominent in both. If it is to become an alliance from below, it will be necessary to bring working and poor people more fully into new movement activism. At a minimum, ways will have to be found to avoid a polarization between metropolitan new movement elites and the working class (which is all too easily drawn to the cultural right). It is anyway troublesome that the new middle classes have come so fully to dominate the commanding heights of progressive politics, and there is a straight (microcosmic) democratic-representational case for widening working class involvement. The Marxist theoretical concern with the proletariat thus remains relevant to the radical politico (Marxist and non-Marxist).

If Marxist politicos draw on Marxist analyses of social forces, they need also to tap Marxism for what guidance it can give to substantive programmes of economic reorganization and governance. For these are what politicos, having come to power through procedural democracy, will have to carry out. The Marxist cupboard is rather bare here. Classical Marxism offered little by way of theorization of the socialist economy, and the attempts under 'actual socialism' to work Marxist economics out in practice were all a failure. Social democracy fared much better, but with little help from Marxism. The Marxist politico will almost certainly have to look to non-Marxist theoretical resources in this area. Still, there are aspects of Marxist theory useful even in economy-building. To name but two general ones, the Marxist concern with the historical character of economic forms, and with which social groups control economic assets and in whose interests, will continue to be relevant in evaluating economic options. Marxist critique might prove particularly useful in decoding, as ideological, economic discourses parading under the banner of neutral technique. Marxism, however scientific in its ambitions, also offers specific and valuable normative considerations for assessing economic programmes. One thinks especially of the theory of alienation and its positive opposites, self-determination at work, the transcendence of socially unnecessary divisions of labour and the flowering of creative work (whether inside or, as Gorz proposes, outside the wage nexus).

The Legislator too can draw upon a particular stock of Marxist theory, even if, as previously noted, Marxism does not classically recognize it as a necessary and separate role. Although the concept of proceduralism is meaningful and politically necessary, it never presents itself in an innocent form. In the real world the Legislator needs to know something about social power relations. Procedural democracy is real because (and insofar as) it is open to the possibility of victory by more than one competing party and institutionalizes a degree of uncertainty as to outcome. Yet its neutrality is inherently limited in at least two ways. First, different voting and decision rules predispose to different political outcomes. The rules cannot predetermine outcomes, but they invariably influence them. Second, there is the matter of procedural democracy's domain. If it is a method of legitimating the making of binding rules and laws, that leaves in contention the question of which domains of power need to be controlled by procedural-democratic decision-making. This is a question to which there is no 'neutral' answer. In the liberal theoretical setting within which the concept arises, procedural democracy is seen as mandatory only for the state and a wide range of areas are thought to be off-limit to state power. Controversially, these include the economy. Here some Marxist critique is in order.

Conscious of the complex interplay of the formal and the substantive, Marxist Legislators recognize that they will, to some degree and unavoidably, be political players. To be sure, they are no more entitled than constitutional designers of other persuasions to set up procedures that unreasonably disadvantage ideological rivals. They will, however, be entitled to press for constitutional measures that lift obstacles to the advance of their movement and supporters, provided that these can be independently justified on universalist and egalitarian grounds. To return to an earlier-mentioned example, Marxist Legislators are legitimately reluctant to define protected free speech in a way that insulates campaign expenditure from state regulation. By leaving room for regulation of campaign finance, Marxist Legislators would in no way be violating common understandings of free speech or giving socialists unfair advantages. They would be assisting their own ideological side (since while capitalism persists socialists will have less financial backing) but, crucially, by levelling rather than tilting the playing field.

Legislators will, in doing all this, be drawing upon Marxist analysis of state power under capitalism. That body of analysis alerts Marxist constitution-designers to the ways in which the power of capital can impinge upon the fair operation of procedural democracy. If 'instrumentalist' accounts of the direct political power of capital inform the way Legislators deal (at the constitutional level) with campaign finance, media control, transparency in donations, and so on, 'structuralist' theories of the capitalist state remind them of the indirect power that comes with large-scale ownership and control of productive assets.[9] Marxists properly do not buy into the conventional liberal depiction of the market economy as a realm of voluntary exchanges between autonomous equals, entitled to protection. Instead they conceive of the economy as a realm of unaccountable power in need of democratization. It is this theoretical understanding that explains their (previously mentioned) reluctance constitutionally to protect productive property from public ownership or procedural democracy. Again, refusing such protection will assist socialists, freeing their hand to seek and implement an electoral mandate for economic democracy. It will, however, be independently justifiable as an extension of the scope of procedural-democratic control and as a legitimate liberty–democracy trade-off in a situation of unavoidably hard choices.

If Marxist theory's realism about power is a necessary antidote to naïve proceduralism, Legislators will of course not find all that they need in Marxist theory. Liberal political thought's own engagement with the issue of power and its restraint will constitute a crucial resource; Legislators will need to read Locke, Madison and John Stuart Mill alongside Marx, Miliband and Poulantzas.[10] Moreover Marxism's focus on class will miss other dimensions of informal power that subvert the claims of naïve proceduralism. No democratic-minded Legislator will wish to lock into the constitution any undue power for experts and bureaucrats. So reading Weber too is in order. Familiarity with feminism will place the progressive Legislator on guard against patriarchal tilting of the procedural playing field. Albeit especially true for the Legislator, no Marxist in any of the three roles can afford, like a Talmudic scholar, to seek all necessary wisdom from one philosophical source.

Conclusion

This paper has not attempted a rescue of Marxism; it could not accomplish that, given its focus on Marxism's metatheory rather than its content. It could be read as advancing a weak thesis and a strong one on behalf of Marxism. The weak thesis is largely negative, and does not actually require that Marxism be true. It is concerned with specifying rules of conduct Marxists must observe if they are to be democracy-friendly. Even so, the thesis is permissive (in the sense of recognizing the democracy-compatibility) of a wide range of Marxist theory including parts of it commonly considered democracy-unfriendly.

The stronger thesis, advanced more tentatively, is that Marxist theory can usefully contribute to democracy construction and other socially desirable projects. Here the permission granted by the translation rules is positive rather than negative, enabling rather than constraining: it allows a valuable body of theory to re-enter the struggle for emancipation. In this respect my concern has been to identify some distinctively Marxist priorities and approaches that can help the politico to win support for socialism and begin to build it, and help the Legislator design a constitution that is at once liberal, universalist and friendly to the egalitarian goals.

Much of this paper is written in the language of democratic theory, which takes the normative and political moments more seriously than Marxism classically does. Marxists convinced that history was pushing inexorably towards socialism did not think of this social order as something that might or might not be chosen, might or might not be choice-worthy. Scientific socialists dismissed such ethical (read: speculative, ideological) consideration as 'utopian'. The reversal of socialism's forward march in the last couple of decades and the full exposure of the Eastern bloc's failures has led many Marxists back to first principles, to a re-examination of why they became socialists in the first place, whether socialism is feasible and desirable, and whether, if it is both, Marxism can make a distinctive input into the struggle for its realization. In this return to the normative the way has been shown by Marx-influenced writers as diverse as Cohen, Elster, Geras, Habermas and Wright.[11] This paper is a contribution to the normative turn. Even so, my concern here has not been to call for a revision of Marxist theory across the board to permit larger scope for the normative (or political and democratic). My more modest strategy has been to propose a metatheoretical firewall that all Marxists and indeed all radicals should respect. The firewall, in the form of translation rules, requires for its justification only the acknowledgement that all theoretical positions, whether structuralist or voluntarist, teleological or contingency-based, centred or decentred, are uncertain to be true. All else follows from that.

Notes

1 Anyone inclined to underestimate this record of human rights abuse should read Courtois *et al.* (1999).
2 For some of the numerous critiques that incorporate these elements, see Kolakowski (1977); Hunt (1980); Cohen (1982); Buchanan (1986); Gordon (1986); Lukes (1986); Pierson (1989); Femia (1993). See also the brief survey of Marxism's anti-utopian critics in Geoghegan (1987: 73–86).
3 Lyotard (1984); Laclau and Mouffe (1985); Kellner (1989).
4 For a recent survey of these positions and their relationship to Marxism, see Walker (2001). The most prominent relatively recent contribution to a Marxist epistemology/ontology that avoids the excesses of relativism and objectivism comes from Roy Bhaskar. See for example Bhaskar (1986).

5 For imaginative efforts to revive Marx as a proto-postmodernist, see Derrida (1994) and Carver (1998). These exercises strike me as strange and rather pointless. What would Marx make of Derrida's renunciation of 'materialist doctrine' in favour of Marxism's 'spirit'? Or of Carver's reading of him as a 'figurative' writer and philosophical idealist for whom capitalism constituted a Foucauldian 'regime of truth' or Wittgensteinian 'form of life' (1998: 20, 27, 59)? For some notable Marxist ripostes to the postmodernists, see Callinicos (1980); Eagleton (1996); Post (1996).

6 For a useful appreciation of Marxism's commitment to individual self-determination, see Forbes (1990). For an earlier take, see Tucker (1980).

7 For other defences of procedural democracy by writers coming from a Marxist background, see Heller (1998); Habermas (1996: 287–28, 463–90).

8 Cohen (1982); Cohen and Howard (1979); Cutler *et al.* (1977); Laclau and Mouffe (1985); Gorz (1982); Habermas (1986; 1990); Offe (1972; 1984; 1985a,b).

9 For surveys of Marxist theories of the state, see Jessop (1982); Taylor (1995); Hay (1999).

10 Keane (1988: 31–68).

11 For Sitton (1996: 15), 'a renewed emphasis on the normative dimension of societal conflict is one of the defining characteristics of recent Marxist theory'. See also Elster (1985: 529–31); Wright *et al.* (1992: 100); Cohen (1995: 1–18); Habermas (1996); Geras (1988).

References

Bhaskar, R. (1986) *Scientific Realism and Human Emancipation*. London: Verso.

Buchanan, A. (1986) 'The Marxist Conceptual Framework and the Origins of Totalitarian Socialism' in E.F. Paul, J. Paul, F.D. Miller Jr and J. Arens (eds), *Marxism and Liberalism*. Oxford: Basil Blackwell.

Callinicos, A. (1980) *Against Postmodernism*. Cambridge: Polity Press.

Carver, T. (1998) *The Postmodern Marx*. Manchester: Manchester University Press.

Cohen, G. A. (1995) *Self-Ownership, Freedom and Equality*. Cambridge: Cambridge University Press.

Cohen, J. (1982) *Class and Civil Society: The Limits of Marxian Critical Theory*. Amherst, MA: University of Massachusetts Press.

Cohen, J. and D. Howard (1979) 'Why Class?' in P. Walker (ed.), *Between Labour and Capital*. Hassocks: Harvester Press.

Courtois, S., N. Werth, J.-L. Pammé, A. Paczkowski, K. Bartošek and J.-L. Margolin (1999) *The Black Book of Communism*. Cambridge, MA: Harvard University Press.

Cutler, A., B. Hindess, P. Hirst and A. Hussein (1977) *Marx's 'Capital' and Capitalism Today*, volume I. London: Routledge and Kegan Paul.

Derrida, J. (1994) *Specters of Marx*. New York: Routledge.

Eagleton, T. (1996) *The Illusions of Postmodernism*. Oxford: Blackwell.

Elster, J. (1985) *Making Sense of Marx*. Cambridge: Cambridge University Press.

Femia, J. (1993) *Marxism and Democracy*. Oxford: Clarendon Press.

Forbes, I. (1990) *Marxism and the New Individual*. London: Unwin Hyman.

Geoghegan, V. (1987) *Utopianism and Marxism*. London: Methuen.

Geras, N. (1988) *The Contact of Mutual Indifference: Political Philosophy after the Holocaust*. London: Verso.

Gordon, D. (1986) 'Marxism, Dictatorship and the Abolition of Rights' in E.F. Paul, J. Paul, F.D. Miller Jr and J. Arens (eds), *Marxism and Liberalism*. Oxford: Basil Blackwell.

Gorz, A. (1982) *Farewell to the Working Class: An Essay on Post-Industrial Socialism*. Boston: South End Press.

Habermas, J. (1986) 'The New Obscurity: The Crisis of the Welfare State and the Exhaustion of Utopian Energies', *Philosophy and Social Criticism* 11: 3–4.

Habermas, J. (1990) 'What Does Socialism Mean Today? The Rectifying Revolution and the Need for New Thinking on the Left', *New Left Review* 183: 3–21.

Habermas, J. (1996) *Between Facts and Norms: Contributions to a Discourse Theory of Law and Democracy*. Cambridge: Polity Press.

Hay, C. (1999) 'Marxism and the State' in A. Gamble, D. Marsh and T. Tant (eds), *Marxism and Social Science*. Basingstoke: Macmillan.

Heller, A. (1998) 'On Formal Democracy' in J. Keane (ed.), *Civil Society and the State*. London: Verso.

Hunt, A. (ed.) (1980) *Marxism and Democracy*. London: Lawrence and Wishart.

Jessop, B. (1982) *The Capitalist State: Marxist Theories and Methods*. Oxford: Martin Robinson.

Keane, J. (1988) *Democracy and Civil Society*. London: Verso.

Kellner, D. (1989) *Critical Theory, Marxism and Modernity*. Baltimore, MD: Johns Hopkins University Press.

Kolakowski, L. (1977) 'Marxist Roots of Stalinism' in R. Tucker (ed.), *Stalinism: Essays in Historical Interpretation*. New York: Norton.

Laclau, E. and C. Mouffe (1985) *Hegemony and Socialist Strategy*. London: Verso.

Lukes, S. (1986) 'Marxism and Dirty Hands' in E.F. Paul, J. Paul, F.D. Miller Jr and J. Arens (eds), *Marxism and Liberalism*. Oxford: Basil Blackwell.

Lyotard, J.-F. (1984) *The Postmodern Condition: A Report on Knowledge*. Manchester: Manchester University Press.

Offe, C. (1972) 'Political Authority and Class Structures: An Analysis of Late Capitalist Societies', *International Journal of Sociology*, vol.: Spring: 73–108.

Offe, C. (1984) *Contradictions of the Welfare State*. Cambridge, MA: The MIT Press.

Offe, C. (1985a) *Disorganized Capitalism*. Cambridge, MA: The MIT Press.

Offe, C. (1985b) 'New Social Movements: Challenging the Boundaries of Institutional Politics', *Social Research*, 52 (4): 817–68.

Pierson, C. (1989) 'Marxism and Rights' in M.Cowling and L. Wilde (eds), *Approaches to Marx*. Milton Keynes: Open University Press.

Post, K. (1996) *Regaining Marxism*. Basingstoke: Macmillan.

Sitton, J.F. (1996) *Recent Marxist Theory: Class Formation and Social Conflict in Contemporary Capitalism*. Albany, NY: State University of New York Press.

Taylor, G. (1995) 'Marxism' in D. Marsh and G. Stoker (eds), *Theory and Methods in Political Science*. Basingstoke: Macmillan.

Tucker, D.F.B. (1980) *Marxism and Individualism*. Oxford: Blackwell.

Walker, D. (2001) *Marx, Methodology and Science*. Aldershot: Ashgate.

Wright, E.O., A. Levine and E. Sober (1992) *Reconstructing Marxism*. London: Verso.

12 Marxisms and capitalisms

From logic of accumulation to articulation of class structures[1]

Yahya M. Madra and Fikret Adaman

As a critique of political economy, Karl Marx's economics and Marxian economics should not be conceptualized as a homogeneous, monolithic, and completed discourse. On the contrary, this rich and vital tradition harbors multiple voices and a multiplicity of theories. Clearly, in this brief chapter, it is virtually impossible to do justice to the richness and the complexity of the different traditions of Marxian economics.[2] In an attempt to make sense of this multiplicity, this chapter will distinguish between two distinct Marxist projects: those that take *the process of capital accumulation* as their center of gravity, and those that take *class exploitation* as their entry point.[3] Whereas the former project is committed to the analysis of capitalism as a crises-ridden process of wealth accumulation, the latter can be described as the institutionally specific analyses of different class structures (capitalist, feudal, slave, independent, or communal) and their articulation. This distinction also informs the structure of the chapter. In the first section, we will briefly introduce some basic concepts of Marxian economics in order to undertake an intelligible survey of the literature. The second section will survey the accumulation theories of capitalism and the fourth section will discuss certain analyses of capitalist and non-capitalist forms of appropriation of surplus in contemporary social formations. The third section is on the Marxist theories of colonialism and imperialism, and as such it will serve as an interlude. Concluding remarks will touch upon some of the implications of different theories of capitalism for imagining and enacting non-capitalist futures.

Some basic concepts of Marxian economics

Value categories

Marx begins *Capital* with an analysis of commodity. He posits that commodity is a condensation of use-value, value, and value-form. According to Marx, "[t]he usefulness of a thing makes it a use-value" (1976 [1867]: 126). Without doubt, not all use-values are commodities. A use-value is a commodity if produced for exchange (be it through the markets or the decrees of a central authority or some other "form of integration"). Nevertheless, in order to be able to determine the value and the value-form of a commodity, Marx will need to introduce a related distinction between *concrete* and *abstract labor* – a distinction that he regards as one of his major contributions (Marx, 1972 [1881]). Whereas the former refers to the fact that each commodity is a product of a specific form of labor, the latter implies that commodities are commensurable with one another only because they are all products of human labor. To put it differently, abstract labor is that which remains of human labor once all its concrete attributes and "sensuous characteristics" are subtracted. Accordingly, "socially necessary [abstract] labour-time is the labour-time required to produce any use-value [commodity] under the *conditions of production* normal for a given society and with the average degree of skill and intensity of labour prevalent in that society" (Marx, 1976 [1867]: 129; emphasis added). The value of a commodity, then, is equal to the socially necessary abstract labor-time that is necessary to produce that commodity at any given moment, under given production conditions, regardless of the actual quantum of abstract labor-time spent on its production.[4]

When discussing the value of a commodity, Marx abstracts from the sphere of circulation and takes only the conditions of production into consideration. The *value-form*, in contrast, is the quantity of socially necessary abstract labor-time that represents the commodity in *the sphere of circulation* (e.g. the markets), given, again, particular conditions of production (Wolff *et al.*, 1982). In fact, the distinction between the value and the value-form is so crucial for Marxian economics that only through this distinction will it be possible for Marx to analyze the relations between the spheres of production and circulation without relinquishing his labor theory of value.

Moreover, this distinction is also inscribed within the structure of *Capital*. Throughout Volume 1 of *Capital*, Marx assumes that commodities are exchanged at their values, that the value-forms of commodities do not deviate from their values – the provisional concept of "exchange value" standing in for both. Although useful as an expository trope, this restrictive assumption makes it impossible to analyze the relations between the spheres of circulation and production. Only in Volume 3 of *Capital*, when this assumption is relaxed, will Marx be able to introduce the concept of *prices of production* as a value-form distinct to capitalism. Prices of production are the social labor-times attached to each commodity in the sphere of circulation under the competitive tendency of equalization of the rates of profit. In fact, much of Marx's analysis of capitalist dynamics is based on the assumption that the prices of production of commodities tend to deviate systematically from their values.[5]

The circuits of capital and many capitals

Canonical accounts of Marx's theory of capital contrast *simple commodity exchange* ($C-M-C$; where C stands for commodity and M stands for money) with the "expansion of value" ($M-C-M'$; where $M' > M$). The former is seen, for instance, as the objective of the worker for selling her labor-power ($C-M$) in order to purchase the means of consumption with the wage received (M–C). On the other hand, the latter, also known as *the circuits of capital*, is usually considered to be the *raison d'être* of capitalist accumulation: The capitalist produces consumption goods for the society not out of goodwill but in order to profit.[6]

There are three basic forms of capital that generate the three circuits of capital.[7] In the first circuit of capital, when capital is in the form of money, it functions as the means of purchase and payment. The first circuit is completed when the means of production (MP) and labor-power (LP) are purchased $\{M-C(_{LP}{}^{MP})\ldots\}$ and put to production. The *value* of the means of production, just like all other commodities, is determined by the average amount of labor-time that is "socially" necessary to produce them. It follows that the *value* of labor-power is also equal to the value of goods and services that are necessary for the laborer to reproduce her labor-power day after day. That is, the seller of the labor-power, with the money she receives in the form of wage-payment, purchases the means of existence of her reproduction, i.e. articles of consumption. From the standpoint of the capitalist, on the other hand, the *use-value* of the labor-power is the labor that will be performed by the worker during the workday. And this brings us to the next circuit.

The second circuit of capital constitutes an interruption in the circulation of capital: $\{M-C(_{LP}{}^{MP})\ldots P\ldots\}$. In this circuit, *productive capital* (P), as the metamorphosis of money capital, takes the function of producing commodities. Productive capital comprises the means of production and labor-power, and from the standpoint of capital they are named as constant (c) and variable capital (v), respectively. Upon entering "into the hidden abode of production" (Marx, 1976 [1867]: 279), we are able to discern the source of profit as unpaid labor: the value of the commodity produced (w) will be above and beyond the value of capital advanced ($c+v$), and the difference between the two will be equivalent to the surplus value (s), i.e. the unpaid portion of the living labor: $w-(c+v)=s$.

Finally, with the third circuit of capital, we exit the sphere of production and enter back into the sphere of circulation. At this final link in the circuit of capital $\{\ldots C'-M'\}$, capital takes the form of commodity, and the surplus labor *materialized* in the mass of commodities will need to be sold in the markets so it can be *realized* in the form of money capital. The moment of *realization* completes the process of self-expansion of value, only to be repeated *ad infinitum*.

With the help of the circuits of capital $\{M-C\ldots P\ldots C'-M'\}$ model, we can distinguish between different types of capitals. For instance, simply by compressing the totality of the circuit to $\{M-M'\}$, the logic of *financial (money) capital* can readily be summarized: lending out money to pocket more money. A relatively more elaborate version of the circuits of capital summarizes the structure of *merchant capital* $\{M-C-M'\}$: buying commodities in order to sell them for profit. Only by entering into the sphere of production (always already enveloped with the sphere of circulation) will it be possible to give an embedded account of *"industrial" capital* $\{M-C\ldots P\ldots C'-M'\}$.[8] What distinguishes the last from the previous two is the particularity of "industrial" capital to capitalism: surplus value is generated *only* as a result of unpaid labor undertaken within the production sphere. Nevertheless, according to Marx the sphere of production always presupposes the sphere of circulation as its condition of possibility. This is because the capitalist production process always depends upon the existence of a market for labor-power, a market for the purchase of means of production, and a market for the sale of the produced commodities (i.e. a market for the realization of surplus value).

Class processes and the capitalist corporation

The notion of class is based on the simple idea that in all social formations, past and present, the performers of labor always produce more than the amount that is necessary to reproduce their immediate conditions of existence. Defined as the performance, appropriation, and distribution of surplus labor, the specifically Marxist notion of *class process* is distinct from other notions of class that designate differences in social status (blue- versus white-collar) or income level (Resnick and Wolff, 1987). Furthermore, it is also distinct from the property-based notion of class that distinguishes between those who own and those who are dispossessed as well as the power-based notion of class that distinguishes between the oppressor and the oppressed. This, however, does not mean that different class structures cannot be conceptualized with reference to these other notions of class. Although these other notions of class predate Marx's novel notion of *class process*, Marx did and Marxists still do continue to refer to other notions of class in order to make sense of the complex relations of inequality, oppression, and exploitation that characterize the different class structures, including the contemporary variants of capitalism.

The identification of the different forms in which the surplus is performed, appropriated, and distributed enables the Marxist social theorist to distinguish between exploitative and non-exploitative forms. For instance, if the surplus labor is performed, appropriated, and distributed by the same individual, Marxists will call this an *independent* class structure. On the other hand, in a *communal* class structure the surplus labor is appropriated and distributed by the same collectivity that performs it. These two are non-exploitative class processes in that the performers of surplus are *not* excluded from its appropriation and distribution. Along with the *capitalist* class structure, in which the surplus is appropriated and distributed by a group of non-laborers, the Marxist canon also refers to *slave* and *feudal* class structures among other exploitative forms (for an early yet solid presentation, see Hindess and Hirst, 1975).

A typical contemporary capitalist corporation is usually an amalgamation of industrial, financial, and merchant capital. Within the class analytical framework, such a corporation is represented as a nodal point of value inflows and outflows. The board of directors of such corporations do not only appropriate surplus value but also receive cuts from the surplus value appropriated in other capitalist corporations. Moreover, such corporations may receive non-class revenues in the form of tax cuts from the government, the interest revenues received in return for the credits extended to consumers, and so on.

In order to secure all these revenues, however, the boards of directors of these corporations need to incur a variety of expenses. For instance, in order to secure the surplus value appropriated within the corporation, it will need to distribute a certain portion of the surplus to its managers, to the marketing division, to the advertising division, to the product development division, and even to unionized workers in the form of union premiums.[9] In fact, in contemporary capitalist corporations the funds allocated out of the surplus to capital accumulation $(\Delta c + \Delta v)$ represent only a subset of the distribution made out of the appropriated surplus.[10]

We are now equipped to elucidate the differences between the capital accumulation and the class exploitation traditions within Marxian economics. At the firm level, whereas the former tradition privileges the funds allocated to the capital accumulation at the expense of all other possible distributions of the surplus, the class exploitation approach argues that it is impossible to predict a priori what destinations (managerial salaries, marketing, capital accumulation, merchanting, trade unions, and so on) will receive what portions of surplus (Norton, 2001). According to the class exploitation tradition, both the amount of surplus appropriated and its various distributions are a contingent outcome of the intra- and inter-firm competitive battles (Amariglio and Ruccio, 1998). At the level of social formation, whereas the capital accumulation tradition emphasizes the capitalist class structures as the dominant if not the only form in which the processes of performance, appropriation, and distribution of surplus take place, the latter approach argues not only that class exploitation may take many forms but also that non-exploitative class structures, with varying degrees of prominence, may co-exist side by side with exploitative ones.

Marxism as a theory of accumulation: crisis theories

In this section, we survey different theories of crisis that identify the logic of capitalism as accumulation of wealth $(\Delta c + \Delta v)$. Theories of disproportionality focus on the sphere of circulation and on the moment of realization of the surplus, whereas theories of the tendency of the rate of profit to fall and the theories of profit squeeze focus on the sphere of production. The last two are further distinguished by their respective emphasis on the forces and the relations of production.[11] We will conclude this section with a discussion of two schools of thought that take the institutional context of the accumulation process into account.

Crisis in circulation: theories of disproportionality

Debates on the dynamics of capitalism early in the twentieth century were based on the different interpretations of Marx's reproduction schema. In these models, there are two sectors (departments) of the economy: one for the production of the means of production and one for the means of consumption. For instance, for Mikhail Tugan-Baranovsky and Rudolf Hilferding the disproportionality between the accumulation rates of the capital goods and consumption goods departments represented the sole source of crises (see, for example, Mandel, 1981). In fact, Hilferding (1981 [1910]) went so far as to argue that, as long as the proportions between the respective rates of accumulation are maintained, there would be no reason for capitalism to deviate from its path of stable expansion. Emphasizing the anarchic nature of capitalist production, such approaches argued that crises come about because it is impossible to coordinate the activities of the producers in the two departments. In these theories, some Marxists (e.g. Nikolai Bukharin) have found a strong case for the planned allocation of resources. Similarly, Hilferding's notion of "organized capitalism," in which a generalized cartel regulates the various crisis tendencies, reflected his understanding of *competition* as the Achilles' heel of capitalism.

A weakness of these early arguments for disproportionality in capitalism was their singular emphasis on the sphere of circulation (Rosdolsky, 1977). In order to maintain the continual expansion of capital, the surplus value that is *generated* in the sphere of production must be *realized* in the marketplace. However, since the conditions for the extraction of surplus value are not identical to the conditions of its realization, a certain contradiction is embedded into the logic of capital. On the one hand, the necessities of realization requires mass consumption, and hence an increase in the income of the wage-laborer. On the other hand, such an increase in the cost of variable capital will translate into a reduction of surplus value[12] and will lower the *value rate of profit* ($r=s/(c+v)$). This *underconsumptionist* argument holds that, since capitalism imposes strict limits on the level of consumption allowed to wage-laborers, sooner or later the system will face a problem of effective demand. Earlier in the twentieth century Rosa Luxemburg and Karl Kautsky, and in the mid-century Paul Sweezy, were among the proponents of this line of reasoning (Sweezy, 1970 [1942]). For Luxemburg (1972 [1921]), in order to overcome the crisis of the realization of surplus value that will inevitably strike the accumulation process, capitalism is obliged to incorporate non-capitalist sectors into the orbit of the capitalist commodity nexus, and to dump all the unrealized surplus to the colonies and the non-capitalist sectors of the world economy. Luxemburg's point is noteworthy as it brings the outside of capitalism into the picture.

The flip side to underconsumption is *overaccumulation*. According to Otto Bauer (see Mandel, 1981: 46), the department that produces capital goods may overestimate the demand for constant capital and this may lead to an excess capacity for the production of consumer goods. Both theories are, in fact, more subtle and fleshed out variants of disproportionality. It is worth noting that these theories purport to identify the triggering mechanisms of the anticipated breakdown of capitalism. According to Ernest Mandel (1978), this is, in part, an outcome of misreading the reproduction schemata as the different representations of capitalism as such and of taking equilibrium as the state in which capitalist accumulation takes place.[13] However, as Mandel correctly argues, for Marx, capitalist accumulation is a process of permanent *disequilibrium*. The crises of disproportionality, leading to devalorization (e.g. cheapening of the means of production), should be seen as the correction mechanisms of the destructive process of competition (Mandel, 1978; Shaikh, 1978; Amariglio and Ruccio, 1998). As such, competition cannot simply be the Achilles' heel of capitalism.

Crisis in production

The debate on the falling rate of profit

The argument that the logic of capital inevitably generates crisis received another theoretical grounding in the so-called law of tendency of the (value) rate of profit to fall (henceforth, TRPF). Based on the assumption that capital accumulation will always lead to the introduction of labor-saving techniques,[14] the law of TRPF states that, owing to the rising organic composition of capital ($k = c/v$), *ceteris paribus* (e.g. the rate of exploitation ($e = s/v$) remains constant), the rate of profit will fall.[15]

Within the Marxian tradition, the law of TRPF has sparked some productive, yet often embittered, debates. Significantly, these have been highly politicized (Cullenberg, 1994). Defenders of the law of TRPF saw themselves as demonstrating the inexorable march to revolution. This, by implication, positioned the critics of the law as reformists. However, it is also possible to see the belief in the "scientific" inevitability of the ultimate breakdown of capitalism as having led Marxists to adopt a wait-and-see strategy, a strategy that tended to make this position ultimately indistinguishable from a reformist one. Critics of the TRPF, on the other hand, because they rejected the inevitability of capitalist collapse, had to devise strategies of social transformation and attempted to actively create the conditions for the revolutionary overthrow of capitalism.

In fact, two distinct methodological clusters of debate can be identified, each with defenders and critics of the law of TRPF.[16] The first cluster involved theorists who conceptualized capitalism as a social totality and identified accumulation as its essence. Here, the debate centered on the strength of counter-tendencies to the falling rate of profit, and on the uncertainties involved in these complex processes, with critics contending that for a variety of reasons it was impossible to treat the TRPF as an inexorable law (Sweezy, 1970 [1942]).[17]

Those involved in the second cluster challenged the characterization of capitalism as a social totality guided by the logic of accumulation. These Marxist economists were convinced that it was theoretically unsound to identify the logic of a social phenomenon without explaining the "properties", "goals," and "actions" of the individuals that participate in it.[18] They argued that no rational, myopically self-interested capitalist would introduce new techniques of production that would lead to a fall in the rate of profit (Okishio, 1961). These critics of the law of TPRF departed from the more traditional Marxist accounts both in the way that they characterized the economic totality and in the way they conceptualized the individual capitalist as a pre-constituted, rational, and optimizing subject. Others, notably Shaikh (1978), argued that, although the capitalist does make "rational" decisions pertaining to the choice of technique, these decisions are not *optimizing* decisions (namely, decisions of economic agents that are situated within a static, perfectly competitive, environment) but, at best, *competitive* decisions (namely, temporary decisions of economic agents that are embedded within a dynamic, uncertain, and imperfect environment). The outcome of such a competitive process offers a clear example of the unintended consequences of rational actions: a rise in the overall organic composition of capital and a fall in the overall profit rate, despite "rational" decision-making by individual capitalists.[19]

The theories of profit squeeze and business cycle

A third cluster of theories of the logic of capitalism underscored the importance of the relations of production in the generation of crises by tracing the ebbs and flows of the *industrial reserve army of unemployed* and their effects on labor militancy (Glyn and Sutcliffe, 1972; Boddy and Crotty, 1975). The argument was that growing trade union strength in times of economic expansion translated into an increase in the share of the social product captured by wages, eventually leading to a profit squeeze. In order to counter this trend, the state, under the direct influence of the capitalist class, would deploy contractionary monetary and fiscal policies that would curtail demand – thus inducing a recession. Although relatively instrumentalist in their depiction of the state power, the political implications of such analyses were to make the unity and militancy of the working class the key to the struggle against capitalism.

Accumulation and institutions: periodizing capitalism

During the 1980s, two innovative schools of thought attempted to move beyond general explanations of the tendencies to move toward capitalist crisis and to look at the specific institutions that helped to account for the long cycles of capital accumulation. Regulation Theory (henceforth RT) originated in France, and the Social Structures of Accumulation Approach (henceforth SSAA) was developed in the US.[20] Whereas RT emphasized the structural dimensions of the process of capital accumulation, the SSAA emphasized power relations and identified class struggle as the propeller of the crises of capitalism.

These differences were most clearly manifested in their respective analyses of the post-war US. To a large extent they arrived at a consensus on identifying the key institutions that had negotiated and stabilized the accumulation process during the Golden Age of capitalist expansion (from the mid-1940s to the mid-1960s): peaceful capital–labor relations, the welfare state, Keynesian expansionary macro-policy, and US hegemony. Nevertheless, they differed in their explanation of how these institutions accomplished their stabilizing mission. RT saw them as helping to counteract the TRPF by enabling wage increases to be geared to a relatively rapid rise in productivity. For the SSAA, these institutions stabilized the socio-political environment, creating a predictable and secure environment for the capitalist investor. Its emphasis on the aspect of "agency" consequently led advocates of the SSAA to analyze the collapse of the post-war social contract as an outcome of political and social resistance (labor militancy, civil rights movement, Third World liberation movements, etc.). On the other hand, RT highlighted the forces of production and the questions of disproportionality, identifying a fall both in productivity and in the rate of profit as the culprit behind the demise of the Golden Age of capitalism.

Although there is still no consensus regarding the exact nature of the institutional arrangements that succeeded post-war Fordism, the idea of *flexible specialization* (Piore and Sabel, 1984) gained considerable currency. According to this notion, the mass production and mass consumption that characterized Fordism was replaced in the 1970s and 1980s by a combination of small-scale production (based on computer and information technologies) and specialized and differentiated consumption patterns. However, as Julie Graham (1991) acutely argued, despite their attention to institutional specificity, both RT and the SSAA, with their emphasis on the stability of the capitalist accumulation process, neglected to produce specific class analyses of the contradictions of capitalism and contemporary social formations. For instance, Alain Lipietz's (1987a) progressive agenda for a new post-Fordist class compromise tended to accept "capitalism" as the only game in town and to abandon consideration of the need for the transformation of class relations (Graham, 1991: 48–9).

Interlude: colonialism and imperialism

Colonialism, according to Marx, can be characterized as a politico-militaristic means for the procurement of cheap raw materials.[21] These reduce the costs of production in colonialist nations and give them a competitive advantage over others.[22] Access to cheaper consumption goods also has the effect of lowering the value of labor-power in the colonialist nations without jeopardizing the direct laborers' access to the means of consumption.

Colonies also serve as a market for capitalist commodities produced in the center, and thereby help to regulate crises of disproportionality. Finally, from the perspective of finance capital, colonies may serve as spheres of influence where financiers of the colonialist nation, without fear of competition, can extend credits not only to the indigenous industrial capitalists of the colonies but also to the agents of other non-capitalist class processes (e.g. slave, feudal, and independent). However, none of the processes described above involves the "exploitation" of the colony by the colonizer in the strict Marxian sense. Nevertheless, all these processes provide the conditions of the existence of capitalist form of extraction of surplus value in the "center" (Ruccio *et al.*, 1990).

Imperialism, on the other hand, involves a much more intensive articulation of the circuits of capital into the colonial territory. One distinguishing aspect of imperialism is the flow of direct investment from imperial centers to the colonies. Through direct investment and by securing direct access to the raw materials and cheaper labor-power, the industrial capitalists of the imperialist nations have begun to "exploit" the workers of the colonies. This is a different form of internationalization of capitalism than the colonial one we have just described. Moreover, this direct investment has two other complementary effects. First, the proletarianization of the indigenous populations opens up new markets for the realization of surplus value for merchant capital. Second, the introduction of the institutions of capitalism in the colonies necessitates the construction of infrastructures (railroads, school, dams, electric systems, and so on) that will be profitably financed by the financiers from the imperial nations.

It would, however, be inaccurate to interpret the Marxist notion of imperialism as suggesting that the world is being transformed into a single global capitalist social formation. Rather, the process is a contradictory one that always involves an encounter between capitalist and non-capitalist class processes. Ernesto Laclau (1977) clarified the terms of this encounter in a pointed criticism of Andre Gunder Frank's analysis of Latin America. For Gunder Frank (1972) and others, Latin American social formations were already capitalist by virtue of their integration into the world market. Laclau countered such theses by introducing into the debate the Marxian distinction between the spheres of circulation and production. According to Laclau, it would be illegitimate to deduce the presence of capitalist relations of productions simply from the presence of commodity exchange. For him, Latin American social formations could more adequately be represented as an articulation of feudal and capitalist relations of production. In fact, capitalist forms not only co-exist with, but may also foster, non-capitalist forms (Ruccio *et al.*, 1990).

The effects of imperialism on the political consciousness of the working classes of the imperial nations have also been a persistent concern for Marxist theorists (Lenin, 1973 [1917]: 118–31; Dobb, 1945 [1940]: 259–69). In particular, it has been argued that imperialist policies may provide the wherewithal to increase the rate of exploitation despite an upward trend in the real wages.[23] *Trade union consciousness*, a political culture that feeds reformism and opportunism, was thus nourished, in part, as a result of the flow of surplus from the colonies to the imperial center.

The question whether imperialism remains a pertinent notion for analyzing contemporary capitalism is open to debate. Michael Hardt and Antonio Negri (2000) have recently proposed the notion of *Empire* to describe the new network of international institutions (World Bank, International Monetary Fund, World Trade Oragization, etc.) that frame, regulate, protect, support, and guide the activities of transnational corporations. Whatever the value of such attempts to account for recent developments may be,[24] it is also arguable that all the economic processes that characterized colonialism and imperialism are still present, albeit in different political and cultural forms, in the contemporary world economy (Ruccio, 2003).

Marxism beyond capitalism

In this section we would like to argue for the possibility and the need to resist the temptation to equate "capitalism" with "the economy" as such. When the economy is theorized to be predominantly, if not exclusively, capitalist, the socialist strategy is also singularly defined as anti-capitalist. We consider this to be a shortcoming as it occludes other possible strategies of social transformation, including class transformation. In what follows we will first establish the need and the viability of class transformative strategies that can move our communities beyond capitalism and then proceed to critically engage with anti-globalization movements from a Marxian class analytical perspective.

Mapping non-capitalism

In the context of the so-called Third World, it may be relatively easier to theorize the co-existence of capitalist and non-capitalist class structures. In contrast, it may be more difficult to argue for the prevalence of non-capitalism in the context of the industrialized social formations of the North. Nevertheless, three areas of research provide ample evidence in support of such a position.

To begin with, recent Marxist-feminist analyses of the household highlight it as a site of economic activity where surplus labor is performed (Kuhn and Wolpe, 1978; Folbre, 1982; Fraad *et al.*, 1994; Gibson-Graham, 1996). In particular, these analyses argue that the performance, appropriation, and distribution of surplus in the context of the household can convincingly be theorized as feudal or independent (single-parent), if not, in some cases, as communal (Fraad *et al.*, 1994; Gibson-Graham, 1996). Second, in recent years, a number of class analytical studies of self-employment, domestic services, and the sex industry has identified a significant degree of economic difference in the "informal sector" – an economic phenomenon that cannot be adequately captured by the capital accumulation model (see the various contributions to the edited volume by Gibson-Graham *et al.*, 2000). And finally, some analyses of the non-traditional economic sites such as "local communities" have argued that, although they are not considered to be a part of "the economy," by contributing to the provision of local public goods through communal labor processes, these sites should be seen as an integral part of our economies (Community Economies Collective, 2001).

Therefore, capitalism cannot be co-extensive with the social formation. A social formation, whether it is a locality, a region, or a nation-state, or the globe, is a site of articulation of multiple class structures. This simple notion opens up a new terrain of possibilities for proposing new strategies of class transformation. Consider the following two distinct left responses in the face of the internationalization of the world economy. On the one hand, some critics of capitalism continue to demand expansionary macro-policies to secure full employment and the reinvigoration of the welfare state. Some Marxists, on the other hand, have begun to distance themselves from such strategies that implicitly accept capitalism as the only game in town (Gibson-Graham, 2006). For instance, they have argued that, however painful deindustrialization may be for laid-off workers and abandoned communities, it may also be an opening for constructing, and experimenting with, communal, non-exploitative forms of appropriation that may serve as concrete points of identification for others who may desire to disassociate themselves from capitalism.

Towards a class analysis of anti-globalization movements

Nevertheless, this shift towards strategies of social transformation beyond capitalism is not as widespread as we wish it to be. In particular, the so-called anti-globalization movements, rather than devoting their energies towards imagining and enacting non-capitalisms, have tended to focus their agenda around various criticisms of capitalism. Some have equated the spread of commodification with the spread of capitalism. Others have argued that the problem is not with capitalism as such but with the democratic deficit in globalization. Still others have suggested that globalization and the newfound mobility of the multinational corporations both undermine the power of trade unions in the North and also secure the cheap labor-power of the workers of the South under deplorable sweatshop conditions.

To begin, capitalism cannot be equated with commodity exchange. Commodity exchange as such predates the spread of capitalist class relations. This is not to deny the devastating effects of the articulation of commodity exchange (a mode of circulation) with capitalist class relations (a mode of production). Without doubt, anti-capitalist movements should engage with the socially, economically, ecologically, and culturally "corrosive" effects of commodification. Nevertheless, to insist on the conceptual distinction between capitalism and commodification extends the scope of the analysis to include considerations pertaining to the sphere of production (Kozel, 2006).

Similarly, to criticize those who stress the democratic deficit of globalization as the fundamental problem does not imply that the deepening and widening of the institutional mechanisms of democratic governance of the world economy (IMF, World Bank, WTO, and so on) is not of the utmost necessity. These approaches are vulnerable to criticism only because the particular way they frame the debate makes it impossible to see the links between capitalist class relations and globalization. In particular, they neglect one of the key impediments to democratization, namely the possibility of the social groups (sometimes designated as "transnational classes") that are responsible for the reproduction of exploitative and undemocratic nature of capitalist corporations to block any serious democratization of the international institutions of economic governance (Wolff, 2000; Odekom, 2006).

Class analysis also helps us gain critical insights into the anti-sweatshop movement. By equating exploitation with the dismal labor practices in the non-Western world, the sweatshop literature has all too often lent credence to a portrait of the working environment in the West as "just," "fair," "humane," and ultimately "non-exploitative." Class analysis and its focus on the moment of appropriation cautions us against such an "Orientalist notion of exploitation" (Erçel, 2006), rendering visible the widespread exploitation taking place here and now in the middle of "the most civilized and advanced" part of the globe.

The point not to be missed here is that capitalism is a peculiar articulation of spheres of production and circulation. From this vantage point the different strands of anti-globalization movements can be seen to take issue with the different components of the circuit of capital. For instance, those who criticize commodification focus on the sphere of circulation and the moment of consumption, whereas those who take issue with the democratic deficit inherent in the international institutions of world economic governance (IMF, World Bank, WTO) focus on the dimensions of the circuit of capital pertaining to finance and trade. The conceptual apparatus of the circuit of capital allows all the different strands of anti-capitalist movements to be grasped in a coherent framework without privileging any single one of them as more fundamental, as more important.

Although lacking the class analytical framework, Hardt and Negri's *Empire* (2000) ends up with an interesting set of leftist demands: the right to global citizenship, the right to social wage, and the right to reappropriate the means of production. For example, for those who seek a rupture with capitalism, the introduction of a social wage (a basic income scheme disconnected from the performance of labor) could provide the wherewithal to experiment with communal forms of production. Without doubt, class transformational projects, on their own, cannot guarantee the arrival of the hegemony of communal forms of appropriation. Nevertheless, they provide new avenues that were not visible from the perspective of theories of accumulation.

Conclusion: theories and strategies

Marxists have long been aware of the dialectical relationship between theoretical practice and political strategies. In this chapter, we have tried to attend to the political implications of different Marxist theories of capitalism. In particular, we have argued that the ways in which we theorize the economy affects the ways in which we devise political strategies of social transformation. Consider, for instance, the way in which the accumulationist theories have emphasized the disorderliness and the crisis tendencies of capitalism. One important implication of such analyses has been to advocate struggles within and against capitalist corporations. Various analyses of the regimes of accumulation, colonialism, and imperialism have brought to the forefront the coordinating and regulatory roles played by the (capitalist) state. Thus these analyses compelled socialists to consider the state as a terrain of social transformative struggles. Class analyses, on the other hand, emphasize not only the multiplicity of forms of exploitation and domination within contemporary social formations but also the possibility of imagining and enacting communal (and maybe even independent) class structures and democratic forms of governance today – as opposed to waiting for the terminal collapse of capitalism or the total overthrow of the capitalist state to begin constructing communism.

Nevertheless, rather than conceptualizing these different strategies as exclusive of one another, the task, today, is to construct an umbrella socialist project that mediates between them. Indeed, a thoroughgoing rethinking entails a strategic lacing together of various strategies of the rich tradition of Marxist political economy. In this context, we believe that it is more urgent than ever to recognize and embrace class transformative strategies as indispensable components of a rainbow of socialist strategies of liberation.

Notes

1 The authors would like to thank Howie Chodos, Kenan Erçel, Stephen Healy, Philip M. Kozel, and Ceren Özselçuk. The usual caveat applies. A longer version of this chapter is available upon request.

2 Inevitably, this will be a particular representation of the Marxian economics, a representation that is influenced and shaped by its authors' particular and thus inescapably partial understanding of Marxism.

3 Bruce Norton (2001: 24) was the first to propose this distinction in stark terms: "My thesis is that whatever détente the two projects managed to maintain in *Capital* and *Theories of Surplus Value*, peace between them broke down after Marx's death. One, the effort to discern capitalism's destiny-determining inner contradictions, became the project of Western Marxian economics and spilled over to inform radical economics more generally. The other, the effort to conceive the historically changing dimensions of class exploitation – and envision associated transformational possibilities – found corresponding less growing room." In fact, Norton's comprehensive work on Marxist theories of accumulation (1988; 1992; 2001) has shaped this paper in more than one way.

4 In this sense, Marxian labor theory of value (LTV) is distinct from other (Smithian and Ricardian) labor theories of value according to which the value of a commodity is equal to the amount of labor-time "embodied" in it.

5 Much has been written on the so-called Transformation Problem (TP) and the scientific validity of the LTV. The TP refers to the transformation of the values of commodities to the prices of production. The Ricardian/Sraffian critics of the LTV argue that, in Volume 3 of *Capital*, Marx has failed to transform the values of the means of production to their value-form (prices of production). More fundamentally, these critics argue that value categories are unnecessary and the LTV should be replaced by a Sraffian linear prices of production model. For a Ricardian/Sraffian critique of the LTV, see Steedman (1977); for the philosophical dimensions of the LTV, see the various contributions to Elson (1979); for a recent classical Marxist defense of the LTV, see Moseley (1993); for the so-called "new" solution to the TP, see Foley (1982); for the anti-essentialist solution to the TP, see Wolff *et al.* (1982).

6 From this, it is possible to conclude that the motive of accumulation is the backbone of capitalism (Marx, 1976 [1867]: 742): "Accumulate, accumulate! That is Moses and the prophets!" Nevertheless, this would involve a mistaken equation of profits with one of its sub-sets, namely the funds allocated for the purposes of accumulation (see the next section, 'Class processes and the capitalist corporation').

7 The following account is based on Volume 2 of *Capital* (Marx, 1978 [1884]).

8 The term "industrial" may be somewhat misleading. By "industrial" capital, Marx is referring not to the industrial (as opposed to agricultural or service) sector, but to the performance of surplus labor. As such, the concept may apply to all the sectors of an economy.

9 Marx writes (1976 [1867]: 709): "The capitalist who produces surplus-value, i.e., who extracts unpaid labour directly from the workers and fixes it in commodities, is admittedly the first appropriator of this surplus-value, but he is by no means its ultimate proprietor. He has to share it afterwards with capitalists who fulfil other functions in social production taken as a whole, with the owner of the land, with yet other people. Surplus-value is therefore split up into various parts. Its fragments fall to various categories of person, and take on various mutually independent forms, such as profit, interest, gains made through trade, ground rent, etc."

10 Again, Marx writes (1976 [1867]: 710; emphasis added): "We treat the capitalist producer as the owner of the entire surplus-value, or perhaps better, as the representative of all those who will share the booty with him. We shall therefore begin by considering accumulation from an abstract point of view, i.e., *simply as one aspect of the immediate process of production.*"

11 In the classical Marxist model of the social formation, the two components of a mode of production are the relations and the forces of production. Whereas the relations refer to classes, the forces refer to technology, ecology, and population. A mode of production, determining the superstructural elements such as culture, ideology, the legal and political system, is the economic base of a social formation. In the 1970s this

base–superstructure model of the social formation was extensively criticized for its economic determinism (Hindess and Hirst, 1975). Later in the 1980s the hierarchical model of the base–superstructure was replaced with a horizontal model of economic, political, natural, and cultural processes (Resnick and Wolff, 1987). In this overde-terminist model no single process is causally privileged and the separation is purely for analytical purposes. The economic processes, however, are further divided into class and non-class economic processes. The latter category includes, among others, processes of distribution and consumption.

12 Unless the rate of exploitation ($e=s/v$) remains the same or rises.

13 Indeed, these models were not intended to depict Marx's vision of the dynamics of capitalism. Rather modestly, and abstracting from the sphere of production, they were intended to demonstrate the possibility and the fragility of equilibrium in capitalist accumulation process.

14 According to Anwar Shaikh (1978: 237–8), the capitalist is compelled to modify the labor process and replace the uppity workers with machines in the face of the social limits imposed on "extending the length of the working day or the intensity of labor, within the given methods of production."

15 The value rate of profit (r) for the economy can be defined as follows: $r=s/(c+v)=(s/v)/[(c/v)+1]=e/(k+1)$.The rising organic composition of capital (k) means that the firm is relying more and more on constant capital rather than variable capital.

16 For a comprehensive survey of this debate, see Cullenberg (1994).

17 To be more precise, Marx did spell out at least five counter-tendencies. These are as follows: (1) increasing rate of exploitation; (2) reduction of wages below their value; (3) cheapening of the means of production; (4) increase in the surplus population; (5) foreign trade (see Marx, 1981 [1894]: 339–48).

18 Also known as analytical, or rational choice, Marxists, this group of social theorists include, among others, John Roemer, Jon Elster, Adam Pzeworski, Samuel Bowles, and Philip van Parijs. With their strict adherence to methodological individualism, in an attempt to furnish Marxism with microfoundations, analytical Marxists have abandoned the methodological premises of Marxian economics and embraced the analytical arsenal of neoclassical economics. Nevertheless, they continued to pose Marxian-inspired questions pertaining to the unequal distribution of means of produc-tion, to the power relations in the labor process, to the collective action problems in the formation of class consciousness, and to the racial and gender-related discrimina-tion in labor markets. For a collection of essays, see Roermer (1986); for critical surveys, see Amariglio *et al.* (1989) and the various contributions to the volume edited by Carver and Thomas (1995).

19 Marx makes this point rather clearly: "No capitalist voluntarily applies a new method of production, no matter how much more productive it may be or how much it might raise the rate of surplus-value, if it reduces the rate of profit. But every new method of production of this kind makes commodities cheaper." Therefore, Marx reasons, the capitalist "pockets the difference between their costs of production and the market price of the other commodities, which are produced at higher production costs. This is possible because the average socially necessary labour-time required to produce these latter commodities is greater than the labour time required with the new method of production. His production procedure is ahead of the social average. But competition makes the new procedure universal and subjects it to the general law. A fall in the rate then ensues – firstly perhaps in this sphere of production, and subsequently equalized with the others – a fall that is completely independent of the capitalists' will" (Marx, 1981 [1894]: 373–4). This is also a summary of Marx's theory of super-profits (or ex-tra-profits), which is based on the systematic deviation between prices of production (the sphere of circulation) and the value of a commodity (the sphere of production).

20 Among the key texts of the RT are Aglietta (1979) and Lipietz (1987a,b). For the key

texts of the SSAA approach, see Gordon *et al.* (1982) and Bowles *et al.* (1990). For a comparative critical review, see Kotz (1990).

21 There is no canonical distinction between colonialism and imperialism; our exposition relies on the writings of Bukharin (1973 [1915]), Lenin (1973 [1917]) and Dobb (1945 [1940]).

22 Both colonialism and imperialism have to be conceptualized within the context of rivalry among colonialist and imperialist nations. The inter-imperialist rivalry, as Lenin would argue, is the key to understanding world economy and its dislocatory and destructive effects on the world. The wars of 1914–18 and 1939–45, according to many Marxists (including Lenin and Dobb), should be understood and analyzed in conjunction with the history of imperialism.

23 In a given social formation, the value of labor-power (v) depends on two variables. The first is the quantity vector of different use-values that are socially considered to be necessary for the reproduction of the worker (q). The second is the value vector of these consumption goods (w). Hence, $v=q*w$. If the values of these consumption goods fall faster (because of imperialist policies) than the value of labor-power, it will be possible for an average worker to consume more use-values even when the value of labor-power falls. In other words, as the rate of exploitation increases so does the "real wage" or the standard of living of the worker. For further discussion, see Wolff and Resnick (1987: 168, 237–8).

24 See the various contributions to the *Dossier on* Empire (2001).

References

Aglietta, M. (1979) *A Theory of Capitalist Regulation*. London: Verso.

Amariglio, J. and D. Ruccio (1998) "The (Dis)orderly Process of Capitalist Competition" in R. Bellofiore (ed.), *Marxian Economics: A Reappraisal. Essays on Volume 3 of* Capital, volume 1: *Method, Value and Money*. New York: St. Martin's Press.

Amariglio, J., A. Callari and S. Cullenberg (1989) "Analytical Marxism: A Critical Overview," *Review of Social Economy*, 47 (4): 415–32.

Boddy, R. and J. Crotty (1975) "Class Conflict and Macro-policy: The Political Business Cycle," *Review of Radical Political Economics*, 7 (1): 1–19.

Bowles, S., D.M. Gordon, and T.E. Weisskopf (1990) *After the Waste Land: A Democratic Economics for the Year 2000*. Armonk, NY: M.E. Sharpe.

Bukharin, N. (1973) [1915] *Imperialism and World Economy*. New York: Monthly Review Press.

Carver, T. and P. Thomas (eds.) (1995) *Rational Choice Marxism*. University Park, PA: Pennsylvania University Press.

Community Economies Collective (2001) "Imagining and Enacting Noncapitalist Futures," *Socialist Review*, 28 (3 & 4): 93–135.

Cullenberg, S. (1994) *The Falling Rate of Profit: Recasting the Marxian Debate*. London: Pluto Press.

Dobb, M. (1945) [1940] *Political Economy and Capitalism*. New York: International Publishers.

Dossier on Empire (2001) *Rethinking Marxism*, 13 (3 & 4).

Elson, D. (ed.) (1979) *Value: The Representation of Labour in Capitalism*. Atlantic Highlands, NJ: Humanities Press.

Erçel, K. (2006) "Orientalization of Exploitation: A Class Analytical Critique of the Sweatshop Discourses," *Rethinking Marxism*, 18 (2): 289–306.

Folbre, N. (1982) "Exploitation Comes Home: A Critique of the Marxian Theory of Family Labour," *Cambridge Journal of Economics*, 6 (4) (December): 317–29.

Foley, D. (1982) "The Value of Money, the Value of Labor Power, and the Marxian Trans-formation Problem," *Review of Radical Political Economics*, 14 (2) (Spring): 37–47.

Fraad, H., S.A. Resnick, and R.D. Wolff (1994) *Bringing It All Back Home: Class, Gender and Power in the Modern Household.* London: Pluto Press.

Gibson-Graham, J.K. (1996) *The End of Capitalism (as We Knew It): A Feminist Critique of Political Economy.* London: Blackwell.

Gibson-Graham, J. K. (2006) *A Post-capitalist Politics.* Minneapolis, MN: University of Minnesota Press.

Gibson-Graham, J.K., S.A. Resnick, and R.D. Wolff (eds) (2000) *Class and Its Others.* Minneapolis, MN: University of Minnesota Press.

Glyn, A. and B. Sutcliffe (1972) *British Capitalism, Workers and the Profit Squeeze.* Har-mondsworth: Penguin.

Gordon, D., R. Edwards, and M. Reich (1982) *Segmented Work, Divided Workers.* Cam-bridge: Cambridge University Press.

Graham, J. (1991) "Fordism/Post-Fordism, Marxism/Post-Marxism," *Rethinking Marx-ism*, 4 (1): 39–58.

Gunder Frank, A. (1972) *Dependence and Underdevelopment: Latin America's Political Economy.* New York: Monthly Review Press.

Hardt, M. and A. Negri (2000) *Empire.* Cambridge, MA: Harvard University Press.

Hilferding, R. (1981) [1910] *Finance Capital: A Study of the Latest Phase of Capitalist Development.* London: Routledge and Kegan Paul.

Hindess, B. and P. Hirst (1975) *Pre-Capitalist Modes of Production.* London: Routledge and Kegan Paul.

Kotz, D.M. (1990) "A Comparative Analysis of the Theory of Regulation and the Social Structure of Accumulation Theory," *Science and Society*, 54 (1) (Spring): 5–28.

Kozel, P. (2006) *Market Sense: Toward a New Economics of Markets and Society.* New York: Routledge.

Kuhn, A. and A. Wolpe (eds) (1978) *Feminism and Materialism.* London: Routledge and Kegan Paul.

Laclau, E. (1977) *Politics and Ideology in Marxist Theory.* London: New Left Books.

Lenin, V.I. (1973) [1917] *Imperialism, the Highest Stage of Capitalism: A Popular Outline.* Peking: Foreign Language Press.

Lipietz, A. (1987a) *An Alternative Design for the 21st Century.* Paris: CEPREMAP.

Lipietz, A. (1987b) *Mirages and Miracles: The Crises of Global Fordism.* London: Verso.

Luxemburg, R. (1972) [1921] "The Questions at Issue" in K.J. Tarbuck (ed.), *Imperialism and the Accumulation of Capital.* London, Allen Lane: Penguin.

Mandel, E. (1978) *Late Capitalism.* London: Verso.

Mandel, E. (1981) "Introduction" in K. Marx, *Capital*, volume 3. Harmondsworth: Pen-guin/NLB.

Marx, K. (1972) [1881] "Marginal Notes on Adolph Wagner's 'Lehrbuch der politischen Okonomie'," *Theoretical Practice*, 5 (Spring): 40–64.

Marx, K. (1976) [1867] *Capital*, volume 1. Harmondsworth: Penguin/NLB.

Marx, K. (1978) [1884] *Capital*, volume 2. Harmondsworth: Penguin/NLB.

Marx, K (1981) [1894] *Capital*, volume 3. Harmondsworth: Penguin/NLB.

Moseley, F. (1993) "Marx's Logical Method and the 'Transformation Problem'" in F. Mo-seley (ed.), *Marx's Method in Capital*. Atlantic Highlands, NJ: Humanities Press.

Norton, B. (1988) "Epochs and Essences: A Review of Marxist Long-Wave and Stagnation Theories," *Cambridge Journal of Economics*, 12 (2) (June): 203–24.

Norton, B. (1992) "Radical Theories of Accumulation and Crises: Developments and

Directions" in B. Roberts and S. Feiner (eds), *Radical Economics*. Boston: Kluwer Academic.

Norton, B. (2001) "Reading Marx for Class" in J.K. Gibson-Graham, S.A. Resnick and R.D. Wolff (eds), *Re/presenting Class: Essays in Postmodern Marxism*. Durham, NC: Duke University Press.

Odekon, M. (2006) "Globalization and Labor," *Rethinking Marxism*, 18 (3): 415–31.

Okishio, N. (1961) "Technical Change and the Rate of Profit," *Kobe University Economic Review*, 7: 85–99.

Piore, M. and C. Sabel (1984) *The Second Industrial Divide: Possibilities for Prosperity*. New York: Basic Books.

Resnick, S. and R. Wolff (1987) *Knowledge and Class: A Marxian Critique of Political Economy*. Chicago: Chicago University Press.

Roemer, J. (ed.) (1986) *Analytical Marxism*. Cambridge: Cambridge University Press.

Rosdolsky, R. (1977) *The Making of Marx's 'Capital'*. London: Pluto Press.

Ruccio, D. (2003) "Globalization and Imperialism," *Rethinking Marxism*, 15 (1): 75–94.

Ruccio, D., S.A. Resnick, and R.D. Wolff (1990) "Class beyond the Nation-State," *Review of Radical Political Economics*, 22 (1): 14–27.

Shaikh, A. (1978) "Political Economy and Capitalism: Notes on Dobb's Theory of Crisis," *Cambridge Journal of Economics*, 2: 233–51.

Steedman, I. (1977) *Marx after Sraffa*. London: Verso.

Sweezy, P. (1970) [1942] *The Theory of Capitalist Development*. New York: Monthly Review Press.

Wolff, R.D. (2000) "Marxism and Democracy," *Rethinking Marxism*, 12 (1): 112–22.

Wolff, R.D. and S.A. Resnick (1987) *Economics: Marxian versus Neoclassical*. Baltimore, MD: Johns Hopkins University Press.

Wolff, R.D., B. Roberts, and A. Callari (1982) "Marx's (not Ricardo's) 'Transformation Problem': A Radical Reconceptualization," *History of Political Economy*, 14 (4): 564–82.

13 Marxism and method

Daniel Little

Introduction

This essay is concerned with Marxist method in the twentieth century. Before proceeding far, however, we have to ask the question: what sort of method are we considering? It is a fact that Marxist thought has inspired research frameworks in many fields – art history, literature, culture studies, philosophy, historiography, and the social sciences. And these influences have proceeded through many different tropes within Marx's thought – the theory of alienation, the concept of mystification, the labor theory of value, the theories of class conflict and exploitation, the theory of the forces and relations of production, and the theory of the mode of production. So the question of Marxist method is complicated in a many-many way: there are many areas where Marxist methods have been employed, and there are many strands within Marx's thought that have given rise to these various approaches.

My focus will be on methodology for the social sciences (within which I include much of historical inquiry). This choice sets two basic parameters to our study. We will be concerned with the ways in which Marxist methods have in the past century helped to shape our understanding of the social world. And we will be concerned with these influences within the domain of empirical research (as opposed to literary, philosophical, or ethical investigations).

Marx is one of the unmistakable founders of modern social science. Throughout a lifetime of research and writing he aimed to arrive at a scientific analysis of modern economic life. Throughout most of his life he emphasized the importance of engaging in a scientific analysis of capitalism as a system. And he consistently adhered to a rigorous commitment to honest empirical investigation of the facts. Marx's own goals were thus undoubtedly framed by his aspiration to construct a scientific analysis of the capitalist mode of production. And social science research and theory today is certainly strongly influenced by many of Marx's contributions – especially in the areas of social history, sociology, and political economy. Here I will survey some of the important avenues through which Marxist approaches to the social sciences have developed in the twentieth century. And I will attempt to provide a perspective on the enduring contributions that Marxist social science has made for the conduct of social research.

The influence of Marx's thought in the social sciences in the twentieth century is ubiquitous: social history and the history of working people (Jones, 1971); institutions within capitalism (Giddens, 1973); political history of revolution and class (Soboul, 1989); the lived experience of the working class (Sennett and Cobb, 1972); alienation and mystification as social categories and real social phenomena (manufacturing and its culture) (Szymanski, 1978; Mészáros, 1972); political economy (Mandel, 1969, 1975); sociology of education (Bowles and Gintis, 1976); the state within capitalist societies (Miliband, 1969, 1982; Poulantzas, 1973). Marx's writings have contributed enormously to how we analyze, conceptualize, and explain social processes and social history.

However, there is no single answer to the question: what is the Marxist methodology of social science? Rather, Marxist social inquiry in the twentieth century represents a chorus of many voices and insights, many of which are inconsistent with others. Rather than representing a coherent research community in possession of a central paradigm and commitment to specific methodological and theoretical premises, Marxist social science in the twentieth century has had a great deal of variety and diversity of emphases. Think of the range of thinkers whose work falls within the general category of Marxian social science: E.P. Thompson, Louis Althusser, Jürgen Habermas, Gerald Cohen, Robert Brenner, Nicos Poulantzas, Ralph Miliband, Nikolai Bukharin, Georg Lukàcs, or Michel Foucault. All these authors have made a contribution to Marxist social science; but in no way do these contributions add up to a single, coherent, and focused methodology for the social sciences. There is no canonical body of findings that constitute a paradigm. Instead, there are numerous signal instances of substantive and methodological writings, from a variety of traditions, that have provided moments of insight and locations for possible future research. And so the graduate student of the social sciences who aims to acquire expertise in "Marxist theory" will find her course of study to more closely resemble that of a literature student than a student of molecular biology, with an open-ended set of encounters with great works rather than a coherent and orderly research discipline.

"Methodology for social science research?"

Why do we need a methodology for the social sciences? Because the social world is indefinitely complex and multi-stranded – thus eluding explanation through simple observation. And because the social world as a domain of phenomena is fundamentally different from the natural world, in the respect of its degree of "law-governedness" (Little, 1993). So neither the methods of ordinary common-sense nor the methods of the natural sciences will suffice to lead us to an ability to recognize the systems, structures, and causal processes that are embodied in the social world. The social world proceeds through the activities of billions of men and women. It embodies institutions, organizations, and structures that propel and constrain individual action, and these social entities give rise to processes that are neither law-governed nor random. The social world gives rise to relations of power, domination, exploitation, and resistance. It produces outcomes that advantage some and disadvantage others. It is the result of complex exchanges between agents and structures, and each pole of this conjunction influences the other. The social world, in short, is complex. The challenge of understanding social phenomena is both important and difficult. This is true in 2000; but it was not less true in 1830, when Engels took up residence in Manchester and undertook to describe and comprehend the confusion of factories, slums, mansions, hunger, and turmoil that Manchester represented. *The Condition of the Working Class in England* is his result (Engels, 1958); and *Capital* is Marx's (Marx, 1977).

What is involved in having a "philosophy and methodology for social science"? It is to have answers to several different domains of questions:

1   inquiry – how to make use of a variety of tools of research to arrive at hypotheses and theories about a domain of empirical phenomena;
2   epistemology – how to employ empirical and theoretical considerations to provide justification for the hypotheses and theories that we put forward;
3   metaphysics – an account of the types of entities and processes of which the domain of phenomena are composed;
4   a theory of the structure of social science knowledge – a conception of the purpose of social science inquiry and a schematic notion of what social science results ought to look like. (Theories? Bodies of empirical findings? Statistical laws? Narrative interpretations of important social processes? Groups of causal hypotheses?)

Marx's methodological thinking, and that of many Marxist social scientists who followed, provide tentative answers to each of these questions. And, as we should expect, these answers add up to something less than a finished and consistent methodology (just as Weber's work does not constitute a tidy theory of social science knowledge and inquiry; Ringer, 1997).

The social science aim of Marxism

Let us begin with Marx's social science contributions themselves. It is fruitful to ask the questions: What are Marx's central aims as a social scientist? And in what does his central contribution consist? Does his work, and the work that followed from it, provide a theory of capitalism and history? Are there specific empirical hypotheses that are subject to empirical investigation in his work? Does it provide a paradigm or research programme, along the lines articulated by Kuhn and Lakatos (Lakatos, 1974; Lakatos and Musgrave, 1974; Kuhn, 1970)? Does Marx adhere to a coherent conception of social inquiry and social explanation? And does Marx have a distinctive conception of social science inquiry – a theory of dialectical reasoning, for example?[1]

Marx's central scientific goals include at least these: to provide an empirically well-founded description of the central institutional features of a market-based property holding economic system; to derive the social implications of these institutional arrangements; and to illuminate the historical process through which these institutional features came to exist in the several capitalist social economies. His central social scientific contribution is *Capital* (Marx, 1977), and this work is a dense mélange of historical description, micro-sociological detail, reasoning about institutions and their implications, and mathematical political economy. (These points are more fully developed in Little (1986).) Marx believed that the institutions of capitalism constituted a mode of production, and that this mode of production has a distinctive historical logic. Ordinary men and women, pursuing their lives within the institutional context of capitalism, make choices in private life, work life, and a variety of organizations (firms, unions, parties) that lead collectively to large-scale patterns of change. Processes of accumulation of capital, acceleration of technological change, and clarification of classes (proletariat, bourgeoisie) are the predictable consequence of the defining institutional setting of capitalist development. Socially constructed individuals within specific institutions behave in predictable ways – leading to a process of social change that can be delineated and explained. There is hence an institutional logic defined by private ownership in the means of production and wage labor, and working out some of the consequences of this logic is one of Marx's central goals. So Marx's social science writings are best understood as constituting a diverse set of lines of thought, explanatory models, and historical interpretations falling loosely under a guiding perspective on historical and social change.

On this interpretation, Marx's contribution to the social sciences is something other than a coherent and simple theory of capitalism. He provides knowledge about capitalism as a social order; but this knowledge cannot be summarized in a formal or mathematical theory with a small number of premises. Rather, it is comprised of an irreducible variety of sociological description, historical interpretation (now often superseded by better knowledge about the feudal world or early capitalism), and quasi-formal reasoning about institutions and economic relations.

Is there at least a coherent theory of social science inquiry in Marx's writings? Marx certainly provides guidance for other historical and social researchers, in terms of where to look for hypotheses. So there is a Marxist "style of inquiry" that has specific origins in Marx's own research. This style of inquiry has a number of features. It is materialist – that is it focuses on the forces and relations of production, and it postulates that technology and power are fundamental with regard to other social formations (e.g. literature, culture, law). It is oriented to the salience of class and class conflict within historical change. It is sensitive to the workings of ideology and false consciousness in our understandings of the social institutions within which we live. And it pays special interest, and offers special concern, to the perspectives of the underclasses at any given time in history.

What about dialectics, and Marx's famous assertion that he has turned Hegel's dialectical logic on its head? Contrary to a number of interpreters of Marx (Ollman, 1971, 1993; Ruben 1979; Schaff 1970), I maintain that the concept of dialectics plays only a minor role in Marx's thinking, and no role at all in his method of inquiry (Little, 1987). The role that dialectics plays is more by way of a high-level hypothesis about institutional change: that institutions have unforeseen and unintended consequences; that processes of change can bring about an under-mining of the foundations of the institutions driving these processes of change; and that there are "contradictions" in historical processes. But this is no more mysterious than Mancur Olson's discovery of the contradiction between private and collective interests (Olson, 1965), Kenneth Arrow's demonstration of the impossibility of a consistent voting scheme (Arrow, 1963), or George Akerlof's analysis of the perverse consequences of information asymmetry in competitive markets (Akerlof, 1970). Social science research has almost always made its more important contributions through discovery of unintended consequences and perverse effects; and this is very much the role that dialectics plays in Marx's writings.

Much of the most constructive work in Marxian social science in the past twenty years has taken place within the framework of "rational choice Marx-ism" – authors such as Elster (Elster, 1982, 1985, 1986), Roemer (Roemer, 1981, 1982a,b, 1986a,b), Brenner (Brenner, 1976, 1982), and Przeworski (Przeworski, 1985a,b, 1986) who have attempted to bring together Marxian historical insights with the methodology of rational choice theory and the new institutionalism (Powell and DiMaggio, 1991; Brinton and Nee, 1998; Knight, 1992). On this approach, it is argued that we can reach Marxian conclusions (about exploitation, class, and the tendencies of capitalism, for example) on the basis of the assump-tion of individual rationality within the specific institutional setting of capitalism. What this demonstrates is that the essential Marxian contribution is substantive, not methodological; it is a set of discoveries about the social world, not an artifact of a particular conception of inquiry.

Is the rational choice approach compatible with Marx's own methodology? I believe that it is. First, Marx's use of the tools of political economy and his central demonstrations of the laws of capitalism depend on the assumption of individual rationality. Second, Marx's approach to method is, as argued above, eclectic. So we would not expect him to reject an approach that promises to provide rigorous empirical and theoretical support for his analysis. And in fact, it is possible to dis-cern the workings of rational choice analysis at the core of Marx's most favored discoveries. Marx's argument for the falling rate of profit, for example, hinges on a very Olson-like argument (Olson, 1965) concerning the contradiction between the individual capitalist's interests and the interests of the class of capitalists as a whole. And this is an argument within the theory of rational choice.

Marx's method of inquiry, then, is unexceptional; it is not sharply distinguished from non-Marxist social science. Marx emphasizes the importance of careful em-pirical and historical inquiry. He values explanatory hypotheses that can be rigor-ously developed in such a way as to explain and predict social outcomes. He is not antecedently wedded to particular interpretations of history (for example recall his agnostic statements about Russian economic development to Vera Zasulich; Marx and Engels, 1975: 319–20). And he constructs his own inquiry around a set of high-level research hypotheses – the salience of class, the importance of the material foundations of social institutions, and the workings of ideology. Finally,

Marx offers what might be called a "galilean" model of social explanation: to explain phenomena in terms of underlying causal conditions rather than crude associations among observable variables. This perspective leads him to engage in careful hypothesis-formation – again, a perspective that is highly consistent with contemporary social science research standards.

Does Marx have a distinctive epistemology for the social sciences? As suggested in this treatment of theory and inquiry, I take the position that he does not. His epistemology is comparable to what we might today call a realist empiricism: that scientific knowledge can arrive at statements about unobservable structures that are approximately true, and that the basis of evaluation of such hypotheses is through appropriate use of empirical methods (observation, experimentation, and historical inquiry). Marx's own writings do not support a relativistic "sociology of knowledge," according to which the validity of knowledge depends on the social class perspective of the investigator; instead, his theory of knowledge is premised on the notion that well-founded beliefs about the social world can be arrived at on the basis of empirical methods and theoretical reasoning.

What about metaphysics and ontology? Here Marx's work is somewhat more distinctive. He presupposes a number of metaphysical assumptions about societies and historical processes: that the social world is a causal order, that social structures have properties and causal characteristics, that individuals constitute social structures through their actions and choices, that "social formations" fall under the categories of "modes of production," that modes of production consist of sets of forces and relations of production, and that classes exist. Each of these assumptions serves as a part of Marx's social ontology. They represent assumptions about the kinds of entities and relations that exist in the world that are, in a sense, prior to specific empirical discoveries. (This does not imply that they are beyond the reach of empirical inquiry, however; the test of the ontology is the empirical success or failure of the more specific theories that are launched within its terms.)

Marx's ontology includes several more specific ideas as well. The ideas of the forces and relations of production are critical to his inquiry; these ideas capture the level of technology and the institutional context in which the technology is utilized that are current within a given society. (This pair of ideas can be summarized as "technology and power.") The concept of exploitation is also crucial in Marx's ontology; it describes a relation within the context of which some individuals and groups are enabled to control the labor-time of others and to derive benefit from their labor without compensation. The labor theory of value, and the theory of surplus value, provide an analytical framework within which to theorize about exploitation. Marx's concepts of alienation, fetishism, and mystification are also foundational in his social ontology. Individuals have consciousness and freedom, but they find themselves always within the context of institutions and ideas that structure their understandings of the relations that govern them. ("Men make their own history, but not in circumstances of their own making" (Marx, 1964).)

The twentieth-century trail breakers

Let us turn briefly to a review of some of the directions that Marxian thought has taken in the twentieth century.

Althusser

Louis Althusser is one of the most important French interpreters of Marx. Althusser attributes to Marxism a philosophical theory, an epistemology, and a series of theoretical concepts, through which he believes that Marxism seeks to view the world. He thus interprets Marx's writings as a philosophical system rather than an empirical or historical theory (Althusser and Balibar, 1970). Althusser defends an "anti-humanist" reading of Marx (Althusser, 1969: 221–247). Contrary to other twentieth-century European interpreters of Marx, he rejects the notion that the theories of human nature and alienation represent core elements of Marx's thought (the central contributions of the *Economic and Philosophical Manuscripts* and other early writings). Instead, he maintains that it is the abstract theory of the structure of capitalism advanced in *Capital* that represents Marx's core contribution.

If *Capital* is the central contribution of Marx's intellectual work, and if *Capital* is about the structure of the existing capitalist mode of production, then is Marx's system an effort at empirical discovery? According to Althusser, it is not. Instead, it is an effort at conceptualizing history in terms of abstract structures and contradictions; it is an effort in structuralist philosophy. Althusser is highly critical of empiricism as a basis for social knowledge. Much of Althusser's thinking about Marx falls within the category of social metaphysics: articulating a series of concepts designed to express the nature of the structures and relations that constitute a historical whole. The concepts of structural determination, overdetermination, and "determination in the last instance" are his central contributions. His notion of "a structure in dominance" is designed to capture the notion that the various spheres of social life – economic, legal, political, etc. – are part of a complex whole in which the economic structure plays a central role (Althusser, 1969: 201). These abstract concepts are intended to provide a highly abstract and non-empirical basis for inquiry into historical processes.

A crucial question from the point of view of this chapter is whether Althusser offers an example of a method for Marxist inquiry. In the sense that is before us here – a method of inquiry designed to probe contingent historical and empirical processes – he does not. He rather constructs a philosophical method of reading and theorizing the thoughts expressed in a complex text. In this respect his work is more akin to literary theory than it is to empirical scientific inquiry. His goal is to extract the "problematic" of a given complex text (*Capital*), rather than inquiring into the empirical properties of a real system (capitalism) (Callinicos, 1976). Althusser emphasizes the "reading" rather than the real object that is read; that is, he emphasizes a reading of *Capital* rather than an interrogation of real, historically given capitalism. In this respect Althusser's version of Marxism embodies a structuralism that verges on idealism.

Althusser's theorizing about Marx influenced several other important figures in European Marxism, including particularly Nicos Poulantzas. Poulantzas undertook extensive analysis of politics within the general framework of Althusser's formulation of the mode of production (Poulantzas, 1973, 1975). His work, however, is based on historical investigation and research in ways that Althusser's work never was; as a consequence, it has the potential to make a significant contribution to our understanding of political power within capitalism. "The object of this book is the political, in particular the political superstructure of the state in the CMP [capitalist mode of production]: that is the production of the concept of this region in this mode, and the production of more concrete concepts dealing with politics in capitalist social formations" (Poulantzas, 1973: 16). Poulantzas attempts to provide an historically informed theory of the state within the framework of an Althusserian formulation of the concept of the capitalist mode of production.

It is fair to ask of Poulantzas whether there is a degree of contingency in the relationship between the political formations he studies and the underlying economic structures. Are there diverging pathways of political development, beginning with the same underlying economic realities of class and property, but leading to significantly different political formations? Are there different political formations, all sonsistent with the same basic underlying economic structure? If the answer is "no," then Poulantzas' work falls in the category of materialist philosophy; if it is "yes," then we can have at least some preliminary confidence that Poulantzas is open to pursuing real empirical social science research. Fortunately for the standing of Poulantzas' political inquiry, there is evidence in his work that he recognizes the contingency of many features of the capitalist state and capitalist politics. He emphasizes the "relative autonomy" of the state – reflecting the notion that the political sphere does not simply dance on the strings of the economic structure (Poulantzas, 1973: 255–74). He makes a serious effort to discover the characteristics of bureaucracy and "state apparatus" – again, a set of features that do not derive from the abstract logic of the CMP (Poulantzas, 1973: 325–50). And in his treatment of the fascist state he makes a genuine historical effort to discover the particular contingencies through which this state form emerged within those historical and economic circumstances (Poulantzas, 1974).[2]

Gramsci

Antonio Gramsci's work can be summarized in several themes, including one significant methodological innovation. Writing in the early years of Italian fascism, his central topic is the question: how was it possible for fascist parties to emerge from capitalist society? International socialists prior to World War I predicted the rise of mass socialist parties of workers; whereas Italy and Germany witnessed the rise of fascism, grounded in other and "non-essential" classes. How could this have occurred within the assumptions of Marxist political theory? In what ways are politics, political consciousness, and political movements autonomous relative to the economic formations of society?

One of Gramsci's most fundamental contributions is his concept of hegemony (Gramsci, 1957). He accords a significant degree of autonomy to the social processes of consciousness formation. There are concrete cultural institutions through which individuals' social consciousness (their "ideology") is shaped, and these institutions are objects of struggle among powerful agents within society. According to a mechanistic theory of ideology, the consciousness of the dominant class determines the consciousness of subordinate classes as well. Gramsci's innovation is to recognize that there is an active struggle over the terms of social consciousness, and that specific institutions – newspapers, universities, labor unions, chambers of commerce, factories, political rallies – have active influence on the frameworks of thought and interpretation through which various groups view the world. These institutions are therefore the object of active struggle among contending groups, and the outcome of these struggles is not pre-ordained. Groups can exercise "hegemony" by establishing the prominence of their guiding assumptions within the core of these institutions of consciousness.

What is the methodological significance of this insight? It is to strike an important blow for relaxing a common Marxist assumption of a relation of determination between the economic structure and the elements of the "superstructure." Gramsci is one of the prominent voices of the twentieth century who sought to reduce the economic determinism of the theory and to leave room for relative autonomy in the spheres of the political, cultural, and mobilizational. His approach gives expression to the role of agency within class politics, and therefore to some extent reduces the primacy of the structural (the economic structure, the mode of production).

It is also pertinent to ask: what is the epistemic basis of Gramsci's theories? He was not a scholarly researcher; instead, he was a thoughtful observer–participant–theoretician. The most compelling aspects of his theories derive from his reflections on the political processes in Italy between the wars in which he was directly involved – the working-class politics of Turin, the socialist and communist movements of inter-war Italy, and his observations of the rise of the fascist movement in Italy.[3] His laboratory was inter-war Italy, and his instruments were his own participation and his powers of observation and diagnosis.

Critical theory

Some of the most important theorists of Marxism in the twentieth century fell in the category of the school of "critical theory," including Adorno, Horkheimer, and Marcuse. This school of thought emphasized the concepts of alienation, fetishism, and critique, and cast strong doubt on the "scientism" of vulgar Marxism. This group of thinkers has not made a substantial contribution to positive thinking about social science methodology, however; their contributions have tended to move Marxism in the direction of philosophy and literature rather than empirical and historical research. A partial exception to this statement is Jürgen Habermas. Habermas succeeds in bringing together a deep philosophical perspective on problems of politics, rationality, and history with a respect for empirical and theoretical approaches to social science research. However, his work too falls at a level of generality that permits it to have little real influence on social science inquiry.

Materialist history

E.P. Thompson was one of the great historians of the twentieth century. And he made a profound contribution to Marxist historiography. His most important book, *The Making of the English Working Class* (Thompson, 1966), provides what is perhaps the single most sustained, historically grounded, and illuminating account of class formation to be found in the literature. His own relationship to a Marxist political movement was complex (Thompson, 1995), and his break with Stalinist politics was unambiguous. The genius of his historical writing, and his outstanding contribution to Marxist method in the twentieth century, is his open interrogation of the historical steps through which a particular class formation, the English working class, came to be. There is no dogmatism in his account, and no simple "orrery" of theory (Thompson, 1995). Instead, there is a highly rigorous and detailed study of the elements of class formation in the circumstances of English history. He provides great insight and detail into the organizations, churches, and associations through which the English working class came to constitute itself as such. And Thompson makes it clear that there is nothing mechanical about the formation of class consciousness – no automatic transition from "class in itself" to "class for itself." Instead, the formation of class consciousness is the result of particular institutions and choices at particular junctures in history. Thus Thompson emphasizes the "subjective" and historically specific evolution of class consciousness. And this approach implies that different circumstances can give rise to different configurations of class.

Other Marxist historians of the twentieth century have shown similar historiographic rigor. Perry Anderson, Albert Soboul, and Marc Bloch, each in his own way, has begun with a broad Marxist perspective, and has then conducted historical research with an open mind and without ideological fixed points. Bloch, for example, begins with a generally materialist view of the influence of technology and property on other dimensions of social development. But he then inquires with historical precision into such topics as the diffusion of the wheeled plow, the property relations that facilitated the adoption of this technology, and the village-level politics that were most well-adapted to these property relations (Bloch, 1966). Soboul begins with the general perspective that class conflict is the key to understanding the French Revolution; he then undertakes the detailed historical research that is needed to track the movements and impulses that led to the stages of the French Revolution. Perry Anderson focuses on the property system and political structure of the "second feudalism" and attempts to explain the course that Eastern Europe took (Anderson, 1974).

In each instance the historian takes his craft with great seriousness. The tools of historical research, and the values of truthful inquiry, drive the historical project; and the authors are prepared to discover connections, contingencies, and anomalies (relative to the theory of historical materialism). Specifically, each author leaves dogma at the door, and expends great effort and openness of mind to discern the institutions and processes that transpire within the historical domain under investigation.[4] At the same time, however, these historians have been guided by the style of inquiry formulated by Marx and extended by others.

Analytical Marxism

The 1980s saw a lively expansion of interest in Marxist theory among analytic philosophers and social scientists. These debates led to a fairly convincing set of answers to questions about a number of important topics: Marx's critique of justice, his theory of exploitation, his ideas about social science method, his economic theories, and his theory of historical materialism. The topics that structured debates throughout the decade largely focused on Marx's theory of history and his economic philosophy. And significantly, these debates drew largely on Marx's later writings, extending from the *German Ideology*, through the *Grundrisse* and *Capital*. Marx is regarded as a social scientist, with a scientific treatment of capitalism as the basis of his critique of modern society and an organized theory of history as context for his theory of historical change and revolution. And much of the work that has emerged from these debates has been as much oriented toward construction of a more adequate social science as it has to formulating a social philosophy. In other words: analytical Marxism has made more of a contribution to the foundations of the social sciences than to social philosophy.

The general approach has been an effort to bring the tools of rational choice theory, neoclassical economics, and contemporary political science models to bear on classic Marxian problems: exploitation, domination, historical change, the workings of a social property system, and the ways in which interests inflect political choices.

Marx's influence on twentieth-century social science

Let us return now to the "style of research" that is embodied in Marxian social science. These points will serve to capture Marx's main contributions to social science inquiry (from at least my perspective). Marx's writings constitute a "style of research" for subsequent researchers that consists of a related family of assumptions and perspectives. Let us now attempt to identify some of the most important contributions of Marx's work for the social sciences in the twentieth century. Seen in broad strokes, important themes would include:

1 emphasis on the significance of class – for people and for social change;
2 focus on institutions of production, technology, property (modes of production, forces and relations of production);
3 concept of alienation;
4 theory of value and surplus value;
5 formulation of an economic theory of capitalism;

6   theory of exploitation;
7   framework for understanding the pre-capitalist history of Europe and sketches of Asia;
8   sketches of alternatives to capitalism – socialist institutions.

These points can be transformed into a series of substantive methodological maxims for social research; as such, they have wielded enormous influence on social scientific and historical research throughout the twentieth century:

1   seek out the "material" institutions – property, technology, labor;
2   examine non-material institutions from the point of view of their role within a social system of production and control – ideology, state, culture;
3   examine the nature of inter-group exploitation, the schemes of domination that these require, and the forms of struggle that result;
4   pay attention to the lived experience of persons within social institutions;
5   examine the centrality of class structures – lived experience, exploitation, behavior and incentive, social change;
6   identify enduring structures – economic, political, cultural – through which the activities of individuals within society are channeled.

On this approach, Marx does not offer a distinctive method of social science inquiry; rather, he provides an eclectic and empirically informed effort to describe and explain the phenomena of capitalism. Marx provides a "style of inquiry" based on a family of hypotheses, hunches, and ontological commitments. Through this inquiry he provides a substantive contribution to social science, in the form of a series of descriptive and theoretical insights; particularly about the institutional anatomy and dynamics of capitalism and social behavior. Dialectical thinking is not a part of Marx's method of social inquiry; at most, a source of hypotheses about "finding contradictions." Finally, the tools of rational choice theory and neoclassical economics are highly consonant with Marxist thinking.

On this approach, Marx's body of research does not represent a catechism; it does not constitute an "organon" in its leather case. It is more akin to a research program in Lakatos's sense: a body of large hypotheses, suggestions for fertile areas to examine, paradigm explanations, theories, and interpretation; some bits of formal theory (e.g. the labor theory of value). To work within the program is to acquire the "tacit knowledge" that emerges from careful study of the many examples of fertile inquiry (Thompson, Bloch, Morishima) and then pursuing social inquiry on one's own domain in a way that is creatively informed by the body of work – but also by the best non-Marxist work – for example, Sabel, *Work and Politics* (Sabel, 1982).

"Method" implies a prescriptive body of doctrines to guide inquiry. Certainly Marx does not offer such a body of doctrines. If anything, he would subscribe to a fairly ordinary prescription – familiar from Mill (1950) or Whewell (Whewell and Butts, 1968) – along these lines:

1   formulate theories and hypotheses;
2   engage in careful study of existing empirical and historical data;
3   discern "patterns" in data that suggest hypotheses;
4   evaluate hypotheses through empirical and factual inquiry.

The more directive parts of Marx's methodology – but now loose and heuristic – look more like this:

1   examine material institutions;
2   look at class, power, exploitation, domination;
3   don't be blinded to effects that violate the materialist dicta;
4   be mindful of "contradictions" that work themselves through historical contingencies;
5   look for underlying causes and structures.

How, then, should we think about the professional preparation of the young social scientist and historian? Is it similar to that of the young biologist or physicist? No, it is not. The social sciences differ from natural science in being inherently more amorphous and eclectic, and this derives from the nature of social phenomena (Little, 1998). There are highly specific research strategies, lab procedures, and foundational theories in the natural sciences. So the young molecular biologist must master a very specific paradigm of precise theories, mechanisms, and structures; as well as authoritative strategies of experimentation and inquiry. But the case is quite different in the social sciences. There we will find no general theory of society, or privileged mode of inquiry for social research. So the best advice for young researchers in the social sciences is to be eclectic and open-minded: learn a variety of tools, explanatory strategies, and foundational hypotheses and powerful examples of social inquiry. And pursue a strong understanding of some of the most imaginative social scientists and researchers of the past generation, whatever their paradigm (e.g. Hirschman or Skinner; Sabel, Tilly, or Scott). Then address the phenomena of interest with an open mind.

Conclusion

Here we have surveyed some of Marx's central contributions to social science research, and some of the most important ideas that twentieth-century thinkers have brought to bear on Marxist social inquiry. Is there such a thing as "Marxist social science"? No, if the point of reference is molecular biology as a paradigm of research. But yes, if we are thinking instead of a loose research programme, inspired by a congeries of hypotheses, insights, and salient powerful interpretations, which the researcher can then have in mind as she sorts through her own research problems.

The root cause of this eclectic nature of the best social research lies in the nature of social phenomena themselves. The social world is not well ordered. It is not a law-governed system of cause and effect. Instead, it is a sum of many different and cross-cutting processes, structures, and institutions, mediated by the purposive meaningful actions of persons, within given cultural and material institutions that bear contingent and sometimes accidental relations to each other.

And Marxist thinking, appropriately eclectically construed, has much to offer as we try to make sense of that plural world.

Notes

1 Many of these questions are explored in detail in *The Scientific Marx* (Little, 1986).
2 For powerful and effective criticisms of another Althusserian effort at social theory, see E.P. Thompson's critique of Hindess and Hirst (1975) in *The Poverty of Theory* (Thompson, 1995).
3 See Carl Boggs' treatment of the development of Gramsci's thought (Boggs, 1976).
4 Other good examples of materialist history include Carr (1984), Finley (1973), Dobb (1963), and Brenner (1976, 1982; Aston and Philpin, 1985).

References

Akerlof, George (1970) "The Market for 'Lemons': Quality, Uncertainty and the Market Mechanism," *Quarterly Journal of Economics*, 84: 488–500.

Althusser, Louis (1969) *For Marx*. New York: Pantheon Books.

Althusser, Louis and Etienne Balibar (1970) *Reading Capital*. London: New Left Books.

Anderson, Perry (1974) *Lineages of the Absolutist State*. London: New Left Books.

Arrow, Kenneth Joseph (1963) *Social Choice and Individual Values*, second edition. New York: Wiley.

Aston, T.H. and C.H.E. Philpin (1985) *The Brenner Debate: Agrarian Class Structure and Economic Development in Pre-industrial Europe*. Cambridge: Cambridge University Press.

Bloch, Marc Léopold Benjamin (1966) *French Rural History: An Essay on its Basic Characteristics*. Berkeley, CA: University of California Press.

Boggs, Carl (1976) *Gramsci's Marxism*. London: Pluto Press.

Bowles, Samuel and Herbert Gintis (1976) *Schooling in Capitalist America: Educational Reform and the Contradictions of Economic Life*. New York: Basic Books.

Brenner, Robert (1976) "Agrarian Class Structure and Economic Development in Pre-Industrial Europe," *Past and Present*, 70: 30–75.

Brenner, Robert (1982) "The Agrarian Roots of European Capitalism," *Past and Present*, 97:16–113.

Brinton, Mary C. and Victor Nee (1998) *New Institutionalism in Sociology*. New York: Russell Sage Foundation.

Callinicos, Nicos (1976) *Althusser's Marxism*. London: Pluto Press.

Carr, Edward Hallett (1984) *The Comintern and the Spanish Civil War*. New York: Pantheon Books.

Dobb, Maurice (1963) *Studies in the Development of Capitalism*. New York: International Publishers.

Elster, Jon (1982) "Marxism, Functionalism, and Game Theory," *Theory and Society*, 11: 453–82.

Elster, Jon (1985) *Making Sense of Marx*. Cambridge: Cambridge University Press.

Elster, Jon (1986) "Three Challenges to Class" in J. Roemer (ed.), *Analytical Marxism*. Cambridge: Cambridge University Press.

Engels, Friedrich (1958) *The Condition of the Working Class in England*. Oxford: B. Blackwell.

Finley, M.I. (1973) *The Ancient Economy*. Berkeley, CA: University of California Press.

Giddens, Anthony (1973) *The Class Structure of the Advanced Societies*. London: Hutchinson.

Gramsci, Antonio (1957) *The Modern Prince, and Other Writings*. London: Lawrence and Wishart.

Hindess, Barry and Paul Q. Hirst (1975) *Pre-capitalist Modes of Production*. London: Routledge & Kegan Paul.

Jones, Gareth Stedman (1971) *Outcast London: A Study in the Relationship between Classes in Victorian Society*. Oxford: Clarendon Press.

Knight, Jack (1992) *Institutions and Social Conflict: The Political Economy of Institutions and Decisions*. Cambridge: Cambridge University Press.

Kuhn, Thomas S. (1970) *The Structure of Scientific Revolutions*, second, enlarged edition. Chicago: University of Chicago Press.

Lakatos, Imre (1974) "Methodology of Scientific Research Programmes" in I. Lakatos and A. Musgrave (eds), *Criticism and the Growth of Knowledge*. Cambridge: Cambridge University Press.

Lakatos, Imre and Alan Musgrave (eds) (1974) *Criticism and the Growth of Knowledge*, reprinted with corrections. Cambridge: Cambridge University Press.

Little, Daniel (1986) *The Scientific Marx*. Minneapolis, MN: University of Minnesota Press.

Little, Daniel (1987) "Dialectics and Science in Marx's *Capital*," *Philosophy of the Social Sciences*, 17: 197–220.

Little, Daniel (1993) "On the Scope and Limits of Generalizations in the Social Sciences," *Synthese*, 97: 183–207.

Little, Daniel (1998) *Microfoundations, Method and Causation: On the Philosophy of the Social Sciences*. New Brunswick, NJ: Transaction Publishers.

Mandel, Ernest (1969) *Marxist Economic Theory*, revised edition. New York: M[onthly] R[eview] Press.

Mandel, Ernest (1975) *Late Capitalism*, revised edition. London: New Left Books.

Marx, Karl (1964) *The Eighteenth Brumaire of Louis Bonaparte*. With explanatory notes. New York: International Publishers.

Marx, Karl (1973) *Grundrisse*. London: Vintage.

Marx, Karl (1977) *Capital*, volume 1. New York: Vintage.

Marx, Karl and Friedrich Engels (1970 [1845–49]) *The German Ideology*, third edition. Moscow: Progress Publishers.

Marx, Karl and Friedrich Engels (1975) *Karl Marx and Frederick Engels: Selected Correspondence*, third revised edition. Moscow: Foreign Languages Publishing House.

Mészáros, István (1972) *Marx's Theory of Alienation*. New York: Harper & Row.

Miliband, Ralph (1969) *The State in Capitalist Society*. New York: Basic.

Miliband, Ralph (1982) *Capitalist Democracy in Britain*. Oxford: Oxford University Press.

Mill, John Stuart (1950) *Philosophy of Scientific Method*. New York: Hafner.

Ollman, Bertell (1971) *Alienation: Marx's Conception of Man in Capitalist Society*. Cambridge: Cambridge University Press.

Ollman, Bertell (1993) *Dialectical Investigations*. New York: Routledge.

Olson, Mancur (1965) *The Logic of Collective Action: Public Goods and the Theory of Groups*. Cambridge, MA: Harvard University Press.

Poulantzas, Nicos (1973) *Political Power and Social Class*. London: New Left Books.

Poulantzas, Nicos Ar (1974) *Fascism and Dictatorship: The Third International and the Problem of Fascism*. London: NLB.

Poulantzas, Nicos Ar (1975) *Classes in Contemporary Capitalism*. London: NLB.

Powell, Walter W. and Paul J. DiMaggio (eds) (1991) *The New Institutionalism in Organizational Analysis*. Chicago: Chicago University Press.

Przeworski, Adam (1985a) *Capitalism and Social Democracy*. Cambridge: Cambridge University Press.

Przeworski, Adam (1985b) "Marxism and Rational Choice.' *Politics & Society*, 14 (4): 379–409.

Przeworski, Adam (1986) "Material Interests, Class Compromise, and Socialism" in J. Roemer (ed.), *Analytical Marxism*. Cambridge: Cambridge University Press.

Ringer, Fritz (1997) *Max Weber's Methodology: The Unification of the Cultural and Social Sciences*. Cambridge, MA: Harvard University Press.

Roemer, John (1981) *Analytical Foundations of Marxism*. New York: Cambridge University Press.

Roemer, John (1982a) *A General Theory of Exploitation and Class*. Cambridge, MA: Harvard University Press.

Roemer, John (1982b) "Methodological Individualism and Deductive Marxism," *Theory and Society*, 11: 513–20.

Roemer, John (1986a) "'Rational Choice' Marxism: Some Issues of Method and Substance" in J. Roemer (ed.), *Analytical Marxism*. Cambridge: Cambridge University Press.

Roemer, John (ed.) (1986b) *Analytical Marxism*. Cambridge: Cambridge University Press.

Ruben, D.-H. (1979) "Marxism and Dialectics" in J. Mepham and D.-H. Ruben (eds), *Issues in Marxist Philosophy*, volume 1. Atlantic Highlands, NJ: Humanities Press.

Sabel, Charles F. (1982) *Work and Politics: The Division of Labor in Industry*. Cambridge: Cambridge University Press.

Schaff, Adam (1970) *Marxism and the Human Individual*. New York: McGraw-Hill.

Sennett, Richard and Jonathan Cobb (1972) *The Hidden Injuries of Class*. New York: Knopf.

Soboul, Albert (1989) *The French Revolution, 1787–1799: From the Storming of the Bastille to Napoleon*. London: Unwin Hyman.

Szymanski, Albert (1978) *The Capitalist State and the Politics of Class*. Cambridge, MA: Winthrop.

Thompson, E.P. (1966) *The Making of the English Working Class*. New York: Vintage Books.

Thompson, E.P. (1995) *The Poverty of Theory, or An Orrery of Errors*, new edition. London: Merlin Press.

Whewell, William and Robert E. Butts (1968) *William Whewell's Theory of Scientific Method*. Pittsburgh, PA: University of Pittsburgh Press.

Index

CPSIA information can be obtained
at www.ICGtesting.com
Printed in the USA
FSOW02n0234281015
12674FS